HOLY TERROR

Also by Flo Conway and Jim Siegelman

SNAPPING:
America's Epidemic of Sudden Personality Change

HOLY TERROR

---

*The Fundamentalist War
on America's Freedoms in Religion, Politics
and Our Private Lives*

Flo Conway and Jim Siegelman

A DELTA BOOK

A DELTA BOOK
Published by
Dell Publishing Co., Inc.
1 Dag Hammarskjold Plaza
New York, New York 10017

for
Jeffrey Brian, Christine,
Robert Vincent and Adam Gregory

Excerpts from this book first appeared in *Playboy* Magazine.
Copyright © 1982, 1984 by Flo Conway and Jim Siegelman
All rights reserved. For information address Doubleday & Company,
Inc., New York, New York.
Delta ® TM 755118, Dell Publishing Co., Inc.
ISBN: 0-385-29286-4
Published by arrangement with Doubleday & Company, Inc.
Printed in the United States of America

Contents

PART II—COVERT OPERATIONS

Preface to the Delta Edition

It has been almost two years since the first publication of *Holy Terror,* a time of economic upheaval for the nation and of anxiety for millions of Americans. Over this time, many of the issues we discuss here have received considerable attention. Some have been the focus of tumultuous, often bitter debate in the nation's courts and legislatures. Others have remained almost constantly in the media spotlight. Still others await even the faintest public airing.

Owing to recent rebuffs at the national level, many in government and the media have been quick to pronounce the downfall of the fundamentalist right crusade. As a result, some may think the threat we describe here has lessened or been set back once and for all.

We believe such assessments are premature. In this century, social scientists have devoted long years to studying fanatical and extremist movements in America. Almost invariably, they have interpreted the rise of such groups as momentary eruptions of the cultural landscape that, over time, inevitably fizzle and decay. In the case of the fundamentalist right—to date, at least—that has not been the story. Since its earliest appearance in rural religion and, soon after, in the political arena, the movement has mushroomed in its reach and power, while the more moderate segments of society that were supposed to absorb it were being drained and divided.

Similarly, other popular works on this subject begin and end on chords of reassurance, promoting the view that the rise of the fundamentalist right is but another swing of the stabilizing pendulum of American society. In slower, simpler times, the metaphor may have sufficed; however, amid today's complexity and change, with the natural checks and balances of our system under mounting stress, we feel that this pendulum assumption breeds a false sense of security and a dangerous complacency.

Consequently, in reviewing this book, we found little of substance that either of us felt impelled to revise for the paperback edition. In a number of places we have made minor changes in tone or style; however, the bulk of our labors was devoted to Chapters 12 and 14. In Chapter 12, we consider events surrounding the 1982 elections and emerging trends for 1984 and beyond. In Chapter 14, we update issues addressed throughout the book. In these expanded sections we have condensed some earlier passages and deleted material we now consider to be out of date. But few of our opinions or conclusions have changed from our original findings.

On the contrary, in our travels across the country during the past two years, we have seen that, on many fronts, the holy war we explore here is only beginning. Yet on our return to the East, we found observers throughout this influential corridor to be unaware of the operations of the fundamentalist right in nearly every other part of the country and largely unconcerned with the impact of the movement on people in the heartland.

Quite apart from its record of successes and failures at the national level, the fundamentalist right has already made a mark on America that will endure for years to come: in the ominous new strategies and technologies it has set loose on the democratic process, and in the emotional toll it is taking on people and families at every level of society.

Increasingly, these individuals and their personal ordeals have become our foremost concern. Since publication, we have received a steady stream of mail from readers nationwide, expanding our view of the personal side of *Holy Terror*. More than any vote, event or headline, the hundreds who responded directly, on talk shows and in local audiences, have guided our reflections as we look to the future. To these many strangers, some now friends, who from the beginning brought the story to our attention, we extend our thanks for their support and continuing inspiration.

FLO CONWAY and JIM SIEGELMAN
New York, New York
September 1, 1983

PART I

HOLY TERROR

1

Holy Terror

---

ter•ror (tĕr′-ər) *n.* 1. Intense, overpowering fear. Anything that instills such fear. 2. Violence toward private citizens, public property and political enemies promoted by a political group to achieve or maintain supremacy. 3. An annoying or intolerable pest; nuisance. Often used in the phrase *a holy terror*.

AS AMERICANS, we don't worry much about terror. Not the way people do in the Middle East or Northern Ireland, where terrorism has become a way of life, or in the Soviet Union, where it has been an instrument of government policy for decades. In the United States, we have seen relatively little organized violence for political ends. But terror is not only about violence. It's about fear and the climate of intimidation, repression and chaos such fear creates.

In the eighties, America has given birth to a new form of terror, a campaign of fear and intimidation aimed at the hearts of millions. It is in two great American arenas—religion and politics—that this new terror has raised its head. In the past few years, a small group of preachers and political strategists has begun to use religion and all that Americans hold sacred to seize power across a broad spectrum of our lives. They are exploiting this cherished and protected institution—our most intimate values and individual beliefs—along with our civil religion—our love of country—in a concerted effort to transform our culture into one altogether different from the one we have known. It is an adventurous thrust: with cross and flag to pierce the heart of America without bloodshed. And it is already well under way.

Much has been written and even more has been broadcast about the rise of the Moral Majority and the ascension of the far

right in American life. Since the 1980 election, public attention
has been focused on this force that has been gathering steam for
more than a decade, on the "new right" and on "the awakening
giant of American politics"—the nation's tens of millions of born-
again Christians who have reportedly reared up in anger and come
charging into the democratic process. The "electronic church" has
become a fixture of mass culture. A "revolution" has swept into
Congress, the White House and the highest offices of government.
And a new style of politics has come into fashion, led by a new
breed of political engineers equipped with their own unyielding
national agenda, a vast array of manipulative tactics and high
technology, and an expressed contempt for the codes of conduct
and civility that have guided public debate in America for two
hundred years.

Yet there is an unspoken element to the fervor that has come
upon the scene. It is the element of terror, the hidden factor of
personal and political intimidation that has become a driving force
in this new climate of change. It is a terror that speaks reverently
of God and Country, of "traditional values," "American morality"
and the "Judeo-Christian ethic," but it has little if anything to do
with religion as we know it. It is no expression of faith or devotion, no act of patriotism or love for America. Instead, it is the exploitation of religion as the vehicle for a larger social and political
movement, a drive for power, not only at the national level, but in
every domain of public concern, in the most intimate areas of our
private lives, and in the volatile arena of world affairs. It is this
broad program of intimidation, manipulation and control in the
name of religion that we call *Holy Terror*.

Holy Terror is all around us in the eighties. It runs like a mean
streak through the "fundamentalist right," the new hybrid of religious and political absolutism that has made Holy Terror its chief
instrument in the seizure of power. But Holy Terror is larger than
the Moral Majority and the insurgent force of the fundamentalist
right. Its shock waves have hit every religion and political party in
America. Already, millions of lives have been touched by it. Much
of our government and our society has come under its shadow.
And every one of us has been targeted.

As authors, we come to this thorny subject fresh from a stroll in
the brambles. Since the mid-seventies, the two of us have been

looking into a number of sensitive questions about the changing nature of religion in America. We began our work in a book called *Snapping: America's Epidemic of Sudden Personality Change,* published in 1978. *Snapping* was a look at the religious cults and mass-marketed therapies that first came to public attention in that decade, and at the powerful ritual techniques they use to bring about sudden conversions and profound alterations of human awareness and personality. Six months after the publication of *Snapping,* this specter of cult mind control swept down with unprecedented horror in the People's Temple massacre in Jonestown, Guyana. The gruesome jungle mass-suicide scene shook one of the most broadly held myths of Americans: that any group which elects to call itself a religion is automatically above suspicion in its conduct and deservingly exempt from public inquiry. In the aftermath of Jonestown, we were drawn to the forefront of a growing national debate over freedom of religion. For two years, we were in constant motion: appearing on television talk shows, speaking before civic gatherings and professional associations, testifying in courtroom proceedings and before a U.S. Senate subcommittee investigating the dangers of the cult phenomenon.

Yet, everywhere we went, the vast majority of questions we received had nothing to do with cults. They came from people who were confused and anxious about changes they saw taking place in larger, more traditional religions, in their own denominations, and in the tide of born-again Christianity that had begun to engulf the nation. On nationally broadcast phone-in shows, we were inundated with calls about personal or family problems relating to various evangelical groups. On virtually every college campus we visited, we heard tales of "open warfare" being waged by descending hordes of proselytizers. Even among many Christians we talked to, we found widespread concern and dissent.

And we felt the sting of Holy Terror ourselves. Before our appearance on "The Tonight Show" with Johnny Carson, we received repeated anonymous phone calls in our hotel rooms in Hollywood warning: "If you say anything about born-again Christians, you'll be sorry." At a state college in Ohio, we arrived for a speaking engagement to find campus bulletin boards papered with handwritten prayer cards imploring God to "use Conway and Siegelman for His greater glory."

Then in 1980, we conducted a follow-up study to *Snapping,* the first nationwide survey on the long-term effects of cult ritual techniques. Of forty-eight groups in our study, we were startled to find that more than thirty—two thirds of those surveyed—had emerged out of fundamentalist or other branches of conservative Christianity. Moreover, these thirty Christian sects combined ranked higher than the most destructive cults we studied in terms of the trauma they inflicted upon their members. Long-term effects included emotional problems such as depression, suicidal tendencies and feelings of guilt, fear and humiliation, and mental disorders such as disorientation, amnesia, nightmares, hallucinations and delusions. The anguished comments we received in personal replies only added to our concern over the effects of some fundamentalist practices on individuals and families in America.

Ours were not the only voices of concern. In the fall of 1980, a new tension began to build. Our mail increased to levels topped only during the period following Jonestown. Christians and non-Christians alike were writing to express their alarm over the growing militancy of hard-line fundamentalist rhetoric and activism. This wing of conservative Christianity, committed to the strictest literal interpretation of the Scriptures, had now merged with political forces on the far right. Together, this coalition had become loud and threatening in its drive to subsume the whole of Christendom under its banner and establish itself, chapter and verse, as the official standard of morality in America.

Suddenly, disaffected born agains started coming out of the woodwork, and we began to see a side of this sprawling movement that no one is talking about. Over the years, we've spoken with many born agains who were sincere in their beliefs and warm-hearted in their desire to make their religion a living part of their daily lives. But we've also met people whose faith had filled them with contempt for their fellow man; people who had been browbeaten and confused to the point of surrender by unyielding preachers and proselytizers. We've seen marriages broken up and families split apart over absurd tests of "true conversion," whole communities turned against one another in heated battles over trivialities of fundamentalist dogma. Worst of all, we've seen real tragedy: people tormented, driven to emotional breakdown and, in some cases, to suicide, while fellow crusaders stood by, un-feeling and uncaring.

This was our first glimpse of Holy Terror, and we have been observing it in abundance ever since. We've seen Holy Terror in the relentless physical and emotional intimidation that permeates every level of the new fundamentalism. There's pressure to con-vert, to be "born again," to receive the "Holy Spirit" in a pre-scribed way. There's pressure to "witness in the faith," to win souls for Christ, and pressure to give money to an endless round of fund-raising appeals. At every level, the bombardment is con-stant, with each new appeal successively more dire in its urgency and more earth-shattering in the consequences of its impending failure. Topping off all this, in the latest push, millions of Chris-tians around the country are now being subjected to a massive social and political assault—in their churches and schools, door-to-door and through the mails, and in a multimedia blitz of fundamentalist print, radio and television—commanding their par-ticipation in a parade of rallies, causes and campaigns to restore "moral sanity" and bring the nation to "repentance."

But something else happened in 1980 that went beyond the moral crusades of the new fundamentalism. The mood of the country turned mean. In the months before the election, we found ourselves in the thick of it. Traveling through the Midwest and the Sun Belt on an extended speaking tour, we felt a rising anger and hostility in our audiences and in many of the towns we visited. Some of it seemed to be a natural response to the frustrations of the day: to the hostage crisis in Iran, to a failing economy, to disaffection with the administration in power. But much of this anger seemed to be engineered and fully orchestrated: the tone, the slogans, the priority of issues and targets were virtually identi-cal from place to place. Across a dozen states, we heard people uncork and fume at their elected leaders in set ways that seemed wildly out of proportion to political reality. And when we sat down to talk with them, we found them unable to account for their rage. Instead, very often, they hurled strings of epithets and all the bitter labels that had been slapped on so many politicians that year, catchphrases like "anti-life," "anti-God," "anti-family" and "secular humanist."

Soon the pieces of a larger picture fell into place. On November

4, 1980, the American political landscape heaved as if in convulsion. In Washington, heads rolled. Most of the veteran legislators who had been targets of so much hostility and derision landed on the Capitol steps in a heap. Before the echoes had died out from the triumphant fundamentalist right's chest-pounding, its leaders had wheeled out a new rack of targets for 1982 and a laundry list of legislation they wanted passed in compliance with their self-proclaimed "mandate for change."

But the pollsters and analysts were divided. To them, the mandate broke down into separate "coattail effects," "pocketbook votes" and a "whiplash of rejection" of an unpopular President. Most puzzling of all was the born-again factor. How many Christians had actually been roused from apathy to activism? How effective were the importunings of those preachers who blessed their pet issues and tilted toward their preferred candidates in their Sunday pulpits, on television and at mass rallies around the country? More importantly, to what extent did the fundamentalist right religious crusade put the fundamentalist right political campaign over the top? And to what degree was the joint effort planned and executed by design? Every faction had its own set of answers, its own interpretation of the final tallies.

Our concern went beyond the numbers. To us, the fundamentalist right onslaught of 1980 marked the formal introduction of Holy Terror into the political arena. Their attempted elevation of Scriptures to the level of public policy, their approach through religion to questions of national values and moral standards, their establishment of overlapping "parachurch" and special-interest political networks, their use of advanced satellite and cable broadcasting operations, along with computerized direct-mail, direct-phone and other closed-circuit mass communications channels—these developments injected unknown quantities into the formation of public opinion and voting patterns. And they upped the scale of Holy Terror, adding to the fundamentalist right's list of victims not just the private citizens whose most intimate feelings and beliefs had been assaulted but, for the first time, elected officials who had been targeted in fundamentalist right "attack"-style campaigns.

We were determined to find out more. So early in 1981 we hit the road again, our intention this time not to talk but to listen, to pursue the flood of personal leads and cries for help that had come to us, to explore the web of interconnection among fundamentalist religious and political forces, and to examine the range of tactics and technology that we believed had been used to reshape people's values, beliefs and opinions—and to move them to act and vote in designated ways. For five months we traveled off the beaten path, sweeping south and west on a route that took us from Massachusetts to Florida, through Texas to southern California, then back eastward through the heartland—covering almost 10,000 miles. Along the way, we talked to public officials and elected representatives at state, local and national levels. We met with clergy of all religions, with leaders of major social, political and charitable organizations, and with experts in the social sciences and related technical fields. But mainly we talked to just plain folks: to Protestants, Catholics, Jews and Americans of no particular persuasion who happened to be farmers and businessmen, life insurance salesmen and telephone repairmen, teachers, housewives, secretaries and students. Together, they told a chilling story of the fundamentalist right's impact on our government and on our culture as a whole.

Along the way, we tried repeatedly to speak with fundamentalist right leaders, but with few exceptions, they were inaccessible. Invariably, when we wrote or called, identifying ourselves and our intentions, we ran into closed doors and brick walls—or to organizational public relations flacks who were similarly impenetrable.

We saw and heard a lot in five months, much more than we could possibly relate here. But after reviewing hundreds of recorded tapes and transcripts, along with hundreds of pounds of documenting books, tracts, notes, letters and press clippings, our initial sense of Holy Terror as a personal phenomenon of mental and emotional manipulation has grown into a far broader picture of mass manipulation on a scale that we believe is unprecedented in both religion and politics in this country. And the big picture is full of surprises. Our tour yielded a string of eye-openers that shocked, saddened and, at times, almost overwhelmed us.

The biggest surprise was the scope of Holy Terror itself. We had assumed that the phenomenon we were researching would be limited among America's various religious groups almost exclusively to born-again Christians. But we found the same pattern of religious and political forces engaged in massive thrusts toward America's Catholic and Jewish populations as well. Another great shock was seeing the sweeping inroads the fundamentalist right has made into our government at many levels. Prior to 1981, most of the pressure being exerted on legislators and other officials seemed to be coming from outside influences: primarily from the ring of fundamentalist right special-interest camps encircling Washington. With the new Congress and administration, however, the force of fundamentalist right pressure seemed to shift from without to *within* the offices of government: led by movement loyalists in Congress, by new agency heads and federal officials who seemed clearly to be using their government jobs and titles to advance fundamentalist right moral and religious positions. And finally, much of the force of Holy Terror in Washington seemed to be flowing directly from the White House, where close aides and advisers to the President, some of whom came to their positions from the cradle of the movement, appeared to be coordinating a broad campaign of government support for fundamentalist right goals and programs. Moreover, their support seemed to have the tacit if not explicit blessing of the President, who had assembled his own machinery for shaping public opinion and exerting pressure on other branches of government, a network that, we soon learned, was tied into the fundamentalist right and availed itself of many of the movement's resources and tactics.

There was more to uncover. As we moved out of Washington, we were struck by the speed with which Holy Terror has spread across the country since 1980. Flushed with success, the national leadership of the fundamentalist right appears to have cemented its hold upon its constituency, unleashing a spate of local affiliate organizations and countless spin-offs that are now replicating the movement's goals and methods at state and local levels. Many of these groups have launched their own moral crusades, using the same strategies of manipulation and preying upon the same deep-seated fears, prejudices and resentments that have proven so effective at the national level. Reaching out across the country, today Holy Terror has leaped beyond politics. It is religion run amok: in the battle over abortion and women's rights, in the teaching of evolution and in the business of elementary, secondary and higher education, in the news and entertainment media, in religious broadcasting and new fields of mass communications technology, in every faith and denomination, across the spectrum of American culture—and beyond into even larger spheres.

For finally, in addressing the threat in its fullness, we were confronted by its least recognized aspect: the growing international character of the terror. In our view, this is the most far-reaching realm of a system of spiritual terrorism that could have the gravest long-range consequences for our society. From this wide angle, the Moral Majority seems like nothing more than an intolerable pest and a nuisance. The sprawl of domestic wrongdoing in the name of religion is dwarfed by the mammoth scale on which some American-based religious organizations have deployed around the world, many of them promoting the same platform of fundamentalist right social and political views and using the same manipulative strategies and sophisticated communications technology. Yet the degree to which some fundamentalist right organizations may be engaged in fueling world tensions and, quite possibly, fomenting high-level international intrigue is intimately connected with the sources of disturbance running loose in the United States. From everything we have seen, in both their leadership and long-range goals, the two levels of operation are inseparable.

On the surface, then, this is a story about religion and politics. It is a tale of two cultures—one fundamentalist, one secular—and of a declared holy war for the soul of America being waged on a society that, for the most part, still refuses to acknowledge that it is being attacked. At its core, however, this is a book about *communication,* the lifeblood of culture. For Holy Terror is not a "shooting" war but a new kind of communication warfare, a guerrilla war on our private thoughts, feelings and beliefs, on our nation's timeless values and historic freedoms, being waged, not with automatic weapons and homemade bombs, but with an arsenal of advanced hardware aimed at the most fragile part of our humanity.

In its grandest designs, Holy Terror transcends the details of religion and politics. As we will be discussing later in this book, and contrary to the high-toned moralizing of the fundamentalist right, their broad plan of social and political control constitutes nothing less than a program of deception and distortion, the use of the instruments of mass communication in a free society in a campaign of total propaganda—a comprehensive information assault on a people and their culture. This idea may be hard for many to grasp. Master plots on this scale are outside our American experience. Yet few of us have any idea how deliberately and systematically many of our private beliefs and national values have already been undermined. This is our foremost concern in this book: to bring to public discussion a greater awareness of the role of manipulative communication strategies in the rise of the fundamentalist right.

In the pages that follow, we will present the phenomenon of Holy Terror in its entirety: the major culprits in the drama, the tactics and mechanisms by which they operate, their targets and victims and their long-range plans, as we have come to understand them. We will also identify what we believe to be a new and potentially destructive pattern of communication. That is the syndrome of ideological fundamentalism, viewed here not as a particular set of religious beliefs, but as a mind-set in opposition to the modern world, to our human nature and, in its extremes, to reality itself. In our view, this closed-minded pattern of social and political reaction poses a threat to individuals and to our society. To us, it is the overriding danger of the fundamentalist right and its program of Holy Terror.

We approach this subject, not as theologians, psychologists or political scientists, but as communication researchers concerned that basic principles of this vital process of human interaction are being violated by the leaders of the fundamentalist right, who, we feel, are also setting dangerous new precedents in communication, in religion and politics and in the use of new media technology. In our view, leaders of this movement have trampled on the primary tenet of a free society: the code of ethics in communication among individuals and groups in public discussion and in the process of government. Once that code is broken, as we are now seeing, people may be thrown into confusion, drawn into the trap of committing the same breaches of conduct; and freedom may rapidly dissolve into a license for anarchy or totalism. Beyond the immediate implications of Holy Terror for any particular issue or election, we feel the larger task confronting our nation will be to reclaim its enduring values and to establish a new code of conduct in communication practices, not just in campaign rhetoric and public debate, but in everyday interactions and in the use of new communications technology.

These are not simply technical issues. They are moral issues of the highest order, and they have everything to do with our beliefs as individuals and with our values as a nation. Big things are happening in the world of communication among people of different faiths, cultures and political persuasions, and the rise of Holy Terror in America is just one reflection of this change taking place on a global scale. Yet when it comes to religion, we have seen, many Americans are afraid to speak their minds at all. Some don't dare even to examine their personal feelings and spiritual beliefs. Like the subject of sex until the fifties and later, candid discussion of religion is still largely taboo in public forums. It is as if people fear they will be branded as "atheists" or "Communists" for simply saying that the world has changed in two thousand years.

But that, too, is part of Holy Terror. In our talks with people around the country, we've found that many Americans, even some of the most devout among us, are hungry for some straight talk on this subject. In the current climate, they seem eager to begin asking the tough questions that must be addressed if religion is to remain a viable institution in America, and if its role in shaping the future is to be a healthy one.

Toward that end, in Part I we turn to the center of the storm, to the individuals whose feelings and beliefs have become targets of a new form of terrorism. Here our aim is not to present every detail, but rather to show the phenomenon in its full form, wherever possible, inviting people on both sides to speak for themselves. In Part II, the assembled picture will serve as the foundation for a deeper discussion, a new communication perspective on the syndrome of ideological fundamentalism. We address that syndrome, not as an attack on the beliefs of any person or group, but in the hope of understanding, and in the spirit of constructive inquiry.

Slain in the Spirit

AMERICA'S BORN AGAINS—they claim to be a majority. Fifty thousand here in a football stadium in New Jersey. Eighty thousand there at a convention in the Midwest. Two hundred thousand on the Mall in Washington. But they are splintered, split and spinning. Evangelicals. They have had an experience of "rebirth in Jesus Christ." Pentecostals and charismatics. They may undergo the "infilling of the Holy Spirit" or receive the "gift of tongues." Fundamentalists. They believe the Bible to be the ultimate authority in all matters, the "revealed, inspired, infallible and inerrant Word of God."

Most use the term "Christian" to refer only to those who have been born again, and their distinction has been widely accepted. But stare into this faceless throng. Who are they? Where have they been hiding all these years?

In the old days, they were spread out across the heartland, most of them rural, poor, undereducated and resting at the bottom of the social ladder. Holy rollers, traveling salesmen, politicians— every sideshow that rolled into town found a new way to play them. With steady acceleration, they were left in the dust of a nation in the process of becoming fast-paced, college-educated and upwardly mobile. For decades, big business, the government and the media treated them as a decaying mass, a kind of cultural compost out of which a rich urban and suburban America came to blossom. But soon those good old days were blown away by the interstates, television and mass culture, and by an outside world that lured away their children, carrying them off to distant places, transforming them beyond recognition, shattering the small-town worlds where families had lived quietly for generations. In their living rooms, on local newsstands and bookshelves, at the neighborhood theater, a new reality was reaching out for them, intruding, confusing, threatening to unravel the plain cloth of work, faith and family from which their lives were cut out in patterns. But that cloth had been fraying for years.

By the seventies, America's born agains were no longer mere country folk. Like the rest of the populace, many had migrated to the cities. Some even spilled over into the suburbs, surrounding themselves with the trappings of the good life and all the gadgetry of consumer society. But most of them still lived a world apart. They prayed in their own churches, studied in their own schools and kept out of politics and fancy nightclubs. And they spread the Word, in accordance with the supreme commandment of their faith: "Go ye into all the world and preach the gospel to every creature." One-to-one, door-to-door, in private and in public, and many-to-one over a burgeoning network of radio and television, they grew to enormous numbers. In some parts of the country, their members amassed great fortunes and rose to exalted positions in real estate, agriculture, business and industry. They achieved the social status conferred upon great wealth and the political power that flows naturally from its empires.

And they became a paradox: a subculture that had become a *super*culture! Scorned in the media, in Washington and their own towns, in many instances rejected by their own children, many grew frustrated and angry. As they had come to see it, nearly every identifiable minority—Jews, blacks, students, women, gays—had come to power. Somehow, America had slipped through their fingers. Meanwhile, high above this grumbling flock, a new corps of avenging fundamentalists reared their self-anointed heads. Their goal: to woo the disenfranchised, to win over their adversaries, young and old, and in the process reclaim the nation for God. The call went out to swell and surge, to *Christianize* America.

There was just one small problem. Most of America's born agains didn't have the slightest idea what was going on. That kind of activism had never been a part of their religion or their lives. In earlier times, this might have been a formidable obstacle. In these times, it called for a modern-day holy war, a rapid call-up and mobilization and a major buildup of advanced spiritual weaponry. As the plan got under way, few realized that they were being drawn into a deadly game. Many, led to believe they were doing battle with the "Archfiend" on native soil, relished the notion of close combat. But again, they were being played. Others, trusting and innocent, were to become the first casualties of this new crusade.

The personal side of Holy Terror is not one you hear about on the talk shows. We first detected it in faint rumblings coming from deep within the Christian community. In the beginning, most of the complaints were hearsay: calls from people alarmed by the behavior of a child or spouse who had forsaken all to join some local prayer or Bible study group, letters from people who had been hounded by proselytizers urging them to leave their own faiths and denominations, reports of people who were driven to emotional breakdowns or suicide by the harsh demands of the fundamentalist life. But few came forward from within the ranks of this hard-sell brand of Christianity. Most of those stories, like many of the lives, were not reclaimable.

Our first insight into the experience came in personal contact with audiences around the country. At the close of our talks on cult mind control methods, we would relate our research to some practices found among America's larger organized religions. This usually caught our audiences by surprise. Very often, people would become uneasy. Some would shift in their seats. Some sat frozen in self-reflection. Others seemed mortally afraid—as if they expected the proverbial bolt of lightning to shoot down from the heavens and incinerate them merely for attending such a discussion.

For some in our audiences, this talk was intolerable. Whole groups from local churches would exit in unison. Organized teams of college evangelists rose to challenge us and "witness in the faith" to our listeners. The inevitable gauntlet would be thrown down: "I have just one question: Do *you* believe in God?" And a chill would descend on the room. People stiffened and withdrew. They were intimidated. The lightning bolt had smacked down.

Only afterward would they approach us: An elderly lady who wanted us to know, "Those others aren't *real* Christians." A college administrator who thanked us for bringing campus tensions out into the open. On one occasion, a stately gentleman who had been sitting grimly in the audience turned out to be a local clergyman. "I've been a Methodist minister for fifty-three years," he said, "and I'll tell you, if the ways of the Lord aren't open to examination, we're all in big trouble."

Then almost without fail, as we made ready to leave, some lone figure would move forward timidly. It might be a fretful student or a frazzled housewife. It might begin: "You have no idea how much your talk tonight has helped me." Or, as on one occasion, "This is the first time anything has made sense to me in five years!" These were our first contacts with the fragile lambs we came to call "ex-Christians." As they told their stories, we learned about the silent suffering of what may be a considerable number of America's born agains.

Diane. Diane was one of the trusting and innocent who almost became a casualty. She didn't approach us out of the audience.

She saw us on television and, soon after, called us in New York and said she wanted to talk about her experience. She said there were some important things she wanted us to know. We knew the tone of anxiety in her voice. We told her she would be among the first people we interviewed on our tour.

Several months later, we arrived in the small town in eastern Pennsylvania where she lived alone with her young daughter. Her house was dingy, with a front porch sinking under the weight of garden pots and children's toys. Waiting at the door, she didn't look like your typical sparkly eyed born again. In her mid-thirties, pale with dark hair, she greeted us softly and motioned us into her living room, an old-fashioned salon. We chatted briefly, then started recording, and for the next five hours she told us about her eight years as a member of different evangelical, charismatic and fundamentalist churches. In her story were all the letters we had received, all the pained faces we had seen, all the rumblings we had heard.

"I never set out to become a Christian," she began, using the general term as most born agains do. "I was a sixties person, but I had been totally disillusioned by that decade. I wasn't searching for anything anymore. I was married. Dan and I lived in an apartment. I had gone back to college and was finishing my last semester when I met this girl in art class, Sarah Ann, and she started talking to me about Jesus. She would set up her easel next to mine and watch me paint, and we would talk. Things weren't going well for me at the time. I had begun to feel that there just wasn't any justice in the world. Everything seemed to be going crazy and sometimes I felt like I was, too. Then one day Sarah Ann turned to me and said, 'I know why you're going crazy, and I know what will help you.' I asked her what and she said, 'Well, if you'd like to, kneel down right now and we'll ask the Holy Spirit to come and indwell you and Jesus can be your Lord and Savior.' I dropped my brushes and started to laugh."

She went on. "I was sure she was kidding, but she wasn't. Then about a week later, she came to me and told me that there was a battle going on for my soul. She said that she was a representative of God and that I had to make a decision because Satan was hot on my tail. This time I thought *she* was crazy. I hadn't thought about religion in years. But as I kept painting, these images came up before me. I began to feel uneasy. I started to worry. She said I should make a decision before it was too late."

Diane didn't make her decision then. She tried to forget about Sarah Ann as she went on to complete her course work. Months later, however, the dark warnings and subtle promises she had been given continued to tug at her.

"So I decided to look her up," she told us. "She sounded happy to hear from me. She said she was having a prayer meeting at her house on Friday and she asked me to come. I pretended I had forgotten. I said, 'A prayer meeting? Aren't you out of that stuff yet?' She said, 'Oh no,' and I heard a voice in the background saying, 'Don't tell her that or you'll scare her away again!' I thought to myself, 'I'm not scared of anything.' I told her I'd come to her prayer meeting. Then I hung up the phone and suddenly I became very, very frightened."

Did she know why?

"No, I just became very frightened of going to this prayer meeting. I was afraid something would happen to me. But then a few days later, I received a letter from another old friend, Jessie. She said she had found true happiness and peace as a Christian. And several weeks before, one of my very best friends had told me that he, too, had become born again. Everyone seemed to be doing it. I decided to go to the prayer meeting."

When she arrived, the scene was bizarre.

"It was incredible, crazy," she remembered. "We all sat around singing songs and then this woman began to talk about how miserable she was because she had been born deformed. Then she said she had gotten into a car accident, which made things worse. I really felt bad for her. I thought everybody else did, too. But then from across the room everyone jumped up and gathered around her and put their hands on her and started praying for God to heal her body. Then they went back to their seats saying, 'Thank you, Jesus. Thank you, Jesus.' They were all so happy. But this poor woman was still sitting there and she was still deformed and she wasn't happy at all. She was very upset, in fact, and she told the group that it had made her even more upset when they did that because all she wanted was a little sympathy. She said she didn't want people praying for her and nothing happening. It was embarrassing. Then they said that if she had no faith, she wouldn't be healed and that put even more stress on her."

The prayer meeting was hardly persuasive, but it drew Diane closer to Sarah Ann and the group. On an intellectual level, she rejected everything she was hearing. Emotionally, however, it was a different story.

"When I left that prayer meeting, I still believed it was a bunch of nothing, but Dan came too, and it made him angry. He started arguing with some of the men there. On the way home, he saw that I had been affected. He said, 'You really do believe it. You're going to become one. You're going to destroy our marriage.' He was very afraid."

Dan was right. Together, Sarah Ann and Jessie applied slow, steady pressure to Diane.

"They started coming over to my house with the Bible," she said. "They would read to me. They started taking me to Bible studies at the gospel temple. It was new and fresh. Their friendship seemed so open and hopeful. They read from the Gospel of John and talked about the true light that came to shine through the darkness and lighten every man on the face of the earth. The imagery began to affect me. I would get an emotional and physical response. Sometimes when I would read some of these Scriptures I would begin to feel light-headed, like I was floating up to the ceiling. I don't know why. Sarah Ann and her friends seemed that way, too, on a high, then I started reading the Bible by myself at bedtime and *I* got high! At first, it didn't last; it would wear off. But soon my life became like that all the time."

In this way, through personal pressure and deep concentration and repetition of Scriptures, Diane became a born-again Christian. The transformation did not take place in a skyrocketing explosion.

"It was a subtle process," she said. "I read the Bible intensely for three weeks and decided that it was true. At that point, I made a decision to follow the Bible, but I didn't want to accept this man Jesus into my heart. That whole idea didn't make any sense to me, but Sarah Ann and Jessie kept telling me that it wouldn't work otherwise, that I had to accept Jesus into my heart. But I was afraid. I felt like something would happen, that I would become somebody else."

Sarah Ann and Jessie would not let Diane become born again in her own way. They redoubled their efforts, showering her with attention and affection. Then they pulled the string.

"They tried to make me feel ashamed. They said, 'Look at your life! You ran your own life and look where it got you. Now, here's your chance. Jesus can take your life and make something out of it.' If I wasn't willing to trust Jesus, Sarah Ann said, I would be lost. Then Sarah Ann stopped talking to me. She said she was mad at me because I was resisting. That upset me. I decided not to see them or go to their churches anymore."

But Diane's anger was fleeting. As it faded, she began to feel rejected and alone.

"That same night this great emptiness came over me. Suddenly, it didn't make me feel good just to be myself and go my own way. Dan wasn't speaking to me at this point; I couldn't talk to him about it. So I called Sarah Ann to apologize and she invited me over to her house to spend the night, and as I was lying in bed, I said, 'All right now, I'm going to do this.' I just said, 'Jesus, come into my heart'—and I fell asleep. When I woke up the next morning, I felt great, really happy and free. I felt like I had gotten rid of my lonely self, like I was no longer just me but now Jesus was inside of me, too, and he was going to fix everything."

This was the beginning of Diane's ordeal. Like many evangelical Christians we interviewed, her famed "born-again" experience was a quiet one. This seems to have become the trend in recent years. The intense atmosphere of the revival tent, with its converging forces culminating in a moment of overwhelming release, seems to be fading from the evangelical scene—even among many charismatics and pentecostals. We were surprised on this tour to find so many people making cool and conscious *decisions* for Christ. As Diane explained, however, from the onset of her new spiritual experience, her decision-making processes had been under attack. She described the process of suggestion that made her think and act in inexplicable ways.

"When something good happened, I was told to attribute it to Jesus having become my Savior," she continued, "but I had so many questions. I would ask them all the time. Always, the reply was that I was just a 'new' born again, that I didn't know anything and that if I kept reading the Bible I would eventually understand. Then I started having these feelings, like messages to do a certain thing, and I'd think it was God or the Holy Spirit talking to me. I was told that I would have all these supernatural experiences for the first few months and then they would go away. They said it was happening because I had started obeying the Scriptures, and that these supernatural things were just for the young—the babes in Christ. They were supposed to be a special gift God gave to new born agains."

Then suddenly, after six months as a "babe," the joyful supernatural world she had entered began to darken. The turn came with her growing participation in the gospel temple.

"They started pulling a lot of new strings," she said. "They wanted us to conform. Everything that had been important to me now became satanic. I had been active in a local women's group, but they began preaching that the women's movement was satanic. They said you couldn't follow Jesus and be a 'women's libber.' They said that rock music was satanic, which shocked me because I always listened to rock music in the sixties. Then they said that the *sixties* were satanic, that Satan had invaded people in that decade through rock music and sex and drugs. Finally, they began to tell us that certain books were satanic and that we were to go home and look through our bookcases and if we found any books that were not Christian we were to burn them because they were demonic. I loved books. I had so many books, all the ones they wanted us to get rid of: philosophy books, psychology books, sociology books—they were all supposed to be satanic, anti-God theories. At the time, that made me very upset. But I was afraid that right here in my own house, Satan would infiltrate the atmosphere. I wanted to be pure, but I couldn't burn them or throw them away. So I took all the books out of my library and put them in boxes and barrels in the basement."

In place of her library, she said, was a single book.

"I started reading the Bible all the time. Early in the morning, in the afternoon, I carried the Bible everywhere I went. I went to Bible studies. They'd pick a subject and pull out all the Scriptures that pertained to it. I memorized them. It became my whole life."

Although it occupied most of her spare time, Bible study was not Diane's only activity as a born again. From the moment she became a babe, she also became an evangelist.

"They told us we were ambassadors of Christ. We were supposed to spread the gospel to everyone. They said the only reason we were living was to bring more people to Christ. They said the only reason God was allowing me, Diane, to live was to bring everybody that I came in contact with to the Lord. That was the idea from the beginning. When the whole world was converted, Jesus would come back in the clouds and pick up all his children and the earth would be destroyed. Everybody would get a chance, but at the 'endtimes' those who refused would be thrown into the lake of fire."

As we talked, Diane's mood grew more somber. She began chain-smoking and fidgeting. We could see she was taking us into territory that was personally painful.

"They started attacking my art," she said, her resentment rising. "They said art had to be just for Jesus. Anything that wasn't just for Jesus should be destroyed. We were to have no other loves besides Jesus. So I began to give up my painting, my reading and writing, my participation in the women's movement. I gave up everything. I cut all ties to the world. I no longer associated with anyone except born agains. Then the fear and guilt really began to get to me. When they told me I had to be a certain way, I couldn't escape. Everyone was watching one another, picking out things that weren't 'Christlike.' Then we had to repent. One day I went to the pastor and told him that these teachings didn't make any sense to me. I was told to leave because I asked too many questions. He said I was obviously a belligerent type of woman. So I started going to another church and the battle began all over again. I asked the pastor: 'If Christ's love was supposed to be so loving, forgiving and merciful, why are you teaching something that is totally the opposite? Show me where it says these things in the Scriptures.' He never answered me. The more I resisted, the worse it became. I felt rotten, like there was something wrong with me. Everybody else seemed so happy."

She looked at us nervously, checking to make sure that we were still on her side. Her eyes brightened as she looked back on her life in the sixties.

"I was a *peace* child," she insisted, "so it was very easy for me to become a disciple of Jesus. It was the *other* person they wanted me to become that didn't seem like Jesus. They wanted me to be a nothing, an empty shell. They wanted me to give up everything that meant anything to me and replace it with Jesus. They said, 'Jesus is sufficient for all your needs. You don't need your friends, you don't need your children, you don't need your husband, you don't need music.' Looking back on it, I can see that everybody was miserable. We had to go to all these prayer meetings and be filled with enthusiasm and the joy of the Lord. But it didn't last. It didn't last for anybody. And I couldn't fake it. I don't know how everyone else did."

Diane got by, however, for months that turned into years, carrying on in all the prescribed ways, yet struggling to retain something of her former self and her former values. Then she was asked to accept something that violated everything she believed to be true.

"They said we weren't supposed to care about anybody who wasn't born again," she said. "It just made me sick to my stomach to be that kind of person. If somebody refused to accept Jesus, we were supposed to turn against them inside. They told us nobody could do good without God, and that if something bad was happening to a non-Christian, we were not supposed to help. We were instructed not to interfere with God's dealings with non-Christians. It was good for them to suffer, they said, because suffering would bring them to Christ."

As much as she rejected these notions, Diane soon found herself believing them. And with each dose of suggestion, her own feeling for humanity receded.

"When I totally succumbed was when I accepted the idea that I was saved and special and I stopped caring about people who weren't. That was the end of the line for me." She turned reflective. "I can't tell you how it happened. It was imperceptible, a gradual thing. I had been an artist, a writer, a feminist; I don't know how I became just a housewife and mother who sat here and read the Bible all day. I never listened to the radio, never watched television, never read a newspaper. I was cut off from everything. I went to Bible study and read Christian books. That was my life."

That life began to consume her and, in her mounting inner conflict, it also began to consume her marriage.

"I had a very unhappy marriage, even before I was born again, but I stayed married because it was forbidden in the Bible to get divorced. Eventually things got so bad that neither of us could take it anymore. We went to a number of ministers and told them it was bad for us to stay married, that we were both depressed and miserable. But they said it was my fault. They said that in my role as a woman, Dan was to be the head of the household and my spiritual leader. I could not conform to that role. I could not be happy just cleaning and cooking and being here all the time. I tried and I tried, then I started becoming depressed. Life became hopeless, it got really terrible, and everyone was telling me it was my fault. So I read the Bible and prayed more. I went to prayer meetings. I did everything you were supposed to do, but I wasn't getting anywhere. Christians I associated with became critical of me because I wasn't joyful. God was not helping me. So I turned on myself. I decided I must be a wicked, evil person."

Her downhill slide was precipitous.

"I got really sick," she said. "I became emotionally ill. I couldn't get out of bed. I had to drag myself to take care of my daughter, who was two at the time. I still went to Bible studies and prayer meetings, but except for that I stayed in my room for eight months. No Christians came to see me. I prayed to God, but He was gone. Then I turned to myself and found out that *I* was gone, too! I was totally helpless. I felt like I was falling into a bottomless pit. I became terrified—"

She stopped abruptly. She was trembling.

"I don't want to talk about that part," she said.

Up to that point, Diane's story seemed reminiscent of many we had heard from former cult members. But as she continued, it became apparent that we were dealing with something larger than the identifiable techniques of mind control. To us, her experience spoke of an added dimension, a frightening new form of *emotional* control. She was the first born again we spoke with who could articulate the conflict.

"You see, the things we had to give up didn't just stop with books and records," she said. "We had to give up thinking *and* feeling. They told us not to think or to question because Satan used the mind to trick you. They told us not to trust our emotions because they were deceptive. That's what happened to me. We were all in this condition, but by then I couldn't stand the emptiness and alienation inside. It was terrible, like looking at yourself and seeing somebody who was totally mindless. All that was inside my head were these automatic answers. I'd struggle with this terrible life and the devastation of not having myself, and all there would be was a Scripture: 'Trust in God,' or 'All things work to the good for those who love God and are called according to His promises.' That one usually caught everything, but this time it couldn't save me from the depression I was falling into."

She took the first steps toward seeking help.

"I went to a number of Christian counselors. They said what I had already heard, that I wasn't being a good wife and mother. I started watching the '700 Club' on television. Every morning I would call the number on the screen and tell them what I was going through, and they would pray for me over the telephone. When they got down on their knees to pray, I got down on my knees to pray. When they said, 'Put your hands on the television,' I put my hands on the television. I sent them money. Nothing helped. Then I met some people from a church of the living word and they decided that I must have demons. They put me through an exorcism. Five people stood in front of me and yelled and screamed at the demons for three hours. They were shouting things like, *'Come out of her! Let her go! Free her! Release her, you foul demons!'* I just sat there. They made me repent out loud every sin I'd ever committed in my life. I felt like my whole self was being totally raped. It was devastating. I felt so terrible."

Softly, she described the events that followed, stopping frequently for reassurance.

"The terror of not finding myself was deep inside," she said, trailing away. "The center of my being was empty, black and dark. So I signed myself into a psychiatric hospital. I told them I didn't know what was wrong with me. I was afraid to talk to them because they weren't born-again Christians. They tried to help me, but I couldn't listen. Sarah Ann called me up and told me that the whole hospital was full of demons, but I stayed for two and a half months, hoping that maybe I could find some answers. They offered me drugs, but I wouldn't take them. I went to group sessions. I saw eight different psychiatrists there and three more at another institution, but when I found out they didn't believe in Jesus, I couldn't listen to them. One doctor told me I was manic depressive. Another said I was schizophrenic. It was all a waste of time and money. I decided I might as well go home.

"So I just came back here to die," she continued. "I was sure that it would happen soon. I thought that I would either kill myself or simply die of pain. I was in total pain, physical and emotional. I sent my daughter to a day-care camp for the summer. I didn't see anybody. Dan would come home and give me dinner, but we never talked."

She talked to no one, but soon someone started talking to her: a hallucination of sorts, as she described it, a voice from inside.

"I was lying in bed one day, all doubled up in pain, and I heard this little voice crying for help. At first I thought it was Satan, so I didn't pay any attention to it. Then the next day I heard it again, this tiny little voice, very faint and weak. Then, I don't know why, I just said, 'I'll help you. I don't have much to offer, but in the time I have left I'll do as much as I possibly can.' And suddenly, I began to think of things that would make me happy."

It was the right move.

"I thought of music," she went on, brightening now. "I thought about fun things I used to do. Then I started reading and writing again. I bought a journal and wrote in it every day. I went out and looked up old friends I hadn't seen in years. I started doing all the things that had been forbidden."

But it was easier said than done. For the next few months, Diane found it almost impossible to make a smooth reentry.

"The world was totally ruined to me. My Christian friends rejected me, and I was afraid to get close to people who weren't born again because they were of Satan. After eight years, I tried to read a newspaper, but everything seemed to point to Satan and the coming destruction of the world. When I tried to think, I would get a pain in my head. Things weren't connecting. I felt like I had lost my mind. I remembered their teaching: 'The mind is the stage of Satan.' I kept looking for some little thing that might poke a hole in everything I had been taught. I thought, if only I could make one little crack in it, I could begin to sort it all out."

That crack came from a most serendipitous source.

"Four months later, I was dusting out my bookcase and I came across an old dictionary with a copy of the Declaration of Independence in the back," she said. "I read it: 'We hold these truths to be self-evident, that all men are created equal, that they are endowed by their Creator with certain unalienable rights, that among

these are life, liberty and the pursuit of happiness.' I looked at
that and I thought, 'Gee, that's really curious! Being a Christian,
you don't have any rights to your life. You certainly don't have
any liberty. And as far as the pursuit of happiness—forget it!'
Then I said to myself, 'Gee, this Declaration of Independence
seems so much more Christian than all the churches I've been
going to.' Then suddenly it dawned on me. I said, 'My God! Our
government is more Christian, more loving, more forgiving, more
free than God's government!' And I said to myself, 'Isn't that interesting!' "

And she continued with her dusting. Those months had been
the hardest yet, emotionally wrenching. Cut loose from her born-
again orbit, estranged from her husband and her daughter, and
without any real guidance, she floated in and out of the twilight
between her born-again self and the old self she was struggling to
reclaim. As it turned out, Diane's "personal encounter" with Jesus
was coming to an end just as America's national encounter was
beginning. In the spring of 1980, things came together for her.

"When I heard about the 'Washington for Jesus' march, something clicked inside my head," she told us. "I remembered all the
things they had been teaching us over the years, and I thought,
'They're marching on Washington. They're really going to do it.
They're going to change democracy.' Of course, they didn't call it
political. They said it was all spiritual. But I remembered the seminars we were instructed to attend, led by fundamentalist teachers
who traveled around the country. They gave us these booklets
about 'spiritual dangers,' which had questions and answers about
democracy. They never actually came out and said that democracy
was wrong. But they said that a pluralistic society was not acceptable to God. They said that freedom of religion was only an illusion, and that democracy could only work if Christians had the
leadership positions."

Word of the march on Washington seemed to fire some long-
dormant impulse in her. With each step, another piece of her missing self seemed to fall into place.

"When I saw that they were going to try to take over the country, I knew that it was possible for them to do it. After all, if they
had *me*, a radical from the sixties, believing all that stuff, they
could get anyone! So I grabbed my tape recorder and took a train

to Washington. I was afraid. I worried about the power they might still have over me. I didn't know if I was strong enough yet, but I had to be. I was determined to confront them."

And so on April 29, 1980, along with 200,000 other born agains, Diane marched on Washington. She filed her report:

"It was exactly as I thought. The followers had no idea that the leaders were directing them down a whole new path, a political one. They began to reinterpret all the old spiritual enemies and make them flesh-and-blood enemies. Satan and evil became legalized abortion, the Equal Rights Amendment and the federal government. But the people didn't know what was happening. They were like sheep being led, totally oblivious. They were just out of it—like I had been. I spoke to dozens of people and asked every one of them, 'Do you think this is political?' And in the face of all the speeches and all the literature and the very fact that it was on the Mall in Washington, every single one of them denied that it was political! They all told me, 'If this was political, I wouldn't be here.' That's when I realized that the leaders could really do it!"

Diane spent a long day talking to born agains at the rally. She found it to be not only exhausting, but unnerving.

"I talked to people from California, from Illinois, from Georgia and Virginia," she said, exasperated. "I tried to reason with them. I said, 'If this isn't political, why did you come to Washington?' They couldn't answer me. They replied with Scripture. The next morning I listened to my tapes. I cried all the way through. I just felt, all those people, they're really good people. I talked with a lot of them; most had only recently become born agains. They sounded so happy. They were so open. They really did love Jesus. I couldn't help thinking about how they would change, how everything was going to die for them, how they were being prepared for something of which they had no idea. That broke me up. I wanted to shake them and say, *'Listen, this is what happened to me! I was a born again!'* But they couldn't hear. They couldn't hear a word I was saying."

We asked Diane what she would say if they could hear her now. She thought for a minute.

"I would say"—she paused—" 'Don't give up your mind. When you make that decision to accept Jesus into your heart, you give up your life. You think you are giving it up to Jesus, but in truth you are giving it up to something else, to your local pastor or church leaders.' I helped myself, but I wouldn't want anybody to go through that. And there are things I haven't begun to deal with yet, big things, like Satan, like the future."

We asked her if she still believed the endtime prophecies she had studied. She nodded.

"Sometimes I still feel that the earth is going to be destroyed, that the whole thing will come to an end. Only now I believe that if that does happen, they are going to bring it about themselves. They'll create the circumstances where we'll have Armageddon. It will be a self-fulfilling prophecy."

It was late. At our request, Diane played some of her tapes from the Washington march. We heard the din of the crowd, the singing, the clapping, the booming speeches. To the naked ear, it sounded like one of the great civil rights marches or anti-war rallies of the sixties. Upon closer examination, however, we could hear a new and throbbing undertone: "THIS NATION WAS FOUNDED ON GOD . . . THE LORD HAS CALLED US HERE TODAY WITH HIS WORD AND PROPHECY THAT WE MIGHT CALL THIS NATION BACK TO RE- PENTANCE. . . . WE'VE COME TO WASHINGTON IN LOVE, BUT WE'VE COME WITH THE MESSAGE OF ALMIGHTY GOD. . . . THIS NA- TION IS GOING DOWN. . . . THE WHOLE NATION IS GOING TO BE DE- STROYED. . . ."

Potomac Fervor

The United States is in no sense founded upon the Christian religion.

—GEORGE WASHINGTON

AS A NATION, we have never been wild about our politicians. We see their job as dirty business. Few professions are held in lower esteem. Nor, for the most part, does our affection for them soar when they become our elected representatives. We make our leaders swear to promote the general welfare, then turn against them for acting contrary to our private interests. We suspect them of every manner of bribery and back-room dealing. We relish revelations of their improprieties. Yet, too often, we forget that politicians are people, too, that their judgments are not divine, that they are vulnerable and sensitive to personal attack—and that they may become victims just like the rest of us.

But as much as we may dislike our leaders, we love our nation's capital, Washington, D.C., the throne of democracy, this cosmopolitan city of stone with the soul of a sleepy southern town. The place is a theater festival of sorts, home to a hundred stages on which popular repertories play out the drama of politics. There is oratory and grand soliloquy. Great tragicomedies have played here, filled with villains and buffoons. There are gala pageants, lavish state dinners, solemn funerals with riderless horses—and fine amateur work, too, with much street theater. On the Mall, at the Pentagon, in Lafayette Park, there have been marches and rallies, love-ins and be-ins, rain-soaked tent cities—and "Washington for Jesus."

Every few years, it seems, there is a new cast of players, a new mixture of government. Titles change, chairs rotate, new faces brighten, old faces fade. But for the most part, the rules stay the same. There has always been a code of conduct to the business of politics and a civility to the task of government. With few exceptions in recent years—most notably Joe McCarthy and Richard Nixon—people here generally play according to the rules. Even in the back rooms and under the tables, there is honor among thieves.

But now there is a new crowd in town, the fundamentalist right, and they have broken all the rules. Their groups with names like the National Conservative Political Action Committee (NCPAC), the Committee for the Survival of a Free Congress, the Christian Voice, the Religious Roundtable, the National Pro-Life Political Action Committee and the Moral Majority have violated something basic in our political process. Born of hastily enacted post-Watergate election reforms and a loophole in a 1976 Supreme Court ruling that permits unlimited campaign expenditures by groups not officially connected with a candidate, the PAC—political action committee—population explosion has introduced into politics the formalized "attack," a campaign style that moves in on a targeted opponent and proceeds to tear away at his voting record and personal reputation until his image among his constituents is riddled with doubt and disdain. In this manner, PACs pave the way for unknown challengers, often their hand-picked candidates, to enter a contest and take the "high road," to mount a heavily funded, professionally managed campaign that maintains a high moral tone with apparent obliviousness to the tactics of their undeclared but allied supporters.

Early in 1981, we spent three weeks in the nation's capital, interviewing spokespersons for a variety of lobbies and special-interest groups, as well as senators, congressmen and their aides, about the impact of the fundamentalist right on the workings of government. Their response was curiously split. Those who had felt the bite of the movement's attacks in 1980 seemed hard-pressed to overstate their concern. Yet the greater portion of those who had not been touched, including many of those who had already been named to fundamentalist right "hit lists" for 1982, were not eager to talk with us. Many denied that they were concerned. One hit list did not make an election, they said. Besides, we were told, most polls showed that fundamentalist right religious and political forces had only minimal impact on the contests they had entered. Economic and other traditional factors were said to be far more significant.

This attitude surprised us, especially in the light of things we had been hearing in our travels. But as we soon learned, this blasé attitude and apparent lack of concern was a cover for a deeper sense of fear and intimidation, a tough new strain of the classic illness known around town as "Potomac fever." In the first months of the new Congress, as legislators busied themselves with the administration's "emergency economic package," Potomac fever was running high in Congress. Across town, however, it had long since broken.

Senator Church. After twenty-four years in the United States Senate, Frank Church was down off the Hill, bounced out of his seat as senior senator from Idaho and chairman of the Senate Foreign Relations Committee, and now working for a law firm in Washington. Church was among the first victims of a coalition of fundamentalist right PACs with names like the Committee for Positive Change, Stop the Baby-Killers, the National Right to Life Committee and the Citizens Committee for the Right to Keep and Bear Arms. Leading the PACs was NCPAC ("Nick-pack"), the National Conservative Political Action Committee, headed by John T. Dolan, and in Idaho, a NCPAC offspring called ABC—Anybody But Church. Along with Senator Church, NCPAC's "Target '80" campaign had zeroed in on four other liberal Democratic senators: George McGovern of South Dakota, Birch Bayh of Indiana, John Culver of Iowa and Alan Cranston of California. All but Cranston lost.

In the campaign, PACs had branded this champion of social progress and the dominant Senate figure during the foreign policy debacle of Vietnam a "baby-killer," an apostle of "appeasement," a "liar" and a "dangerous man." For his role in the Senate Intelligence hearings of 1975, NCPAC had dubbed him "the radical" who "single-handedly has presided over the destruction of the FBI and the CIA." Church fought back in 1980, lashing out at his accusers for what he called their use of "the big lie technique."

Idaho newspapers termed the attacks on him "cheap," "deceitful," "venal" and "pigweed." But like so many Democratic incumbents, he lost ground steadily and was buried in the Reagan landslide.

"I don't know what to make of their motivation," he confessed, referring to this new breed of political adversary, "except to say that in Dolan's case, he's very brazen. To say that he's careless with the truth would be using much too mild a term. I think he would acknowledge that he has no compunctions about twisting the truth, reshaping it and presenting it in ways that are intended to discredit an incumbent in the eyes of his constituents."

He recalled an example from the early days of the campaign.

"NCPAC commenced its attack on me by running television commercials which showed a local legislator, a very conservative Republican closely affiliated with the new right, standing next to the open hole of a Titan missile silo. He was pointing down into the silo and saying 'This silo is empty and the women and children of Idaho are in graver danger of a Russian attack because Frank Church almost always votes against a strong defense.' "

Church's eyebrows went up. "Now, from a factual standpoint, there were several things wrong with that commercial. First, I had not emptied the silo. That had been done by a decision of the Air Force, owing to the fact that the Titan missile had become obsolete. Secondly, the obsolete Titan missile had been replaced by a much more advanced, more accurate and more dependable Minuteman missile. I had voted *for* the Minuteman missile, not against it! And finally, the empty silo hardly made the women and children of Idaho more vulnerable to a Russian attack, because if the Russians ever engaged in such an insanity, the last place they would be likely to target would be an *empty* silo! From every standpoint, the message was ludicrous and false."

Church ticked off a list of other distortions and misrepresentations of fact that he claimed were used to discredit him in 1980. Among the charges: that he had taken money from Chrysler Corporation executives, then voted for federal loan guarantees for the foundering company; and that he had received "influence buying" money from California and Arizona irrigators to vote for a Senate bill in their interest. A NCPAC newspaper ad accused him of voting to increase his Senate salary by $13,000, when in fact he had voted against the proposed increase. At that point in the campaign, Church, who had until then been silent, called a press conference and pointed to the record. NCPAC took out a second ad, retracting the claim.

"But I was left to wonder whether they did it deliberately," he mused, "knowing that the retraction seldom catches up with the original lie."

The same NCPAC ad also distorted Church's vote for federal aid to bail out New York City's sinking finances.

"New York City was cited again and again in the campaign," he said. "NCPAC claimed that I had cost the taxpayers $1.3 billion of federal money. But, here again, the truth was that I hadn't cost the taxpayers anything. By the time they ran the ad, all of that money had been repaid to the Treasury, plus about $32 million in interest. The taxpayers had actually *earned* a modest amount, but when I pointed this out, NCPAC refused to retract the charge. From then on, they really exhibited very little interest in whether their charges were distorted or even false. They just kept repeating them in different forms."

We asked Church if he had ever faced strategies like this in his political career.

"No, nothing as brazen as this," he said. "They start in early on incumbents, sometimes a year before the campaign gets under way, with enough money to use television and radio long before people are even focusing on the next election. Then through this constant repetition of certain themes, they can erode the base of support for anyone they choose to target."

In his race, Church saw the large nationwide groups, such as NCPAC, acting as master strategists, central coordinators among various fundamentalist right organizations with allied social, political, economic and religious goals.

"Some of those who are targeted may not appreciate how this coalition of far right organizations works together and how closely it is attuned ideologically," he said. "For example, there was no logical reason, no plausible reason, no earthly reason why I should have been selected by the right to life organization as one of their five targeted senators. Now, by NCPAC, yes. I can understand why they would want to include me in their top five. But my position on abortion is very conservative and always has been. It's far from abortion by choice. I was ninety-five percent on their side of the issue, but the right to lifers moved in against me anyway and circulated the churches with literature on the Sunday before the election. I have no doubt that had a very real impact on the outcome of the race."

Church pointed out that one week before the vote, polls showed him nine points ahead of his Republican opponent, Congressman Steven Symms, despite the efforts of Dolan and NCPAC. As the race came down to the wire, however, other groups jumped in to help finish him off.

"Moral Majority, Christian Voice and the rest didn't move in until the last stages of the campaign," he said. "Then they closed ranks to reinforce everything that NCPAC had been doing. They took out advertisements that read: 'Don't vote for Frank Church—Pray for him!' They leafleted the churches the Sunday before the election. They put literature on the cars. There was a terrific blitz at the end. The money behind it was immense. In the end, I came within one percent of winning—that's only four thousand votes. But when a switch of twenty-five hundred might have swung the election, any one group alone probably did me enough damage to make the difference."

In the profusion of PACs, however, Church saw the fundamentalist groups as the most dangerous.

"You can say, accurately, of Terry Dolan and his associates, that truth is the first casualty in their campaigns, that they are simply engaged in manipulating public opinion," said Church. "They have come to believe that if you use these methods, if you have the money, if you repeat the themes, you can cut into the base of support of any incumbent and have a powerful influence on electing your own candidates. But the fundamentalist wing of the movement, to me, is the most insidious part of this new phenomenon. It's not that we haven't had episodes of intolerance and fanaticism in the past, but the witch burnings in Salem were pretty much confined to Salem. Now we have these pulpiteers reaching out to an entire nation over the largest media network in the world!"

He was referring to the newly politicized preachers of the televised "electronic church," but he went on to say that he was not opposed to religious leaders getting involved in politics. In

Church's view, however, the fundamentalists were crossing over a line that had not been breached before.

"The difference is that the fundamentalist ministers of the right are absolutists," he said. "They believe that they possess the ultimate truth which has been revealed through the Bible and that their interpretation of Scriptures constitutes the irrefutable will of God. Now you can say that the Catholic Church or other churches believe that their doctrine or creed is the ultimate truth, but until now, even absolutist churches have confined their doctrine to the salvation of the soul for those who believe, and that doesn't trespass on others. Such authority rests on the belief that you either adhere to their creeds and thus win eternal salvation, or you don't and are damned to eternal condemnation. The fundamentalist right is going beyond, seeking to change the laws of the country to conform to their religious beliefs, so that everyone must comply under penalty of punishment. They are exhibiting a kind of fanaticism that leaves no room for those who may disagree, for nonbelievers, for Jews and other minorities in this country who may not be practicing Christians."

This question of fanaticism was one we would confront often. Church elaborated on his sense of the term.

"They are not satisfied to have their go in the arena of the democratic process," he said, "where you win or lose, but you do so with a certain grace and with a certain respect for the motivation of those who may disagree with you. Their bigotry and intolerance toward those who disagree is extreme. They see themselves as the great force of the future, destined to dominate the whole political, economic, social and religious agenda for this country and perhaps the world."

The nonreligious nature of the movement seemed obvious to Church. He cited the "morality index" issued in 1980 by the Christian Voice.

"About half the issues on their index were purely secular: Taiwan, the Panama Canal, the Rhodesian sanctions. They could not be logically related to their religious beliefs. So you got the bizarre result that Father Drinan, a congressman who was a Catholic priest, got a zero morality rating, while Congressman Kelly, who admitted taking a $25,000 Abscam bribe, got a one hundred percent morality rating."

He saw his own targeting by the movement as equally political. "In my case, it had nothing to do with morality," said Church. "The fact was, quite simply: they wanted me out of the chairmanship of the Senate Foreign Relations Committee."

As we talked about the campaign, Church came back to the role of fundamentalist preachers in the political process. Long after the campaign, his personal concern was still growing. He had recently given an address in New York on the fundamentalist right's "theo-political" goals.

"Have you read the statement of purpose of the Christian Voice?" he asked, reaching for a copy of his speech. He read: "'We believe that America, the last stronghold of faith on this planet, has come under increasing attack from Satan's forces in recent years. . . . The standards of Christian morality (long the protection and strength of the nation), the sanctity of our families, the innocence of our young, are now under the onslaught launched by the "rulers of darkness of this world" and insidiously sustained under the ever more liberal ethic.' "

"Shades of the Ayatollah Khomeini!" he said. "Dissenters are devils to be pursued, condemned and exorcised!"

He eased back in his chair. "You know," he reflected, "I think the separation of church and state has served this country exceedingly well. When you consider what a disparate, polyglot land this is, were it not for that principle and the capacity we've demonstrated to tolerate differences among us, we could never have maintained a free society all these years. Even today, tradition in this country still works against any effort on the part of fundamentalist preachers to lead a political movement directly. Their method is one of *indirection*. They speak from the pulpit to a tremendous number of people every week. They make it clear how 'good' Christians should vote on religious grounds, and thus they control the political process by indirection. I have no doubt that many a close election in 1980 was decided in this way, by true believers who went to the polls thinking that they were carrying out the will of God."

Church's thoughts returned to the Hill, which had been his life and home for a quarter century. "I can't imagine that anyone is genuinely indifferent up there," he said. "Of course, states may vary—my state might have been far more susceptible to this kind

of appeal than others—but when you see how much influence this
movement has gained in nearly all of the Bible Belt of the South
and Midwest, in all of the intermountain West—in Alaska, they've
taken over the Republican Party completely—you just have to take
this seriously."

We asked him what countermeasures he would recommend.

"I think the method for dealing with this thing has still to be
devised. When all the information is put out, when people see why
it poses a danger to a free society like ours, when targeted incumbents realize how vulnerable they are to attack, I think we'll see
some enterprising countermeasures begin to emerge."

Church's mood deepened. His tales of intimidation reminded us
of others we had heard about targeted senators, reports of fear-
filled committee meetings, of Senate sessions dominated by unspoken threats of political retribution, and of congressional prayer
breakfasts conducted, as one senator told us, in an atmosphere of
"inquisition."

"Are you glad you're out of there?" we asked him.

For a moment, he was silent. Then he nodded.

"Yes," he said, metering his words. "I began to think . . . in
the later days of my career in the Senate . . . that the place had
become a kind of asylum . . . and that I was one of the inmates."

Congressman Synar. Mike Synar licked them in 1980. Singled
out for defeat by Moral Majority, this freshman Democrat from
Muskogee, Oklahoma, was reelected by fifty-four percent of the
voters in his district. With House and Senate heavyweights falling
like flies in his own and nearby states, the Honorable Michael J.
Synar, a born competitor, fought back hard and won. Back on the
job in 1981, Synar was not likely to call in sick with Potomac
fever. A New York *Times* article had pegged him "an angry
young man," openly fearful of the impact of special interests on
Congress and the political process. Yet at thirty, his boyish good
looks and tousled hair made him something less than an imposing
political figure. When we met him in his office across from the
Capitol, he looked more like a first-draft-choice ballplayer, standing solid, shirtsleeves rolled and ready for action, as he leaned into
our conversation.

"I want the whole free world to know we've been targeted," he said. "That's one of the things we've learned about these groups. The classic incumbent's strategy when you're attacked is don't respond, because you turn one newspaper story into two and enhance your opponent's 'name identification.' Well, these guys have got so damn much money to pour into TV and they are so well organized in the churches that the technique a lot of incumbents used in their campaigns backfired in 1980. We've decided to meet them head on."

Synar was a straight shooter. He spoke plainly, with a hint of Midwestern twang that put a stamp of authenticity on his words. He talked of his campaign experiences with pad and pen in hand, drawing diagrams and jotting down numbers as he referred to "media buys," "beefed-up samplings" and other advanced tools and methods that have come to dominate the campaign process.

"The style of politics has changed radically," he said, referring not only to these mass-media and polling techniques. "Thanks to the new right, incumbents and favorites can no longer play their traditional roles. Look at my state. As far as Moral Majority was concerned, there were two focuses of attention in Oklahoma in the last campaign: the U.S. Senate race and my race. Andrew Coats, the Democratic Senate candidate, took the high road. We, on the other hand, did not take what I would call the low road, but we did take on the challenge. We won. He didn't."

Synar cited a number of instances in which he and Coats were forced to confront charges made by the Moral Majority and other groups. Coats was accused of "smelling of alcohol" when he delivered a speech to 117 Baptist preachers—a charge he declined to respond to. Synar, on the other hand, faced up to similar threats from the beginning.

"Their first media buy was centered around Moral Majority issues," he said, "prayer in school, abortion, things like that. It was one of the healthiest media buys early in a campaign that any of us had ever seen. On school prayer, they twisted my position. They said that I was opposed to voluntary prayer in school, which was not the case. Six weeks later, we found that we had dropped roughly ten points in the polls. We were bleeding to death. At that point, we decided not to ignore them any longer."

Synar and his team "went on the attack," but their response was larger than any single issue or group.

"We did not attack the Moral Majority per se," he pointed out. "The first thing we said was that we had a lot of Christian men and women supporting us—which was true. We did not even attack them for their *right* to get politically involved. But we identified the Moral Majority for what they were. They are not a religious group; they are a political group. Then finally we challenged the accuracy of their information. Our counterattack was quiet, a person-to-person type of thing."

Synar cited other instances of what he called Moral Majority's "horrendous distortions." Besides the school prayer vote, he said, his opponents twisted his record on the Panama Canal treaty, defense spending, abortion and other social issues—as Church told us NCPAC and others had done to him. As Election Day approached, Synar continued, advance polls showed a drift over to his underdog opponent, a newcomer named Gary Richardson. He recalled their initial confrontation.

"Richardson was not considered to be in the race until the day before the filing deadline," said Synar. "It had taken us eighteen months to organize our district, then he jumped in with no money and no name identification. Well, all of a sudden this unknown, unfinanced candidate had a ton of money, a ready-made organization and every known right-wing group backing him. Three weeks out, at the chamber of commerce forum in Muskogee—my hometown and the largest city in the district—I took off the gloves."

Synar relived the moment with obvious joy.

"He went through his basic speech about me being against prayer in school and the whole smear. Then I stood up and said very clearly, 'Good afternoon, ladies and gentlemen. Welcome to the Muskogee Chamber of Commerce Congressional Debate, better titled "Truth or Consequences."' I said, 'My opponent, Gary Richardson, has said I'm against prayer in school. That's a lie and Gary Richardson *knows* that's a lie.' I went through each attack they had made and said, 'That's a lie and Gary Richardson *knows* that's a lie.' Well, his face turned about fifteen shades of white. He couldn't believe that I had gone on the attack. Then I called him a *Superchristian*. I said he was using his religious credentials as a lay minister to express a political posture, which was improper. I broke his back! My hometown polarized against this religious movement and we won Muskogee by fifty-five hundred votes."

Synar laid out the fundamentalist right's grand strategy as he saw it.

"Now, I don't know about other campaigns, but this is what we were able to chase down and piece together," he began. "In districts like mine, they start with their base group, which is the religious community of small-town churches. They may bring someone in from the national office of Moral Majority who will meet in a small local church with maybe no more than twenty ministers, basically fundamentalist. Then they'll show a film filled with horrors about the Russians and welfare cheaters, one of those really scary right-wing movies, and the Moral Majority man may get up and make a speech pointing out that their congressman has not supported these issues and has to be defeated because he is not representing the family unit, 'the moral and ethical fiber' of the district. Afterward, they may hand out a scorecard sheet rating the congressman on the morality of his voting record."

Once that base group is established, Synar explained, fundamentalist right forces may proceed to build what he called "satellites."

"Now this is important," he said, drawing lines on his pad, "because that's where they get their troops. You see, for many years the right has always had unbelievable amounts of money. But they never had the soldiers. This marriage between the religious community and right-wing money has given them the two tools it takes to win: all the money you could ever want and all the soldiers you need to deliver. Well, we can fight money, but when they pull in four hundred workers from the youth groups and churches who have been all fired up, it's an impossible thing to match."

Synar explained how the fundamentalist right also reached beyond the religious camp into larger circles of small-town life.

"Now, in my particular case, we found them involved with another active core group in the community, the Amway Corporation, the national home product sales company. Amway is a great system of organization in rural areas because they use the pyramid theory to build their local sales force. It may turn out that their head man locally starts having meetings with all his people, and they literally have a rural political organization overnight. I have a lot of close friends in Muskogee who are in Amway. Their kids are still in school and they like to make a few bucks on the side. I lost them all, because Amway people were getting to them more often than I could. They had people living down the street who've known my family all my life really thinking that I was some kind of villain. They spread rumors—the underground is very active out there—and being single, you can imagine I was hit with all the things that go along with that. I felt a sincere anger, I must say, but I never really believed in my heart that we would lose. So I did not overreact. They were better financed, they outspent us; but even with their huge organization, they couldn't out-organize us. I made myself available. I went home thirty-three weekends last year. I really worked the district. In the final analysis, that may have been what put us over."

Synar paused. His pride was unassuming. He included his staff in each detail of his campaign efforts. Yet, clearly, he was hurt by these personal attacks. His frequent use of the term "We were bleeding" seemed to be more than mere polling jargon.

"The emotionalism was so great," he continued. "I saw I could not take on the far right, particularly the religious right, using logic and reason. I would walk into a hot town meeting and the hatred for me was so great I couldn't hope to overcome it. The answer always took longer than the attack. For example, on the abortion issue, I am not for abortion on demand, but I am for abortion in cases of rape or incest or to save the life of the mother. I can get up there and give you an eloquent explanation of the Supreme Court decision on abortion. I can show the beauty of that whole argument by Justice Blackmun. I can make it as emotional as you want—would you turn down a little child who had been raped? Or your own sister? I can pour on the emotion as well as they can, and I can turn people around on the issue. But it takes fifteen minutes, not ten seconds. Then what did we see on the last Sunday before the election? Leaflets on every car in every church parking lot with dead fetuses and a slogan that says, in effect: 'Your congressman kills these kids!' That was *me* they were talking about!"

The experience left Synar with a cutting impression of his opponents.

"Look," he continued, "these people are fanatics. They have

one policy: win at all costs. They'll push any issue that will get them a vote, any issue that will raise them a buck. They'll say anything. They'll do anything. They'll use any tactic that's available to them. They have no principles, no morals, no ethics. They will say anything, regardless of whether there's an iota of truth to it. They'll play to any group."

Synar shook his head in dismay. "You know, it is regrettable that the media let them run rampant in the last election. I think we lost a good ten to fifteen Democratic seats that would not have been lost if these groups had been revealed for what they really are: a front, a loose-knit group of front organizations for the Republican National Committee."

It was a serious charge, one we had not heard voiced until then. "Don't you know what the Republicans are doing?" he explained. "They're setting the stage for this. They sit in the House of Representatives making up all these crazy amendments—and you can quote me on this—to get Democrats on the record against them. Why do you think they voted seventeen times on abortion and prayer in schools? To use in their propaganda! Take defense. I'm very pro-national defense, but I'm also for spending *smart* defense money. Well, each of these religious and right-wing groups used my voting record to try to show me as anti-defense. The five votes they used were all Republican substitutes to budget authorization and appropriation bills. They were not even defense votes. But they ran commercials saying I voted against national defense. Every one of these groups had handouts mentioning these votes. Now, it's pretty hard to believe that they would have all seen all five of these budget votes and used them as defense votes unless somebody told them to twist it. This same commercial was run in congressional districts nationwide and paid for by the Republican National Committee. I saw commercials for three other Republican candidates around the country. Each had the same slogan and the same pictures as my opponent's. I mean, you've got to ask, don't you?"

As we talked more about the opposition, our conversation turned from campaigns to Congress itself. It was here, on the Hill, that Synar was seeing the end result of fundamentalist right tactics at the grass-roots level.

"I'm very worried about the future of the United States Congress," he said. "These groups have become a petrifying force. You can see it in the House right now. We are literally legislating out of fear. People are afraid of what will happen if they do not kowtow to the right. Let me give you an example: I have a friend in the House from a midwestern state who is a moderate, personally a little bit liberal, but he's a hard-liner when it comes to abortion. He's anti-abortion right down the line. I went to him and I said, 'Why this one issue? Is it something in your background?' And he said, 'No, it's very simple. Since I've been in Congress, I have never won an election by more than seven percent of the vote. Seven percent of the people in my district are anti-abortion, and they all vote. If they turn on me, I'm not here."

Synar began slowly tearing sheets off his notepad.

"Look," he continued, "it's bad around here. It's frightening. My colleagues, some of the closest friends I've made over the last two years, are really frustrated. They don't know whether to go on with the fight or to just go home and forget it. The fire, the enthusiasm, the aggressiveness of a lot of my colleagues are gone. Legislation that should be authored is not being authored. Issues that should be discussed are not being discussed. It's not only the natural change in power from Democrats to Republicans that has caused this. It is a sense that the Democrats and even Republicans opposed to these groups do not know how to fight them. And because they don't know how to fight them, they do nothing."

Synar offered another example of how the fundamentalist right has succeeded in spreading fear through Congress.

"There are a number of issues where these right-wing groups cannot win in the Supreme Court or on certain legislative committees. So now they are trying to change the forum of debate in order to gain control. Last term I served on the Judiciary Committee, which is like Death Row in the U.S. Congress. It's the most controversial committee. That's where you get all the issues in one place: abortion, school prayer, busing. As a midwestern, moderate congressman, it has become very dangerous to sit on this committee. I had an opportunity to leave it, but I stayed. I was not going to let them run me off Judiciary. There were twelve other openings and Democrats had to be recruited to fill them."

Synar explained how, in his view, such tactics threaten to undermine the lawmaking process.

"As a congressman, I have a mandate from the people of my district to make the most responsible decision based on the facts," he said. "In doing that, I satisfy my conscience and represent my district at the same time. Well, that's not the way the right sees it at all. They want to tell my people what they want. They want to set the issues. As congressmen, we used to say, 'We're here to represent our people whether they're informed or not.' But now we have to go one step further. We've got to say, 'We're here to represent our people, but we've got to recognize that they may now be *misinformed!*' We may get fifteen hundred letters on some issues, all on the same little perforated postcards. We know that there has been a conscious effort to misinform the public. But we have to launch a barrage of media and personal appearances explaining the issues and our votes. It's not enough to be a legislator anymore. You have to be an information-provider."

Synar thumped his desk. "Let me tell you something," he said. "There's only one way to deal with the new right. You don't go in there and try to out-yell them and out-scream them and out-holler them. The way you're going to beat them down is the way you beat down any extremist group: with better information and better ideas. When you go in there, you've got to have your facts in order. You need to have good sound reasons for your position that people really do believe in. Then you've got to prepare your people for what they're going to hear. You've got to let them know they've been targeted, so it won't take them by surprise."

As Synar talked, we saw the stark picture he was painting. The new session of Congress had scarcely begun, and as he described it, the fundamentalist right was already a steamrolling force. We asked him how serious he thought it might become. He answered without hesitation.

"It's the future of the whole American democratic structure as we know it," he said. "We've always had extremist groups in this country, on the right and on the left, but thankfully they have always played themselves out. Never before have we had such massive amounts of money combined with precision targeting. If enough people surrender, if enough people give up, if enough people say, 'The challenge is not great enough, just let them have it,' if enough people turn their heads, you're going to see a change in the focus of this country that may take generations to recover from. We are heading toward a point where reason, compassion and understanding will no longer be the order of the day. It will be emotion and deception—fear and lies. It's up to the American people to decide whether they will accept that type of politics."

He stopped, breaking his own stride.

"It's a funny thing," he said, his mood softening. "You may find this ironic. Last year, I was depicted as immoral and unethical, the anti-family candidate. In 1972, my family was chosen the outstanding All-American family in the United States by the National Conference of Christians and Jews! I am a two-time national winner in the 4-H Club. My sister and brother are two-time national winners. I am a former state president of the 4-H Club, former state chairman of the Episcopal Young People's Organization, state Junior Classical League president, state Farmer's Union speech winner, state American Legion speech contest winner, national state winner in debate, chairman of the student congress of the University of Oklahoma. And I'm being painted as unethical, immoral and anti-family!"

Synar pointed to some of the personal trappings around his office. "All my life I've had one tag: the All-American boy," he said. "I knew when I was fourteen years old that I wanted to be a U.S. congressman. I've led my life so I would have nothing to hide. I'm a farmer and a rancher. I come from a small town. I have a model family. My parents are immigrants. Now I'm being painted as the devil himself!"

The contrast was apparent. We asked him for his outlook for the future.

"The real emphasis in the next year or so is going to be at the state level," he said. "We're going to see a real power play by the Moral Majority at the bottom of the political spectrum, in races for state representative, state senator, county commissioner and so on. If they succeed there, all bets are off. It will be over. Because if they can break the states, they'll break the foundation that elects people like me.

"It's a sad commentary on America," he said dejectedly. "A lot of good men and women were defeated in 1980 who were honest, legitimate, hardworking, dedicated public servants. They were defeated because they were outspent and lied about, and this country will be the less for that. I've asked myself many times since the election, 'Is this going to change my voting patterns? Is it going to make me watch myself more carefully?' The answer is no. I love this job and I'll fight anybody, particularly these groups, to keep it. But I won't kowtow to them. I know I'm playing with fire. I know I'm inviting it—the misery, the headaches, the money, the extremist organizations—but I have faith in the American people. I really do. No matter what, they are not going to make me fear my own constituency."

As we rose to leave, Synar backed away from his desk. On the wall behind him there was a huge Indian headdress studded with bright blue-and-white feathers. He said it was an authentic Cherokee warbonnet, specially made in his campaign colors.

"You know," he said, "the only thing every voter in this country wants to know about the person they send to office is that he's a fighter. Well, this may be the issue I've decided to fight. I would much rather fight in other areas. I'd rather be an expert on energy or education or economics. But I can't, because everything in those areas is now tied into this area. This may be *the* issue. This may be the challenge of my whole political career.

"Moral Majority said they would not have a hit list in Oklahoma in 1982," he said keenly. "They said there was only one person they wanted to defeat: Mike Synar."

And Mike Synar licked them again in 1982.

Big Fathers

"Let me count this day, Lord, as the beginning of a new and more vigorous life, as the beginning of a crusade for complete morality and the domination of the Christian church through all the land. Dear Lord, thy work is but begun! We shall yet make these United States a moral nation!"

—SINCLAIR LEWIS—*Elmer Gantry*, 1927

EACH IN THEIR OWN WAY, Diane, Senator Church and Congressman Synar described to us this new form of intimidation, manipulation and control by indirection advancing under cover of religion. After talking to its victims and targets, we began looking for our own pathways of insight into the movement. Soon we discovered how much of it was right before our eyes: on television, in the pulpit of the "electronic church," where the magic of technology had turned so many ministers and preachers into Big Fathers, front men in the modern business of Holy Terror.

For decades, mainline America ignored its sanctimonious TV preachers. We trucked them to the dump of television, Sunday morning, where they wrung tens of millions from their extended flocks, piling dollar upon dollar and brick upon brick until they had built great media empires that reached into space. Like all things electronic, the electronic church has come a long way in fifty years: from the first crackly radiocasts of tent-show holy rollers like Aimee Semple McPherson in the twenties, to the hate-filled sputterings of Father Coughlin in the thirties, to the kindly smile and flowing vestments of Bishop Sheen in the fifties. No longer just for the aged and the handicapped, today the electronic church is the preferred form of religious exercise for housewives with small children, working people on the go, college students, truckers and traveling salesmen. It commands space beside the networks in daily TV logs. It has its own slot on the dial in motel rooms. It plays in bars.

The electronic church, we are told, is a colossal structure: 1,400 radio stations, 3,500 local television and cable systems, 4 all-religious satellite networks, with new Christian radio stations signing on at the rate of 1 a week, new TV stations at 1 a month. Altogether, they rake in over $500 million—*half a billion!*—in small donations, tax-free, every year. More than 115 million Americans are said to tune in each week. Forty-seven percent of the country now prays better electronically. Only forty percent attend church regularly. Surely, this is a force to be reckoned with.

Or is it? The numbers are not gospel. Until recently, much of the data on the electronic church came from the electronic church itself: from boastful TV preachers; from spokesmen for the National Religious Broadcasters, a trade association of Christian programmers; or from polls commissioned by its members. Many of those figures now appear to be inflated or misleading. Using data from A. C. Nielsen, the nation's best-known television research organization, Rice University professor Dr. William Martin found that the ten most popular TV evangelists had a combined audience of only 13.7 million. Adjusted downward for those who watch several shows back to back, said Martin, a total of only 7 to 10 million Americans could be counted among the mainstay audience of the electronic church. The statistics may be turned and seasoned according to taste; there is little doubt that, in the early seventies, the electronic church more than doubled in size, ballooning from 10 million viewers in 1970 to just under 21 million in 1975, when it leveled off. Yet, ironically, as its brightest stars were rising, its combined ratings began slipping—by nearly a million in a three-year period.

Now, from all indications, the electronic church has begun to collapse upon itself, as power becomes concentrated in the hands of a few. Like a star in the process of transformation, it is growing smaller and hotter. For those who possess the greatest armories of high technology—the latest satellites, the biggest studios, the fastest computerized fund-raising operations—success is sweet. To the small fry go the spoils and the loose change, the weak and the infirm. Across the board, however, the projected picture is still one of pomp and sanctimony, complete with live audiences, lavish sets, splashy musical extravaganzas and ritual glitter. More than ever, in its metamorphosis, the electronic church is the flagship of the fundamentalist right in its bid to establish a separate Christian culture with a separate, all-encompassing mass medium, ideologically pure, unlimited in its potential and, for all practical purposes, beyond the reach of regulation.

At the helm are the Big Fathers, religious broadcasting personalities who bear little resemblance to clergymen as we have always known them. Few if any perform weddings, funerals, christenings or other acts of personal counseling and consolation. Their ministries rarely extend beyond their state-of-the-art broadcast facilities. Mainly, they seek to win converts, to build ever larger headquarters with still newer technology, to buy great tracts of real estate and to found Christian universities in their names. And with increasing enthusiasm, many are now using their enormous wealth and popular followings to mount strident social and political crusades.

People are worried about the rise of the Big Fathers and their electronic church. Community church leaders claim they are driving local religions off the air. This may be true: in 1959, half of all religious programming was nonpaid time donated by local stations to many faiths and denominations. Today, ninety-two percent is bought time, paid for by Christian, mostly fundamentalist, Big Fathers. The Federal Communications Commission has investigated a number of them on charges of fraudulent and deceptive fund-raising, yet most have survived unscathed. To date, no one has looked deeper into the way in which so much technology is being used in the name of religion to manipulate the beliefs and actions of millions on a daily basis.

As we began delving into the fundamentalist right, we realized that, in all the talk about the electronic church, few useful distinctions were being made. Moral Majority's Rev. Jerry Falwell with his "Old-Time Gospel Hour" was not the only stop on the dial, nor was he the industry leader. Many Big Fathers had been on television and radio far longer. Other TV ministries had larger facilities and viewing audiences. Still others had higher annual incomes. But were they all part of the picture of Holy Terror?

To find out for ourselves, we began watching the electronic church—religiously. Sundays from morning until evening, weekdays at seven, afternoons at one. For a solid month and then regularly, we watched Big Fathers until our eyes began to blur. We came to know their TV faces and families, their styles and sales pitches, and we began to note distinctions: between the old-timers and the newcomers, the good guys and the bad boys, the country bumpkins and the city slickers. All seemed firmly rooted in the same foundation of big-money, high-technology Christianity, and in the unyielding evangelical imperative: to go and make disciples of every creature and all nations. Yet, as we watched, out of the swirl, a sharp division came into view between those Big Fathers who appeared to use their pulpits for political ends and those who did not. For the most part, the old-timers seemed dedicated to creating a television version of faith and devotion, however lucrative, slick and imperfect. The newcomers, on the other hand, seemed to be using the privileges of religion and the power of mass media to build a broad base for ulterior ends. In order to understand their divergence, we sought to place them within the larger establishment of the electronic church, which most Americans still assume to be quite benign.

THE OLD-TIMERS

Oral Roberts. Most of the old-timers predate television, but their empires rest on their success in the medium. Oral Roberts, for example, the granddaddy of Christian broadcasting, has been around so long doing exactly the same thing that most people forget he is still on the air. Yet, until recently, no other video ministry claimed an annual income as high as his estimated $60 million, and to date no other TV preacher holds sway over a city as large as Roberts's Tulsa, Oklahoma. Through the fifties, Roberts won fame and followers as a tent-show faith healer from the "buckle" of the Bible Belt. In the early sixties, he founded Oral Roberts University, ORU, "the campus where miracles are a way of life." Tulsa's number-one tourist attraction, ORU is the prototypical fundamentalist TV preacher's university, complete with Bible-oriented curriculum, a rigid dress code, a campus singing group

that appears on Roberts's TV show, and a basketball team that
acts as a drawing card for students and symbolizes Roberts's
image of wholesome, robust Christianity.

Faith and health go together in the world of Oral Roberts. In
1977, he announced plans for his $120-million City of Faith com-
plex that included a thirty-story hospital, a twenty-story research
tower, a sixty-story clinic and a medical school devoted to merg-
ing "God's healing streams of medicine and prayer." Like ORU
Law School, which has been charged repeatedly with religious bias
in its selection of students, since its inception, Roberts's City of
Faith has been surrounded in controversy, legal battles and divine
defenses. In 1980, Roberts claimed he had received assurances of
the project's success when a looming 900-foot Jesus Christ spoke
to him in a vision. The following year, the complex opened with
much fanfare and no organized opposition.

At the center of the conglomerate stands Roberts and his
weekly television show, currently titled "Sunday Night Live." On-
camera, he is an old-time faith healer, offering little more than
simple inspiration and crusty sermonizing. Yet his positive slogan
—"Something *good* is going to happen to *you!*"—and his surefire
sales pitch of "seed faith"—give *first,* then expect miracles in your
life—may account for much of the sixty-four-year-old preacher's
staying power, and for the fact that, in 1980, his program topped
the Nielsen ratings among religious broadcasts. All this, from what
we could see, on the strength of nothing more complicated than
this homily by Richard, Roberts's son and heir apparent:

> We love you, we believe in you, we're praying for
> you. . . . We as a family love you and care for you and
> want you to share with us what your needs are. Where you're
> hurting, we'll pray for you and expect miracles in your life,
> physically and financially. Not only that, we'll write you
> back. That's a promise from our family to you.

Though his latest ratings have begun to falter in the face of
growing competition, Roberts is still going strong. Watching his
big-time professionalism, listening to his sermons and singers, we
saw little in his studio sets that went beyond the tent show or the
country church. But the world behind the cameras was another

story. Jerry Sholes, a former scriptwriter and producer for Roberts, offered a rare insider's look at the workings of the electronic church in his book, *Give Me That Prime-Time Religion*. His report on the Oral Roberts Evangelistic Association described the machinery and duplicity that may be characteristic of many religious broadcast enterprises. Among other things, Sholes pointed out that this brand of high-volume TV religion can barely keep up with its correspondence. Roberts, who has claimed to answer every letter personally, received as many as 20,000 letters per day when Sholes was with him, each of which required opening, sorting, accounting for contributions and preparation of a response. If Roberts did this personally, Sholes maintained, he would have had to read and answer twenty-four letters *per minute*! Instead, incoming mail was run through mechanical letter openers and sorted into two categories: money enclosed or no money enclosed. From there, it was distributed to more than a hundred "letter analysts," who scanned the letters and coded them according to the type of problem mentioned by the writer: health, finances, marriage, spiritual, family, etc. Computers then matched the codes with stored paragraphs containing brief replies to each category of problem, messages written, not by Roberts, but by OREA staff writers and edited by OREA vice-presidents before they were sent to Roberts for approval or modification. Similar mechanisms intervened in Roberts's pledge to pray personally over the letter requests he receives. According to Sholes, Roberts prays over computer printouts containing only the names of the writers sorted according to problem category. "It is my contention," wrote Sholes, with a note of bitterness, "that this is not what people expect when they write to Oral Roberts and ask him to pray over their problems."

Sholes had other bones to pick with Roberts and his high-rolling ministry. He criticized the star evangelist's $500 Brioni suits, his $25,000 Mercedes and his $250,000 home in Tulsa as trappings unbecoming a country faith healer who loves to talk about his humble origins. But to us, these excesses seemed common among the old-timers. Watching them, we saw an electronic church that was only superficially religious, not at all political, merely big business; and in their country ways, the old-timers strived to look and play the role of executives.

Rex Humbard. The medium's other leading old-timer has built his business on the same product line. At sixty-two, Rex Humbard has been around as long as anybody in religious broadcasting: forty-nine years on radio, thirty on TV. Born in Hot Springs, Arkansas, the son of itinerant preachers, he was saved at thirteen and has been evangelizing ever since. In 1958, he opened his $3.5-million Cathedral of Tomorrow in Akron, Ohio, a 3,500-seat, futuristic marble-and-glass extravaganza, equipped with a hydraulic stage and a 100-foot cross containing 4,700 red-white-and-blue lightbulbs. Humbard claims to minister to 100 million each week in six different languages over 620 stations, but his figures are doubtful. Among the big breadwinners, his estimated $25-million annual income seems rather paltry for a ministry the size he claims. Nevertheless, over the years Humbard has managed to accumulate his share of electronic church assets. In 1973, his holdings included a $10-million office complex in Akron, a college in Michigan and a girdle factory in Brooklyn, New York.

Like Roberts, Humbard's show is a family operation—a mix of gospel singing, traditional sermonizing and prayer—hosted by Rex and wife Maude Aimee, with the help of their children and grandchildren. Humbard also has a massive direct-mail operation to follow up on the requests for books and other materials he offers on the air. Yet his pleas for support have not always meshed with his needs of the moment. In 1979, Humbard claimed on the air that his ministry was $3.2 million in debt. Shortly thereafter, he and his two sons purchased a home and condominiums in Florida for $650,000. "I'm facing a financial lion, bills that are trying to devour this ministry," he had declared earlier. The following spring, he was singing a different tune: "My people don't give a hoot what I spend the money for," he told a reporter.

A simple family man and head of a multimillion-dollar ministry, Humbard moves with the times. In 1980, when his ratings started to slip, he spiced up his act, unveiling a new multicolored logo and uprooting his Akron set location in favor of an outdoor garden scene at Georgia's lush Callaway Gardens. Through the exotic greenery, however, his message remained homespun:

> And we go to a place called heaven. We walk inside those pearly gates and down those streets of gold, and there we

look! There's a mansion on the hillsides of glory. But that's
not what's going to make heaven beautiful. There'll be no
twisted limbs. There's no blinded eyes. There will be nobody
hungry in heaven. There'll be no broken homes. There'll be
no funeral processions.

Like Oral Roberts, Humbard steers wide of involvement in politics. "Jesus would never get into politics," he has said. We found
his folksiness and family style excessive, his "You Are Loved!"
slogan transparent. Yet, among Big Fathers, Humbard seems benign, if unabashed. He once donated a carload of TV sets to a
leper colony in the Philippines.

Robert Schuller.   After Roberts and Humbard, we came upon a
different breed of old-timer. No preacher on television exudes
more sheer joy than Rev. Robert H. Schuller of Garden Grove,
California. The fifty-five-year-old pastor of the Garden Grove
Community Church is something of an oddity among religious
broadcasters. Where most of his colleagues preach a uniformly
glum vision of earthly life, Schuller is an exuberant apostle of op-
timism. His weekly show, "The Hour of Power," has only been on
the air since 1970, but Schuller claims it has the largest Sunday
morning viewing audience, according to the Arbitron ratings, of
any religious program.

It also has perhaps the most unusual set in the world: the
$18-million "Crystal Cathedral." Designed by world-famous ar-
chitect Philip Johnson, the Crystal Cathedral has been called "the
most important religious structure to be built since the Cathedral
de Notre-Dame de Paris." Shaped like a four-pointed star, it is
400 feet long, more than 120 feet high and consists entirely of
white steel trusses covered by 10,000 one-way mirrors. Open to
the sky in daylight, perked up at night by the twinkling of 11,000
ceiling lights, with seating for 2,800 and a choir of 120, it is un-
deniably impressive and a growing southern California tourist attraction.

At its pulpit stands Schuller, the physical embodiment of all this
sparkle. Silver-haired, with aviator glasses, he strikes a beatific
pose in the center of his 185-foot red marble altar. Where most
evangelists wear plain, dark suits, Schuller dresses like the late

Bishop Sheen, in long, rich-colored robes with velvet trim. No hard-liner, Schuller is urban, West Coast and breathless in his inclination toward catchphrases, as in his series of sermons, entitled *Strive to Arrive and Survive and Thrive in 1981!* His business pitch, "a Christian celebration in possibility thinking," is to Schuller what "seed faith" is to Oral Roberts: a promise of hope and good things to come. Schuller takes up where Rev. Norman Vincent Peale leaves off:

> This is a ministry with a positive thinking focus. . . . For all who join us, we automatically list you in the Possibility Thinkers Club, which means, among other things, that you will receive some of our most inspiring gifts. . . . I have in my hand a beautiful cultured pearl, an authentic pearl. A grain of sand entered an oyster and around that grain of sand an oyster slowly, preciously created out of the obstacle an opportunity. Out of the intrusion, a gem. And so the pearl in the shell is like God's extended hand, reaching out to give you a problem that you can turn into a pearl.

Schuller has survived, thrived and positively arrived in the quarter century since he came to California from Iowa and started preaching atop the concession stand at a drive-in theater. His theme of success runs consistently through his sermons and best-selling books, and no doubt much of his popularity derives from the fact that his message is universal. Despite his huge audience and his glass house, Schuller's annual take is estimated to be only about $16 million, but he prides himself on his low operating budget. His position as a salaried pastor, with a volunteer choir and other services donated by his congregation, makes it possible for him to produce, in his words, "the least expensive international religious telecast on television." Watching him, however, we got the impression that he, too, is feeling the squeeze of Christian video saturation. His recent dire appeals for funds stand out in contrast to the overall upbeat tone of his ministry. Although we had come to view all cries of financial desperation by TV preachers as part of the show, Schuller's pained on-air admissions were an early indication to us that the shrinking electronic church pie may force some old-timers off the air.

Jimmy Swaggart. One old-time ministry that is healthier than ever is the Jimmy Swaggart Crusade, in comparative terms, a modest little $20-million-a-year operation. Headquartered in Baton Rouge, Louisiana, like most media ministries its expressed goal is one of "world evangelization." On the screen, however, few ministries project such a convincing down-home country style, complete with traditional "camp meetings," "altar calls" and pentecostal "baptism in the Holy Spirit." Although younger than Roberts and Humbard, Rev. Jimmy Swaggart is a holy roller in the classic mold. An accomplished country and gospel singer (and cousin to rock and roller Jerry Lee Lewis), in his weekly televised crusades, Swaggart sits spread-eagled at the piano and sings closeup into the mike, accompanied by an impressive contingent of polished backup musicians.

The music is sweet and smooth, but Swaggart's sermons are pure hellfire: stomping, shouting, sweating, good-book waving, brow-mopping tent shows. Small-town audiences appear awed by his mastery of the idiom, his bombast and grisly imagery. They call out along with him as he preaches sermons with titles like: "The Blood, the Basin and the Bosom," "All Satan's Apples Have Worms," "Hell Is No Joke"—and one we tuned in one Sunday night, "The Destructive Power of the Gospel of Jesus Christ." When Swaggart is cooking, he gets red-hot:

> Now, we're living in a dirty age, a filthy age. I mean, it's *dirty!* Twenty years ago, you turned on television, you would not have heard the profanity! . . . Now . . . you turn on television and it's one curse word after the other. It's one profanity after the other. Besides that, the—I want to say *ladies*—but the women are so indecently dressed that it's so vulgar that it defies description. It is *inane!* It is *absurd!* It is a *LUDICROSITY!* It is *stupid!*

Yet, in all we watched, Swaggart did not step over the line that separates old-time religion from newfangled political agitation. As he put it:

> You say, "Jimmy Swaggart, are you opposing television? Are you opposing the industry?" No. No. No. No. No. *No!*

And I'm not trying to get these gracious pastors to draw up
some list of rules in our churches. That won't do any good!
But I'm telling you this: when you feed on that trash, and it is
trash, when you feed on that garbage, and it is garbage, when
you feed on that rot, and it is rot—it will get in your mind
and start to take root. And then you wonder why the ner-
vousness, you wonder why the illness, you wonder why the
oppression. . . . I'm saying this: get so close to God, get so
full of the Word, get so full of Jesus Christ that that trash
holds no attraction for you anymore.

Perhaps the best instance on television of holy rolling as pure
art form, Swaggart is hard, gruesome, but never mean. He stands
head and shoulders above minor competitors like Rev. Ernest W.
Angley, the Akron, Ohio, faith healer who drives a pink Cadillac,
wears a slippery toupee and places his hands on the TV camera
while shouting, *"Heal! Heal!"* And he has been mentioned as a
likely successor to Rev. Billy Graham. Graham, the undisputed
king of the old-timers, has no regularly scheduled television show
but has become world-famous for his televised outdoor crusades.
Graham has had his political ups and downs over the years. He
took a strong stand apart from politics after his support for Richard Nixon crumbled embarrassingly during Watergate. More recently, he drew fire for his anti-nuclear views and a widely criticized trip to Russia. Graham's career is a saga unto itself, but not
to be told here. For the days of the old-timers appear to be numbered. With the transformation of the electronic church into a political tool, most of the old-timers' stars are setting, as others are
rising and changing in hue.

THE NEWCOMERS

The newcomers have introduced a previously unknown world to
people who tune in to the electronic church for prayer and devotion. In contrast to the simple, stark and generally soothing world
of old-time religion, the newcomers bring a world of anger, rage
and supernatural horror to mass-media Christianity. Under their
influence, the electronic church has become a different kind of

force with a different kind of message. As we watched them in a
spreading climate of social and political upheaval, the newcomers
emerged as stalking-horses, high-strung and charging.

James Robison. Unlike his contemporary, Jimmy Swaggart, who
at times can be downright likable, Rev. James Robison *is* mean,
and he makes no bones about it. This thirty-nine-year-old, tall,
dark and chubby Ft. Worth, Texas, preacher has been called
"God's Angry Man"—an emotion that may be the secret of his
success as an evangelist and the key to his sudden rise to national
prominence in 1980. In the pulpit, Robison displays a piercing,
barking preaching style that can be painful to the ears. He snarls.
He spumes. He slashes and twists as he cuts away at the onrushing
hordes of satanic forces he sees threatening America: "Soviet
blackmail," "homosexual perverts," "the vile cesspool of sex education" and "the slaughter of millions of innocent babies." His
common theme: "America will not survive as a nation . . . unless
we repent of our sins against God. We have already begun our last
slide into slavery and debauchery."

Robison speaks often of debauchery. An illegitimate child, at
times he seems proud of his wayward past. "When I was a kid,"
he has said, "I planned rapes and plotted crimes. I considered everything but murder. I was mean. I'm talking about sadistic!
Cruel! I killed animals . . . deliberately. I killed a dog—just threw
it on the floor until it died. I killed a cat. Put it in a fire. . . .
God, I was bad. I was filthy!" By eighteen, however, he had decided to become an evangelist. Five years later, after a brush with
higher education, he was on his way, kindling his fiery style in
Bible Belt revival meetings. In 1965, he launched the James Robison Evangelistic Association, and in 1970, a modest half-hour
television ministry, but the crudely produced "James Robison Presents" left him far short of the big leagues for which many felt he
was destined.

Then in 1977, in his pugnacious style, he railed against a local
"queer ministry" and was unceremoniously kicked off the air in
his hometown. The boot propelled him into national headlines and
eventually into the Religious Roundtable, a newly formed fundamentalist right lobby. Robison became its mouthpiece as the
preachers-into-politics movement provided him with a custom ve-

hicle and second showcase for his rage. In 1979, he began patching together coarse documentary footage of World War II concentration camps, Vietnam war atrocities and clips of kiddieporn and child abuse for a series of syndicated television specials on moral decay in America. His 1980 hour-long "Wake Up America, We're All Hostages!" was a turning point in the growth of the electronic church as an instrument of social and political agitation. The show was airing around the country while Robison was stumping on behalf of the Roundtable. The multimedia effort culminated in Dallas in August 1980, when Robison addressed 15,000 fundamentalist preachers at the Roundtable's "nonpolitical" national affairs briefing, saying:

> I'm sick and tired of hearing about all the radicals and the perverts and the liberals and the leftists and the Communists coming out of the closet: it's time for God's people to come out of the closet, out of the churches, and change America! We must do it! . . . Our preachers are to warn the people, we're to warn the people the enemy comes . . . we're being attacked by satanic forces.

From this pulpit in Dallas, Robison made one of the most-quoted remarks of the 1980 campaign:

> If necessary, God would raise up a tyrant, a man who might not have the best ethics, to protect the freedom interests of the ethical and the godly.

Although not officially connected, Robison's political activities appeared to take a toll on his ministry and its finances. Following the election, he announced that heavy losses were forcing a one-third reduction in his staff and the elimination of ten stations in major markets as outlets for his weekly show. When we watched him in early 1981, his politics were submerged as he struggled to regroup and build support for his upcoming politically oriented specials. Yet, in his televised crusades, we heard the note of intimidation we had come to recognize as the unmistakable ring of Holy Terror:

If you died tonight, do you know you'll go to heaven? I
talked to a boy one afternoon about giving his life to Christ.
He said, "You know what, I'm going to do it in the morning!
Tonight I'm going to a movie." I said, "Before you go to the
movie, let's pray." He said, "I told you, I'm coming in the
morning." I said, "Listen, we could pray and you could trust
Jesus now." He said, "I told you, I'm trusting Jesus in the
morning." He got on his motorcycle at 12:30 A.M. on his
way home from the theater. He hit a car head-on and
died. . . . I talked to a boy working in his front yard on a
car, changing the oil. He slid out from under the car. I said,
"I'd like to talk to you about the Lord Jesus Christ." He
said, "I'm busy working on my car." I said, "It'll only take a
few minutes." He said, "I told you, I'm busy." I said, "All
right." I went two blocks. He slid under the car. The jack
slipped. The car fell. Crushed him. I could take the next two
hours and, without breaking the momentum, I could tell you
story after story after story where I preached to people like
you and they rejected Christ and died lost.

Jim Bakker.   Across the dial of the electronic church, there is no
greater contrast to the hard-bitten Robison than the diminutive
Rev. Jim Bakker of the "PTL Club"—the initials have been said to
stand for Praise the Lord, People that Love and Pass the Loot.
Short, childlike, forty-year-old Bakker and his petite wife Tammy
rank with the superstars of the electronic church. In 1979, their
daily Charlotte, North Carolina-based broadcasts aired over more
than 200 TV stations, 3,000 cable systems, and grossed more than
$52 million. Yet, watching this pair, we saw that even in its public
face, the smiling world of big-time television evangelism has a
dark side that cannot be completely hidden.

Bakker is a pioneer figure in the development of the "Christian
talk show," religious broadcasting with an entertainment tilt and
today the centerpiece of the new electronic church, complete with
oozing hosts, gushing guests, splashy musical numbers and com-
puter-generated color graphics. In this expanded format, more
diversion than devotion, Bakker has packaged the image of born-
again happiness and perfection, adding his own cast of stock characters to the revolving core of reborn celebrities and athletes who
work the Christian circuit.

Each show we watched was unvarying, as overstuffed businessmen, teary-eyed housewives and reformed prostitutes recalled the dire circumstances that brought them to Jesus. To each discussion, Bakker summoned an appropriate passage from the Scriptures, breaking the pace with light entertainment and frequent commercial appeals for money and membership in "the club." Cast in the "Tonight Show" mold, the "PTL Club" has its own roly-poly guest host, Henry Harrison, who plays Ed McMahon to Bakker's Johnny Carson. Bakker even opens with a Carson-style born-again monologue. Occasionally, though, his cheery banter takes a swan dive:

Hello, everyone. Thank you. Well, I just got back from California and it's nice to be back. . . . Tammy's doing so much better and she's anxious to be back. . . . It's kind of strange to visit your wife. I feel like I'm dating again. I go out and visit her on weekends. . . . In fact, she wants to be back, but the doctor said, "No, you are going to rest some more," and we know that Tammy will be much stronger and feeling much better after she goes through this time of rest and rebuilding.

Apparently, Tammy had suffered a nervous collapse, something that could happen to anyone. But as Bakker described it, the breakdown seemed to have resulted, at least in part, from the demands of the job and the pressures of living a perfect born-again Christian life. We wondered, was her story similar to Diane's in any way? Tuning in regularly, we saw the fragility of PTL's stars laid bare often, and further exploited for sympathy, soul-winning and financial support.

Jim and Tammy got their start in television doing Christian puppet shows in Portsmouth, Virginia, in the mid-sixties, during the first days of expanded-format Christian talk and variety. One night, toward the close of a fund-raising telethon that was far short of its $120,000 goal, Bakker discovered in his own emotional repertoire the media tactic that soon catapulted him to stardom. He started to cry:

Listen, people, it's all over. Everything's gone. Christian television will be no more. The only Christian television station is gone, unless you provide us with the money to operate it.

The phones lit up. Jim Bakker had become the Jack Paar of Pray TV! The Bakkers were to have their highs and lows over the years, however. Driven in their "fire for the Lord," in 1969 he suffered a nervous breakdown from overwork. Now, apparently, it was Tammy's turn:

> I probably shouldn't say too much about it, but the doctors told me that the FCC problem was almost too much for Tammy to go through, and that that was one of the things that totally became an exhaustion to her.

Among top Christian broadcasters, Bakker has been the only one to date to run into lasting trouble with the authorities. In 1978, he nearly went under from $6 million in debts brought on by too-rapid expansion of his broadcast facilities, and by exorbitant construction costs on his $100-million Heritage USA recreation and entertainment complex. In 1979, newspaper reports that he had diverted $337,000 in donations solicited for overseas missions to pay his domestic bills brought down an FCC investigation. Subpoenas to open his financial records prompted howls by Bakker of government-sponsored religious persecution—and gave him something else to cry about in his never-ending quest for funds. Through 1981, as the legal battle dragged on, we watched his resistance harden and his pleas become almost pathetic:

> I desperately need to hear from you, and if anyone can slip an extra five or ten into that envelope to help me pay this airtime. . . . We are right on the brink of disaster in our affiliates. . . . If we could just have some help from our friends in the next few days, it would really help us. We've gone through quite a time. The enemy tries and tries and tries, but we can stand together. It's not time to go off the air. It's time to stay on the air and continue to take the world.

But apparently, the FCC was less of a problem than the competition. Bakker's 1980 audit showed a decline in income of $12 million from the year before, one of the largest drops in the electronic church league. Nevertheless, Jim and Tammy squeaked by, drawing up to $90,000 a year in salary and fringe benefits. On the show, Bakker continued to trot out testimony from his stable of "new creatures in Christ": pop singers, ex-cons, "Christian psychologists," the once-blind and once-lame. As we watched, however, he returned repeatedly to the theme of emotional collapse:

> You know, Jesus went aside and rested, and so often we feel so obligated to you, our partners, that we don't want to miss being here. . . . It seems like we're having to learn some ways to rest and to have some folks help us to understand that if we don't take the rest someday, we'll be resting six feet under. . . . A little baby chicken, to get away from fearful things, crawls under its mother's wing. And you know what? It's *dark* under that chicken!

Big Fathers, strong and weak. Before our eyes, they were changing television, and thereby, reality as it was defined for many Americans. This new world the electronic church unveiled to us was as foreign as anything we had encountered in our travels. Gradually, day by day, it was changing the message and meaning of religion and the atmosphere of the culture as we knew it. In our absorption, although more professional than personal, we soon realized that, like many in its audience, we, too, were being removed to another world, drawn between two cultures, two different Americas. It was an eerie sensation. Like Diane, Frank Church and Mike Synar, we felt as if we, too, had become targets—and in the comfort of our living rooms. What was going on here? Curious, we prepared for our first excursion to the imperial capital of the electronic church.

THE WIZ

If there is a monster force in the electronic church, it is CBN, the Christian Broadcasting Network, with its flagship program, the daily, internationally syndicated "700 Club." CBN is *big*. In fact, it is the largest noncommercial broadcasting network in the world.

In the United States, it reaches more than seventy-five percent of all homes with television, over 150 local stations and 2,500 satellite-cable systems. Internationally, its programs are aired in Japan, Puerto Rico, the Philippines, Colombia, Chile, Peru, Costa Rica, Honduras, Guatemala, the Dominican Republic and over the Armed Forces Radio and Television Network. In 1980, CBN's income exceeded $60 million. At one point, it was reported to be gaining 73,000 new subscribers every day. Other Christian broadcasters may claim more local stations or more viewers, but their fortunes are sinking. Roberts and Humbard have lost a million viewers. Robison is out of his largest markets. Bakker's income is down nearly a quarter. Chances are, their losses were CBN's gains.

The host of the "700 Club" is CBN's founder and president, Dr. Marion Gordon "Pat" Robertson. At fifty-two, Robertson's image is still that of the boy next door, a little kid with a perpetually wide-eyed look and a chipmunk smile. One media analyst we spoke with likened him to "Howdy Doody grown old." But Pat Robertson is no sawdust-head. He is a Yale lawyer, an ex-Marine lieutenant who saw combat duty in Korea, and a scion of one of Virginia's most prominent families. He claims kinship with President William Henry Harrison, and his father, the late U.S. Senator A. Willis Robertson, was chairman of the Senate Banking and Currency Committee. Unlike his distinguished ancestors, however, for the moment at least, the younger Robertson has kept his hat out of the ring of elected office. He has set his sights higher, aiming to bring the whole world to Jesus Christ.

Robertson's primary instrument for effecting this mass conversion is the "700 Club," first aired in 1963 and named for its initial 700 donors. Through the late sixties, Robertson and Jim Bakker, then his employee, shared the host's spot and other duties. Following Bakker's resignation in 1972, the show became increasingly sophisticated, reaching beyond the usual born-again circuit riders—such as entertainers Pat Boone, Efrem Zimbalist, Jr., Roy Rogers and Dale Evans—to literary heavyweights—such as Alvin Toffler and Malcolm Muggeridge—and to secular topics ranging from dieting to home gardening to martial arts. Regardless of the guest or topic, however, Robertson almost always manages to steer the discussion toward his own social and political interpretation of Scriptures, a version that is inevitably pegged to current events. One day as we watched, for example, Robertson shared with his black cohost Ben Kinchlow a privileged and ominous revelation:

> Ben, I was sitting—it was the most moving thing—you know, there are times that you think that God speaks to you, and you hope that you're hearing from Him and not just daydreaming. . . . This was a time when I *know* God spoke to me. . . . He said, "There's going to be a crash," you know, stock market crash, other kind of crash. And He said, "Only the securities of your government will be safe." . . . He said, "The Soviet Union is going to get in very bad trouble internally." . . . The next thing He said was that Fidel Castro is going to fall, and when he does—I'm not going to tell you because that's something I'm not going to talk about on television.

Despite its religious adornments, the "700 Club" may be as blatantly political as any program on television. Aided by a team of roving correspondents, Robertson offers news and features on domestic and international affairs. He presents in-depth discussions, complete with charts, graphs and supplementary film footage, on topics ranging from world economic trends to Mideast conflicts to the agricultural and industrial problems of developing nations. He also features live and taped interviews with politicians, elected officials and other controversial figures, among them: Senators Mark Hatfield, Jesse Helms, William Proxmire, and anti-Equal Rights Amendment activist Phyllis Schlafly. The chat may be light, but the message is always heavy—and scary. In one show we watched, Robertson welcomed, live via satellite from CBN studios in Washington, D.C., Virginia Republican and U.S. Senator John Warner:

> SENATOR WARNER: I'm delighted to be here with you, my dear friend. You were too modest to say that I have the privilege of occupying your father's seat in the U.S. Senate. . . .
> ROBERTSON: Well, we appreciate you, and I know my fa-

ther would be delighted to know that such an able individual
was filling the seat he occupied for twenty years.

For fifteen minutes, on religious television, Robertson and Warner conducted a wide-ranging discussion of U.S. foreign policy
and military strategy, dwelling on the arms race, the enormous
sums the superpowers are spending on weapons development, and
the imminent threat of nuclear attack. Then Robertson raised the
question that pops up as frequently on the "700 Club" as it does
on "The Tonight Show." "How bad is it?" he asked, referring to
Warner's claim of U.S. nuclear inferiority. Warner built his case
out of a smattering of history and statistics, citing his personal experience as Secretary of the Navy, as he put the ultimate fear into
Robertson's viewing audience:

> SENATOR WARNER: We've been going downhill. . . .
> We're at that point, what we call the "rocky crevice" . . . we
> never realized that the Soviet Union could build a missile
> with the guidance system literally to come across the ocean
> and go right down the smokestack, so to speak, of our land-
> based missiles.

The only alternative that day, according to Warner, was the
now-scrapped plan for a mobile MX missile system. The two
spoke in technical jargon about the "time of maximum peril" and
the famed "window of vulnerability." Then as Warner signed off,
Robertson turned to the audience and began to rephrase the entire
defense discussion in apocalyptic terms:

> ROBERTSON: Now, he's not some right-wing fanatic. He
> isn't some religionist who is trying to drum up a cause . . .
> and he says exactly what I've been saying and many others
> have been saying. We're entering a period of maximum crisis
> where our entire civilization is in the balance, and where the
> converging events taking place in the Soviet Union, in our
> economy, in the military balance, in the world food supplies
> and oil supplies, make a maximum opportunity for military
> adventure . . . which could possibly launch a chaotic situa-
> tion in the whole world.

In support of his claim, he recited a verse from the Bible:

And so the Lord says, "I will pull out my anger upon you. I will consume you with the fire of my wrath. I have heaped upon you the full penalty for all your sins. . . ." We need God because our nation is still with sin. . . . That's why we call for repentance, not because we're bluenoses that say, "well, we don't like you to have fun," but I don't want you or me to be *incinerated!* That's the bottom line.

Robertson and Kinchlow bowed their heads. "Let's pray and let's ask God . . . Father—let's just kneel down, Ben." They knelt, closing their eyes tightly:

We kneel before you right now on this broadcast and we pray for men like John Warner. And we pray for Ronald Reagan and we pray for his Cabinet and we pray for the leaders of our nation. O God, may the members of Congress turn from partisanship and may they turn to the Lord today. And may they know that, O God, the situation is much more critical than we'd like to think. . . . Thank you, Father, we believe . . . that you will come and bring righteousness to this land. In Jesus' name. Ay-men—and *Ay-man!*

Robertson opened his eyes and commanded:

Continue to pray. Call upon the Lord. The situation is serious. . . . Call a fast; weep at the altar. . . . *We'll be back with more right after this message.*

Unlike other TV evangelists, apart from periodic fund-raising telethons, Robertson seldom asks for money on the air. Instead, after each segment of the show, Robertson cuts away to commercial messages that tout his various interests in subtle ways. This one, after a half hour of saber-rattling and fervent prayer, was soft-sell, with matching imagery and camerawork. The young male protagonist was urbane and sophisticated. The voice-over pure Madison Avenue:

You've really got it all. A low, fast car. And a new house.
A lot of friends in your life and no commitments. You're
well fed. You're in great shape. You've got the best back-
hand in the club. You're quick and confident, and you're the
boss's favorite. You're young. Face it: you're everything. But
happy! You can be happy. Read the Bible and find out what
you've really been missing.

The "700 Club" is just the tip of the CBN iceberg. Beneath the
prayer, politics and slick marketing ploys is a vast network of
Christian culture. The nerve center under Robertson's command
consists of eighty-three phone-in "prayer counseling centers"
through which, in 1980, 10,000 volunteer counselors made contact with almost two million callers. Over numbers flashed frequently on the "700 Club" screen, CBN claims, tens of thousands
each year are brought to Christ. Others, presumably already
Christians, phone in their "spiritual, physical, social and emotional" needs. Each caller's name and address are dutifully logged
on colored forms: orange "prayer requests," green "answer to
prayer" sheets, pink "crisis" slips. These go to CBN's direct-mail
department, which may then begin sending timed-release pamphlets, computerized letters, "personally" signed notes from "Pat"
and inevitable requests for money.

But there is much more to the CBN empire. Moving up on the
"700 Club" is "Another Life," the first Christian soap opera, first
marketed for national syndication in 1981. In addition to the nonprofit religious CBN, there is a secular commercial clone, also
called CBN. The Continental Broadcasting Network, Inc., CBN's
wholly owned subsidiary, consists of local television stations in
Atlanta, Boston, Dallas and Portsmouth, Virginia. These commercial outlets carry other religious programs, old reruns of "wholesome, family-oriented" shows; and, seven times daily, they air
"CBN Update News." As on other commercial stations around
the country, "700 Club" spots are run along with the other commercials.

Robertson also has his own Christian college, CBN University,
located at CBN headquarters in Virginia Beach, Virginia. Offering
state-approved Master's degrees in communication and education,
with more programs to come, CBNU is advertised as "An Equal

Opportunity Institution" that does not discriminate on the basis of race, color, national or ethnic origin. According to its catalog, however, like students at Oral Roberts and other fundamentalist universities, the CBNU student is one who "has confronted and accepted the claims and teachings of God's Son, our Saviour, the Lord Jesus Christ."

And there is *Pat Robertson's Perspective,* a monthly newsletter with a circulation of 247,000. The second-largest newsletter in the United States (only the *Kiplinger Washington Letter* reaches more), it is even more explicit than Robertson's TV show in its discussion of social, political and economic issues in the light of "Biblical prophecy." Sample forecasts:

> The Bible long ago recognized the incredible nature of compound interest.
> High-quality bonds would be a good buy at this time. . . .
> By 1982, there may well be a crash of major proportions.
> Surely, if mankind sought God together, He would give them an abundant energy supply and an abundant food supply.

One 1980 *Perspective,* entitled "Proposal for Radical Change," offered explicit solutions for a "Radical Tax System," "Radical Arms Control," "Radical Compassion" and "Radical Freedom," concluding:

> Above all else, we need a national resolution—a constitutional amendment if necessary—reaffirming our Judeo-Christian heritage. We must take back the religious freedom that the Supreme Court has taken from us.

Such are the vital organs of the CBN giant. Yet, despite its tax-free status and its close connection with millions via television, telephone and direct mail, CBN doesn't see itself as an electronic "church." Rather, its self-image is that of a "parachurch" ministry which "supports and strengthens" the local church. In a press release apparently aimed at easing the fears of local pastors, Robertson maintained that, in 1979 alone, CBN counselors referred 40,000 callers to more than 5,000 local churches; also that an independent survey of his supporters revealed that CBN "spurs donors to increase giving to the local church." Both claims are questionable. After a nationwide survey of local congregations by the independent Institute for American Church Growth, the institute's vice-president concluded that "shows like the '700 Club' are almost insignificant in making people active in the local church."

Either way, there is little doubt that CBN holds a position of unrivaled influence among broadcast ministries. But what is Robertson doing with his giant operation and its power? Apparently, he is patiently carving out for himself a far-sighted niche in the social and political hierarchy of the fundamentalist right.

CBN claims to be apolitical, but Robertson's words and deeds have been contradictory. In 1980, when Robertson served as co-chairman of the "Washington for Jesus" rally, he was widely quoted as saying "We have enough votes to run the country. And when people say, 'We've had enough,' we are going to take over." Later that year, however, he resigned abruptly from his key position in James Robison's Religious Roundtable, proclaiming, "God has been leading me in a different direction." At the time, he expressed his "personal belief the Lord is to change society through spiritual, rather than political, means." Yet his television show and newsletter remained as topical as ever, advancing virtually every Biblical and moral position that other fundamentalist right groups had vowed to enact into law. A year later, he was listed as co-chairman of the second "Washington for Jesus" march, planned for the spring of 1984.

Following his formal split, Robertson kept his distance from more visible leaders of the fundamentalist right, while his network branched out in its efforts to attract new viewers with secular-style programming. And his electronic ministry became more puzzling than ever. What kind of spiritual enterprise was this that was entering into competition with the networks? What were the long-range political designs of Robertson's parachurch operation? What kind of high-tech mass communications empire was he building? What was in it for human beings? And what did all this have to do with religion? With these questions in our minds, we ventured south to Virginia Beach.

Down the yellow tollway that led to this resort town in the coastal kingdom of Tidewater, the year-round crowd knew all about Pat Robertson. Many remembered him from the early sixties, when CBN was just getting off the ground. They told us stories of his attempts to wring donations and free services from local merchants. A salesman recalled some office equipment he had demonstrated for Robertson. "He wanted it for *nothing*," he told us, "completely without charge!" Years later, he was still astonished at Robertson's nerve. "I told him it was out of the question, but the implication was, 'You're doing it for the Lord.' That upset the devil out of me!" We asked him about the atmosphere at CBN. Had they tried to bring him into the born-again fold. "Not me, I'm already a Christian," he said, "but the *feeling,* you get that feeling there," referring to their steady pressure to join the club. "I felt it coming every time I opened my mouth. It pervaded every conversation."

We talked to a young mother who was not born again. She was furious at Robertson and CBN. "Have you been over there? Have you seen what he's got there?" she asked, her voice rising. She was upset because they ran commercials for the "700 Club" on CBN's nonreligious station in Portsmouth. "They run them on Saturday mornings, during the cartoons," she said. "I don't want my kids watching that stuff."

A young couple, who had been members of the "700 Club" for two years, were disillusioned. "We found strength in it," they said, "but it started to bother us, seeing Pat Robertson's face on everything. We'd get phone calls and they would say, 'Oh, just a minute. Pat has a special message for you.' Then they would play a tape recording of Robertson asking for money. When they came back on the phone, we said, 'You can tell Pat Robertson to go jump in the lake! We think these money-raising tactics aren't Christian. They're disgusting and we don't want to support you anymore.'" We asked them how powerful Robertson was locally. "He has a lot of influence around here," they agreed, "but he probably has more outside this area. He's become pretty authoritarian. A lot of people have left after running into that hard-nosed thing and all those prophecies."

We wanted to see for ourselves. We had written a month ahead, requesting an interview and a tour of the facilities, but we received no reply, and when we called, no one had a record of our letter. Finally word came back: Robertson would not see us, but we

were welcome to view the show, and someone would be there to
meet us.

We drove through sand and shrubs to CBN headquarters.
There, in a clearing flanked by tall trees, was Pat Robertson's empire: two buildings, a security booth and a construction trailer. It
was not the dynasty we had expected. The larger structure, CBN
studios, consisted of two windowless wings joined by a red-brick
Colonial façade with stone columns and a modest steeple. In its
shadow, two great dish antennas pointed skyward. The main lobby
was like a warp between two worlds, spotless, with milky marble
floors and a curved double staircase of rich-colored woods. Beneath the stairway, double doors opened into a round chapel with
a pointed ceiling, a hard-shell revival tent with concentric pews
and recessed lighting. In the center of the chapel, a life-sized
wooden cross dangled precariously from a heavy chain. Other visi-
tors proceeded directly into the studio as we waited under the
watch of two receptionists. In a small sideroom off the lobby was
a table with books for sale: *Pilgrim's Progress,* Robertson's auto-
biography, a book about Elvis, and a cookbook by Robertson's wife Dede—*My God Will Supply*—with recipes for "faith
hamburgers," "love waffles," "self-control chili" and "gentleness
beans."

It was past the hour when we were met by a tall, attractive
young woman from CBN's public relations staff, another Diane.
She gave us a thick press kit and hurried us upstairs, where we entered the main studio from the rear of the balcony. The audience
was half full. The show was already in progress. Ben Kinchlow,
Robertson's strapping sidekick—and according to Diane, "a former black militant"—was introducing the star. On cue, the audience applauded as Robertson walked onto his powder-blue parlor
set.

Robertson addressed the camera, not the audience, as he and
Kinchlow joked about news reports on the perils of cancer-causing
substances. Downstage left, fifty telephone counselors sat in the
shadows at a multitiered phone bank, talking quietly to one another. Their phones lay silent.

Next, Robertson conducted an interview with a project director
for the World Bank. The man wasn't in the studio. He was sitting
in Washington, for no apparent reason, before a color backdrop of

the U.S. Supreme Court. The studio camera pulled up within inches of Robertson as he sat on the deserted set asking questions into the lens. When the red light atop the camera was lit, he appeared chatty and casual. When it went out, the other man's face came on the overhead monitors as Robertson conferred with his stage directors and floor managers. As in any secular television studio, the audience was superfluous and seemed to sense it, paying little attention to the images flashing above them or to the disembodied voices booming around the cavernous room.

So far, we had seen nothing to justify CBN's existence as a religious enterprise. Then slowly, the atmosphere changed.

Back on-stage, a young male singer was lip-synching in tongues, a kind of pentecostal scat. The audience came eerily to life. Several pairs of arms floated up, reaching limply in the traditional charismatic pose. Some sat rocking with their eyes closed. A few shouted faint "Amens" and "Praise the Lords." Then Robertson reappeared to talk about miracles: a man who had been healed from a hunting accident; a woman whose faith had lengthened her short leg. The fervor mounted as he invited home viewers to call in. Numbers flashed overhead and, instantly, the phones started to ring. In their bleachers, the counselors sprang into action, grabbing their colored forms, praying into the telephones; some appeared to be speaking in tongues. For several minutes, the place was in an uproar. Then the ringing stopped and the noise subsided. For the audience, it had been cathartic.

After the show, Robertson stepped forward to greet the audience. We asked Diane if we might have a few words with him, but she said he had to leave right away. She hustled us out the back door as Robertson lingered with the crowd. Outside, two gentlemen from CBN's technical division were waiting to show us around. Christened in 1980, CBN's broadcast center was a "state-of-the-art facility," they assured us, making their case in a flood of numbers. Costing $20 million, and purportedly larger than some network facilities in Hollywood, the complex contained not one but two identical 12,000-square-foot studios, each equipped with four $100,000 RCA computerized color cameras. Nearly everything at CBN was computerized, they said. The religious broadcasting outfit had the nation's first fully automated production facility, right down to its microprocessor memories—capable of simultaneously controlling 53 different pieces of scenery and 846 lighting fixtures in each studio. These breakthroughs, we were informed, had virtually eliminated the need for stagehands.

With our tour guides in front and our good shepherd behind, we ambled over the 2,200 miles of electrical cable that ran under the building. In the depths of the machine, we passed through airlocks protecting more computers in editing, production and other technical areas. Here, forty-eight video machines were whirring quietly, churning out high-quality tapes for distribution. Space-age editing machines were running on six-day, ninety-hour per week schedules. In the master cubicle, a single engineer controlled program distribution to all U.S. time zones. As we rolled past room after room and rack after rack of high-tech apparatus, our tour guides rambled on in dollars and metric figures; and when we interrupted to ask how they liked working at CBN, they began to witness. One had been an engineer at CBS. The other came to CBN from RCA's satellite communications division. Both spoke interchangeably of the marvelous environment at CBN. Both offered similar testimony about the abundant love they had found there. And they sang of their admiration for Pat Robertson as we stepped through a fire door into the sunlight.

Before us were CBN's giant 10-meter dish antennas, the powerful microwave transmitters that beam CBN signals to RCA *Satcom II* and Western Union *Westar* satellites parked 23,000 miles up in "geosynchronous" orbit. The system operates around the clock, they said, relaying pictures and sound for distribution to CBN's 2,500 broadcast and cable outlets. Behind the dishes, at the door of a bunkerlike control house, sat a polished granite tombstone fixing in space and time the moment when "Earth Station" CBN first spoke to the heavens. Inside the bunker, yet another lone engineer sat before a bank of meters and monitors. As we crowded into the tiny hut, the twin dishes beamed invisibly upward and our guides beamed visibly outward.

"You could jam any signal of any station," said the man from RCA, adding quickly, "but of course, that's not what we're here to do."

As they walked us back, we heard loud voices and clapping. In the lobby, a hundred people came streaming out of the chapel. What was this? "Fellowshipping," said Diane. Every day at noon, there was a prayer meeting for CBN's staff and guests. At the edge of the crowd, an elderly southern gentleman was waiting to meet us for lunch, W. LeRoy Harrelson, CBN's vice-president for public affairs.

A mile away, at the local restaurant-salad bar, we learned that Harrelson had only been at CBN just over a year and, like Diane, he knew practically nothing about what went on at the top. In his late sixties, white-haired with a halting drawl, Harrelson had been a small-town newspaper editor, then press secretary to U.S. Senator Ernest F. Hollings of South Carolina before moving into public relations for a national textile company.

"Then the call came about a year ago to come up here, and here I am," he said happily. "If you'd have asked me two years ago, I never would have thought I'd be here, but you just have to do what you think God wants you to do."

Lunch was slow-paced and low-key.

As we ate, we asked Harrelson about Robertson's political position in the fundamentalist right camp.

"Now, he never was part of the Moral Majority, never," Harrelson protested, adding, "of course, we love *all* ministries. Each has its own calling of God. We were being drawn, just naturally, I suppose, into the political arena, so to avoid any confusion on the part of our members or the media, he just decided to resign from the Roundtable."

Had Robertson seen something in the Roundtable that disturbed him?

"No, no. He just wanted to clear the air. It's my own feeling that you can drop a political veil between you and somebody else, then it's very hard to reach them spiritually."

It was the CBN party line. If Robertson was apolitical, we asked, why had he co-chaired "Washington for Jesus"? Harrelson looked shocked.

"You know, it was difficult for the media to understand that 'Washington for Jesus' was a dedicated, sincere effort on the part of religious leaders across the board, who came together and felt that it would honor God if our people would humble themselves and ask God's forgiveness and guidance by coming to the nation's capital to pray."

We mentioned some of the literature that was passed out at the rally and asked if some Christian groups might have been using the occasion for political gain.

"Now, don't hold that against 'Washington for Jesus,'" he said. "Naturally, when you get a group that size together, things are going to be passed out. But I know that 'Washington for Jesus' was nonpolitical, and I believe it could be a turning point for our nation, in the sense that God honored that."

"God honored that?"

"God told us to do that," he declared. "All through the Bible, there are cases where nations have done that. When David was running up against the Philistines, he inquired of the Lord and won a great victory. In Jehoshaphat, when Israel was in such terrible condition, the whole nation came together on their knees and inquired of the Lord, and the Lord honored that. Now, you can make any kind of political thing you want out of that, but Pat did a beautiful job of explaining to the Washington Press Corps that this was not political. These are devout, honest Christians who came to pray for their nation."

We had few doubts about the rank and file, we said, it was the leaders of the march and their motives we were questioning.

"Now, you say *march,*" Harrelson interrupted. "In a sense, it's a march, but you know, we don't consider it a march. This was an expression from deep within our country. We know we have sinned as a nation. We see filth and violence and immorality. And we know that through history God has punished nations who have not listened to His word. The question is, do we deserve punishment now?"

But could he understand how this descending mass of sincere Christians might be viewed as an attempt to intimidate elected officials in Washington?

"Well, that's America for you," said Harrelson. "I mean, that's freedom. Nobody can stop people from making any interpretation they want."

We changed the subject, asking if, in order to work at CBN, you had to be born again. Again, the question seemed to catch Harrelson by surprise.

"Well, there's no rigid policy," he said, "but I don't think anybody would be comfortable really, if they didn't fit in." He chewed on the idea for a moment. "They could come, I suppose, but I don't know whether they'd last too long."

"That was our point," we said. "In a pluralistic society like the United States, why have a *Christian* broadcasting network that might make many people uncomfortable?"

"To serve God," said Harrelson, "to carry out the Great Commission, which is to take the gospel to every nation."

Was that his hope, that CBN would bring everyone on earth to Jesus Christ?

"Yes, yes," he said without hesitation, "that's what we call the Great Commission. I've just come back from Japan—do you know there are a hundred and fifteen million people there who know nothing of God? They have completely different cultures—Buddhism and Shintoism—but they are very shallow, very materialistic. Missionaries have been plowing up rivers and jungles and doing great work, but they've been reaching only a very limited number of people. Here we've got a medium that can reach beyond all physical barriers. It crosses all bounds."

We asked Harrelson a question that was of growing concern to us. "When you go into other nations and present your Great Commission," we said, "do they ever resent it? Do they ever say, 'Sorry, but we have our own perfectly good religions and we don't want to be brought to Jesus'?" The prospect didn't faze him.

"No," he said firmly, "you see, you're not dealing with nations over there, you're dealing with *individuals*. You buy your time, you have your program, those who want to listen, listen. Those who don't, don't."

Yet could he see how, even in the United States, some people might object to Pat Robertson using all this technology for the purpose of converting others to his religious beliefs?

"I don't see the point here," he said, getting riled. "Are you saying that we don't have the *right* to do this? That we don't have the right to be on the air? You know, the Lord has given the mass-communications media. Are Christians not supposed to use it? This is the way to reach people. It is the Great Commission. And then the end will come!"

He veered off on an endtimes tangent. We steered him back. "No," we said, "we aren't denying anyone's rights, but at least in America the airwaves have always been considered a resource for the public good, not an advocate of any one religion." But now, we suggested, people of many faiths were finding CBN's purely Christian network to be intolerant.

"Well, if they do, they can start their own," he said. "It's a free country."

We suggested that many Americans felt that their religious beliefs were private and should not be made into a slick mass-media product. Harrelson wasn't listening.

"The point is, do you believe in *God*?" he said. "As long as people are led to their final relationship with God, so that they're saved and not condemned, that is all that's important."

We had other serious questions, but each drew the same response. With so much technology, we asked, how big could CBN grow?

"It will expand to the point God wants it to expand to," said Harrelson.

Where did he see the operation ten years down the line?

"We'll be where God wants us to be," he said, "so long as we stay in His will. That's why we're getting into the secular market, because we feel that God wants us to do that in order to reach people who are not interested in religious programming. Because if we can reach them through programming that is not religious per se, we'll be able to expand God's kingdom. And that's our mission."

The meal ended amicably, but despite the outward show of dialogue and openness, we felt no connection with these two congenial people. As we talked, they seemed unable to grasp our concerns and oblivious to the idea that others might find their views narrow or extreme. Yet we wondered.

In our day at CBN, we had only grown more mistrustful of the global enterprise being conducted behind Pat Robertson's noble façade. It seemed to us that by removing himself from the forefront of fundamentalist right politics, this well-bred Yale lawyer had made the smartest move of all, allowing other fundamentalist right preachers to take the heat while he proceeded to use the nation's airwaves, apparently, for grander religious and political designs.

THE PRINCE OF THE POWER OF THE AIR

At the hands of its Big Fathers, the electronic church has become something more than a new form of devotion. For those in command of the new technology, it has become the communications battlefront of Christian culture, with orders from God—the Great Commission—to capture America and win the world for Jesus Christ. But while their goals are virtually identical, Big Fathers vary widely in their means and priorities. Media wizards like Pat Robertson appear intent on working slowly, assembling their high technology to form international parachurch empires. A simpler, more immediate approach has attracted far more attention for its grass-roots efforts on a national scale, and for the adventures of the most controversial Big Father of them all.

Everybody's heard of Rev. Jerry Falwell. Since early 1980, he and the national media have been carrying on a torrid affair. Pastor of the Thomas Road Baptist Church in Lynchburg, Virginia, star of "The Old-Time Gospel Hour" on television, and founder and president of Moral Majority, Inc., the fundamentalist right lobby that has sought to influence legislation and elections at state, local and national levels, Falwell has become synonymous with the new right and the preachers-into-politics movement. On every divisive issue that pops up, from abortion to school prayer to sex and violence on television, Falwell's name and face are there. In Congress and the administration, he has become a roving representative-at-large, self-appointed leader of the nation's born-again Christians, consulted by everyone from lawmakers to the President to foreign heads of state on everything from Supreme Court nominations to international arms sales.

Close up, on the weekly television show that provides him with a national pulpit and power base, he appears larger than life, venting his spleen at liberal politicians, public educators, pro-abortion "murderers," homosexuals, "smut peddlers," atheists, "humanists," "godless Communists" and his critics in the media. With the changeover of power in Washington, he has become bolder and more explicit in his televised remarks. Yet, after watching him week after week and observing his public style, we found little about him that seemed worthy of so much attention. Even more astonishing to us was the fact that so many statesmen, politicians and members of the press bow to him—indeed, that they take him seriously at all. For, in the larger picture of Holy Terror, Jerry Falwell is small potatoes.

As a TV preacher, he may be the supreme religious huckster of the era. Jerry Falwell will sell you anything to float his various fundamentalist operations. He may give you, absolutely free and without obligation: two bronze "Jesus First" lapel pins, a "Faith Partner Pocket Secretary Appointment Book," a "memorial brick" in one of his buildings in Lynchburg, or a copy of his latest book. For the same price, he will send you a "Congressional Petition on Moral Issues," a beautiful parchment reproduction of his "Christian Bill of Rights," and for your other lapel, an "Old Glory" flag pin. The gimmicks work. In 1980, Falwell claimed to have taken in more than $60 million, putting him right up there with the electronic church industry leaders. But his diversified efforts have cost him dearly, perhaps more than any other television evangelist. Falwell's 1980 audit showed that, in one year, he spent more than $23 million—half his ministry's total expenses— just to raise money, and even then, he wound up more than $19 million in debt. By late 1981, amid his political triumphs, the letters of desperation were going out. Falwell's televised pleas for donations became more strident as he asked his "Faith Partners" to double their regular contributions to help overcome his secular "enemies," and mounting expenses in his political operations forced him to lay off more than a quarter of his Moral Majority staff—leaving him more dependent than ever on the national media.

Unlike Pat Robertson, Falwell has no income-producing satellite empire. To maintain his image, to keep his "Old-Time Gospel Hour" on nearly 400 television and 500 radio stations, to fuel the Israeli Jet Commander that carries him 300,000 miles per year to speaking dates and political rallies, Falwell needs to generate a constant flow of more than $1 million per week. While much of this sum continues to pour in through his television show and direct-mail appeals, without the national publicity he receives for his Moral Majority crusade, in all likelihood, Jerry Falwell would be back in Lynchburg to stay by now.

Yet he remains a political power and a media superstar. Falwell knows how to play the media. He knows how to catch their eye, standing proudly in his dark vested suit with an American flag nearby. And he knows how to catch their ear. He has a million punchlines. On homosexuality: "God created Adam and Eve, not Adam and Steve!" On his political affiliation: "I'm not a Democrat. I'm not a Republican. I'm just a noisy Baptist." On national defense: "Jesus was not a pacifist. He was not a sissy."

And he knows how to get their goat. Falwell has succeeded in the media in large part because he hits the press where it lives—in the First Amendment. Falwell assails the media regularly. In 1981, he spearheaded the nationwide drive to boycott the sponsors of television programs judged objectionable by fundamentalists. When *Penthouse* magazine ran an interview with him, obtained under spurious pretenses, Falwell swept into federal court and won an injunction—albeit a brief one—preventing nationwide distribution of the publication. Around the country, Moral Majority spokesmen have called for the banning of textbooks and sued libraries to obtain the names of borrowers of materials they sought to censor. Through actions such as these, carried out under the broad banner of morality, Falwell monopolizes the media, winning prime-time exposure and color cover stories while other movement heavyweights go unnoticed.

But by any other measure, Falwell fails in his claim to speak for a significant segment of American society. He has claimed to represent a television constituency of 25 million, yet at the height of his public exposure, Arbitron ratings revealed that his gospel hour broadcast had an audience of only 1.6 million. He has bragged about the 70,000 fundamentalist ministers in his Moral Majority network, and about his broad base of popular support, yet nearly every poll taken shows that most Americans oppose his efforts. In one national survey, only 6.6 percent of those polled said they considered themselves members of his proclaimed majority. In another, only 7 percent of those surveyed looked favorably upon him, while more than ten times that figure agreed that a person's religious convictions should not be a basis for political action. The verdict has been consistent. How then has Jerry Falwell managed to convert so little raw material into so much power?

Much has been made of Falwell's humble beginnings: of his

grandfather, who was an avowed atheist; of his father, who had
been a bootlegger, then a drunkard and died of cirrhosis of the
liver after he shot and killed his brother in a feud over the family
business; of his God-fearing mother, who listened devotedly to
Rev. Charles E. Fuller's "Old-Fashioned Revival Hour." Young
Jerry Falwell was said to be a straight-A student, baseball hero
and practical joker who, in 1950, was denied the valedictorian's
podium at his high school commencement for, among other things,
leaving a rat in a teacher's desk and locking another in a supply
closet. At eighteen, listening to Fuller's revival hour, he became
born again via radio and promptly enrolled in the Baptist Bible
College in Springfield, Missouri. Then, in 1956, he drove home
and founded the Thomas Road Baptist Church in a soft-drink
plant once owned by the Donald Duck Bottling Company. That
same year, he started his own local half-hour radio broadcast and,
soon after, a Sunday afternoon television show. At the outset, he
made the discovery: "Those early contacts with radio and television," he has said, "were a springboard to my realization of the
potential power of the media."

For the next quarter century, however, few outside of Lynchburg heard of Jerry Falwell, yet his empire was growing steadily
through a technique he called "saturation evangelism," defined by
Falwell as "preaching the gospel to every available person at
every available time by every available means." The strategy
called for more than door-to-door and word-of-mouth efforts. He
bought a printing press and ran off handbills, notices, leaflets and
his own newspaper. He installed a telephone bank, launched a
direct-mail operation and began marketing mass-produced tape
cassettes of his sermons. And he honed his radio and television
skills. The saturation campaign clicked. By 1979, his Thomas
Road complex claimed 17,000 members, making it the second-
largest congregation in the country. It included a private school,
Lynchburg Christian Academy; a college, Liberty Baptist; a summer youth camp and an alcoholic treatment center.

Beneath his hard structures, however, Falwell's financial foundation was shaky. In 1973, the U.S. Securities and Exchange
Commission sued his ministry for "fraud and deceit" and "gross
insolvency" in the sale of $6 million in church bonds. All debts
were repaid, the fraud and deceit charge was erased, but only after

Falwell agreed to let an independent board of managers take over his ministry's financial affairs. In 1977, the board was disbanded, but Falwell's debts continued to mount. Two creditors filed liens on his ministry. He went to court over an $81,000 tax bill, and in 1980, he was forced to borrow another $6.5 million to stay afloat.

Atop his ministry's massive debts, Moral Majority, a wholly separate enterprise, allowed Falwell to stay on the offensive. On the hustings in 1980, he spoke freely on issues that, back then, he was only making vague references to on television, roaming from state capital to state capital decrying the sins of ungodly people in government. As he emerged from the electronic church to lead the fundamentalist right political crusade, recruiting local preachers to help him and staging a nationwide Christian voter registration drive, Falwell stepped seemingly at will across the line between religion and politics, addressing moral issues as a preacher, advancing his political platform as a lobbyist and endorsing candidates as a private citizen. His strategy included flashy media events like his "I Love America" rallies, and other political tactics. For example, a 1980 Moral Majority-sponsored multimedia presentation, *America, You're Too Young to Die,* shown widely around the country, roused thousands by mixing images of Charles Manson, atom bombs exploding, homosexuals embracing and aborted fetuses lying in bloody hospital pans, with these words falsely attributed to Gus Hall, former head of the U.S. Communist party: "I dream of the hour when the last congressman is strangled to death on the guts of the last preacher." Hall never made the statement. Similarly, Falwell gained strong support in Alaska, where Moral Majority took control of the state Republican party, when he spoke publicly of a personal conversation with then-President Jimmy Carter in which Carter, in effect, confessed and endorsed the presence of homosexuals on his senior staff. Tapes of the conversation proved the alleged exchange never took place. Falwell later recanted the charges and backpedaled on a number of positions he had taken, but the interim publicity served him well, helping him recruit more preachers for his coalition and raise more funds for his lobbying efforts.

Not surprisingly, Falwell's political adventurism belies even his own earlier preacher's terms. Until 1979, when Moral Majority was founded, like most evangelicals Falwell shunned involvement in politics. In fact, one Sunday night in 1965, he denounced such activity from his Lynchburg pulpit in a sermon, "Ministers and Marches," which soon became the talk of the town. At the time, he was disturbed by the involvement of black ministers in the civil rights movement and, in particular, by the work of Rev. Dr. Martin Luther King, Jr. That spring night, Falwell drew upon the Scriptures and, verse by verse, built an airtight argument for abstention by preachers from social and political activism. His words have since come back to haunt him:

> As far as the relationship of the church to the world, it can be expressed as simply as the three words which Paul gave to Timothy—"Preach the Word." . . . Nowhere are we commissioned to reform the externals. We are not told to wage wars against bootleggers, liquor stores, gamblers, murderers, prostitutes, racketeers, prejudiced persons or institutions, or any other existing evil as such. . . . Our only purpose on this earth is to know Christ and to make Him known. Believing the Bible as I do, I would find it impossible to stop preaching the pure, saving gospel of Jesus Christ, and begin doing anything else—including fighting communism, or participating in civil rights reforms. . . . Preachers are not called to be politicians but soul-winners.

In 1980, however, Falwell rejected "Ministers and Marches" as "false prophecy." At the same time, he began sending out signed letters for Moral Majority, under a fluttering red-white-and-blue banner, in which he declared:

> In recent months, God has been calling me to do more than just preach—He has called me to take action. I have a divine mandate to go right into the halls of Congress and fight for laws that will save America.

What does Jerry Falwell truly believe? As with many fundamentalist right leaders, who say different things to different crowds at different times, it's hard to tell. His clearest statement to date can be found in *Listen, America!*, his 1980 manifesto. There, Falwell opened with the same tactics he used in his slide show, detailing a trip to Thailand where he read in a local newspaper about an eight-year-old girl who was reportedly raped by a hundred Communist pirates. Another teenage victim "watched the Communists chop off her parents' heads and then carry them around by the hair," wrote Falwell. Further along, he told stories of other atrocities:

> The teacher who had taught the children about Jesus Christ was tortured by the Communist guard. His tongue was pulled out with a pair of pliers and cut off. He was left to drown in his own blood.

As with many fundamentalist right preachers, fear of "godless communism" appears to be a staple of Falwell's doctrinal diet. So is advocacy of the free-enterprise system, which Falwell was quick to deem divine in nature:

> The free-enterprise system is clearly outlined in the Book of Proverbs in the Bible. Jesus Christ made it clear that the work ethic was a part of His plan for man. Ownership of property is biblical. Competition in business is biblical. Ambitious and successful business management is clearly outlined as a part of God's plan for His people.

Belief in democracy, however, does not appear to be part of Falwell's creed. In a chapter entitled "Our Republic," he drew a damning distinction, held by many on the fundamentalist right, between a democracy and a republic:

> Today we find that America is more of a democracy than a republic. Sometimes there is mob rule. In some instances, a vocal minority prevails. Our Founding Fathers would not accept the tyranny of a democracy because they recognized that the only sovereign over men and nations was Almighty God.

Like Pat Robertson and nearly everyone else on the fundamentalist right, Falwell claimed that America's leaders must reach for God in the act of government:

If a man is not a student of the Word of God and does not
know what the Bible says, I question his ability to be an
effective leader. . . . Only by godly leadership can America
be put back on a divine course.

Falwell harped on this theme as he deprecated America for
what he sees as widespread moral bankruptcy and spiritual decay:

We must, from the highest office in the land right down to
the shoeshine boy in the airport, have a return to biblical
basics. . . . Will it be revival or ruin? There can be no other
way.

Falwell has stated publicly that he does not want to "Christianize" America, yet his writings suggest otherwise:

When we as a country again acknowledge God as our Creator and Jesus Christ as the Savior of Mankind, we will be
able to turn this nation around economically as well as in
every other way.

Statements such as these do little to support his public position
in favor of religious pluralism. He wrote:

Each and every man and woman alive today needs a new
birth experience. Man must be born again; he must be regen-
erated and believe in the death, the burial, and the resurrection of Jesus Christ and accept the shed blood of the Savior as the atonement for his sin in order to be complete.

Falwell claims his Moral Majority is a political operation, not a
religious one, but his scriptural beliefs lie at the root of almost
every item on his social agenda. Similarly, he claims interde-
nominational support for his platform, but his activist network
consists almost exclusively of fundamentalist preachers and their
followers, many of whom believe they are carrying out the will of
God. In his public postures, Falwell has made gestures to distance
himself from his freewheeling, often embarrassing Moral Majority
state chairmen who, he claims, operate totally independent of his

national organization. Yet, with so little real support, his band of
fundamentalist foot soldiers may be his only source of power over
local communities, liberal and minority groups, state legislators
and other officials. In the end, however, the illusion of power may
continue to be his greatest weapon. As he continues his attack on
the secular world, aided by fundamentalist right forces more formidable than himself, his surviving clout will in all likelihood remain in his ability to launch public attacks and threaten his
opponents with political retribution. Indeed, in Falwell's moral
republic, the drive for revenge seems to emerge as the highest aim
of policy. As he wrote:

> A politician, as a minister of God, is a revenger to execute
> wrath upon those who do evil. . . . The role of government
> is to minister justice and to protect the rights of its citizens by
> being a terror to evildoers within and without the nation.

We quote Falwell at length because there is no interview with
him or spokesmen for his organization in this book. In 1981, as
we did with many on the fundamentalist right, we wrote requesting
an interview and a tour of his ministry. Less than a week later, we
received separate form replies requiring our signatures before our
requests would be considered. The form was a printed legal document demanding, among other things, that we agree to grant to
Falwell "a common-law copyright on the words, phrases and images he uses in said interview," and that we promise not to supply
any material obtained in an interview "for or to any other publication other than that stated above" without first obtaining his written permission. The document concluded:

> Any violation of this agreement shall entitle Jerry Falwell
> to compensatory damages and reasonable attorney fees.

The paper, still warm with the heat of Falwell's *Penthouse* flap,
seemed clearly designed, not only to intimidate, but to circumvent
journalists' First Amendment guarantees by forcing them to sign
contracts with Falwell as a precondition for mere consideration of
an interview. We called Lynchburg and spoke with the woman
who had sent us the contracts, telling her that neither of us would

sign the document, but that we were coming to Lynchburg and would be interested in speaking with anyone in the organization. But apparently the contract was meant to cover Falwell's entire organization. "Someone will be happy to see you," she said, "as long as you've signed the form." We declined again. Two months later, a Washington *Post* article reported that Falwell's public relations office said that so far, no journalists had balked at signing the agreement.

By that time, however, we had lost our interest in interviewing Falwell. We had already caught his act at the Copa. Early in 1981, Falwell came to New York to address a luncheon gathering of network television producers and broadcast executives at Manhattan's famed Copacabana nightclub. It was not the kind of place in which you would expect to find a staunch Baptist preacher. We arrived downstairs at the Copa to find Falwell standing at a flood-lit podium in the center of the dance floor, amid white plaster palm trees and gaily colored papier-mâché tropical fruit, bathed in purple disco lighting.

The performance was classic Falwell. To every challenge and accusation made by the broadcast bigwigs in attendance, Falwell had a ready-made answer. In the course of a ninety-minute talk and discussion, we watched Falwell disarm his challengers a dozen times, using one of the few original techniques in his arsenal, a device we have come to refer to as the "Falwell Goosestep." That afternoon, Falwell repeatedly drew analogies between fundamentalist right social and political tactics and those employed over the years by groups on the left. No mention was made of his record of distortions, his contradictory public statements, or his implied scriptural requirements for public officeholders, which, if enforced, would violate federal law. Instead, Falwell laid out his easy analogy: "I think it's fair for the conservative goose to do what the liberal gander does." Then, as we had observed many times before, he uncorked a flood of variations on the theme that left his usually savvy audience virtually helpless. To wit:

The Falwell Goosestep on censorship:

> Now, some feminists—I was reading, coming over—are advocating censorship in the pornography field. I think it's a mistake.

The Falwell Goosestep on morality-based boycotts:

The ERA proponents, for example, do not support states that haven't ratified it yet. I think that's fair. Some disagree.

The Falwell Goosestep on preachers in politics:

I think that a minister, whether it was Bill Coffin as chaplain at Yale or Martin Luther King as a Baptist pastor in Atlanta, has the right to take off the pastoral cap . . . and fight the battles they have fought. I also think Jerry Falwell has that right.

The Falwell Goosestep on the First Amendment:

As a matter of fact, while I believe in the separation of church and state, there are many constitutional attorneys who do not.

The Falwell Goosestep on his relationship with President Reagan:

I don't attempt to tell him how to run the White House. If I did, I think I know what he would do. And he doesn't try to run Thomas Road Church. I *know* he knows what I would do!

And finally, the Grandslam Falwell Goosestep on the rights of atheists, focusing on America's foremost crusader against school prayer:

Madalyn O'Hair and I are not—let me just say we don't have any social times together—but I was in Austin, Texas, last year for a rally on the state capitol steps, which the governor was very much for . . . and he had his aides there to help us. We were contacted a day or two ahead, saying Madalyn wanted to have a competitive rally on the grounds . . . I said, "Please do. We promise not to interrupt her and I don't think she'll interrupt us, because although we disagree with her message, we would die for her right to preach it."

And although Falwell wouldn't speak with us without a signed contract, he did prove to be a good correspondent. One day after watching "The Old-Time Gospel Hour," we called his 800 number to request two free "Jesus First" lapel pins. The young voice on the phone was polite. He took Flo's name and address and didn't ask for a donation. Several weeks later, the pins arrived with a letter from Falwell requesting money:

> Maybe your financial situation seems impossible. . . . Try putting "Jesus First" in your stewardship and allow Him to bless you financially.

We sent no money and made no reply, but it didn't matter. We were on Falwell's mailing list, cranked into his direct-mail machine that reportedly sends out 500,000 letters a week to fundraising targets drawn from his pool of 4.5 million names. For the next six months, every two weeks there was another letter. Each one came in a different envelope from a different Falwell ministry. Most contained computer-written messages such as:

> Dear Florence:
>   I want to personally thank you for requesting your "Jesus First" pins. . . . And now, Florence, I want to minister to you in yet another way . . . a very special booklet. . . . It is free . . . *The Future, the Bible and You.* . . . I want every God-fearing person like you, Florence, to know what the Bible says about these coming events. . . . There's no cost, no obligation. You don't have to make a gift if you don't want to. . . .

We sent in the return envelope, requesting the book, but without a donation. It never came. Later, we received a "Faith Partners Acceptance Form." For a minimum of ten dollars a month, it said, we would receive a giant-print Bible, a copy of Falwell's "Sermon of the Month," a special guide to daily Bible-reading, *three* "Jesus First" pins—two bronze, one 24-karat-gold-plated—a "Faith Partner Pocket Secretary Appointment Book" and an exclusive monthly newsletter from Falwell "sharing my feelings on controversial issues too hot for me to talk about on television."

The accompanying letter told of a dying man who was converted in his hospital room as he watched "The Old-Time Gospel Hour" and died the next morning. Falwell wrote:

> So for the sake of thousands of souls like the man with the brain tumor who was saved twenty-four hours before he went out into eternity, won't you please become a "Faith Partner" immediately?

The mail kept coming. "THE BATTLE IS RAGING . . ." read a red-white-and-blue envelope. Inside was a second sealed envelope containing an "OFFICIAL BALLOT FOR: FLORENCE CONWAY" and instructions to "CAST YOUR VOTE FOR CREATION OR EVOLUTION." "WE ARE LIVING IN THE LAST DAYS!" began another. "I sincerely believe we are living in that last generation before Jesus returns," wrote Falwell. "That's why I've rushed you this membership card." Possibly his most outrageous pitch, however, went out during an earlier financial squeeze. He wrote:

> I have become the victim of a vicious, orchestrated attack by the liberal politicians, bureaucrats and amoralists. . . . You will never read it in the newspaper that Jerry Falwell quit. You may read that someone killed me—but that is the only way I can be stopped. . . . Opposition is becoming more and more violent. Our enemies are hitting us from every side. And we are certain that right now there are key individuals in our country who are plotting to close down this ministry.

Lynchburg's Thomas Road Baptist Church is located on what is commonly referred to as the "other side" of this worn-out industrial town. The main structure, a great red-brick hexagon, stands atop several acres of parking space. There is parking everywhere: in the upper lot, in the lower lot and along nearby streets. In the far corners of the property, the day we visited there, more than a hundred yellow school buses were nested in rows. Beyond them sat several highway trailers from Falwell's "I Love America" rallies.

We passed between the great columns at the church entrance and were ushered quickly to the rear of the main chamber. It looked more like a broadcast studio than a house of worship. Television cameras manned by men in headphones rolled along the aisles trailing black cables. Up to the left, above the balcony, there was a glass-windowed control booth. At center stage stood Falwell, telling the home viewing audience how his congregation had "packed the house" for the third time that morning. There were dozens of empty pews. We took one to ourselves. Several moments later, a young couple came over and sat beside us.

Falwell's message today was about world hunger. "There are sixteen million refugees in the world," he said, "and most of them are products of Communist aggression." His guest that day reiterated the point that these people were hungry as "a direct result of Communist rule." Then the center cameraman closed in tight on Falwell as he made the morning's first appeal for money:

> As Bible-believing Christians everywhere, would you write a check to "The Old-Time Gospel Hour" and mark it FOR WORLD HUNGER DAY . . . ? The first $100,000 that comes in will go to the East African project in Somalia.

It was another classic Falwell appeal: committing himself to give only the first $100,000. The request would probably bring in ten times that amount, the excess of which he admitted in a later appeal, was to be used for other ministry operations. Then Falwell delivered his Sunday sermon, more of the same sales pitch. "Does Jesus care if people are hungry and hurting?" he began, ending with, "Make your check payable to 'The Old-Time Gospel Hour.'" Following a song by Falwell's SMITE singers (Student Missionaries in Training for Evangelism), he went back to fundraising, finally revealing the underlying motivation for the hunger project:

> What's our ultimate purpose out there in Somalia, in Pakistan, in parts of the world where people are starving and dying? What's "Food for the Hungry" doing, just feeding mouths? Yes, so ultimately they can feed *hearts*. They're earning the right to be heard. You can't tell a starving man, "God bless you, let me preach the Bible to you." You feed him first.

During a break in the taping, Falwell called out the collection plates. As he worked the house crowd, he talked them through the added attractions seen by the home audience. When he talked about May Day in the Communist world, he said, "We actually fed into the master tape . . . last year's display of the Russian armaments in Moscow . . . Nikita Khrushchev with his shoe up there beating on the UN desk." The final plea for donations was followed by a traditional altar call:

> While our heads are bowed . . . I want to challenge you to come. . . . If you're still struggling with this matter of becoming a Christian, why don't you give up and give in to God and just come down . . . ? Sometimes the crowd is a hindrance . . . forget the crowd. Just you alone. Isolate yourself . . . you're not joining anything.

The scene was peaceful, the chorus monotonous and relaxing. Falwell ended the service with a blessing. We rose slowly, watching the audience. They looked pleased with their celebrated pastor and privileged to be in his famous church. When the room was nearly emptied, the young man beside us turned and said, "You're reporters. Are you working on a newspaper article?" He introduced himself as Rick, an associate director of Falwell's rallies. "Are you from New York?" he asked.

Falwell remained on the podium, chatting with members of his congregation. Like Pat Robertson, he seemed to be in no hurry. We asked Rick if we might be able to have a word with him. As we moved down the aisle, we noticed a dozen men positioned between the pews and the podium, blocking the stairs. One was carrying a heavy walking stick. They were Falwell's bodyguards, Rick explained, part of a permanent security force which, he claimed, was larger than the Lynchburg Police Department. "Dr. Falwell gets forty to fifty death threats a week," he said. Rick spoke with one of the bodyguards, who then mounted the podium and conferred with Falwell. We waited. No word came back. Rick apologized and said he would be glad to answer our questions if we waited until the next day.

Out in the sunlight, the parking lots were nearly empty. We asked a young girl if she would take our picture in front of the church. She looked petrified as she reached an outstretched arm to take our camera. These were not the same kind of Christians we had met at the "700 Club." The air in Falwell country was heavy. Behind us, Jerry Falwell and his bodyguards strolled across the blacktop to their cars.

We spent the rest of the day talking to "Lynchburgers." We visited other churches and talked with local ministers, most of whom had little love for Jerry Falwell. "There's no way he could have seventeen thousand people in there every week," said one. "Take away those students and the Sunday school kids, and I'd say if they have six thousand in church, that's a lot." That morning, across town at the city's stately First Presbyterian Church, Rev. John Killinger had delivered a sermon entitled "Could Jesus Belong to the Moral Majority?" It was his second in a series of scathing attacks on Falwell and his activities. Killinger answered in the negative, as in his earlier sermon, "Would Jesus Have Appeared on 'The Old-Time Gospel Hour'?" in which he speculated tongue-in-cheek on what Christ might have told Falwell and his associates: "You appear to be very religious before your television audiences," said the mainline pastor, "but inside, you are rapacious, unconverted wolves, seeking only a greater share of the evangelical TV market without really caring for the sheep you devour."

The rest of Lynchburg society seemed to be maintaining what Killinger referred to as "a discreet silence." Few people we spoke with were willing to be quoted by name, yet all had strong feelings about Falwell. "There is a fear that he's helped engender that God will get you if you criticize him," said one. "If I were sitting in his congregation, I'd hesitate to say anything." On the local scene, we got a picture of Falwell quite different from his national image. "He doesn't care what the media says about him," said one gentleman, "but he's supersensitive to local criticism. He cannot afford to have his own people see him in a bad light." A local businessman drew another line in the picture. "From an economic point of view, he's really been a boon to the town," he said. "He's Lynchburg's fourth-largest employer. He's got a small industry over there. There's fifty million dollars a year passing through here, through the banks, the motels, the restaurants. No wonder people are reluctant to speak out against him."

One woman who was not reluctant was a local teacher named Rachel Wilson. A native of Lynchburg, she had been watching Falwell's interactions with the town over the years.

"It's just been a tragic horror story, from A to Z," she told us. "People here couldn't care less about the man. They're embarrassed by him, but they won't say so because the money is too big. He brings too much business here." A government and history teacher in the Lynchburg middle schools, Wilson recently formed an opposition group called INFORM—Individuals Needing Facts on Right-wing Movements—but the level of local participation was not high.

"When I organized INFORM," she said, "people by the dozens came to thank me. They said, 'Oh, it's time somebody around here did something.' But they wouldn't join up. I received so many contributions saying, 'Here's my twenty-five dollars, but I cannot allow my name to be made public.'"

She did not share their fears.

"I mean, he has *used* this town for his own gains," she said, offering an example from her own field. "He attacks the public schools. He's out to get us all the time. But where do you think his Liberty Baptist student teachers have been training? In the public schools!" She made light of Falwell's posturing before the national media. In her view, many of his public actions were publicity stunts designed merely to elevate him in the eyes of his congregation. She spoke of Falwell's jousting with the skin magazines that have drawn so much of his wrath.

"He laps it up," she said. "When I heard he was in one of those magazines, I went to the drugstore immediately to buy it. When I got there, they said the lady before me had just bought two hundred copies! The report going around town was that Jerry was sending people out all over the state and buying them up himself."

Yet the battle against the "smut-peddlers" seemed to be central to Falwell's media strategy. A week before, we saw him launch a new attack on "The Old-Time Gospel Hour":

I heard that in the last couple of issues of *Playboy* magazine, they had written about me. I don't subscribe to *Playboy*. . . . As a matter of fact, I don't know a real Christian

who does. I'll repeat that: I don't know a real Christian who
does subscribe to *Playboy* or any such smut magazine.

Early the next morning, we called Rick and made an appointment to speak with him that afternoon. He told us to meet him in
the small house across from the church that served as headquarters for Falwell's rallies. We were on time, but there was no
sign of Rick. We waited. After a half hour, the door opened and a
young crowd burst into the house. It was Falwell's singing group
from the college: wholesome, clean-scrubbed and not very
friendly. In a corner of the room, a young man muttered, "I'm
getting sick and tired of these reporters coming around here."
Still no sign of Rick. After an hour, we left, about to head out
of town. Finally, hoping to find somebody in the Falwell organization who might answer our questions without a contract, we
made our way across Lynchburg to the national headquarters of
Moral Majority, Inc. We found it in a small storefront by a truck
loading dock, across from the Lynchburg Weenie Stand.
There were three tiny offices, all empty and dark. In the recep-
tion area, a secretary sat behind a desk piled high with mail. We
asked her if there was anybody around who would speak to us. She
told us someone might be back in an hour or so, if we wanted to
wait. We declined. We looked down at the piles of mail on her
desk. Poking out of one stack was a piece of paper with a little
bunny in the corner and the words "Please allow 8–10 weeks for
delivery" running along the bottom. It looked to us like a *Playboy*
magazine subscription invoice. The billing address had been typed
by a computer. It read: "Rev. Jerry Falwell . . . Lynchburg,
VA."

Religion and the Rise of the Fundamentalist Right

History offers few examples of fanatics suffering from scruples.

—ALBERT CAMUS

IT'S A SHORT TRIP from Lynchburg to Washington. Driving through Virginia, the spirit of the "Old Dominion" seemed mocked by the state's new religious fiefdoms. Pat Robertson's empire in Virginia Beach was high-tech and lifeless, his people distant. In contrast, Jerry Falwell's operation was a real church, but the people inside it were stiff and hostile. In both places, a mere handful of people manned the controls. From airless booths, they manipulated rows of push buttons and rooms of machinery. Looking out on this terrain of hardware, we realized: *There's nobody here! This is no grass-roots movement.* It is a figment of the satellites and memory banks run by a tiny core of ambitious men. The massive electronic church was a shadow in a box: already it was beginning to flicker. So, too, we soon discovered, the "new right" was another illusion, merely the old right with computers and a new religious twist: fundamentalism.

It should come as no surprise. Zealotry has always been a feature of the far right in American politics. In its faith, fears and prejudices, the old right's list of evils was short and classic: blacks, Jews, labor unions, Communists at home and abroad. Yet, from the modern resurgence of the racist Ku Klux Klan in the twenties to the birth of the anti-Communist John Birch Society in the fifties, the old right remained a marginal or at most a regional threat to American life, a bristling of the lunatic fringe. Its organizations were primitive, its leaders frenzied, and although they invoked God and Country, with few exceptions, the old right's crusades remained social and political, its boogeymen and luminaries mainly secular. And in the end, for the most part, the old right was a dismal failure. Time and again, its campaigns were soundly rejected by the overwhelming majority of the American people.

But not so with the fundamentalist new right, the cluster of ultraconservative forces that swelled to victory in 1980. In its newfound fullness, the fundamentalist right is a diversified agglomeration of negativity. Atop traditional old right pilings of anti-communism, anti-socialism and anti-labor—which it tends to equate indiscriminately—it has built a platform of reaction to social developments of the sixties and seventies: anti-busing, anti-welfare, anti-gun control, anti-abortion, anti-feminism, anti-gay rights, anti-sex education and anti-pornography. Over all this ideological hardwood, it has laid a film of cryptic "pros": pro-life, pro-America, pro-family—pro-God.

God is the voice in the fundamentalist right whirlwind. Religion has given the far right in its reincarnation the power it always needed to bewitch, bewilder and bother: the pull of "the Word," the magic of television, and an army of obedient Christian foot soldiers. Improving on the extremism of the cranky old right, which most of the nation saw through, the upstart fundamentalist right has wrapped its central issues in religious swaddling. In this way, it has put the old right's rejected social and political agenda back on the map: renamed, reborn and crisply recoded in terms that are vague, misleading—and irrefutable. In the language of the recoded right, for example, communism is condemned, not as an objectionable political or economic system, but as a purveyor of "godless atheism." Welfare and social programs for the disadvantaged are opposed, not on racial, ethnic or even economic grounds, but as a government-sponsored evil that "undermines the moral fiber of the community." Abortion and equal rights for women are denied as violations of the biblical roles of wives and mothers. At the same time, free enterprise and a strong military posture are lauded, not as pathways to progress and security for the nation, but for their remote scriptural underpinnings.

Devices like these work well to arouse anger and passion in

people who have thought little about such matters, and in people who may be vulnerable to simple slogans and catchphrases. Yet this recoding process that has targeted so many Christians, clergy and Americans of many faiths and occupations was not the brainchild of Jerry Falwell, James Robison or even Yale-educated Pat Robertson. From takeoff, the course of the fundamentalist right has been carefully plotted and tracked by remote control. At the core of the movement, beyond the showmen and their technicians, lie the master strategists, the tacticians who write the programs, plot the charts, manage the money and call the shots.

The collaboration is no conspiracy. The individuals and organizations in the movement are all known, as are most of the interconnections among them. By design, in fact, little has been kept secret. Yet, as we saw often as we crossed the country, the connection between the new right and fundamentalist Christianity is obscure to many Americans. While they remain transfixed on Jerry Falwell, they miss the real meaning of the movement, at the same time becoming ever more vulnerable to the operations of a few men who have launched a dozen PACs, a hundred candidates, a thousand write-in campaigns and millions of carefully targeted votes. To understand their place in the politics of Holy Terror, religion run amok in its most "civil" form, it is important to consider the brains behind the fundamentalist right—the personalities and the mind-set—and the marriage of religion and politics which they arranged.

THE GANG OF THREE

Viguerie—Mail Chauvinist.   Practically speaking, Richard A. Viguerie may be the most important individual in the fundamentalist right network. Forty-nine years old, blue-eyed and balding, Viguerie is the moneyman. Without him, most of the movement's most influential PACs and organizations would never have come into being. Without his continued efforts, in all likelihood, they would cease to exist.

Unlike older benefactors of the right, however, Viguerie's power is unrelated to his personal or family wealth. Rather, it flows from the system of computers operated by the Richard A.

Viguerie Company of Falls Church, Virginia. Huddled in its memory banks are the names of 25 million Americans, approximately 4.5 million of whom are known supporters of right-wing causes. Every year, Viguerie sends 100 million letters to the concerned citizens on his lists, requesting money and other forms of support for the forty different groups he represents. Reportedly, they respond to the tune of almost $15 million, mostly in small gifts of ten to twenty dollars. With these small checks, Viguerie has helped turn esoteric special interests into central interests. Over the years, his firm has hauled in millions for groups such as the Panama Canal Truth Squad, Gun Owners of America, the American Security Council and Citizens for Decency Through Law. At the same time, he has drawn successfully on his lists to provide vital support for archconservative politicians, including Senators Jesse Helms of North Carolina, Jim McClure of Idaho, Orrin Hatch of Utah and Congressmen Philip Crane of Illinois, Mickey Edwards of Oklahoma, Larry McDonald of Georgia—reportedly a national council member of the John Birch Society—and Phil Gramm of Texas.

Perhaps Viguerie's greatest personal commitment, however, is to the multi-issue umbrella groups that make up the political core of the fundamentalist right: Terry Dolan's NCPAC (the National Conservative Political Action Committee), the Conservative Caucus and the Committee for the Survival of a Free Congress. Viguerie played key roles in the launching and initial fund-raising of each of these groups, and through his continuing efforts and close personal relationships with their leading figures, he sees that their interests remain allied and their operations tightly coordinated. With the emergence of the fundamentalist right in 1980, Viguerie stepped into the role of chief publicist for the movement as well. His book, *The New Right: We're Ready to Lead,* is at once a guide to its key figures and a sentimental greeting card to all his friends. It is also a diatribe against "liberalism"—the mortal enemy of the fundamentalist right.

In his book, Viguerie bitterly attacks liberalism as "devious elitism" and "socialism on the installment plan." He claims it favors "a society based on state regulation, supervision and coercion." According to Viguerie, liberals advocate "compulsory unionism, government-imposed racial and sexual discrimination, and oppressive taxes." They have "defended and even promoted pornography and abortion." They attack "our allies rather than our enemies" and encourage American women "to feel that they are failures if they want to be wives and mothers." His alternative: the new brand of political absolutism he calls conservatism which, although grounded in some traditional principles, rapidly departs from conservative thinking as it has found its expression in American history. Viguerie's conservatism is really *ideological fundamentalism,* a move to impress his social thinking and religious beliefs on others.

With the rise of the movement, Viguerie has been intimately connected with its candidates, issues and organizations. He has worked with the multi-issue groups since their inception. He has championed other single issues and spun off whole organizations through single mailings. Yet his life-sustaining services are not cheap. Since 1965, when he began the Viguerie Company with a $400 investment, he has reaped a corporate and personal fortune, in large part due to the extraordinarily high fees he charges his clients. In 1971, for example, he raised $1.2 million for an anti-pornography group called Citizens for Decent Literature—and claimed fees and expenses of eighty-four percent. In 1977, he raised $802,000 for a fundamentalist outfit called Bibles for the World and charged them $889,000—one hundred and twelve percent! Viguerie cites high postage, printing, copywriting and computer costs, yet other professional fund-raisers manage to keep their expenses below twenty-five percent of their clients' yield. Viguerie has also made six-figure loans to groups whose principles he values, sharing in their political triumphs and gathering new names for future use—some of which he re-rents to approved candidates for one-time use. Viguerie's own description of the "internal dynamics" of the insurgent movement testifies to the new levels of sophistication reached by the far right in America:

> Some people think we are a big conspiracy. Others think we meet and vote on everything we do. Others think I give orders to everyone. These are all false ideas. . . .
> When we get together, we never vote on anything. . . . We exchange information. We brainstorm new ideas. Some people volunteer to do something or commit their organi-

zation to do specific things. But no one gives orders like a commander-in-chief, or a Godfather. . . . We meet to work on specific projects, say a piece of legislation. . . . We are creative in convincing different groups that their interests are the same as ours in particular battles. . . . Our informal way of operating is very frustrating to liberals who would love to have us tied up in formal organizations that would be easier to attack.

Viguerie's personal rags-to-riches saga parallels the rise of the fundamentalist right, offering insight into the way the new mindset has taken hold in the political arena. He was born during the Depression in Texas, where his father worked his way up from a construction job to an executive position with Shell Oil Company while his mother kept house, canned vegetables and toiled at odd jobs to supplement the family income. A poor student in high school and college, Viguerie failed in his early attempts to become first an engineer and then a lawyer. During those years, his heroes were "the two Macs"—General Douglas MacArthur and Senator Joseph McCarthy—both of whom helped fuel his loathing of communism. Viguerie rambled through the fifties, becoming involved in Republican party politics and working for Dwight Eisenhower's 1952 and 1956 presidential campaigns. In 1960, he wrote his first fund-raising letter for Texas U.S. Senate candidate John Tower.

Then, in 1961, he answered a cryptic ad in *The National Review* seeking "field men" for a "national conservative organization" called Americans for Constitutional Action. Shortly thereafter, Viguerie came to New York City to find that he had, in fact, been recruited for the position of executive secretary of Young Americans for Freedom (YAF), a student organization founded a year earlier at the Connecticut home of columnist William F. Buckley, Jr. During their heyday in the sixties, YAFers served as campus radicals of the far right, opposing the eastern Rockefeller wing of the Republican party, all Democrats and liberals—particularly those in the emerging counterculture and anti-war movement.

The call to arms came after the 1964 presidential election, a crushing defeat for conservatives of every degree in America. Watching the overwhelming rejection by the larger public of their platform and their champion, Senator Barry Goldwater, was a brutal experience for many YAFers in their first major political campaign. For many, the pain was intolerable and indelible, nurturing in their formative political years a deep-seated desire for revenge against the liberals who, they felt, unfairly depicted Goldwater as an extremist. One month after the election, Viguerie started his direct-mail company. In a story that has become a fundamentalist right legend, he assembled his first mailing list sitting in the office of the clerk of the House of Representatives, copying by hand the federally required file of names and addresses of each of the 12,500 people who had given fifty dollars or more to the Goldwater campaign. During the next ten years, Viguerie plied his trade by trial and error, building his lists through fund-raising efforts for different conservative causes and candidates. In 1973, he acquired another prized list of core contributors when he was asked to help Alabama Governor George Wallace retire his 1972 presidential campaign debts.

By 1974, the Viguerie machine was well oiled and productive. At the same time, events in Washington and around the country were firing another head of steam on the far right. Foremost among them were passage of the Equal Rights Amendment in Congress and the Supreme Court's 1973 *Roe* v. *Wade* decision legalizing abortion, judgments which angered traditionalists and conservative Christians and gave impetus to the militant Stop ERA and Right to Life movements. Hard-liners were further enraged by the final blow in the stinging Watergate affair: President Gerald Ford's selection of Nelson Rockefeller to be his vice-president. Then came the 1976 election, and Jimmy Carter's campaign for the presidency stirred the first political rumblings of America's born agains. But, upon his inauguration, Carter quickly lost their favor by his advocacy of new social programs and campaign reforms, his opposition to prayer in schools, and in the move that sounded his political death knell among conservatives, his diplomatic initiatives that resulted in the Panama Canal treaty.

The Carter years were a boon to Viguerie and the rising fundamentalist right. Through his mailing lists and allied PACs, Viguerie raised millions from the shared discontent of wealthy businessmen and modestly endowed Middle Americans. Those efforts were augmented by two new publications started by Viguerie, the *New Right Report*, a newsletter for political activists, and *Conser-*

vative Digest, a slick monthly aimed at hard-liners like those Viguerie acquired for his lists through his efforts on behalf of George Wallace. From early 1977, Viguerie and the fundamentalist right hammered away at the Carter administration from the pages of *Conservative Digest,* condemning the President for campaigning as a conservative Christian and then showing liberal colors after his election, also for failing to appoint many conservative Christians to high posts in his administration.

However, it was the furor over the Panama Canal treaty that gave Viguerie and the fundamentalist right their first symbolic victory. Though they lost in their effort to dissuade a majority of senators from ratifying the pact, their lobbying and direct-mail blitz proved that they could raise an impressive clamor. Between the summer of 1977 and the Senate vote in April 1978, fundamentalist right forces mailed almost nine million cards and letters urging Americans to oppose the treaty. They chartered a Boeing 737 jet to fly their "Truth Squad" of anti-treaty senators and congressmen around the country. They bought time on television and radio, took out newspaper ads, distributed countless leaflets. The effort cost $3 million and probably changed few minds in Congress or among the public—but it netted Viguerie and his allies more than 400,000 new names for their mailing lists!

Those names proved immediately useful several months later when they were cranked into the fundamentalist right's first coordinated election effort, which helped elect five new right senators— Humphrey of New Hampshire, Jepsen of Iowa, Armstrong of Colorado, Warner of Virginia and Simpson of Wyoming—and more than two dozen allied congressmen. For the first time in a national campaign, the small circle of fundamentalist right strategists proved it could have sweeping impact on American politics through a heavily funded, closely coordinated coalition of umbrella groups and special interests.

Central to the entire effort, in Viguerie's view, is what he refers to as the "new technology": "using computers, direct mail, telephone marketing, TV (including cable TV) and radio, cassette tapes and toll-free numbers, among other things, to ask for contributions and for votes." Of the new tools, Viguerie considered direct mail to be the most formidable. "Frankly," he wrote, "the conservative movement is where it is today because of direct mail. Without direct mail, there would be no effective counterforce to liberalism, and certainly there would be no New Right." For Viguerie, direct mail is "the one method of mass commercial communication that the liberals do not control." Like far right spokesmen have for years, Viguerie bemoaned the ills caused by what he moderately referred to as the "liberal-leaning news media" which, he claimed, have a "virtual monopoly on TV, radio, newspapers and magazines." His panacea: the high-speed, computerized letter-writing, addressing, stamping and mailing apparatus that has for years been the third most effective mass-marketing force in America—behind television and print advertising.

"You can think of direct mail as *our* TV, radio, daily newspaper and weekly magazine," he wrote, referring to the U.S. mail repeatedly as "the advertising medium of the underdog":

> We sell our magazines, our books and our candidates through the mail. We fight our legislative battles through the mail. We alert our supporters to upcoming battles through the mail. We find new recruits for the conservative movement through the mail. . . . Without the mail, most conservative activities would wither and die.

Viguerie uses this mass medium as more than a mere fund-raising or advertising channel. From his description, he sees it as his own private commercial network and a tool for programming a wide range of personal actions:

> Raising money is only one of several purposes of direct-mail advertising letters. A letter may ask you to vote for a candidate, volunteer for campaign work, circulate a petition among your neighbors, write letters and postcards to your senators and congressmen, urging them to pass or defeat legislation . . .

If he has done anything in his career, Richard Viguerie has raised the institution of "junk mail" to new heights of social and political control. Reading some of his letters, however, we found them lacking in ethical standards. Viguerie's direct-mail solici-

tations employ many of the same gimmicks used by Jerry Falwell
to exploit the beliefs and emotions of their readers. An early letter
from the Conservative Caucus, for example, included two flags in
its attack on the SALT II arms limitation treaty: "the red-white-
and-blue of Old Glory—and the white flag of surrender." Another
Viguerie letter, from the Free Congress Research and Education
Foundation, played heavily on the "pro-family" strategy pioneered by the fundamentalist right as yet another pathway to people's emotions:

Dear Friend:
    Do you believe that children should have the right to sue
their parents for being "forced" to attend church?
    Should children be eligible for minimum wage if they are
asked to do household chores?
    Do you believe that children should have the right to
choose their own family?
    As incredible as they might sound, these are just a few of
the new "children's rights laws" that could become a reality
under a new United Nations program if fully implemented by
the Carter administration.
    *If radical anti-family forces have their way, this UN-spon-
sored program is likely to become an all-out assault on our
traditional family structure.*

Other Viguerie letters employ even more cynical subterfuges. In
Thunder on the Right, Alan Crawford, a young conservative journalist who once worked for Viguerie, revealed that during Representative Daniel Crane's 1978 congressional campaign in Illinois,
Viguerie mailed out 100,000 copies of a mass-produced form letter designed to look like they were individually handwritten by the
candidate's wife. Enclosed in each letter was a photograph of
Crane, his family and his dog. The "wife letter," said Crawford,
was routinely used by Viguerie and became his "single most effective fund-raising gimmick for congressional campaigns."
    Like Falwell and other mass-mailers, Viguerie's efforts seem to
take for granted the attempt to deceive audiences concerning the
real authors and the impersonal nature of the mass-produced letters. Viguerie and his clients have also been charged with using

ploys that are more plainly deceptive and, in some cases, illegal. Viguerie mailings have displayed the names of U.S. congressmen without their authorization. A 1970 fund-raising letter for a Florida senator gave his Senate office for a return address—a violation of federal law. In 1977, Viguerie was charged by the state of Ohio with failing to register as a fund-raiser and temporarily barred from operating in both Ohio and Connecticut.

Yet, despite his subtle deceptions and transgressions, his apparent low regard for the intelligence of his audiences, and his fees, which one state attorney general has called "unconscionably high," Viguerie talks about religion and morality as much as any strategist on the new right. His frequent moralizing offers still another example of how fundamentalism has become ingrained, not only as the religion, but as the political ideology of the movement. Raised as a Catholic, Viguerie sent his children to a private fundamentalist school after withdrawing them from Catholic parochial schools when he heard they were being shown films on ecology. Reportedly, he keeps a Bible on his desk and views religion as a central feature of his self-declared effort "to save the Western world." "We believe we should be in politics as a way of improving the world from a religious concept," he has said. Like Falwell, however, his political outlook appears to revolve around the notion of retribution. "We're going to look *very* carefully at the votes when all this is over and do an *awful* lot of punishing next election," he said during the Panama Canal fight.

By 1980, he was walking yet another fundamentalist line as, around the time of "Washington for Jesus," he called upon readers of *Conservative Digest* to petition Congress to proclaim a "National Day of Prayer and Fasting." Invoking Washington, Lincoln and Christ in the same breath, Viguerie urged millions to pray together "for a common goal" and to "symbolize America's desire to return to God." In his book, he stepped up the call: "Those who want to play a leadership role in saving America and bringing freedom to the world should set aside, not just one day a year, but one or more days a month exclusively devoted to prayer, fasting and meditation." If they did, he believed, "miracles will come to pass in our lives and in our country."

And apparently, for Viguerie, in 1980 that miracle was named Falwell. In assessing the movement's triumph, Viguerie was quick to embrace the electronic church as the new right's "own ready-made network," praising Falwell's Moral Majority as the new right's "most important asset." Viguerie credited Falwell with recruiting 2.5 million previously unregistered evangelical Christian voters and with re-registering up to 1.5 million more. Falwell in turn lauded Viguerie, writing a glowing introduction to his book and praising Viguerie's courage in the face of the "godless minority of treacherous individuals who have been permitted to formulate national policy."

Looking ahead to 1984 and beyond, Viguerie hoped to more than double his 4.5-million-name mother lode, primarily by mining the still untapped potential of the nation's born agains. Bogged in his own debts, however, Falwell's continuing value to the movement seemed to lie less in his capacity as a fund-raiser than in his talent as a hell-raiser, leaving Viguerie and his allies to find new born-again followers as they had unearthed their first strike. That was done, not through Falwell, but through the efforts of the second member of the fundamentalist right triumvirate, the individual who, more than any other, created the Moral Majority and forged the bands marrying religion and politics in the eighties.

Weyrich—"Mr. Big."   If there is a head man in the syndicate of Holy Terror, it is Paul Weyrich, the architect of the preachers-into-politics movement. Weyrich is the organizer who brought together many separate religious and political forces and united them in a comprehensive network of shared interests and nonoverlapping activities. An Eastern-rite Catholic and son of German immigrants to Wisconsin, thirty-eight-year-old Weyrich is officially listed as director of the Committee for the Survival of a Free Congress (CSFC), a top new right PAC founded in 1974 and benignly described by Weyrich as "a bipartisan political committee aimed at electing conservatives to the House and Senate." But the scope of his activities is much broader and less innocent. In fact, he appears to be the driving force behind nearly every religious, social and political concern of the movement.

A former journalist, Paul Weyrich's political career traces back to the rebirth of the old right as a fundamentalist crusade. In 1971, while serving in Washington as press secretary to former Colorado Senator Gordon Allott, Weyrich met and formed an alliance with multimillionaire entrepreneur Joseph Coors, head of the Golden, Colorado-based Coors brewery, the nation's fifth-largest seller of beer. The archconservative Coors was well known in the West for his support of far-right organizations, foremost among them, the John Birch Society (named after a young fundamentalist preacher purportedly killed by Communists in the Korean war), and for his traditional right-wing opposition to organized labor. In the early seventies, Coors's family-owned company endured a bitter two-year strike by brewery employees who claimed they were searched without warning and required to submit to preemployment lie detector tests. In reaction, Coors reportedly set out to break the trade union movement in the West, contributing hundreds of thousands of dollars to existing hard-line organizations.

He also began funding new ventures of his own. In 1973, Coors and Weyrich formed the Heritage Foundation, the first of many new right "think tanks" oriented almost exclusively toward making old right ideas more respectable and acceptable to a broader spectrum of Americans. Weyrich, although lacking a college degree, served as its initial president, and with heavy funding from Coors and other wealthy backers, the foundation was able to attract a number of conservative scholars with impressive credentials. Then in 1974, the Coors-Weyrich team collaborated in the birth of the Committee for the Survival of a Free Congress, and with the help of Richard Viguerie's direct-mail machinery, the aggressive PAC got off to a running start. Unlike other PACs, however, which engage primarily in direct funding of candidates and campaign advertising, CSFC made few outright contributions to favored candidates. Instead, it used its money to play an activist behind-the-scenes role, seeking out and organizing sympathetic individuals and groups and training them in coordinated political strategies.

With the new right's first election triumphs in 1978, many of which Weyrich and his organization claimed credit for, the money began rolling in and Weyrich's activities blossomed among a number of formal and informal groups. First, he set up the Free Congress Research and Education Foundation, a tax-free subsidiary of the parent political committee. Next, in the summer of 1979, he was instrumental in convening the Library Court group, a coalition of more than twenty PACs and special-interest lobbies that met in offices along the alley behind the Library of Congress where Weyrich's CSFC was headquartered.

But it was to the arena of religion that Weyrich soon brought his most creative organizational energies. This work began when new right pollsters identified America's born-again Christians as the largest bloc of unregistered voters in the country. In 1976, it was estimated, between five and eight million of them came out to vote for a born-again presidential candidate who they believed to be a devout conservative Christian. Seizing on their disillusionment, Weyrich took steps to round up the flock.

The first person he called upon was Rev. Robert Billings, a fundamentalist and former Maryland public school principal. Years earlier, Billings and his wife had set out across the country by car and trailer to help Christians organize private schools in reaction to what they saw as a growing trend of immorality and creeping "secular humanism" in public education. Following the 1976 election, after a failed run for Congress, Billings was "persuaded" by Weyrich, whom he had met during his campaign, to come to Washington and start a lobbying operation that would represent Christian schools and fundamentalist political positions. At the time, Weyrich was attempting to build his political network by copying the organizations and strategies that had been used successfully for decades by liberal think tanks and political committees, and he was hoping to found a fundamentalist organization that would play a right-wing role similar to that played by the National Council of Churches and other moderate and liberal religious public affairs committees.

The catalyst in this interaction was Weyrich's next find, Ed McAteer, a Christian lay leader from Memphis, Tennessee, who had recently completed twenty-five years as a salesman and sales manager for the Colgate-Palmolive Company. In his job, McAteer covered the South, making personal connections with fundamentalist preachers and denominational leaders throughout the territory. In the mid-seventies, he worked as national field director for the Christian Freedom Foundation, a tax-free religious and educational foundation financed by J. Howard Pew, founder of the Sun Oil Company and another active supporter of the John Birch Society. McAteer found his way to Weyrich through Howard Phillips, a conservative Republican and founding member of the Young Americans for Freedom who served in the Nixon administration. Amid the wreckage of Watergate, Phillips, a disillusioned Republican-turned-Democrat, played a key role in the emergence of the fundamentalist right network. In 1975, with the help of his old YAF cohort Richard Viguerie, he founded the Conservative Caucus, a lobbying organization patterned on the liberal group Common Cause which hoped to mobilize grass-roots constituencies to influence their legislators and thereby affect the course of national policy. McAteer, with his extensive contacts in the South and his organizational background from the Christian Freedom Foundation, became field director for the Conservative Caucus and, at a quickening pace, the seeds of fundamentalist religion and politics began to mix.

One of the first hybrids to emerge was Christian Voice, formed in early 1979. Christian Voice began as an openly political fundamentalist organization and within a year claimed 187,000 members, a fifth of them clergy. Its congressional advisory committee included some of the fundamentalist right's newest prizes from the 1978 elections, Senators Humphrey and Jepsen, along with Senators James McClure of Idaho and Orrin Hatch of Utah. Christian Voice, whose legislative adviser had been associate director of Weyrich's Committee for the Survival of a Free Congress, served as an early prototype for future fundamentalist political action groups.

Before it was overshadowed by newer and larger coalitions, Christian Voice had its hand in a number of political operations. In 1979, it helped introduce an unsuccessful piece of legislation in Congress that would have proclaimed the United States a "Christian nation." In 1980, it issued its famous "moral report cards" on U.S. senators and congressmen, rating the legislators according to a mixed bag of religious and political criteria that defined the fundamentalist right platform: school prayer, abortion, "security for Taiwan," opposition to "forced unionization of teachers," "Rhodesia sanctions," etc. Also in 1980, Voice dropped all pretense of impartiality, establishing a subsidiary group, Christians for Reagan, with a $1 million budget earmarked for recruiting fundamentalist support for the former California governor's White House drive.

But the hard core units of the movement were yet to come. On the surface, Moral Majority and the Religious Roundtable were separate organizations, yet in their overlapping founders, principles and directorates they functioned as a diversified whole. Moral Majority, ostensibly created by Rev. Jerry Falwell, was really the product of a portentous meeting arranged by Ed McAteer between Falwell, whom McAteer knew from his traveling days, and the new right team of Weyrich and Phillips. In fact, it was Weyrich, not Falwell, who coined the name Moral Majority. He also gave the group its first executive director, Robert Billings. From the start, Billings ran the show while Falwell played the media with his state capital rallies. Then in mid-1980, Billings left Moral Majority to join the fundamentalist right's man of the hour, Ronald Reagan, becoming a key campaign figure and Reagan's official liaison to the religious community.

The Religious Roundtable, on the other hand, was McAteer's baby. Launched in September 1979, its initial two-day meeting was attended by Weyrich, Phillips, Viguerie and a panoply of fundamentalist right honchos, all of whom were apparently looking to the religious group for big political payoffs for their special interests. Prominently displayed on the Roundtable's board were stars of the electronic church, such as Falwell, Pat Robertson (who was later to resign) and the angry James Robison, who stepped in as vice-president and PR up-front man for the group. When the Roundtable held its national affairs briefing for 15,000 fundamentalists in Dallas in August 1980, it was Robison, not McAteer, who fired the crowd, warming them up for a headline appearance by Ronald Reagan, the only presidential candidate to accept the Roundtable's invitation.

Yet the unseen hand behind it all was Paul Weyrich. As central organizer of the meeting, he was determined to make the fundamentalist vote count for the new right in 1980. "I'm going to make a substantial effort to refocus the efforts of those folks," he told a reporter. In another Dallas effort, Weyrich laid out his grand vision and master strategy. "You are the pastors who have been chosen by God Almighty to lead; we are talking about Christianizing America," he told an audience from the pulpit of Dallas's First Baptist Church. He continued his revealing overture:

We are talking about simply spreading the gospel in a po-

litical context. We share the guilt, because many of us have
fallen into the heresy of division of God's program. We have
ceded certain areas of endeavor to the devil. . . . My
friends, what we're talking about here is making ourselves
felt. Make no mistake about it. Even if we should prevail in
every possibility, from the presidency on down to the lowest
state official in the November election, our job will just be
beginning. We are in this for the long haul. We are in this
until the Lord Himself comes back and rescues all of us.

In his book, Richard Viguerie cites Weyrich's role in midwifing
the birth of the fundamentalist right. "He and Howard Phillips
spent countless hours with electronic ministers like Jerry Falwell,
James Robison and Pat Robertson, urging them to get involved in
conservative politics," he wrote. But Weyrich's political fundamentalism appears to go deeper still, by his own admission, well
beyond traditional principles. "We are different from previous
generations of conservatives," he has said. "We are no longer
working to preserve the status quo. We are radicals, working to
overturn the present power structure of the country."
The broader thrust of Weyrich's radical game plan can be
found in the "pro-family" movement, the catch-all political alliance of which Weyrich is generally assumed to be *de facto* head.
Weyrich's pro-family movement is central to fundamentalist right
strategy, predating even Moral Majority in its inception. Published
reports locate its birth in Washington in December 1978, following the movement's first election victories. At the quietly held
meeting, Connie Marshner, head of the Family Policy Division of
Weyrich's Free Congress Research and Education Foundation,
and forces from a variety of fundamentalist right factions came together to draft a piece of legislation they titled the Family Protection Act. According to journalist Johnny Greene, the act was to be
introduced in Congress to serve as a smokescreen for a broad
range of social and political initiatives. In a controversial article in
Playboy, he quoted Gary Potter of Catholics for Political Action,
one of the leaders of the meeting, who later summed up what
Greene saw as the ultimate goal of many of those present:

When the Christian majority takes over the country, there
will be no satanic churches, no more free distribution of

pornography, no more abortion on demand and no more talk of rights for homosexuals. After the Christian majority takes control, pluralism will be seen as immoral and evil and the state will not permit anybody the right to practice evil.

Weyrich's own comments on the pro-family movement in *Conservative Digest* suggest that he shares Potter's orientation. Lauding Nevada Senator Paul Laxalt, who introduced the finished Family Protection Act in Congress, Weyrich proclaimed, "If Laxalt will lead, God will punish less." Several months later, he described at length his personal commitment to the movement, commenting on the opposition, which he characterized as the "anti-family" movement:

> This is really the most significant battle of the age-old conflict between good and evil, between the forces of God and forces against God, that we have seen in this country.
> We see the anti-family movement as an attempt to prevent souls from reaching eternal salvation, and as such we feel not just a political commitment to change this situation, but a moral and, if you will, a religious commitment to battle these forces. I don't mean to be simplistic about it, but there is no other way to view what is happening, especially if you read, believe in and understand Holy Scripture.

In his masterworks of political engineering, Weyrich emerges as the embodiment of the fundamentalist right mind-set in its all-consuming religious quest. As the guiding force behind so many separate political groups and endeavors, each working in its own way toward his expressed theological goals, Weyrich's brand of ideological fundamentalism shows the insurgent movement in its most ominous form. But not in its most ruthless. Beyond religion, the movement has pioneered a new form of pure political terrorism, under the direction of its most hard-biting personality.

Dolan—Leader of the PACs.   At thirty-three, despite recent setbacks both personal and political, John Terry Dolan remains one of the most dreaded figures in Washington. A lawyer from a middle-class New England home, this stone-faced young man with a drooping mustache is frequently referred to as the "hit man" of the new right. In his duties as chairman of NCPAC, the National Conservative Political Action Committee, Dolan presides over one of the largest and most powerful PACs in the nation. In 1980, NCPAC raised $7.5 million—more than any other PAC—to defeat its ideological enemies. In 1982, it brought in an unprecedented $10 million—although many of its efforts went for naught.

Like most fundamentalist right groups, NCPAC is a compact organization. Founded in 1975 by Dolan and two like-minded political operatives, Roger Stone and Charles Black, using Richard Viguerie's direct-mail expertise, NCPAC raised millions, largely on the strength of kickoff endorsements from Ronald Reagan and Senator Jesse Helms. Reagan called the fledgling organization "our best bet to keep the liberals from seizing total control of Congress." Helms signed a NCPAC letter requesting urgent contributions "because your tax dollars are being used to pay for grade school courses that teach our children that *cannibalism, wife swapping* and the *murder* of infants and the elderly are acceptable behavior." However, Stone and Black soon left the organization to become consultants (Black became political director of the Republican National Committee and, later, of Reagan's presidential campaign), and NCPAC quickly became Terry Dolan's one-man band.

From his headquarters in Arlington, Virginia, the self-styled media expert used sophisticated polling methods to identify key voting patterns and campaign issues. Then he set out to recruit and groom NCPAC-approved candidates to run in carefully selected races. However, Dolan's most significant blow to the political process has been his development of NCPAC's "attack"-style campaign. Through polling and analysis, Dolan sought to identify weaknesses in the images and voting records of liberal incumbents, which NCPAC then proceeded to target without mercy in saturation publicity campaigns.

By these means, in 1978 NCPAC scored its first major successes with the defeat of Democratic Senators Dick Clark of Iowa, Floyd Haskell of Colorado and Thomas McIntyre of New Hampshire. New Hampshire was a particular triumph for Dolan, who used Boston television to reach New Hampshire voters and hand victory to his hand-picked selection, Republican Gordon

Humphrey, a former airline pilot with virtually no political experience. In Dolan's view, unknowns like Humphrey make ideal candidates. He has said he prefers candidates like ministers and businessmen who have no political enemies and no public records that can be attacked by the other side. In recruiting, Dolan actively seeks out candidates who are attractive, articulate, ideologically pure, and who display the "stubbornness" to endure uphill and often ugly battles. He then proceeds to turn them into credible candidates through a process he calls "image-building." At the same time, NCPAC endeavors to destroy the credibility and popularity of targeted opponents, using every media technique available to what Dolan proudly calls his "gut-cutting organization."

More than anyone on the fundamentalist right, election night 1980 was Dolan's moment of triumph. For two years he had been working day and night to insure the success of NCPAC's "Target '80" assault on liberal Democratic senators. NCPAC began its attack in early 1979, a full year before the traditional start of most election campaigns, using the media to "soften up" its targets' public images long before it had candidates to offer as alternatives. In his initial fund-raising letter to known conservative donors, Dolan announced his then farfetched intention to "actually seize control of the U.S. Senate." Through Viguerie's owned-and-operated network, using all the language and imagery of the old right, Dolan attacked George McGovern as "the radical senator from South Dakota who favors recognition of Communist Cuba." He hit Frank Church (as Church told us earlier) as "the radical chairman of the Senate Foreign Relations Committee who single-handedly has presided over the destruction of the FBI and the CIA." He called John Culver, a freshman Democrat from Iowa, "the *most radical* member of the entire U.S. Senate." He slammed Birch Bayh of Indiana "for his extremist support of the Equal Rights Amendment extension and abortion on demand." And he labeled Alan Cranston of California "one of Big Labor's staunchest allies in the U.S. Senate."

"Just imagine the added beneficial side effects of this plan," wrote Dolan:

- First, it will rid us of the most radical members of the U.S. Senate and the ringleaders for almost all liberal legislation that comes up in Congress.

- Second, it will put all the other liberals on notice that if they step out of line . . . the voters will rise up and oppose them. . . .
- Finally, it will let other good conservatives in the Senate know we can win key strategic battles.

The letter's comprehensive five-fold game plan provides a key to NCPAC's strategy of using new right money and fundamentalist grass-roots activists to advance its old right platform. Step one: voter surveys for "discriminatory issue selection. . . . It is far more profitable for us to attack the liberals on those issues that particularly will annoy their constituents," wrote Dolan. Step two: the hiring of full-time field representatives to begin "marshaling" the opposing forces—anti-abortion groups, anti-tax groups, anti-gun groups, etc. Step three: a massive direct-mail campaign to every registered voter in each state, designed to "expose each liberal senator's 'Record of Radicalism.' " These letters would also seek to get each person personally involved, not only through contributions and votes, but through "a number of small but important tasks, such as writing letters to editors, walking a precinct, sending postcards and other letters to their friends, consenting to list their name on newspaper advertisements . . . and a host of other activities." Step four: "immediate and extensive" advertising via television, radio and newspapers "to exploit the weaknesses of each incumbent." Only then, after heavy independent expenditures, would NCPAC undertake Step five: final candidate recruitment, following which, wrote Dolan, "all resources developed during this independent campaign will . . . be turned over to the candidate we decide is the best able to represent the conservative viewpoint."

In theory, Dolan's plan was bold and unprecedented. In practice, it was devastatingly effective. In South Dakota, NCPAC blazed the trail for groups as varied as the National Right to Life Committee, the National Right to Work Committee, the Citizens Committee for the Right to Keep and Bear Arms, the National Tax Limitation Committee, the Committee to Save the Panama Canal, the Committee to Defeat the Union Bosses and the John Birch Society. It presented polling data to Republican Congressman James Abdnor that convinced him to take on McGovern —prompting McGovern to charge that Abdnor and NCPAC had conferred in violation of federal election laws. In Indiana, NCPAC commercials showed a large baloney being sliced by a cleaver. The voice-over began: "One very big piece of baloney is Birch Bayh telling us he's fighting inflation." In every state, similar slogans were used: "If Church wins, you lose!" "If Culver wins, you lose!" The coordinated assault worked.

Dolan was unapologetic. "There's no question about it," he had said earlier, "we are a negative organization." When caught spreading false information, only on occasion would NCPAC retract its claims, and then, apparently, not until after its commercials had registered their maximum impact. Reveling in his victory, Dolan seemed determined to multiply NCPAC's successes using the same tactics: one week after the election, he unveiled a new hit list of twenty-one senators targeted for defeat in 1982, and during later 1981 budget battles in Congress, NCPAC launched scathing campaigns against Democrats who opposed the Republican Administration's proposals. Yet, like other fundamentalist right leaders, Dolan denied that his efforts were in any way affiliated with the Republican party. He termed his years as a member of the GOP "perhaps the lowest ebb of my political career."

Dolan describes his brand of politics as "constitutional libertarianism," which he defines as government doing "as little as possible." He seems to delight in watching targeted liberals and moderates go down in flames. Yet, almost alone among fundamentalist right leaders, Dolan seldom talks about religion, although his group runs on the same ideological track as Moral Majority and other fundamentalist groups. Dolan claims to be uncomfortable with the social issues of the fundamentalist right. He once stated that "the government shouldn't be concerned with trying to wipe out sin."

Nevertheless, Dolan is a champion of Holy Terror. He admits that his fund-raising appeals are designed to "make them angry" and "stir up hostilities." "We are trying to be divisive," he has admitted. "The shriller you are, the better it is to raise money." And although he denies the intention, he has been widely quoted as having confessed: "A group like ours could lie through its teeth, and the candidate it helps stays clean."

In our research, we tried repeatedly, by mail and phone, to arrange interviews with fundamentalist right strategists. Viguerie was too busy. Weyrich requested more information, then turned us down. Others were tied up in meetings or out of town. Left to assemble our own picture of the Gang of Three, we had only their printed statements and public appearances to go on. Those appearances, on leading news and commentary shows, left us with a chilly feeling. Watching Viguerie, Weyrich and Dolan, we thought they seemed like aloof, coolly efficient personalities. They attacked issues that were multifaceted and complex as though they were cosmic battles between good and evil that could be engaged on an unthinking and unfeeling plane.

As we learned more about their goals and methods, it was hard to put traditional terms on what these men were practicing in Washington. Certainly, it was not the art of politics, for the fundamentalist right was not open to compromise. Nor did it strike us as public debate, for the individuals we observed seemed unwilling or unable to listen to those who disagreed with their ideological positions. Instead, they were obvious in their dislike for their enemies and in their desire for revenge. Like their counterparts in the electronic church, these leaders of the developing movement seemed to have become joint products of their absolutist beliefs and their all-powerful technology. It seemed they were being shaped by their strategies. And their beliefs were becoming neutral tools, in the end, no different from the hardware in which they placed their faith.

Target Practice

*Onward Christian soldiers,
marching as to war,
With the cross of Jesus
going on before.*

—(Traditional)

WITH THE RISE of the fundamentalist right, religion and morality in America have turned into something new: an insurgent drive, not simply to stage a bloodless coup and seize the government, but on a broader scale to bring about a sweeping cultural transformation. In the process, many sensitive issues have been turned upside down: censorship, pornography, homosexuality, sex education, prayer in schools. But the attack goes beyond any one book bonfire or television boycott, beyond any set of moral judgments.

In its war on the richness of American life, the fundamentalist right is reaching for command over our sense of ourselves as human beings, over our culture's guiding definition and image of mankind. The following issues, in our view, make up the fulcrum of the thrust. Cutting across all faiths and deeply into our private feelings and beliefs, they give the movement leverage beyond its size. They also offer new angles of insight into the fundamentalist right mind-set.

RITES TO LIFE

No single issue so vividly dramatizes the manipulative emotionalism of the fundamentalist right as the national uproar over abortion. At the start of the eighties, the abortion controversy was a live grenade, an unprecedented force for rousing individuals to social action. For movement organizers, it was the "paramount" moral issue of our time. For feminists, it was a symbol of a woman's right to determine her personal and biological destiny. For disadvantaged minorities, it was more dismal evidence of the government's receding commitment to social welfare. For doctors, it was rapidly becoming a professional nightmare. For clergy, the issue was leading to bitter divisions within and among faiths.

And for politicians, it was Holy Terror. Abortion was ripe for plucking by the fundamentalist right. Long before the 1980 election, new right strategists like Paul Weyrich and Terry Dolan identified its political potential. As a single-issue cause, the case against abortion could be quickly, simply and graphically presented. As an already controversial social issue, it offered movement leaders busloads, picket lines and whole marches full of concerned clergy, impassioned housewives and idealistic young student activists. As a public relations weapon and grass-roots organizing tool, it was the perfect smokescreen for the launching of larger political salvos. Demographically, abortion was almost guaranteed to ignite the apathy of unregistered born agains, and equally likely to sway for conservative Republican candidates ethnic voting blocs with long-standing Democratic sympathies.

Once these patterns were traced, it took only light tailoring to stitch together the loose coalition of anti-abortion groups that sprang up in the early seventies into a single-minded "pro-life" movement with custom-designed PACs and lobbies such as the National Pro-Life Political Action Committee, the Life Amendment Political Action Committee and the American Life Lobby. Working closely with new right organizers at the grass-roots level and in Washington, selectively in 1978 and with wholesale slaughter in 1980, "pro-lifers" had significant impact in dollars, volunteers and votes on state, local and national elections. A 1980 postelection study by NCPAC found abortion to be the most effective single issue to prompt Democrats to vote Republican, and a major factor in the defeat of four of NCPAC's five targeted liberal senators.

The object of all this fuss is no insignificant thing, yet it has been almost lost in the shuffle of big-time organizations and power politics. It is also difficult to identify, for the furor over abortion is in large part a war of names and labels. Anti-abortion forces refer to the "preborn baby" or, more popularly, the "unborn child." Pro-abortion forces prefer accepted medical designations such as "fetus" or "embryo." Both trails lead quickly to a bog of imprecision, but that is what the battle is all about: our culture's definition of what it means to be a human being. Is a "preborn baby" a human being? Is a fetus? Or an embryo? Or a mere fertilized ovum? These questions are not trivial. Their answers determine whether the medical procedure of abortion is nothing less than "murder," an act of homicide committed by mother and doctor against a living and defenseless person, or whether at certain stages and under certain circumstances, abortion is simply "the induced termination of pregnancy."

The puzzle seems to call for a medical solution. Yet scientific debate on the question is as heatedly divided as public opinion. Some scientists equate the start of human life with the onset of biological life, when egg and sperm unite. Others refrain from calling the living object human until it displays human characteristics: the first faint heartbeats or a developing nervous system, which may be evident as early as four to six weeks after conception. Not until the second month does a fetus begin to take on recognizable human form, yet most medical experts still link full human status to the concept of "viability," that stage where the developing being is capable of surviving outside the womb. But viability is a troubling guideline. It may be reached in as many as seven months or as few as five, and progress in infant medical care and life-support systems are rapidly making this practical criterion all but irrelevant.

The medical argument is intricate and under constant revision, yet medical considerations have little to do with the fundamentalist right battle over abortion. Pro-lifers seek to protect the unborn, *regardless* of viability or stage of development, to grant full human status and equal protection under the law to the fertilized egg from the moment of conception. This means, according to the agenda shared by most pro-life organizations, a ban on *all* abortions, without exception. This is the unyielding pro-life stance: that all life is sacred, a gift of God, a process which is not to be interfered with by mere mortals for any earthly reason.

Most Americans disagree, more than two thirds of the country, according to nearly every poll. To varying degrees, they feel that there are circumstances under which a woman should have the right to choose abortion: in cases of rape or incest, where there is evidence that the child will be born with a gross deformity or genetic defect, when the mother's life is in danger or when, for personal reasons, a woman simply does not want to bear a child. In each instance, the decision requires a judgment on the nature and value of human life.

Who then should have the final say? The scientist? The lawmaker? The Bible? Or the individual? The United States Supreme Court says the individual. On January 22, 1973, it handed down its fateful *Roe* v. *Wade* decision, granting women the constitutional right to have an abortion, more or less on demand, through the first six months of pregnancy. Writing for the seven-to-two majority, Associate Justice Harry Blackmun explained the court's reason for ruling in two related cases that the human fetus was not entitled to full legal personhood and that, in most instances, denying a woman's right to have an abortion would be a violation of her right of privacy. The overriding factor in the decision was the court's refusal to dictate a pat answer to a profound question. Wrote Blackmun:

> We need not resolve the difficult question of when life begins. When those trained in the respective disciplines of medicine, philosophy and theology are unable to arrive at any consensus, the judiciary, at this point in the development of man's knowledge, is not in a position to speculate as to the answer.

And so the Supreme Court upheld the principle that no American would be forced to accept the strictures of any sect or group on matters that, in the end, came down to personal belief or religious faith.

For pro-abortion forces, many of them members of the awakening women's movement, *Roe* v. *Wade* was the culmination of a brief but spectacular quest, a fitting postscript to the consciousness explosion of the sixties and its rejection of stereotyped social and sexual roles. Until that decade, abortion had been illegal in the

United States, forcing women who refused to bear an unwanted child to travel to other countries or to seek illegal abortions, often performed by amateur surgeons in sordid back-alley settings. In both instances, the procedure had been expensive, humiliating and, very often, life-threatening. *Roe* v. *Wade* ended all that. The decision promised greater personal freedom for all Americans and was quickly hailed as a breakthrough in the movement for women's rights.

But for another segment of America, *Roe* v. *Wade* was seen as a moral Pearl Harbor. The sudden reversal of long-standing laws and social norms touched off a fire storm among members of conservative religious groups and their political allies. Many opponents saw the decision as an assault on traditional morality and family values. Others viewed it as granting mothers and doctors a "license to kill." Still others viewed the decision as, in the words of dissenting Justice White, "an exercise in raw judicial power." Almost instantly, the "right to life" movement was born. Local citizens groups and grass-roots coalitions began picketing abortion clinics and working through legal channels to roll back *Roe* v. *Wade*. Statewide and national right to life groups received the blessings of major religious bodies. The Roman Catholic Church, a consistent opponent of abortion, nursed the movement through its infancy. In 1975, the National Conference of Catholic Bishops approved a *Pastoral Plan for Pro-Life Activities*, which combined anti-abortion educational and counseling programs with political action "to ensure legal protection for the right to life." As other conservative denominations joined the fight, pressure began to build on elected officials to support or initiate anti-abortion efforts. While pro-abortion activists slacked off, assuming the battle had been won, pro-lifers marched steadily onward, claiming victories across a widening spectrum of court and legislative fronts. Step by step, pro-life activists and their supporters in Congress succeeded in cutting off federal funds for abortions for the poor, for military personnel and their dependents, for Peace Corps volunteers and recipients of U.S. foreign aid programs and, finally, for many government employees. State laws and court rulings brought additional curtailments on the stage of pregnancy and the locations in which abortions could be performed.

But the flurry of initiatives did little to curtail the practice of abortion. After 1973, the yearly figures for abortions in the United States rose steadily, reaching nearly 1.5 million by the end of the decade, and with public opinion leaning more heavily against them than ever, some pro-life sympathizers resorted to more militant and, on occasion, violent means. In numerous cities, women were forced to cross angry picket lines to enter abortion clinics. Doctors were harassed and their patients plagued by anonymous phone calls charging them with murder. In some abortion clinics, nurses and administrators were reportedly bribed to obtain the names of clients. And more than a dozen clinics were firebombed. In St. Paul, Minnesota, staff members of Planned Parenthood, the national family planning organization, reported repeated incidents of arson, attempted bombings, kidnap threats and random acts in which bullets were fired at the clinic, windows broken with cement blocks and walls spray-painted with obscene graffiti. In 1978, unidentified "vandals" broke into a Cleveland, Ohio, women's clinic and severed electrical cords, smashed glass containers and splattered iodine on walls, chairs, beds, floors and carpets. In both cases, as in others around the country, no arrests were made and no charges filed, but pro-abortion forces charged their pro-life opponents with instigating the "reign of terror."

Of all the fundamentalist right issues we explored, the heated anti-abortion crusade was the only one where tactics approached those of terrorism in its classical sense of physical violence. The pro-life movement pioneered the fundamentalist right's use of personal intimidation and gruesome scare tactics. Its promotional literature, circulated among closed groups and through the mail, was routinely decorated with photographs of aborted fetuses and filled with grisly descriptions of abortion procedures. But with few exceptions, before the larger public, pro-life efforts took the "high road" of morality and legality. By the late seventies, the narrowing focus of the movement had become centered on a campaign to pressure Congress into passing a Human Life Amendment to the Constitution, one that, if ratified by the states, would overturn *Roe* v. *Wade* and grant full legal status to all human life from the moment of conception. The drive set off the fundamentalist right's first concerted attempt to terrorize the U.S. Congress.

From the outset, pressure on senators, congressmen and their staffs was intense, climaxing yearly on the anniversary of *Roe* v. *Wade* in an anti-abortion "March for Life" that brought tens of thousands to the capital wielding banners, posters, black crosses, coffins and toy babies on sticks. Following the giant rallies, marchers swarmed over Capitol Hill, confronting legislators on the street and in their offices. Delegations from every state descended on their representatives and combed the halls for additional support. By early 1980, nine versions of the proposed amendment had been introduced in congressional committees. Across the country, seventeen states had called for a constitutional convention to force the issue. Yet, despite the onslaught, the pro-life effort fell far short of the two-thirds vote in Congress required to propose an amendment to the Constitution.

Then came the 1980 election and, like so many other issues, the disfavored pro-life cause was born again with new money and new muscle. Fundamentalist right preachers and strategists locked arms with other special-interest groups, championing the pro-life cause on television, in books, articles, brochures and direct mail. Rev. Jerry Falwell made the issue a prime plank in his Moral Majority platform. Rev. James Robison delivered the opening prayer before a record 100,000 at the 1980 "March for Life." Down Library Court and across the Potomac, new right strategists made the pro-life concern a top priority of their budding pro-family movement, seizing upon the issue as an effective springboard for other "pro-morality" drives. According to their calculations, the well-organized movement offered rare opportunities to shatter traditional religious and ethnic voting blocs and fuel public disenchantment with liberal policies that had long supported medical funding for the poor. Although he had expressed little interest in the moral issues raised by the pro-life cause, Terry Dolan assigned NCPAC operatives to coordinate their targeting efforts with those of state and local pro-life groups.

The flow of funds, marchers and media mixed smoothly. Cornered at its convention in Detroit by leading pro-life senators, Jerry Falwell and the entire fundamentalist right hierarchy, the Republican party adopted platform planks endorsing pro-life judges and passage of the Human Life Amendment; and Ronald Reagan became the first serious presidential candidate to favor the constitutionally shaky position. With the coming of the new Congress and administration, pro-life advocates rejoiced. Although public opinion was hardening against them, for the first time they had a sitting President on their side and a slew of ardent supporters in Congress. Following his inauguration, President Ronald Reagan welcomed pro-life leaders to the Oval Office. In a later meeting, he and his budget director, David Stockman, received a "white paper" prepared by two pro-life groups which claimed that nearly $4 billion a year could be saved by eliminating most government family planning, birth control, sex education, teenage counseling and world population control programs. Within weeks, the President nominated two pro-life activists to head major federal health and social service agencies.

And on Capitol Hill, a volley of new initiatives was fired. In both houses of Congress, bills were introduced to reverse *Roe* v. *Wade* by legislative fiat. A proposed Human Life Statute sought only majority support, not the two-thirds vote required by the faltering constitutional amendment proposal. But the proposed statute was legally questionable and politically explosive. As the public and the media became aroused, pro-life forces began squabbling among themselves over tactics. A senator and two congressmen quit the board of the National Pro-Life Political Action Committee after it named nine of their colleagues to 1982 election hit lists. Later in the Senate, a splinter faction introduced a competitive but watered-down amendment proposal intended, not to enshrine the right to life but simply to strip the courts of authority over anti-abortion legislation. Hard-liners protested, the administration turned cool on the issue, but the pro-life drive plunged on, despite its setbacks, having succeeded at least in turning its religious crusade into an almost wholly political affair.

In our travels, we had many conversations with people on both sides of the abortion fight. They were among the most sensitive, thought-provoking and infuriating talks we held in our research. Predictably, our contacts with representatives of the pro-life side were the more emotional. We listened to the familiar arguments, we read the literature, we looked at the drawings and photographs of dead fetuses, and we were moved by people's commitment to a cause they seemed to consider the most burning issue of our time. We also picked up an all-too-familiar pattern in the movement.

The first time we discussed abortion with many pro-life activists, we found their recitation of facts and arguments impressive. Their citing of documentary evidence and authoritative names was thorough, and as researchers trying to weigh both sides of the issue, at times we found ourselves helpless even to raise a plausible point for the opposition. The pro-lifers we met had been prepped. They had the leaflets, badges and bumper stickers, the mimeographed testimony and graphic aids. Yet, in most instances, we found, like their cheap-shot pamphlets, their personal understanding of the issue was paper-thin.

The most vehement discussion of our trip took place in the suburban living room of an evangelical Christian family we met during a stopover in a small southern town. The couple we will call Larry and Sue, both in their thirties, were leading figures in their local right to life movement. They held positions in chapters of national pro-life organizations and helped organize Christians of all denominations in their area for larger campaigns, and when we called they graciously invited us to their home for lunch and talk. The meeting began on the warmest of terms. Our opening conversation was wide-ranging and easygoing. As the talk turned to abortion, however, our cordial interaction quickly dissolved into a bitter one-sided argument. A recent born-again convert, Larry built his case against abortion on biblical assumptions framed as legal arguments.

"It is illegal to be a homosexual," he declared. "It's illegal to commit adultery. I don't approve of premarital sex, and that, too, is illegal in most places. When you're talking about abortion, you're talking about human beings being *killed,* and that, very simply, is a human rights issue."

Larry discoursed at length on the currently fashionable pro-life analogy to the anti-slavery debate of the nineteenth century, taking his lead from area pro-life group brochures which proclaimed: "The unborn baby is the modern Dred Scott."

"I think you can relate abortion to the civil rights of blacks," he said, referring to pre-Civil War laws depriving black Americans of full legal status. He cited the Fourteenth Amendment as a precedent for the Human Life Amendment, to which he and Sue had devoted long hours of volunteer efforts.

"Of course there are problems with the amendment," he admit-

ted. "I'm not being simplistic about them. I recognize them and
I'm all for working them out. I just don't think killing an innocent
human being is an option. Human life has to be the premise and
priority of our society."

Flo questioned his premise and priority. "Aren't you making a
big assumption here?" she asked.

"What's that?"

"You're assuming that you can define what human life is and
when it begins."

"I'm not assuming that at all," he said. "Aren't you assuming
that *you* can say?"

"No," we both replied, but he wasn't listening.

"Well, the Supreme Court said that human life begins at birth,"
he contended.

"What court was that?"

"The Supreme Court."

We asked Larry if he had read the *Roe* v. *Wade* decision. He
didn't answer. He listened quietly as Jim summarized the majority
opinion. "Their decision, therefore," said Jim, "was that the question of when human life begins . . ."

"Viability!" Larry interrupted.

"No," Jim continued, "the decision was not based on viability."

"Well, they mentioned it," he protested, taking off on a tangent
of questionable facts and twisted logic. "There's a guy saying right
now that we shouldn't consider human beings human until a
month *after* birth. What's the difference between that and drawing
the line at birth? And what about a minute *before* birth?"

We tried to return the discussion to the wording of the Supreme
Court decision, citing the justices' conclusion that the matter
should be left to personal conscience and conviction.

"I believe there's a human life that's being killed," said Larry.

"Would you deny another individual the right to his or her own
belief?" we asked.

He sidestepped the question. "I believe in *your* human life and
I would deny another human being the right to kill you," he said
threateningly. "What makes you more valuable than an unborn
baby?"

"Do you realize the judgment you're making in what you just
said?" Flo asked.

"I can say what I want," said Larry. "This is my house."

Tempers flared. All pretense of politeness vanished. At this point, Sue, who had been listening quietly, stepped in to mediate. Born again at fourteen, from a pentecostal background, she was six months pregnant and didn't want any arguments in her home.

"Now, this is obviously a very controversial issue," she said softly. "We feel very strongly about our position and obviously you do, too."

We didn't have a position, we told them, we were simply trying to understand theirs. Larry went on.

"I think this is an issue that society needs to be based on. I believe that human life begins at the moment of conception," he repeated.

"Tell me," Jim asked, "*why* do you believe it?"

"Why do I believe it?" The question struck him as a *non sequitur*. He paused to think.

"From medical evidence I've read, from considering it personally, just from the sensibility of it."

When we asked, Larry denied that his religious beliefs had anything to do with his pro-life stance. Like many pro-lifers we spoke with, he seemed reluctant to assert the religious point with members of the secular world. We asked him if he knew that, according to most polls, the majority of Americans held different beliefs and were strongly opposed to his position.

"Why does everyone keep saying, 'Hey, who are you to impose your beliefs?'" he said, genuinely baffled. "This is a society. Society does that. I have things imposed on me all the time."

We suggested that, in a democracy, questions of morality can only be legislated when there is a broad consensus of majority and minority views.

"You talk about democracy and its responsibility to protect the rights of the minority," said Larry. "Well, what about the rights of the unborn? You're talking about snuffing out *all* the person's rights! Before you know it, there will be groups that want to kill their dependent parents and, under your logic, we'd have to let them do it."

We listened patiently—and sometimes not so patiently—until the middle of the afternoon. After lunch, Larry had to leave and we talked with Sue for a while longer. In his absence, she was more conciliatory, explaining that new converts were usually more fervid than born agains who were more "mature" in their beliefs. Then we, too, had to go.

"We have thought long and hard about how we feel," she said. Then an icy stare came over her eyes. "Obviously, you find our position very offensive. Well, we find your position just as offensive."

As we drove away, we were relieved to be gone from a home where our lives were given no more value than that of a fertilized egg in the womb. Neither of us believed that. Like most Americans, and in agreement with the Supreme Court, we felt that with limited restrictions a woman's reproductive choice should be her own. But more importantly, we felt strongly the distinction between biological life and human life. For years we had asserted that man's humanity is not just a matter of biochemical machinery. On the contrary, our understanding of communication in nature and society had convinced us that humanity lies, not in submicroscopic realms, but in the space *between* human beings: in the relationships among people that, from birth, govern the development of our thoughts, feelings and personalities.

But that was *our* belief. That value of human relationship seemed absent from this Christian home, as it was missing, we felt, in the electronic church and the computerized politics of the fundamentalist right. In their fixation on dogma and ideology at the expense of real people and life as it is lived every day, it seemed to us, the pro-lifers showed little respect for their fellow men and women or for the sanctity of human life. We pressed on, looking to trade so much talk of the soul for a little heart.

We met other pro-lifers whose defensive postures were riddled with contradiction and hypocrisy. Although they claimed to be for life, most were strong advocates of the death penalty. Most endorsed the massive buildup of America's life-threatening nuclear arsenal. Overall, their concern for life seemed to stop abruptly in the delivery room. Callous toward the needs of those already born, most favored depriving poor mothers of health care and hungry children of a hot lunch at school. Others we met were clearly using the abortion issue to fight personal battles for marriage, family and born-again morality, or as an outlet for their own unhealthy sexual preoccupations. Some, both men and women, had obviously joined the pro-life movement to combat the rising tide of feminism or to secure for themselves greater comfort in their traditional life-styles or sexual roles.

To be fair, we found many on the other side of the issue to be guilty of their own excesses and rhetorical flourishes. But there was no Holy Terror. For the most part, people's pro-abortion positions were rooted in serious real-world considerations. In their attempt to refocus their role in the battle away from the pro-lifers' implication that their stand was somehow "anti-life," they framed their defense as "pro-choice," supporting the larger right of individuals to make their own determinations of conscience. The pro-choice designation lacked the emotional impact of the pro-life tag, but it was more honestly reflective of the real dichotomy over the political issue.

Yet, on both sides of the pro-life / pro-choice battle line, we found a reluctance to talk openly about religion. Pro-lifers dressed their cause in grandiloquent medical and legal terms, only admitting among each other that their crusade remained a religious one. Pro-choicers held fast to the Constitution and the Supreme Court, but stepped lightly around religion, put off and cowed by their opponents' public piety. At times, many seemed to lose sight of the fact that the pro-choice position is a moral one, too, based on beliefs firmly rooted in the undergirding religions of American society. In fact, the pro-life position held jointly by many Christians and Catholics represents not only a minority of public opinion but a bare fraction of America's religious denominations, many of which have openly endorsed the pro-choice position. Like their anti-abortion counterparts, America's pro-choice denominations share a deep belief in the sanctity of human life. Yet, without contradiction, under a variety of circumstances, their teachings permit and at times defend a woman's right to have an abortion.

Few Americans have heard of RCAR ("Ar-car"), the Religious Coalition for Abortion Rights. It did not score the stunning court victories of the late sixties and early seventies that were largely attributed to NARAL, the National Association for the Repeal of Abortion Laws, now renamed the National Abortion Rights Action League. It hasn't been targeted for picketing and firebombing like some chapters of Planned Parenthood. Yet

RCAR has been around as long as most of its opponents. It was established in the months after *Roe* v. *Wade* by leaders of more than two dozen organizations representing a variety of religious denominations that differed widely in their beliefs, yet stood firmly united against any attempt to overturn the Supreme Court decision. Through the seventies, as the abortion issue became an organizing tool and rallying point for fundamentalist right political action, RCAR and its affiliate groups stepped up their activities, too, monitoring pro-life targeting efforts at the federal level from their offices in Washington, and mounting regional efforts in key states where abortion rights laws had come under attack.

Despite fundamentalist right pressure and the deep divisions that have taken place over the abortion issue, as of 1981, more than 3,000 clergy and officials of twenty-seven national religious bodies had signed RCAR's "Call to Commitment." Their list of affiliates is a testament to the American notion of religious pluralism: Lutherans, Baptists, Presbyterians, Methodists, Episcopalians, Quakers, Unitarians, Jews, members of the United Church of Christ—even a group of devout Catholics. None takes the issue of abortion lightly, and their positions vary on when it is morally justified, yet it is not in spite of their divergent views but because of them that each of RCAR's member groups wholeheartedly endorses the Supreme Court's view that abortion must remain an individual decision, to be made on the basis of conscience and personal religious conviction, and without the threat of government interference or punishment.

In itself, the diversity of doctrines among RCAR members shatters the pro-lifers' presumed monopoly on morality. In fact, more than half of RCAR's member bodies are Christian groups with strong pro-choice views. The American Baptist Churches, for example, whose National Ministries division is an RCAR affiliate, stand in direct opposition to their fundamentalist relations, stating: "Because Christ calls us to affirm the freedom of persons and sanctity of life, we recognize that abortion should be a matter of responsible personal decision." So does the Christian Church (Disciples of Christ), which resolved in 1975 to "respect differences in religious beliefs concerning abortion and oppose, in accord with the principle of religious liberty, any attempt to legislate a specific religious opinion or belief concerning abortion upon all Americans." The official United Methodist position is even more explicit: "We believe that continuance of a pregnancy which endangers the life or health of the mother, or poses other serious problems concerning the life, health or mental capability of the child to be, is not a moral necessity. In such a case, we believe the path of mature Christian judgment may indicate the advisability of abortion." RCAR's Jewish organizations uphold ancient Hebrew teachings that the fetus is not considered a person. As a United Synagogue of America resolution stated: "In all cases, 'the mother's life takes precedence over that of the foetus' up to the minute of its birth. This is to us an unequivocal position." Abortions, "though serious even in the early stages of conception, are not to be equated with murder, hardly more than is the decision not to become pregnant."

Even RCAR's Catholic affiliate, a dissident group organized as Catholics for a Free Choice, adheres to a religious tradition that has long been respected by their faith. "We affirm the religious liberty of Catholic men and women and those of other religions to make decisions regarding their own fertility free from church or governmental interventions in accordance with their own individual conscience." Their position is not as rebellious as it might seem. The Catholic Church is, by its own standards, a relatively recent convert to the absolutist position that human life begins at the moment of conception. Saints Augustine and Aquinas believed that "ensoulment" did not occur until several weeks after conception, and from the thirteenth century until 1869, the official Church position allowed abortion until fetal "animation"—approximately four months after conception.

In the morass of religious contention surrounding the issue, RCAR stands unparalleled as a voice of tolerance and pluralism, yet even among pro-choice activists we spoke with, its existence was not widely known. To learn more, in our rounds about Washington, we visited RCAR's Capitol Hill headquarters in a stately old building angled almost catercorner between the U.S. Supreme Court and the Capitol. There we met Pat Gavett, RCAR's director, an attractive woman in her late forties, with light, fluffy hair and a cheery smile.

"Oh, we have a terrible time with the press," she said, as we sat down around her desk to talk. "The press still does not perceive the controversy over abortion as a religious issue. They see it as a *women's* issue, so they go to the National Organization for Women, or to Planned Parenthood. But most pro-choice groups keep their hands off the religious perspective. They leave that to us because they believe we are the only organization that can legitimately speak to it."

She peered curiously at us over the top of her glasses, describing her organization to us as if we were the first people in the media to take RCAR seriously. She told us about an RCAR counterrally held in Washington the same day as the anti-abortion "March for Life."

"On January 22, we brought together the leaders of every one of our member organizations and denominations. It was probably the first time all these people had been in the same room, much less that they were standing together on a very sensitive, volatile issue. It was amazing, nothing short of remarkable, yet the press did not cover it."

Gavett described a bizarre confrontation that took place that day between pro-life marchers and pro-choice clergy.

"After the rally, the pro-lifers were all up here on the Hill waving their huge crosses with the baby dolls dangling from them. They knew we were having all these religious leaders here, so they came and held a pray-in in our downstairs lobby. About fifty of them came into the building and got down on their knees and began conducting a very loud prayer service for the souls of all these religious leaders who were in there. When we came out of the conference room, they were still on their knees praying. It was an incredible scene. Our people—ministers, priests, rabbis—had to thread their way through all of them."

We asked her why so many media and pro-choice people shied away from the religious aspects of the debate. She gave us the first straight answer we had heard on the subject.

"Most of them are afraid they will appear to be anti-Catholic," she said without blinking. "It's only within the last three or four years that many of our own denominational leaders were willing to talk about it. When I came here in '77, it was very difficult to get clergy to come out front on this issue. The big thing then was ecumenism, and people felt they would be upsetting the very sensitive relationships they had worked to establish with other denom-

inations if they came out in support of abortion rights. They just
didn't think that the issue was worth it at that point. And to be
frank, maybe it wasn't. Four years ago, it looked as though the
battle was over."

Gavett went on to describe the gradual "erosion" of the pro-
choice position: the newly restrictive court precedents and legislation, the upsurge in marches, picket lines and personal harassment; and finally, the growing intimidation of elected officials.

"I think the new right saw a good thing when it crossed their
path," she said. "Ours isn't the only emotional issue they picked
up on as a way to swell their ranks—they've collected a whole
barnyard full of issues. But ours is the *most* emotional, the most
easily manipulated, because it's so easy to call someone a 'baby-
killer' and make emotional hay."

Gavett described the broad scope of fundamentalist right exploitation of religion in the abortion issue. "You see them going in
the back door of each of the major religions," she said. "In every
denomination, there is always a small group of fundamentalists
who they can use to get the entire denomination to change their
stance. Within the Methodists, for instance, you have the 'Good
News' people. Within the Presbyterians, there is an extremely conservative laymen's group. Among the Catholics, there are the
charismatics."

Gavett's frankness was a welcome turn from all the veiled
charges we had been hearing. We asked her to distinguish among
the roles of various activist denominations on each side. For
starters, she contrasted the early Catholic right to life position
with the fundamentalist right's pro-life political approach.

"In the beginning, the Catholic Church came at this issue out of
a genuine theological position and a sincere belief," she said. "It's
true, they were well organized from the parish level up to the precinct level. But the Catholic position was predictable. It was man-
ageable. You could talk to them—they were *reasonable*. The new
right is something else again. I think most of their leadership
doesn't care a fig about abortion rights personally. Frankly, I
don't think they have *any* deep personal convictions. They have a
lot of money; they're looking for votes—and their belief, where it
exists, is irrational."

She underscored the discrepancy. "A lot of Catholics have

come to recognize this," she continued. "They realize they're doing a great disservice to Catholic principles by working to unseat members of Congress or state legislators who disagree with them on abortion but who support every other issue of social justice that the Catholic Church has traditionally endorsed."

We asked Gavett to describe the tactics she had seen among pro-life activists on the Hill.

"They pray," she said with a helpless shrug. "And they try to get others to pray with them. That happens all the time, not only during the 'March for Life' but also during 'Washington for Jesus.' One group went to see a senator who was later defeated in the election. They walked into his office and commanded him to get down on his knees and ask for forgiveness for his votes on abortion. He refused. I'm sure he was baffled."

She motioned to the area where we were sitting. "I've had them come in here and pray for me," she said. "They'll line up in front of the desk and ask me questions. 'Don't you know that abortion is killing?' 'Don't you read the Bible?' 'Are you born again?' Then they'll say, 'We're going to pray for you now,' and they'll bow their heads very ostentatiously and ask that I be forgiven for my sins for murdering innocent children."

We asked her how that made her feel.

"Proud of what I'm doing," she said quickly.

More directly, we asked Pat Gavett for her impression of the kinds of people who were so fervently dedicated to the pro-life cause.

"There are two kinds," she told us. "A lot of them are young and idealistic, and they're looking for someplace to channel that idealism. Maybe in an earlier day they would have been in the anti-war movement. Now the prospect of saving babies and finding Jesus is the answer. But these are college students, most of them. When they grow up, when they are faced with real-life situations, when they meet women who are desperately in need of an abortion, or when they get pregnant themselves, they'll realize that there are hard situations and they'll want to make those decisions for themselves, not to have somebody else make their choices for them."

She went on. "The second type are the older people who are really afraid of what is happening to society as they know it, and, to some extent, I suppose, their fears are justified. They see drugs, pornography, crime in the streets, and all these things just scare them to death."

We asked her how she dealt with both types.

"You can't deal with the kids," she said, "because you cannot reason with them. They're not listening to you. They're angry. But you can get through to some of the older people. You can calm their fears. You can invite them in to talk, and they're amazed to find out that I don't have horns or anything. You can say, 'Yes, I agree with you that young people should not be having irresponsible sex. But don't you think it's the role of the Church to help them not to do that?' And they'll say, 'Yes, of course.' And I'll say, 'Well, don't you think we ought to be concerned about that rather than about banning abortions for women who need them?' In fact, one fundamentalist person came in here, and by the end of the meeting, he confessed that he really had no problem with the abortion issue at all, not theologically. He was really afraid that it was ripping apart the fabric of the family. I pointed out to him that it couldn't really strengthen a family to have a teenage daughter with an illegitimate child. Then he confessed to me that what he was *really* worried about was the ERA, and that the reason he was worried about the ERA was *really* because it would give homosexuals equal rights—and *that,* the Bible says, is a sin!"

Gavett described the emotional contortions that seemed to tie many pro-lifers into fundamentalist right knots. We listened as she defined Holy Terror to a *T*.

"You see, they need to build that fear," she said. "They need it to frighten people into action, to scare the daylights out of people who have never voted before. They have to twist and distort—the fetus pictures themselves are a gross distortion. Most of them are not even medically accurate, they're a good six to eight weeks off the gestation periods they put on them. But they have to put that image in the public's mind that these are live children. They don't want people to think of a developing fetus, but rather of a six-month-old baby with a full head of hair and a set of diapers. I've heard their leaders say it over and over again. 'Never say "fetus"; always say "baby." Never say "terminate a pregnancy"; always say "kill the baby, kill the baby, kill the baby." ' Then people will go out and register to vote for this guy who's running on the pro-life, pro-family platform and promises to straighten everything out."

As targets of pro-life intimidation, Gavett told us, many politicians had been reluctant even to be seen publicly at pro-choice rallies or meetings. "We're right across the street from Congress," she said, "but we cannot get these people to come and speak at our conferences. It just makes them too nervous to be associated with a pro-choice group."

She drew back in frustration. "I don't understand their thinking. Many of them have been tarred as pro-choice legislators, and there's no way they can become *untarred*. If they would just go ahead and face up to it, they would probably win support from many of the disaffected millions who didn't vote at all in the last election. Most of those people are on our side, but politicians think that if they walk the fence and remain very quiet, nobody will pay any attention to them. Well, once they've been targeted, forget it. They'll never get off that list, even if they voted for the Human Life Amendment, because this thing has nothing to do with the Human Life Amendment anymore. It has to do with whether or not the senator or congressman voted the right way on defense policy or economic or tax issues."

Pat Gavett peered out through the window through the trees to the whiteness of the Capitol. In Congress, she said, a representative of the Catholic Bishops was on hand virtually all the time. Legislative advisers for the Christian Voice were reported to be lobbying constantly. Pro-lifers with posters and crosses and toy dolls paraded regularly through the House and Senate office buildings. She looked at us plaintively.

"We are so rational," she said. "We are so calm. We are so well behaved. We are so colorless. We had a thousand people here in January—that's pretty good for a pro-choice rally. We had the leaders of every major denomination in America sitting together on the same dais. We put together a gorgeous volunteer choir. It was quite a story. Nobody used it."

She let out a last lingering sigh. "I don't know how colorful you have to get. We do not carry dead fetuses around in bottles, and I don't think we want to start carrying dead women around in bot-

tles either. But you know, one really wonders what you have to
do."

As we left Pat Gavett, we made our way down the Hill and out
across the Potomac, heading for the heartland. From well into
Virginia, we could still make out the Capitol dome in all its bril-
liance. Beneath it, America's lawmakers were being forced to do
something that no nation had ever done before: pass judgment on
life itself, which all living things possess, and distinguish between
mere life and *human* life. This untimely burden and its consequences had been put upon them by the fundamentalist right as
part of a political plan that had little to do with that momentous
philosophical issue. As the debate raged on, tossed by wild tides,
we wondered if the victor would be life in its smallest chemical
process—the growth of cells—or in its grandest human form—our
capacity to choose.

MONKEYSHINES

The pro-life movement, as we came to understand it, was the emotional key to the fundamentalist right. Playing on medical distinctions and theological disputes, fundamentalist right leaders had
fanned this outpouring of feeling into a major political conflagra-
tion and harnessed its power to help eliminate their enemies and
break traditional religious affiliations and party loyalties. But the
pro-life campaign was only one arm of the attack. The other was
just as emotional, fueled by the same fears, but with higher intellectual aspirations. Its target: the core institutions of our national
life, education and science. As we moved into these areas, we
came to understand yet another aspect of the fundamentalist
mind-set: the rejection by many Americans of the value of knowledge, not only for society, but for their own survival.

In the long run, the fundamentalist right's attack on education
may be its most deadly blow to the body of America. Public education has always been the first corollary of democracy. Our
Founding Fathers knew that the system would not work without
an informed populace capable of making reasoned, independent
choices. Yet, historically, the battle between religion and education has been more heated than any other in American life. Since

the start of public education in the early 1800s, the system has been plagued by bitter divisions over the methods by which the minds of the young would be trained, over the range of ideas and influences that would be permitted in the classroom and, perhaps above all, over the degree to which the nation's schools should function as inculcators of moral values and religious belief. For almost two centuries, the course of public education progressed steadily in the direction of basic skills and instruction in the humanities and sciences. Increasingly, the teaching of values and religion was relegated to home and church.

Then, as in the abortion debate, a series of U.S. Supreme Court rulings touched off a fire storm. In 1962 and 1963, the court held in two separate decisions that daily prayer, Bible reading and other religious exercises should not be permitted in public schools. The judgment enraged conservative Christians who, unlike America's Catholics, had no well-organized parochial system to turn to; and many began looking for alternative schools that would mold their children in ways more consonant with their traditional beliefs and mores. In many communities, particularly in the South, wildcat "Bible-based Christian schools" were formed, with programs weighted heavily in fundamentalist dogma and old-style discipline. In the sixties' era of permissiveness, rebellious youth culture and court-ordered racial integration, many parents saw in fundamentalist schools a way to shield their children from a changing world—as they were trying just as desperately to shield themselves.

The trend caught on. Like the electronic church, fundamentalist schools became big business for independent operators. One outfit, ACE, Accelerated Christian Education, Inc., grew into a $10-million-a-year business that supplied complete class curricula, study aids and teacher training for more than 160,000 students nationwide. By 1980, independent fundamentalist schools had become the fastest growing segment of American education, with over 14,000 private institutions already established and, according to one estimate, new schools opening at the rate of three per day! The network was separatist and militant. When state officials in Nebraska, Iowa and elsewhere ordered church schools closed for failing to meet enrollment and education requirements, fundamentalist teachers defied court orders, claiming the First Amendment gave them authority to educate their children in accordance with their beliefs.

Yet, despite an eroding base of support, public schools still account for almost ninety percent of elementary and secondary education, and for the fundamentalist right, the American public school system has become the whipping boy for many of their frustrations and complaints against the secular world. In addition to their drive to put prayer back in the classroom, there are a number of items the fundamentalist right wants *out* of school: such as sex education, which they believe fosters teenage promiscuity and pregnancy; co-ed sports, which they feel promotes immoral physical contact between the sexes; and drug education, which they think similarly stimulates experimentation.

But without question, for many fundamentalists the most dangerous substances in public schools are ideas, specifically, any notions that violate their unbending interpretation of the Bible. In the last decade, fundamentalist right fervor has divided school districts across the country. Led by a handful of national activists and organizations, local parents' groups and "concerned citizens'" councils have arisen to promote censorship of textbooks and other materials they consider to be "anti-Christian, anti-parent, anti-government, immoral and obscene." Books tarred with this designation include classics such as *Of Mice and Men, A Farewell to Arms, The Grapes of Wrath* and *The American Heritage Dictionary*—alleged to contain 70 entries in 155,000 rated "obscene or otherwise inappropriate for high school students." More revealing have been attempts to ban the works of modern authors known for their radical social or political views. George Orwell's *1984* has been widely banned for its nightmare vision of a controlled society. Kurt Vonnegut's *Slaughterhouse-Five* and Joseph Heller's *Catch-22* have come under attack for their anti-war themes. Eldridge Cleaver's *Soul on Ice* and other fiery writings by black authors have been repeated targets, as has *The Diary of Anne Frank,* condemned by extremist anti-Semites as false documentation of a Nazi Holocaust they claim never happened.

One elderly couple, Mel and Norma Gabler, have converted their home in Longview, Texas, into "the nation's largest textbook review clearinghouse." Since 1961, the Gablers' mom-and-pop foundation, Educational Research Analysts, has distributed thousands of textbook reviews to parents' groups and local school boards, citing line-by-line objections to alleged attacks on "Christian values," "negative thinking," and passages said to foster communism, socialism and "internationalism." One Gabler complaint cited a textbook mention of showman P. T. Barnum's famous statement, "There's a sucker born every minute," as "a depressing thought." Another condemned a favorable mention of UNICEF, the United Nation's children's fund, because "it is a known Communist front." Through such efforts, the Gablers have made an impact on public education; in one year alone, Texas officials removed ten books cited by them as unsuitable for school use. Parents in more than a dozen states have used Gabler materials to challenge courses and texts, forcing some of the nation's largest educational publishers to alter books and other teaching materials or risk being closed out of lucrative school markets.

Worst yet, the censorship mania has spilled out of the classrooms into the nation's public libraries. An American Library Association spokeswoman reported that, beginning in late 1980, "literally on Election Day," reports of censorship attempts reaching her desk multiplied almost fivefold.

The most ferocious censorship fight of all time continues over the fundamentalists' perennial foe, Charles Darwin, and his embattled theory of evolution. Only, in the eighties, evolution has become a code word for a much wider assault on the secular world.

Darwin's theory of evolution has been a target of attack by religious forces since the publication of his *Origin of Species* in 1859. From the outset, his thesis that mankind evolved from apes and lower species through biological processes of random mutation and natural selection—often gravely oversimplified as "the survival of the fittest"—was intolerable to devout Christians who believed that man stands apart from the earth and its lesser inhabitants as the favored creation of a divine supernatural being. In fact, opposition to the theory of evolution was one of the primary contributors to the rise of modern fundamentalism. The battle peaked first in 1925 in the famous Scopes "monkey trial" in Dayton, Tennessee, in which celebrated trial lawyer Clarence Darrow clashed with fundamentalist statesman and former presidential candidate William Jennings Bryan. Darwin lost in court. John T.

Scopes, a local schoolteacher, was fined $100 for teaching blasphemy. But the public spectacle drew the eyes of the nation and exposed the absurdity of the fundamentalist stand.

Thereafter, times grew tough for believers in the biblical account of creation, which held that the world was created less than 10,000 years ago in a rapid succession of supernatural acts that lasted six days and delivered each species of creature intact. In the passing decades, a surge of scientific research has all but confirmed the view that the universe was born approximately 20 billion years ago and that the earth alone is somewhere around 4.5 billion years old. Current scientific opinion is that the miracle of life is only slightly more recent, having arisen spontaneously from organic building blocks and evolved progressively through the chain of being to the species of man, *Homo sapiens,* which is believed to have been around for more than 50,000 years.

But fundamentalists continued to reject these findings. In their own churches and schools, they clung fast to the creation account as the first word and last hope of their literal faith. And through steady pressure and intimidation, they chipped away at establishment support for the Darwinian view. In the late fifties, more than three decades after the close of the monkey trial, the nation's most widely used biology text contained no treatment of evolution. (In 1929, the same book had a picture of Charles Darwin on its cover!) In 1959, however, the launching of a Russian *sputnik* satellite jarred the United States into a burst of technological development, placing emphasis on science at every level of public education; and in the sixties, Darwinian concepts and evolutionary thinking triumphed.

America's fundamentalists, however, viewed the re-emergence of evolution as a flare on the road to moral decay. This time their reaction was more sophisticated. Forbidden by law to bring religion into the classroom, the movement framed its response in terms of "scientific creationism," a self-styled discipline with its own body of purported "facts" and corroborating evidence that were said to constitute *proof* of the biblical account of creation. To the learned world, the ploy was transparent. The scientific and educational establishments denounced the creationists' claim as a myth and "dangerous" nonsense. One prominent science educator condemned creationism as "the big lie," declaring, "There is not a shred of evidence to indicate any scientific basis for the creationist view."

But to devout Christians in the heartland, and to many undereducated teachers, the creationists' approach was often persuasive. Through the establishment of creation "institutes" and "research centers" around the country, they gained credibility among local school boards, college administrators and state education departments. Their real breakthrough, however, was not theoretical but tactical. Leaders of the crusade chose not to seek the complete repeal of the Darwinian perspective, only to demand "equal time" for their viewpoint in state schools and colleges. The request had a seemingly reasonable, marketplace-of-ideas kind of appeal and won wide support from legislators, judges and public officials.

By 1980, legislation requiring equal time for creationist teachings had been introduced in seventeen states, and under attack from the fundamentalist right's network of grass-roots censors, the nation's science textbook publishers retrenched again. Sellers of one leading textbook reduced its section on Darwin from 1,373 words to 45. Its text on evolution was cut back from 2,750 to 296. At the same time, school boards were recommending or mandating the use of texts which used the "two-model approach." And suddenly, without any mention of the Bible, schoolchildren were being taught as science a view of mankind's emergence that described the origin of life in terms of supernatural acts, mystical interventions and a "great flood" that drowned the primitive creatures known today as fossils.

Through it all, like the fundamentalist schools movement, the creationist cause was becoming big business, as local school boards and state education departments were required to buy new curriculum instruction and course materials. Not surprisingly, many of the young creation research centers also had active textbook publishing and educational divisions, but the products they sold in great quantities only demonstrated the weakness of creation science. Most treatments were mere polemics attacking the Darwinian model by seizing on areas of contention currently under debate in the scientific community: gaps in the fossil record, for example, or questions about the accuracy of radioactive dating techniques. Some creationist proofs were nothing more than word magic. In one case, creationists argued that because scientists refer to Darwin's contribution as a *theory* of evolution, it is therefore something he merely "dreamed up." In fact, no term in science is more highly regarded than "theory"—a reasoned explanation of a phenomenon based on observation, experimentation and an ongoing process of scholarly debate. Other alleged proofs distorted the laws of science for religious purposes. For example, the Second Law of Thermodynamics is a basic principle of nature which states that all physical systems tend to run down to states of lower energy and higher disorder. Yet creationists claim the Second Law makes evolution impossible, demanding "intelligent supernatural intervention" to reverse the inevitable decline of physical systems. Like most creationist arguments, however, their error ignores new knowledge which has given science a broader perspective, in this case denying recognized distinctions between closed physical systems, which do tend to disorder, and open biological systems, which function on a different set of natural principles.

Far from offering a coherent alternative, creationists have been hard-pressed to explain why their biblical account should outrank the dozens of colorful creation myths found in every major religion. Hindus claim the universe began with the hatching of a great "cosmic egg." The ancient Babylonians believed the universe was born of *two* parent creators. Even the Bible has two different accounts: the six-day version in the beginning that put plants and animals on earth before Adam and Eve, and a later tale that placed Adam in Eden before the animals were created and brought to him for naming.

Yet the creationists pressed forward in a series of legal initiatives. Echoing fundamentalist hostility for the secular world, a sympathetic Georgia judge declared, "This monkey mythology of Darwin is the cause of permissiveness, promiscuity, pills, prophylactics, perversion, pregnancies, abortions, pornotherapy, pollution, poisoning and proliferation of crimes of all types." In Arkansas, after failed attempts in other states, creationists won passage of a bill, signed immediately by the governor, requiring use of the two-model approach in public schools. The American Civil Liberties Union moved promptly to challenge the law in court, and after a highly publicized trial, Federal Judge William Overton threw out the Arkansas law and exposed the charade. He ruled:

Since creation science is not science, the conclusion is inescapable that the only real effect of [the law] is the advancement of religion. . . . It was simply and purely an effort to introduce the biblical version of creation into the public school curricula.

Judge Overton went on to invalidate the scientific pretenses of the two-model approach:

The two-model approach . . . is simply a contrived dualism which has no scientific factual basis or legitimate educational purpose . . . [the creationist model] is not science because it depends on supernatural intervention which is not guided by natural law. It is not explanatory by reference to natural law, is not testable and is not falsifiable.

The decision had immediate impact as school boards in Arkansas and elsewhere refused to act on creationist laws, but pending court challenges in other states promised to keep creationism on the public docket for years to come. Although their arguments have been judged to be not a scientific discipline but a branch of Christian apologetics, the "big lie" proliferates, fueled by zealotry, intellectual chicanery and a broadening economic base. And few realize the extent to which the continuing scam is an integral part of the larger picture of Holy Terror in America. In fact, as we found, to a large extent, creationism is a wholly owned and operated subsidiary of the fundamentalist right political network.

As we went west, we were surprised to learn that the nation's largest creation "research" operation, the Institute for Creation Research in San Diego, was launched by one of the three founding members of the Moral Majority, Rev. Tim LaHaye, former pastor of San Diego's Scott Memorial Baptist Church, and that, until recently, this aspiring center for objective inquiry was a branch of LaHaye's Christian Heritage College.

To learn more, we headed for San Diego. Several years earlier, we had spent two months researching along the city's shores from which the cults of the seventies plucked their first catches of young runaways and vacationing students. Now, on the beaches, the mood was repentant. The drug culture was awash in beer, and talk had turned from enlightenment to endtimes, from the dawning of the Age of Aquarius to the coming battle of Armageddon.

Ten miles inland, in the rural district of El Cajon, we found the three-story Institute for Creation Research, a typical San Diego structure of stucco and red tile surrounded by tall palms and leafy tropical splendor. Inside, in his second floor office, Dick Bliss was equally exultant. After twenty-three years as a high school science teacher and director of science education for a large midwestern school district, this jovial man with a round face and thinning white hair held the prestigious position of director of curriculum development for the internationally known institute. At the time, just months before the celebrated Arkansas trial, he sat confidently holding the creationists' trump card. For perhaps more than anyone else, Dr. Richard E. Bliss was the man behind the two-model approach, which he helped pioneer in the Racine, Wisconsin, public school system.

Down the institute's main hallway, past its one-room "Museum of Creationism" and its small library overflowing with creationist texts, Bliss greeted us in a burst of enthusiasm and began to explain his two-model approach. The ploys that wooed Arkansas and much of the nation were soon laid out before us.

"The evolution model is, of course, a random, mechanistic process," he offered disparagingly, "while the creation model is a nonrandom, *creative* process. The two are mutually exclusive. But models are *faith entities*. They are frames of reference or paradigms within which you can correlate and integrate scientific data. Now, when we understand this, we can also understand that I have no business as a teacher programming a child toward my belief or anybody's belief."

He spoke in basic phrases, not like a scientist, but like the high school teacher that he was. In one short summation, he had reduced all of Darwinian theory, including the body of evidence that preceded Darwin and the decades of experimentation and documentation that have followed, to the level of a seemingly arbitrary belief system. For the moment, we did not protest.

"I'm a little bit biased *toward* science," Bliss continued, terming his creationist model "excellent, excellent education and excellent science." Creationists were meeting all the demands of science, he claimed, including the ultimate prerequisite of "unfettered inquiry."

"I look at the same scientific data that any evolutionist would look at," he said, "only I look more strongly at a lot of data that he throws out."

That data, considered irrelevant or extraneous by evolutionists, pointed in Bliss's model to the inevitable existence of a "Creator." We asked Bliss exactly what, in scientific terms, he meant by a Creator?

"I have no idea, in *scientific* terms," he said, raising a qualifying finger. "I have no idea other than an intelligence, a force or being that can in fact create man as man, dog as dog, cat as cat . . ."

But, assuming the creationist's declared scientific approach, we asked, how could he make that leap from the observable evidence to the existence of an entity he could not identify or define? Bliss repeated his opening argument.

"Yes, we're making a leap from scientific evidence that seems to demand a designer and design. But the evolutionist is doing the same thing on his part when he talks about random processes. He's looking at the same evidence and taking a leap of *astronomical* faith!" Dismissing virtually all of modern quantum physics, he began rattling off facts from biology, genetics and chemical thermodynamics which, he claimed, comprised the evolutionist's "houseful of assumptions."

As in our talks with pro-life activists, we had not come to defend the opposition. Evolutionary scientists were indeed battling out profound issues in their respective disciplines. Yet we questioned Bliss's premise that both models were faith entities. Was he admitting that creationist claims were based on religious beliefs?

"Not necessarily," said Bliss, reminding us that "in scientific creationism, you cannot tie yourself to a scriptural position." He added: "That's *scientific* creationism. That doesn't mean I throw the Scriptures out as far as my philosophy of life is concerned."

We tried to pin him down. For the record, how would he define the relation between scientific creationism and the biblical account of creation?

"I would make no connection with that right now," he said.

So the two were not related?

"Not at all," he said flatly, adding, "not when I'm practicing as a science educator."

The cat-and-mouse game went on. Bliss took the offensive, picking out inconsistencies and imperfections in evolutionary theory, at the same time dismissing greater flaws in his own argument. Flo asked him how creationists accounted for the documented history of biological change within species, including man. Bliss offered the only available explanation for change in nature: the evolutionary view.

"We accept change one hundred percent," he said. "We accept the same change that the evolutionist is accepting, only he's calling it microevolution and we're calling it *variation*. But we're saying this: 'A frog is always a frog and a dog is always a dog.' You're not going to see a frog become anything but a frog."

He pulled another animal out of his hat. "I can go into the rock pigeon," he said. "The rock pigeon in itself is a gene pool for the fantail, the pouter pigeon—beautiful, *beautiful* birds! You can outbreed and inbreed, backbreed, and you come right back to the rock pigeon. Who knows the variety you can get? But you'll always get a pigeon."

He tossed other species into the ring, birds, bacteria, the famous "horse series" of related fossils. Some of his examples were familiar to us; others came out of nowhere and were presented in detail. We could imagine how parents and students, teachers and administrators, judges and legislators, all for the most part untutored in science, would be impressed by this carefully selected and heavily weighted argument. If the creationist case was so convincing, we asked, why does virtually every scientist not affiliated with a creationist institute emphatically reject it as completely lacking in scientific evidence? Bliss took on a hurt look that turned intense.

"Well, I'll tell you a couple things that I think," he said, "and you can agree with me or disagree. But there is no way that some of these men who are avowed atheists—*they* say it, I'm not saying it for them—"

We stopped him. "What does a person's religious belief or lack of it have to do with the merits of his opposition to an alleged scientific argument?"

"Aw, but wait a second," he threw back. "It has the same thing to do with what you're referring to here. I'm saying that there is no way under the sun that they are going to tolerate a God, a Creator, an Intelligence, or any kind of thing like this. They are not going to tolerate it!"

"But what is this sudden injection of religion into the scientific process?" we asked. We had thought we were talking about unfettered inquiry and the collection and analysis of data. Did he really believe members of the scientific establishment were refusing to accept valid data because of personal religious bias?

"I have a hunch, a strong hunch," said Bliss, "that for the *anti-*creationists—and these are the ones you're hearing from, the ones who are delivering all the polemics and the vitriolics—I believe this is a *philosophical* argument. This is not a scientific argument to them."

Bliss told us that reputable scientific journals and institutions had rejected papers submitted by creationists. He chastised the establishment, declaring that their actions would "do immeasurable harm to the scientific enterprise." We prodded him with the charge that was later confirmed in Arkansas.

"Dr. Bliss, with all due respect, isn't the creationist perspective a religious crusade moving forward under the cover of science?"

Bliss bridled. "Well, if you would say that, *in all due respect,* the evolutionists, the anti-creationists are really an atheistic movement against a Creator, if you would accede to that, then I would say, 'Yeah, maybe there's an equivalence.'"

He tried again to throw the bias claim back on the evolutionists.

"The point I'm getting at is that we have a situation here where they are programming young minds, through their textbooks, their instruction and everything, to a singular point of view which is a *no-God* point of view."

"But when you frame your argument in scientific terms, aren't you taking God out of the whole system?" we asked. "Aren't you as guilty of that as the so-called atheists you're challenging?"

Bliss was taken aback. "Not true," he protested. We continued.

"But suppose we believe that we're alive because God breathed life into us. Aren't you denying that, from the scientific point of view you're talking about here?"

"No, not at all," said Bliss. "What we're doing in fact is adding another dimension, another very exciting dimension, from the dimension of looking at everything as a random process to looking at everything through the eyes of *created* process."

We pressed forward. "Couldn't God just as easily have created a *random* universe as a nonrandom one?"

"Well, yeah, God could have created it at random. But then, uh . . ." he laughed weakly. "Yeah, He could have, but you don't expect, at least in our mentality, you don't expect that from intelligence. You expect from intelligence order, design, and purpose. Wouldn't you expect that?"

"I don't know," said Jim. "I think there's something really elegant about randomness."

"Okay," said Bliss, recovering, "and I would have to answer you this way. God could do anything He wants to do. But when it comes to the scientific data . . ."

And he was safely back to his scientific defense. We asked Bliss, if creationism is such good science, why had there been so much public controversy. He attributed the furor to a "tremendous grass-roots ground swell."

"Look, we're not making it among scientists," he admitted. "That's very slow and painful. But you poll almost any community throughout the United States and you'll find that about eighty percent of all the people say they would like two models taught to our young people."

We asked, "Since when has scientific inquiry been conducted in the court of public opinion? If their science is valid, why not make their case in accordance with the standards of the scientific enterprise?"

"Well, we could, if there wasn't so much bias."

"Bias or not," we continued, "why go to courts and state legislatures to have your view mandated for teaching in science classes?"

Bliss leered. "Yeah, but who's doing that?"

Hadn't his group been instrumental in having equal-time bills introduced in more than a dozen states?

"Not at all," said Bliss. "We have nothing to do with any court cases. We have nothing to do with any legislatures. If I am invited as an expert witness in science education, I will go and testify, but you can be sure, as an educator, that I think it's very unfortunate to have to go this way. But why is it? That's the question you have to ask. It starts out with parents petitioning their school boards and administrators and the schools give them a deaf ear. And the parents are frustrated, they're screaming, so they go to their state legislator and get him all excited. Now you've got this eighty percent writing letters to the state education committee and the state says, 'Okay, you invited this, find out how in the world you are going to teach a creation model without teaching the Book of Genesis.' So they invite me over."

He was only partly correct. According to press reports, the Institute for Creation Research had drafted the creationist bill that was passed in Arkansas, and later, its chief counsel pushed unsuccessfully to co-defend the statute with the state attorney general. Now we could see how the grass-roots brushfire spread, much as it did in fundamentalist right election campaigns: from the organizations whose newsletters and publicity materials fire up preachers around the country; into the churches, where parents are urged to petition their school boards; and on to the state legislatures, whose members have no place to turn for advice except back to the creation research centers, many of which are affiliated with fundamentalist churches or colleges. "Isn't that a closed circle?" we asked Bliss.

"They go to other places," he said, "but we're the most fluent writers and the largest institute, there's no question about that. But I don't see anything wrong with it."

We said it struck us as an unorthodox approach to science.

"I don't see anything unorthodox with parents wanting their kids to be taught something other than a humanistic, no-God philosophy, which is incorporated into the random mechanistic process of evolution."

He was back to that. Was he saying that random process was a code word for atheism?

"I'm not saying it's a code word for anything," he answered. "I'm saying no-God philosophy. If you want to call that atheistic, go ahead."

Our talk wound down as we touched on other tactics used by each side. Apparently, some members of the scientific community were beginning to rise up in their own anger over creationist pressures. Bliss recalled a painful incident.

"Do you know what I was called?" he asked. "A 'broken-down

old retired educator.' And this was on the floor of a state senate!"
He laughed, wincing at the remark by a leading scientist. The low
blow had obviously been a searing one, and deeply revealing of
the frustration members of the scientific community have been
feeling as targets of a slickly packaged, well-financed attack.
Faced with their own research problems in times of dwindling
public support and government funding, it seemed likely that, in
many states, the secular establishment would fail to beat back the
creationist surge. We asked Bliss what the consequences will be
for science if the evolutionary model is defeated.

"I think it will be exciting," he said breathlessly. "Because now
man is going to have a conscious view of God. He'll have a God,
whatever that God might be, and he's going to be accountable to
that God."

Bliss also revealed the larger purpose behind the fundamentalist
right drive on the hard sciences. Twice earlier, he expressed
grander designs.

"If we establish a two-model approach and the inquiry that
goes along with it, it's going to spill over into the social sciences
and history," he said.

The prospect of a spillover was even more frightening. Bliss's
vision exposed the creationists' role in the long-range plan of Holy
Terror.

"Oh yes," he said, "the breakthrough has to come in science.
You ought to remember, evolution and evolutionary philosophy—
that *type* of philosophy—would never have permeated the social
sciences if it hadn't first come in through the sciences. And the
reverse process, I'm convinced, has to happen if it's going to un-
hook itself."

Was that the goal: to expunge all critical thinking and nonfundamentalist philosophy from the culture? If so, in its reaction to
change and its assault on the image of man, the fundamentalist
right could not have found a more precise target than evolution.
Back then, Bliss was cool. His side had the numbers, the money
and the momentum, and despite later setbacks, we questioned
whether even the federal courts could trim the creationists' sails.
Bliss gestured to the stacks of mail on his desk.

"I've got some real good friends in social science and history," he boasted. "And they're saying, 'You know, Dick, we agree with you. We might even take the initiative on this round.'"

THE WORLD'S GREATEST EVIL

In their holy war on the culture, the pro-lifers' and creationists' attack on science is only one arm of a larger fundamentalist right pincer movement. The other, the drive against the humanities, is being conducted as an independent attack on "secular humanism." To most Americans, secular humanism is a vague, ho-hum tag. The term has no emotional component. But to millions of fundamentalists, it has become a rallying cry and object of blind rage. Most have no idea what secular humanism means, yet they feel it is their mortal enemy. The confusion may be deliberate, for as a catchall code word, secular humanism stands for a long list of fundamentalist right targets.

Rev. Tim LaHaye is the foremost purveyor of fundamentalist hysteria over secular humanism. Co-founder of Moral Majority and godfather of the Institute for Creation Research, LaHaye is southern California's answer to Jerry Falwell. Yet his name is almost unknown outside the fundamentalist world. Like Falwell, LaHaye heads a local church conglomerate, a hard-line establishment with three separate complexes around San Diego. He is also founder of the city's Christian Unified School System, comprising four grammar schools and two high schools, and of Christian Heritage College, initially the parent foundation of the ICR. In addition, LaHaye has gained national recognition among America's born agains as founder and president of Family Life Seminars, a two-day sex-and-marriage counseling session which he and his wife Beverly conduct before large audiences in churchgoing communities coast to coast.

Lately, LaHaye's political activities have come to eclipse his preaching duties. In early 1981, he stepped down from his head pastor's position to devote more time to his leadership roles on the national board of Moral Majority, as head of its California state chapter, and as founder and president of a parallel group, Californians for Biblical Morality.

But it is as an author in the lucrative world of Christian book publishing that Tim LaHaye has made his mark. His sixteen titles include *Ten Steps to Victory over Depression, How to Be Happy Though Married, Spirit-Controlled Family Living* (with Bev La-Haye) and *The Unhappy Gays.* Outstripping all past successes, however, is a small volume with a title identical to a secular classic in the literature of brainwashing, *The Battle for the Mind.* The original, written in 1957 by British wartime psychiatrist Dr. William Sargant, explored in depth how intense physical and emotional experiences may bring about sudden changes in religious and political belief. LaHaye's book, which makes no mention of Sargant, is neither scientific research nor psychology. Rather, it is a relentless attack on the bugaboo of secular humanism, which LaHaye defines as "not only the world's greatest evil but, until recently, the most deceptive of all religious philosophies." Published in mid-1980, the book is a 237-page clarion call for fundamentalist involvement in politics and government, and its impact on the movement has been profound. In the months preceding the 1980 election, LaHaye sent 85,000 copies to fundamentalist pastors around the country, and throughout the following year, the book remained among the top five Christian best-sellers.

LaHaye's *Battle for the Mind* is a classic piece of *agitprop—* political writing that stirs up anger and hatred. Addressing his fundamentalist audience, LaHaye simplifies and inflames, endeavoring to characterize virtually all of nonfundamentalist society as a victim of the spell of secular humanism. Repeatedly, LaHaye depicts humanism as "the enemy" and a form of "religious evil." He writes:

> Most people today do not realize what humanism really is and how it is destroying our culture, families, country—and one day, the entire world. Most of the evils in the world today can be traced to humanism, which has taken over our government, the UN, education, TV and most of the other influential things in life.

Humanists, LaHaye says, are the enemies of Christians, and they have designated the 1980s for "the battle against religious rights." Unless Christians wake up to the evil, he continues, "the humanists will accomplish their goal of a complete world takeover by the year 2000." His battle plan is equally short-winded: "We must remove all humanists from public office and replace them with pro-moral political leaders."

LaHaye's argument might be amusing if he were just an isolated voice, but as a leading spokesman for the fundamentalist right, tied into its vast network of PACs and grass-roots activists, his abomination of the secular world borders on incitement. So, too, his ignorance of his subject would be merely pathetic, if he were not spreading misinformation and loathing. Mimicking the creationist tactic, he couches his attack in pseudo-science. "A major portion of your 1,800-gram brain consists of your intellect (or mind)," his argument begins. "Your mind has phenomenal potential, which is almost beyond belief." According to LaHaye, the mind is most heavily influenced by the eyes and ears. He stresses: "It is difficult to exaggerate the importance of using these receptors properly." Through improper use, LaHaye goes on, millions of parents have "lost their children's minds to rock stars, atheistic-humanistic educators, sensual entertainers and a host of other anti-God, amoral, anti-man influences."

"The second significant part of your brain is your heart, or as scientists call it, your emotional center," says LaHaye, which is not really heart-shaped but "walnut-shaped" and "located behind your forehead and between your temples." The heart, too, is influenced by the eyes and ears. As evidence, LaHaye cites an account of a sixteen-year-old who "had committed a sex crime that startled everyone who knew him." In his room were found "two thirds of a drawer filled with pornographic filth," LaHaye notes quantitatively. His diagnosis: "At a time when he was beginning to experience new sexual passions, he *artificially* fanned them by the misuse of his eyes, until his emotions were ignited beyond control."

Building on this premise, LaHaye goes on to label those associated with "almost every major magazine, newspaper, TV network, secular book publisher and movie producer" a "committed humanist." For the first time, he defines humanism as "man's attempt to solve his problems independently of God"—in his view, a futile task. He concludes:

> Today's wave of crime and violence in our streets, promiscuity, divorce, shattered dreams and broken hearts can be laid right at the door of secular humanism.

Fanning his own flames, LaHaye claims that humanists are "vicious in their expressed hatred of Christianity and its absolutes." Christian thought is the humanists' "mortal foe," and biblical revelation their "public enemy number one." Throughout history, notes LaHaye, humanists have worked relentlessly for their destruction. Reaching back through the ages, LaHaye blames the Renaissance for the birth of modern humanism. In Florence, Italy, he says, Michelangelo's "magnificent 'David' stands nude," in violation of orders from the Creator, "who followed man's folly by giving him animal skins to cover his nakedness." Due to skeptics like Jesuit-trained Voltaire and Rousseau—whom LaHaye describes as a "moral degenerate"—the Enlightenment was a total failure. But God's lesson was lost on the wretched humanist mind, perhaps because, as LaHaye claims, "intelligent people tend to be largely of the Melancholy temperament."

Next LaHaye defines the five basic tenets of contemporary humanism as he sees them: atheism, evolution, amorality and concepts of "autonomous, self-centered man" and a "socialist one-world view." Drawing heavily on critiques of humanism by born-again apostle Dr. Francis Schaeffer, and pulling quotes from the writings of American humanists such as John Dewey and Corliss Lamont, LaHaye attempts to characterize the philosophical school as a formal religious denomination, referring to a thin pamphlet, the *Humanist Manifestos I and II* as the humanist "bible." Citing a much-quoted article in the 1978 *Texas Tech Law Review,* "The Establishment of the Religion of Secular Humanism and its First Amendment Implications," coauthored by former Arizona Congressman John Conlan (an early supporter of the Christian Freedom Foundation), LaHaye declares that humanism has become entrenched as America's official religion. His urgent remedy: fundamentalist political action. Two elections, he claims, "could dramatically change the climate of national government" and return "moral sanity" to America. The remaining third of his book is a field guide to the Moral Majority and its affiliates, giving precise instructions on voter registration, grass-roots organizing and "the truth about the separation of church and state." Americans still baffled by the political uprising of angry Christians in recent elections may find some unsettling insights in this book, only one among many widely distributed and studied in churches, weekly Bible studies and other fundamentalist groups and gatherings.

Tim LaHaye has come a long way from Pumpkintown, South Carolina (population twenty-five), his first pastoral assignment after graduating from the ultrafundamentalist Bob Jones University. His wife Beverly, herself an author and founder of an anti-feminist group, Concerned Women for America, was an early appointment to the Reagan administration's Family Policy Advisory Board. Most of the candidates LaHaye supported in 1980 are now in office. But some of his more audacious moves have backfired.

In 1980, it was reported that LaHaye's Scott Memorial Church was supporting and giving financial aid to a militant anti-Catholic evangelical organization, Mission to Catholics, distributors of scurrilous literature. One Mission pamphlet, written by LaHaye's former university chancellor, Bob Jones, described the late Pope Paul VI as the "archpriest of Satan, a deceiver, and an antichrist, who has, like Judas, gone to his own place." It also called the Catholic Church "the old harlot Church still sitting on the seven hills of Rome, drunk with the blood of martyrs and fornicating with the political leaders of the world." During the controversy that surrounded news of the connection, LaHaye's minister of missions claimed that Scott Memorial had severed its financial ties with the group, but refused to disavow its goals or methods. "We're still friends to Mission to Catholics," he said. "We're not enemies by any means."

Tim LaHaye's enemies list is not confined to secular humanists and Catholics. His church bookstore sells materials that attack Mormons for "posing as Christians" and preaching "heresies." He has been outspoken in his denunciation of homosexuals, and he and his wife agree that women should be "totally submissive" to their husbands. In a manner more akin to James Robison than Jerry Falwell, meanness drips from LaHaye's pen and floods his various ministries and political crusades. His tough talk mirrors Robison's as well.

"I haven't punched anyone's lights out since the service," he once told a reporter, "but I got into some fistfights then and got beat up. I've had a lifetime problem fighting anger."

We bumped into Tim LaHaye, of all places, in a roomful of humanists. We found ourselves in southern California the week the American Humanist Association was holding its annual convention at the old Hotel San Diego, a hundred-year-old relic still standing proud at the edge of a crumbling inner-city district. It was odd finding LaHaye in this part of town in the company of his avowed enemies, such as Corliss Lamont, the reigning dean of American humanists, Paul Kurtz, former editor of *The Humanist* magazine and author of the 1980 *Secular Humanist Manifesto,* and Rev. Paul Beattie, president of the Fellowship of Religious Humanists, a nationwide group whose very existence deflated LaHaye's claim that all humanists are atheists. LaHaye was not there as a closet humanist. He was listed on the program as a participant in a fundamentalist-humanist "dialogue" scheduled to precede the convention's main event, presentation of the AHA's "Humanist of the Year" award to astronomer and author Dr. Carl Sagan. After seeing Jerry Falwell live at the Copa, we could not pass up an opportunity to catch Tim LaHaye downstairs at the Hotel San Diego.

They were a sad lot, these vicious humanists who were going to take over the world by the year 2000. On our way into the hotel, we watched them gather, these power-hungry one-worlders. As a group they were old and pale and thin, plodders not plotters, survivors of the thirties heyday of organized humanist thought and social action. Most looked like retired academicians and librarians: the men in tweedy sweaters, baggy corduroys and soft-soled shoes; the women mostly gray-haired with neck-chains around their glasses.

The Continental Room was floodlit and overflowing. The crowd chuckled and fidgeted. In one corner of the dais sat LaHaye, in a drab brown suit. In the opposite corner sat the humanist contender, Dr. Gerald Larue, professor of biblical history and archaeology in the School of Religion at UCLA. A nationally known expert on the Bible and an excavator of sacred sites in the holy land, Larue looked only mildly pleased to have received this assignment.

LaHaye fired the opening shot, hailing the meeting in this basement ballroom as a historic occasion, a confrontation between "two diametrically opposed positions" that "comprise the major philosophical battleground which will exist between now and the twenty-first century." Then he proceeded to give the humanists a short course in fundamentalist thinking, which he described as identical with "traditional moral value thought": belief in a living God, and in the conviction that man is a sinful creature, that he needs a Savior, that the world needs "a vital relationship to the Christ we believe in," and that the world is a "temporary place." His talk was illuminated by slides projected on a small screen behind him showing a cartoonlike figure from his book with a large *S* on his chest—for "Sinful"? He went on to tell the humanists what *they* believed. Above a chorus of snickers, LaHaye characterized most humanists as atheists, or atheists "at least from a Christian perspective." Their cartoon character had an *A* on his chest—for "Atheist"? LaHaye ran through his humanist tenets of atheism, amorality and evolution—"a natural result of atheism"— which held that man is an animal and "therefore he can live an amoral life as animals do," since "there is no one up there telling you what's right and wrong." He compared their "autonomous, self-centered" philosophy to that of the Soviet Union, "where they literally worship the memory of Lenin. They took God out of their beliefs and then found that people couldn't exist in a vacuum . . . and that's why you see these statues and they come and stand at his shrine and so on." In his closing plea, he called for the last six of the Ten Commandments to be adopted as federal law. The crowd stiffened as LaHaye said, "I don't think that man is capable yet of managing social order and individual decency without fear of some supernatural being overlooking him and able to punish him."

Then Gerald Larue rose and assumed his full stature. He looked down at LaHaye and shook his head. "That's quite an act to follow," he began. He was seething, but under control. Like most of the audience, he was insulted by LaHaye's attack and by his ignorance of humanist thought. "I think that if you continue your investigation of us, you'll find that we are among the most caring and *humane* people that you will find anywhere," he said. Then he moved to reclaim the high ground, rejecting LaHaye's argument that humanists and fundamentalists were diametrically opposed on moral counts.

"We, like you, are deeply committed to morals and ethics and to human welfare," he said. "Like you, we have deep concerns over the state of the nation and the state of the world. But we are concerned, not because of rules and regulations that come from the ancient past or from the outside. Our responses are the result of love, the result of caring, the result of sensitivity to human needs and human hurt."

Yet, beneath his conciliatory tones, Larue was furious at the planners of the "dialogue." He blew the whistle on their attempts to shackle him.

"I was told this cannot be a *debate*," he continued, "and I will tell you, when I signed up for this, I really didn't want to do it. . . . I was told that you are a representative of 'nice people' and that I shouldn't offend you. Okay, I had no intention of doing that. . . . I was also told—and you may smile at this as I did—that you are not very well educated and that I shouldn't be too *philosophical*. But, you see, I've been dealing with LaHayes in my classrooms for the last twenty-five years, and believe me, when they come out of my classroom they *are* educated!"

With that off his chest, Larue proceeded to decimate LaHaye's biblical contentions. "You're telling us that between two and three thousand years ago, the divine will was revealed once and for all, sufficient for all humans from that time on? Is that fair? . . . You would not accept the fact that millions of Moslems believe that God spoke again through the angel Gabriel to Mohammed . . . you would reject the revelation that came to Joseph Smith . . . you would deny Mary Baker Eddy's *Key to the Scriptures*. . . . We humanists don't have this kind of problem." Larue accepted much of the wisdom of the Bible, not as divinely revealed, but as an expression of "concepts that seem to be timeless": the cry for justice, the cry for kindliness, the Golden Rule. "But that's found in practically all religions," he said. "There's nothing uniquely Christian about it. It's simply a human expression of relationships."

Then Larue got tough. He turned to address LaHaye directly. "Where we would differ with you, sir, is that we would deny the right of people who have been dead for two thousand years to control and to condition our time and our space and our opinions. We are not where they were. They are not where we are. Their thoughts are not our thoughts. Their moral codes belong back where they originated—in Palestine, in Babylon, in Egypt, in Rome and in Greece."

LaHaye sat quietly as Gerald Larue continued to lacerate his comic-book theology. The audience liked Larue and so did we. After hearing the same litany of evils from TV preachers, new right manipulators, pro-lifers, creationists and now LaHaye, we were at last happy to hear someone take a stand for human beings. For a moment, immersed in this amiable old crowd, the negativity we had been absorbing for months subsided.

The Gospel According to Bunker Hunt

There is nothing wrong with making money. Thank God for people who have the ability to make money, who acknowledge that it all belongs to the Lord and it is not theirs to hoard, but it is theirs to pass on for the kingdom's sake.

—BILL BRIGHT—Campus Crusade for Christ

THE PATH OF HOLY TERROR is a closed loop, firing issues and causes from fundamentalist right bases in Washington, Virginia, California and elsewhere into the heartland, where millions of Americans, on faith and in fear, shoot back at the institutions the movement seeks to control. But the terror spreads far beyond the domestic plane, sinking deep into the grass roots and springing outward from America's native soil.

Perhaps the most active force on the fundamentalist right is an organization whose name means nothing to most Americans and which has been virtually ignored by the pundits and pollsters: the Campus Crusade for Christ, International. Campus Crusade, as it is known, has made big business out of bringing people to Jesus, and like most big businesses, it has become a multinational enterprise. Our investigation suggests that it may be the largest, richest and most ambitious group on the fundamentalist right.

Dr. Bill Bright, founder and president of Campus Crusade, looks like an unassuming man. At sixty, he appears in his press photographs like a trim figure maybe ten years younger, with dark eyes, black hair and a wrinkled smile. Except for those photographs, however, he is scarcely visible. He has no weekly television show. He seems to shy away from interviews. And with two notable exceptions, he has kept out of the spotlight of the fundamentalist right's descent on Washington. Yet, from his place in the shadows, Bill Bright commands the ultimate fundamentalist right tactical unit: the Great Commission Army, a corps of 6,000 staff members and hundreds of thousands of volunteers in 131 countries. Their stated purpose: "to share the gospel with every person on earth." The phrase is no exaggeration. With the help of some of the richest men in the world, the Great Commission Army is heading toward its immodest goal, not merely to Christianize America, but to "make disciples of all nations." In so doing, Bill Bright may fulfill his dream: "to change the course of history."

It has been more than three decades since Bright identified America's college students as "the greatest source of manpower immediately available to accomplish this objective." In 1951, he founded the Campus Crusade for Christ at the University of California at Los Angeles, targeting the "leadership people" who, he recognized, commanded the most respect on campus and exerted a "subtle, shaping influence" on the rest of the student body. In its first years on campus, several hundred UCLA students "came to the Lord," including the president of the student body, the editor of the campus newspaper and top campus athletes, among them Olympic decathlon champion Rafer Johnson and All-American linebacker Donn Moomaw. Moomaw later passed up a career in professional football to become a minister. In 1981, he delivered the invocation at Ronald Reagan's presidential inauguration.

Unlike Moomaw, however, Bill Bright is not an ordained minister. He is a businessman, a candy salesman. Born in 1921 on a ranch in Oklahoma, in the early forties he went West and started Bright's California Confections. Soon after, he followed acquaintances in the Los Angeles business community to a church in Hollywood, where he pursued a growing interest in Christianity. Then one night in 1945, he knelt quietly by his bed and committed his life to Jesus Christ.

It was not an emotional experience. There was no blinding, overwhelming revelation and he felt no different afterward. As he described the process, it was "a transaction of the will." After a year at Princeton Theological Seminary, he returned to southern California and enrolled in Fuller Theological Seminary, where he noticed that Christian missionaries were "standing in line" for tra-

ditional assignments in prisons, hospitals and skid-row missions
while important leadership groups, such as students and businessmen, were being ignored.

UCLA was only the first step. Bright's next task, "as in any expanding business," he has said, was to recruit a corps of dedicated, qualified personnel who were "fruitful in their witness for
Christ." As he traveled from campus to campus, harvesting fruit,
Bright's confection grew sweeter still, claiming large gifts from activist Christian businessmen and other nationwide ministries. At
the same time, he undertook a development program that soon
turned Campus Crusade into a miracle of modern marketing. That
program, begun in 1958 with the aid of a professional sales consultant, started with the shaping of a simple "sales pitch," first
formulated as "God's Plan," a positive presentation of the claims
of Christ. Eventually, it was refined into the "distilled essence of
the gospel," Bright's *Four Spiritual Laws,* a seventy-seven-word
capsule course in fundamentalist Christianity which Bright had
printed in palm-sized booklets, complete with diagrams.

In the beginning, Bright claims, he was not attracted to the slick
marketing methods of the "intelligentsia." "The very thought that
a man needed to resort to what I considered Madison Avenue
techniques to do the spiritual work of God was repugnant and
offensive to me," he said. But he came around. Over the next
three decades, more than 250 million copies of the *Four Spiritual
Laws* were printed in 100 languages. Other sales innovations
quickly followed that made Campus Crusade the brand leader in
"evangelization and discipleship"—conversion and training in the
fundamentalist life. These included a series of nine small pamphlets, called "transferable concepts"—Christian "truths" which,
according to Bright, could be "communicated from one person to
another and then to another, spiritual generation after generation,
without distorting or diluting"—and a set of simplified workbooks
titled *Ten Basic Steps Toward Christian Maturity,* covering subjects such as "stewardship," "witnessing" and "obedience."

The direction of the crusade, as Bright conceived it, was toward
"aggressive evangelism," culminating in a process he called "spiritual multiplication." Spiritual multiplication is the secret of fundamentalism's exponential growth. Multiplication improves on the
traditional missionary's aim of converting others one by one by

"teaching witnessing disciples to make other witnessing disciples," thus creating the need for capsule sales pitches and simple instructional materials. As with most of his business-oriented methods, however, Bright was not the originator of the concept. It was developed in the early thirties by founders of the Navigators, a missionary organization that began in the U.S. military and, following World War II, spread quickly to college campuses through veterans studying under the G.I. Bill. Navigators and other campus missions such as the InterVarsity Christian Fellowship deployed similar evangelizing materials, but none sounded the charge of multiplication with such single-minded zeal.

Before long, with the success of his techniques, Bright unveiled the most ambitious religious marketing campaign of all time: to "fulfill the Great Commission of the Lord in this generation." Bright interpreted the concept of the Great Commission as proclaimed in the New Testament—to "Go therefore and make disciples of all nations"—to be the Scriptures' supreme command. As Campus Crusade's numbers multiplied, Bright sent thousands of "newborns" streaming into local churches, and with the influx, many local pastors began to adopt his methods and materials. Soon the ministry begat training seminars for ministers and institutes for lay evangelists, and subsidiary ministries blossomed: Athletes in Action, amateur basketball, weightlifting and track teams whose members entered national competitions and witnessed to spectators during halftime breaks; a Military Ministry for armed services personnel at home and abroad; an Executive Ministry of wealthy businessmen who hosted "evangelistic dinner parties" where select guests were presented with the claims of Christ and urged to be born again. Bright formed a High School Ministry, a Camping Ministry, a Prison Ministry, Drama and Music Ministries, and a twenty-four-hour "Prayer Chain." His Special Ministries included traveling lectures by an illusionist who illustrated the *Four Spiritual Laws* "by magic," and by a best-selling Christian author whose biggest drawing card was a lecture entitled "Maximum Sex." In each ministry, Bright strived to use the group's broader activities as the means to get people to accept Jesus Christ as their Lord and Savior.

Then in 1974, with the help of a communications consultant from Michigan State University, Bright began to expand his Mass

Media Ministry. One multimedia production, *The Paragon Experience,* used nine film projectors and three screens to synchronize his gospel message with rapidly flashing images and lyrics from contemporary music. The main addition to his product line, however, was called "mediated training," a discipling method that employed slides, film and tape cassettes, and reportedly increased the efficiency of Crusade techniques from five to eighty percent!

Throughout the sixties, as Bright's banner unfurled, it became apparent that his crusade was more than just religious. With the rise of the counterculture and the anti-war movement on campuses across the nation, Bright's mission became overtly *counterrevolutionary.* On every campus, his students became the embodiment and, in some cases, the last vestige of clean-cut, wholesome Christian youth. As drugs, rock music and talk of revolution began to flood the campuses, Bright hit upon a new sales pitch that capitalized on the youth revolt: a fundamentalist gospel of revolution. In 1967, as he retells it, Bright tested the strategy at "the fountainhead of the radical movement," the University of California at Berkeley, which was then riding the crest of the Free Speech Movement that had begun several years earlier. At the height of the turmoil, Bright moved into Berkeley with six hundred Campus Crusaders for a week-long evangelization push. Using the slogan "Solution—Spiritual Revolution," the group held rallies, banquets, prayer breakfasts, dinner parties and off-campus meetings with students and faculty promoting "a new kind of revolution" which, they claimed, would change the course of history, creating the social reforms students were fighting for by "reshaping the lives and attitudes of individuals."

A Berkeley professor told Bright "the back of the radical movement was broken" that week, and in the heat of the sixties, "Revolution Now!" became Bill Bright's battle cry. Traveling from college to college, he called meetings and announced: "I am not a religious speaker, nor am I here to talk about religion. As a matter of fact, I am opposed to religion." Then, having captured the attention of his audiences, he proceeded to portray Jesus Christ as "the most revolutionary Person the world has ever known, a Person who made revolutionary claims for Himself and revolutionary demands upon all who would follow Him." "Revolution Now!" played well on tumultuous campuses and became a popular Christian book title that brought author Bright nationwide attention. In the fall of 1970, during the campus uprising that followed the Nixon administration's escalation of the Vietnam war, Bright launched another invasion, sending four hundred Crusaders to counter an anti-war rally at the University of Texas at Austin. "Campus Crusade for Christ smashes Student Mobilization Committee," a local radio station declared. Proclaiming victories at Berkeley and Austin, Bright prayed "for God to do it again and again throughout the entire world."

The fundamentalist counterrevolutionary machine was in gear. During college vacations, Bright sent teams of Crusaders to beaches, resort areas and inner-city and overseas locations to conduct meetings, parties, recreational activities and "community surveys"—all of which provided them with opportunities to witness to potential converts with the *Four Spiritual Laws.* In every setting, Bright's occupation troops carried out their missions in insurgent style. In fact, their operating procedures appeared to be modeled on the tactics of leftist guerrillas. Bright's description of a summer project reads like a page from Che Guevara's diary: "A select team of students comes to the resort area, locates jobs and settles into a normal work routine . . . the Christians find housing together. Usually, they secure a common meeting ground to sponsor outreaches." From the high school level on upward, Bright talked about "developing goals, strategies and materials to penetrate and influence the youth culture most effectively." After successful presentation of the *Four Spiritual Laws,* he stressed the importance of swift "follow-up appointments" in which Crusaders sought to "disciple" new converts through frequent Bible studies and "small discovery or action groups."

But without a doubt, Bright's greatest domestic coup was his 1976 "Here's Life, America" crusade, the nationwide television, radio, newspaper, billboard, telephone, door-to-door and bumper-sticker blitz that spawned the cryptic proclamation: "I Found It!" If "Revolution Now!" was Bright's answer to the cultural revolution of the sixties, then "Here's Life, America" was his great leap forward, a breakthrough in the mass-marketing of fundamentalist Christianity with increasingly political overtones.

Bright's expressed goal for "Here's Life" was evangelistic: to "saturate" the nation city by city and "fulfill the Great Commis-

sion in the United States by the end of 1976." But his real purpose, again, appeared to be counterrevolutionary, to solve the
problems of society through "a spiritual and moral rebirth in our
land." Every person in the United States would be given an "opportunity to respond," said Bright, and "as these people were
trained and discipled, change would occur in the moral fiber of
our country." Again the gospel message was reduced to a simple
slogan—"I Found It!"—the brainchild of a young Harvard Business School graduate and former ad man for Coca-Cola who
served as Bright's special assistant. After test-marketing in the
South, the program was launched in 246 major cities and thousands of small towns. In each locality, the operation followed
Bright's two-pronged plan of "spiritual warfare." "Proclaiming
the gospel is like a military offensive," he wrote, "with the mass
media serving as the Air Force—softening up the objective—so that
the ground forces can come in and capture an area." In the case of
"Here's Life," the ground troops were local pastors and congregations who had been enlisted in Bright's Great Commission
Army—the basic strategy that Moral Majority, NCPAC and other
fundamentalist right organizations would soon adopt as their own.

Following an initial campaign of saturation bombing via media
messages designed to arouse local curiosity, target cities and
neighborhoods were broken down into blocks of fifty homes, each
assigned to a different Crusade volunteer who would witness to
occupants and attempt, first, to get them to accept Jesus and, second, to steer them into the nearest participating church. Special-
ized squads approached students, businessmen and members of
the singles community. Homemakers were trained in conducting
"evangelistic coffees and teas" for women in their neighborhoods.
Ideally, Bright hoped, the saturation campaign would set off a
"chain reaction" and his Four Spiritual Laws would conquer the
community.

The impact of "Here's Life, America" has been widely dis-
puted. At one point, Bright set a goal of converting 25 million
Americans, but by his own count, the final tally reached only
532,000. Like every Crusade military offensive, victory was measured in terms of a Vietnam-style body count: 10,000 in Atlanta;
9,000 in Washington, D.C.; 27,600 in Greater Los Angeles. According to figures released by Bright's spiritual war department,

179 million Americans were bombarded by his "I Found It!" slogan; 7.7 million were contacted personally by 325,000 trained witnesses from 15,000 cooperating churches. But the numerology is suspect. According to a study of "Here's Life" in Fresno, California, and Indianapolis, Indiana, conducted by the Institute for Church Growth, of the thousands who purportedly made decisions for Christ after being telephoned by Bright's follow-up volunteers, ninety-seven percent never made it into a local church.

But Bright rolled on, undaunted, determined to saturate the nation "on a continuing basis." At the same time, in the 1976 election year, he took what were among the fundamentalist right's first steps into the political arena. Like many movement leaders, the origin of Bright's activism dates back to the Supreme Court's fateful school prayer decisions of the early sixties. According to Bright, those rulings were responsible for all the turmoil of the decade. He wrote:

> God began to chasten us. It was as though the plug was pulled, and evil came upon us like a plague of locusts. Within a brief period of time, President John F. Kennedy was assassinated in Dallas, the drug culture swept up millions of our choice young people, the black and white racial controversy bordered on civil war in city after city, the campuses were aflame with riots, violence and revolution and the war in Vietnam divided our country.

According to Bright, only a nationwide spiritual rebirth could stem this hemorrhaging process. In a 1976 pamphlet, he became one of the first fundamentalist right leaders to urge America's born agains to elect "men and women of God" to public office. Also at the time, he became associated with the Christian Freedom Foundation in its early attempts to mix religion and politics. That tax-exempt group had been growing increasingly political since 1975 when a number of right-wing businessmen, including Amway Corporation President Richard DeVos, a Crusade supporter, and Art De Moss, then board chairman of the National Liberty Corporation and a longtime host of Crusade executive dinner parties, teamed up with ultraconservative Arizona Congressman John Conlan and Ed McAteer, then CFF's field director, to tilt the organization in a direction the emerging fundamentalist right would soon follow. The fledgling movement sought to use local prayer groups, Bible studies and Sunday school lectures to organize the "Body of Christ" into a new political party. Much of its literature was supplied by the controversial far right Third Century Publishers, which distributed "Good Government Kits" and issued the first Christian voting "indexes" in more than thirty hotly contested Congressional districts.

Bright's political ambitions were also proceeding independent of the growing fundamentalist right network. In 1976, with more contributions from wealthy business interests, he purchased a lavish mansion in Washington, D.C., and opened a "Christian Embassy." Staffed largely by Campus Crusaders, the "embassy" held prayer breakfasts, luncheons and dinner meetings for U.S. senators and congressmen and their wives and reached out to federal workers throughout the government and the military. In Bright's own efforts, he visited with congressmen in their homes, coaxed one senator to attend a fourteen-hour mediated training session, led another to Christ in his Senate chambers and prayed with one congressman and knelt with another in their Capitol Hill offices. Later, Bright expanded the embassy to include a similar mission to members of the United Nations in New York. Reaching out to the world, his goal was no different than when he began at UCLA: to approach "leadership people." As his embassy director explained, by witnessing to people in government, at the UN, the World Bank and in foreign embassies and consulates, "the lives of leaders on each continent will be changed and doors of opportunity for spreading the gospel in many nations will open."

The international effort soon grew beyond mere pamphlets and bumper stickers, demanding massive organization and big money. As national organizers took charge of the fundamentalist right's domestic political crusade, like Pat Robertson (with whom Bright co-chaired the 1980 "Washington for Jesus" rally), Bright appeared to withdraw from the electoral trenches. Following his guerrilla-style outline, in 1977 he announced plans to take the fully tested "Here's Life" program worldwide. It would be, his spokesmen said, "the most extensive Christian social and evangelization mission in recorded history," an all-out effort to "share the gospel with every person on earth." The price tag for the grand body count: a cool $1 *billion*.

And who better to help him raise it than the richest man on earth!

Back in 1977 when "Here's Life, World" was unveiled, the name of Nelson Bunker Hunt was not widely known. Yet, already, the rotund, bespectacled Hunt was far from your typical multimillionaire Texas oilman. As elder son of the late mythical Dallas entrepreneur H. L. Hunt, along with his brothers, William Herbert and Lamar, Bunker Hunt presided over the largest family fortune in the world, an empire with financial holdings estimated at $5 billion. Much of this wealth lay in oil and natural gas interests inherited from their father, who died in 1974. But the other Hunt brothers, all shrewd businessmen, and Bunker, considered by many to be a financial wizard, quickly parlayed their initial assets into a mammoth, widely diversified portfolio of profitable investments.

At one time considered by his father to be a failure, he usurped the old man's title and, at the age of thirty-five, became the richest private individual in the world, at least on paper. His holdings included, at one time or another, the biggest oil field in Africa, more than a million acres of Western ranchland, 1,000 thoroughbreds (the largest string of racehorses owned by an American), and, with his brother Herbert, the 400-unit Shakey's Pizza Parlor franchise. But all that seemed like petty cash next to the Hunt brothers' biggest deal of all time: their perceived attempt to corner the silver bullion market that culminated in the Silver Crash of 1980. After a spectacular runup, the price of silver plummeted as commodities dealers panicked at the Hunts' bold strokes, leaving the brothers, due to risky financing, on the brink of financial collapse. Bad publicity and a government inquiry followed, and Bunker Hunt was branded as the villain whose hoarding almost touched off a worldwide financial crash.

Throughout the ordeal, Bunker Hunt continued in his volunteer position as chairman of the International Executive Committee of Bill Bright's "Here's Life, World" crusade. At the top of his short list of duties was the task of helping to raise "Here's Life's" $1 billion war chest. Like a good oilman, Hunt primed the pump with an initial contribution of $10 million. Brother Herbert gave $1 million of his own, and Bunker raised him with an unknown follow-up gift listed only as "considerably more." In addition, Bunker agreed to provide some $5 million in financing for a feature-length film, titled simply *Jesus,* to be distributed for profit by Warner Bros.—with "missionary rights" reserved for Campus Crusade.

But Hunt's munificence was only beginning. At the height of his high-level silver dealings, he was also sending out personal letters to fellow millionaires around the country inviting them to attend a series of weekend gatherings sponsored by "Here's Life." The formal solicitations were polite and momentous:

> You, together with your wife or husband, if convenient, are cordially invited to be our guest at a very important meeting that could help determine the destiny of civilization. . . .

Those who attended the meeting were advised that they would "hear and discuss plans and strategies that are not only having a profound moral and spiritual impact upon many nations but are also a critical deterrent to the avalanche of evil that is threatening to engulf the world." Later letters, signed by Hunt, were similarly urgent, grandiose and cryptic. The purpose of the messages, however, was to invite those so endowed to become part of "History's Handful," a select club of one thousand individuals, each of whom had pledged $1 million or more toward "Here's Life's" billion-dollar goal.

By mid-1980, Hunt's own brand of spiritual multiplication had increased his original investment tenfold, raising $170 million for "Here's Life" from his millionaire friends and Texas acquaintances. By early 1981, the total was approaching $220 million. Donors' names and amounts were closely guarded, but an indication of "History's Handful" could be seen in the list of those who endorsed the project in its initial phases: U.S. Senator William Armstrong of Colorado, former President Gerald R. Ford, Watergate Special Prosecutor Leon Jaworski, astronaut James Irwin, cowboy star and fast-food entrepreneur Roy Rogers, former Nixon supporter W. Clement Stone, Dallas Cowboys owner Clint

Murchison, Jr., football quarterbacks Roger Staubach and Terry Bradshaw, controversial Texas industrialist Cullen Davis, former Texas Governor John Connally and California Lieutenant Governor Mike Curb.

The global program was a multinational, multimedia, miltilingual version of the "I Found It!" blitz. When the project was launched, Bright named a former president of McDonnell Douglas Astronautics to head a special "task force on technology." The unprecedented plan for global saturation included a program to place cheap television and radio sets in more than two million villages around the world and to create special "circuit-riding" portable theaters in vans and on motorcycle caravans to take the *Jesus* film and other Crusade materials to remote areas lacking electricity. Other task forces included yet another Bright spin-off called Agape Ministries, referred to as the "Christian Peace Corps," which helped place Christians working in professions such as agriculture, engineering, teaching and medicine on two-year tours of duty in underdeveloped nations—with directions to witness for Christ while both on and off duty.

The final task force on "diplomatic relations with national governments" was central to Bright's global plan. In a press conference, "Here's Life" International Chairman Wallace E. Johnson, co-founder of the worldwide Holiday Inn motel chain, spoke freely about the "urgency" expressed by foreign business leaders he had visited concerning "inroads of communism" in their governments. Like Bright, Johnson denied that the mission had an overt political posture, and he ducked the question of whether "Here's Life, World" was really a thinly veiled attack by wealthy capitalists and free-enterprisers on the old far-right Satan of world communism.

"We're selling faith in the Lord and Savior Jesus Christ, and that will take care of it," said Johnson.

Despite the group's official denials, the spirit of counterinsurgency seemed to hover over Bright's billion-dollar baby. In Bright's *Come Help Change Our World,* an overview of Campus Crusade with a big windup for "Here's Life" funds, Bright described repeatedly the counterrevolutionary orientation of his global outreach program. When he arrived in Pakistan, he wrote, the country was "in a state of political turmoil. Even though riots were raging all around us, with buses and trains being burned and people being killed, the Christians still came to the meetings." At the same time, the group showed no aversion to provoking a few uprisings and incursions of its own. In Malaysia, a Muslim nation, the law is clear, wrote Bright: "Christians are not allowed to approach Malays with the gospel." Nevertheless, "Here's Life" moved in on the country's large Chinese population. "Although threatening telephone calls were received every day, and vehicles bearing 'I Found It!' bumper stickers were maliciously damaged, campaign workers remained undaunted." In Colombia, nine volunteers and staffers embarked on what Bright termed a "sacrificial mission" to rural areas, while his "mission impossible" team "developed a ministry among government officials in Bogotá."

Other "Here's Life" efforts aimed advanced technology at backward regions. In the Kilungu hills of Kenya, where three quarters of the natives are nonliterate, tape recordings were employed to train local pastors in the use of specially designed picture versions of the *Four Spiritual Laws*. Elsewhere in Africa, caravans equipped with loudspeakers blared "I Found It!" translated into a native language chant as children trailed along behind, singing the jingle. In other remote areas, loudspeakers called villagers to dubbed versions of the *Jesus* film, while further afield, Crusaders on foot used battery-powered bullhorns to summon people to small gatherings where they might see *Jesus,* the magic film or other Campus Crusade presentations.

In each country, Bright boasted astronomical body counts: 9,242 recorded decisions for Christ in Pakistan; 10,260 in San Cristobal; 28,174 in Hong Kong; 1,850,982 in India! Social and political windfalls were also dutifully reported. Crusade publications credited "Here's Life" with the "unexpected impact" of "creating the kind of spirit in Kenya that made a peaceful transition to a new government possible following the death of President Jomo Kenyatta" in 1978. A press release described how "Here's Lifers" went underground in Uganda after being declared "subversive" by former dictator Idi Amin.

As the project moved forward, in each locale, "Here's Lifers" employed the same guerrilla-style procedures used by Crusaders in the United States. Major foreign cities were sectioned off geographically and volunteers were assigned to "saturate specific blocks." Before traveling to their assignments, Agape workers received special training in "evangelization and disciple-making, cross-cultural communication and interpersonal relationships." Then they were deployed according to a carefully conceived plan of "strategic placement." "Doctors, nurses, teachers, agricultural workers, engineers and financiers can go many places that missionaries cannot," wrote Bright. "The need for trained people like this is so great that they are allowed into many countries where missionaries are banned, even though the authorities know that they will be sharing their faith in Christ while doing their assigned tasks." The goal, according to Bright, was the "multiplication of nationals, vocationally and spiritually."

The aim was fully in line with the evangelical urge of fundamentalist Christianity, but for Bunker Hunt, the harmony appeared to strike even deeper chords. Like his father before him, Bunker Hunt has long been involved in right-wing politics. The old man's participation, however, was largely confined to blistering public attacks on communism and glowing defenses of the free-enterprise system. When asked why he never joined the extremist John Birch Society, H. L. Hunt answered, "I always thought they should have joined me." The younger Hunt, however, was a joiner. As his own fortune accumulated, his growing interest in right-wing politics led him down the path his father refused to tread: into the John Birch Society. In his Hunt family biography, *Texas Rich,* author Harry Hurt III described John Birch Society founder Robert Welch as Bunker's political "mentor." Welch, said Hurt, became Hunt's "surrogate ideological father," schooling him in the Bircher's paranoid style of anticommunism and ultraconservative politics. Bunker, in turn, began pouring undisclosed amounts of money into the Society. In the mid-sixties, he was said to be one of its largest contributors. In 1976, he joined its national council and was reportedly giving $250,000 per year. But Hunt's merging fundamentalist and political interests went back even farther. In the early sixties, he backed an organization called the International Committee for the Defense of Christian Culture, a short-lived venture founded by an ex-Nazi turned militant anti-Communist with the declared goal of "resistance against [non-Christian] regimes and political concepts."

It can be said, if not in defense of all Christian culture, at least in support of Bunker Hunt, that his mixture of Christianity and capitalism seemed to be in good faith. A slow-moving and simple man, like his father, Bunker in middle age has gained a reputation as an eccentric and penny-pincher in everyday matters. When it comes to religion, however, his fervor seems sincere and his spending has been profuse. He once supported an expedition to find Noah's Ark, and his silver purchases were said to be motivated, at least in part, by his belief that the price ratio of gold to silver would someday reach its biblical era proportion of five to one.

As it blossomed worldwide, however, "Here's Life" seemed to offer Hunt and many others a unique approach to the social, political and economic goals of the fundamentalist right. Here, at last, all vital aims and concepts had been recast in Christian terms. In a single stroke—the move to share the gospel with every person on earth—all competing interests and opposing forces were targeted. Domestic squabbles over preachers in politics and the separation of church and state were trivialized. And the alarming implications of a worldwide fundamentalist drive for social and political control were defused by the unassailable rhetoric of the evangelical imperative.

Today, in the gospel according to Bunker Hunt, as on television according to Pat Robertson and Jerry Falwell and in the computerized mailings of the fundamentalist right, the same supernatural world view rules—above men, governments and the laws of nature; over high finance, high technology and hardball politics. As Bright declares, his is a "supernatural ministry." "Miracles must happen for the Great Commission to be fulfilled." To facilitate this, he advises his followers to "think supernaturally" in an effort to become "a different kind of person"; to "pray supernatural prayers" that our nation might experience a spiritual awakening; and to "plan supernatural plans" that God might comply with miracles.

It is the foremost expression of the fundamentalist mind-set. In these supernatural suggestions, the movement finds perhaps its greatest tools for personal control. As Bright says, to help fulfill the Great Commission in our generation, "you must first turn over your life completely to God." The obvious corollary, as he instructs, "Our finances must also be turned over to the Lord":

> If I understand Scripture correctly, God expects us to care for our families. But beyond that, Christians are never to

hoard. They are to invest in the kingdom. The very process of hoarding causes souring, just like the manna in the wilderness. . . . As you study the lives of Christians who hoard, you find that their money has cursed them, and it has cursed their children because they have disobeyed God.

Reading the above sales pitch made by Bright in the closing paragraphs of his book, we wondered if the same appeal was used at the banquets hosted by a man who once owned 155 million ounces of silver bullion. With Bunker Hunt's help, the Campus Crusade for Christ has become perhaps the richest fundamentalist enterprise in the world. In 1980, its worldwide revenues totaled more than $71 million—with future pledges yet to be paid. The annual figure is higher than that of any electronic church ministry, higher than that of any evangelical or missionary group we surveyed.

Men and money go together in the supernatural order of the fundamentalist right. In his books and "transferable concepts," Bill Bright reminds his readers that "every great movement has started with only a small number of truly committed men." Repeatedly, he draws the unlikely comparison that "Lenin took Russia, a land of more than one hundred million people at that time, beginning with just seventeen men." On a hunch, we counted the number of people on the "Here's Life" International Executive Committee whose photographs appear in Campus Crusade's 1980 *Annual Report*. They included Bill Bright, Bunker Hunt, Roy Rogers, W. Clement Stone, Dr. Jacob Malik—former president of the United Nations General Assembly—Wallace E. Johnson from Holiday Inns, the chairman of the J. C. Penney Company, the wife of the president of the Exxon Corporation, and businessmen and financiers from Switzerland, Canada and South Africa.

Altogether, there were seventeen.

Since 1978, in our travels to nearly fifty college campuses, we have run the gamut of Campus Crusade's self-described style of aggressive evangelism. To people in the Northeast, the organization is scarcely known, but it is omnipresent in most Midwest college towns and throughout the South and Sun Belt. Over the years, we've received many complaints about the Campus Crusade, maybe ten or twenty times the number we have received concerning its near equivalents, the Navigators and the Inter-Varsity Christian Fellowship. Perhaps Campus Crusade takes its Great Commission more seriously. Perhaps among young lay evangelists, none do it with more zeal than Bright's magic Christians. Whatever the reason, Campus Crusaders have upset a lot of people around the country. On a state campus in Maryland, a young freshwoman told us, she had been reduced to tears by local Crusaders who had harangued her repeatedly in an effort to get her to kneel and accept Jesus in the manner prescribed in the *Four Spiritual Laws* pamphlet. In a small college town in Pennsylvania, local clergy told us that Campus Crusaders had created a state of "open warfare" as they pursued converts from other campus ministries and the town's established churches. In a town farther south, we met a young wrestler who had gone into a local gym to train, only to find that it was a "proselytizing front" for Campus Crusade's Athletes in Action ministry. One of the leaders of the gym was a relentless witness. "I was told that I was going to burn in hell, that God was going to strike me down," our muscular contact recalled. "Believe me," he said, "if I were to see this guy on the street today, I can assure you, there would not be future generations from his seed."

We heard of more blatant deceptions. On campuses in Missouri and Arizona, we were told of Campus Crusaders who planted themselves in the doorways of fraternity and sorority houses in an effort to lure students to evangelistic meetings described only as "leadership rallies." On other campuses, we heard of teams of Crusaders who approached people with requests to take "opinion surveys" that opened with questions about "the state of the world" and ended with: "Have you heard about the *Four Spiritual Laws?*"

Some of the complaints we heard came from one-time Campus Crusaders. "They sent us out too soon," said a young man who had spent two years in a Crusade "action group." "We had to memorize Scriptures; we didn't even have to understand them, just be able to blurt them out. I used to argue with them all the time. I said, 'Paul spent three years out in the wilderness studying the Word of God before he went to spread the gospel, so how come we don't even spend three *months* on it?' But they went so fast, there was such an urgency. They said, 'Jesus won't come back until the whole world has heard about Him.' "

After two years away from the group, he told us, his feelings were decidedly mixed. "I look at myself in the mirror now and I see that I've got some aggression toward them. It's like they stole something from me, some *time*." His parting comment on the movement made us think back to our first interview with Diane. "I have to say, on the average, Campus Crusade probably makes people a little better than they were before they came in. They become a little kinder, a bit more conscious of their interactions, just like anybody who gets religion. But I also believe that they are not real people. They don't have real feelings for people. They're lying to themselves and to others, and the worst thing about it is that I don't think they even know it."

We had our own share of run-ins with members of the group. During our earlier research on *Snapping,* we had been alarmed by Crusade tactics that displayed disturbing similarities to cults we had studied: their aggressive recruiting style, their use of subtle forms of deception, Bill Bright's command—nearly identical to the cults'—calling for the "surrender of the intellect, the emotions and the will—the total person." We never called Campus Crusade a cult, yet when we raised our concerns about the group, our published comments brought down the wrath of Crusaders and their supporters around the country. Our contacts with these aggressive troopers, often angry and more than mildly intimidating, only deepened our concern. They seemed to have strayed far from one of Crusade's foremost principles of evangelism: "Nearly everyone responds to love," said an official handbook. "We give them an opportunity to pray, but we never 'bruise the fruit.' "

John Jones, Jr., sounded faintly thunderstruck when we identified ourselves on the phone. As director of communications for Campus Crusade, Jones had been hearing about us since he came to his job four years ago from a small-town newspaper in Tennessee. In the wake of the Guyana tragedy, due in part to general observations we had made, Campus Crusade was being lumped in with the cults by some critics, and although the organization had a generally good worldwide reputation, we had given Jones quite a headache. He had made our lives difficult as well, in tough-talking letters, phone calls and Crusade press releases. Among other things, he had accused us of failing to get both sides of the story. Now here we were on the phone requesting a meeting, and Jones turned suddenly hesitant. "If you're going to put us in a line with all these strange cults, like just another animal in the zoo, I'm not interested," he told us. "But if you're going to present us as an organization that's been around for thirty years with a clear position in Christianity, for whatever we are, then that's fair. That's okay." He invited us up to Crusade headquarters at Arrowhead Springs, in the mountains above San Bernardino.

In its heyday, the spa at Arrowhead Springs was one of California's renowned resorts. Rudy Vallee, Al Jolson and Judy Garland entertained at its gala opening in 1939. Esther Williams filmed a movie in its cliffside pool. Elizabeth Taylor spent her first wedding night in a suite high atop the Art Deco hotel. Then, as new roads and airports were built, Hollywood's early jetsetters leapfrogged to fancier spots in Palm Springs and Las Vegas. The resort foundered and, in the early sixties, Bill Bright collected enough donations to buy the six-story concrete-and-steel hotel complete with china, silverware, spare linens and more than 1,700 acres of scrub hills and landscaped grounds.

We entered headquarters, a great bulkhead of a hotel, its main lobby looking like something out of an old Astaire-Rogers movie. The former newsstand was now a Christian bookstore. The porters had been replaced by uniformed patrolmen. A medium-sized man with thinning hair came scooting across the black-and-white marble floor. The mood was sober and businesslike as John Jones ushered us through back hallways to his modest office.

We opened with a question about the aggressiveness of Crusade's evangelizing methods. Jones responded with an exegesis on the biblical origins of the Great Commission.

"It's the part where Matthew reports on the last meeting between Jesus and the Apostles," he said, "when he says, 'Go into the world and make disciples of all nations,' you know . . . and 'Lo, I'm with you always till the end of the age.'" He continued. "All right, I would say that is interpreted by most Christians as a *directive,* not an option."

Jones tried to portray Crusade in the mainstream of evangelicalism. He described the group as a "service ministry." He spoke of what Bright termed "aggressive evangelism" as *initiative* evangelism. He noted the group's cooperative efforts with local churches in the United States and abroad. He went on to explain Crusade's supernatural orientation.

"See, the idea is that the essence of Christianity is coming into a dynamic, personal relationship with the living Jesus Christ," he said. "You have to start from the premise that Jesus is not dead but He's alive. He's not visible. He's not here on this earth, but He's alive—obviously, you don't have a relationship with a dead person."

Jones described how born-again Christians may be, as Bright referred to it, "filled—empowered and controlled" by the Holy Spirit. "Jesus did die," he continued, "but defying everything that we know of the way the natural order operates, He was outside that order as well as inside it. He was *supernaturally* raised from the dead and He is eternally alive today. He hears prayers. He knows where we are. He's *sensitive*. And we're saying it's Jesus that is meant to inform your conscience and direct your activities throughout your life."

We asked Jones how something so holy could be reduced to catchy slogans and slick marketing strategies.

"You know, some people say that using billboards and telephone banks and tease campaigns and bumper stickers is like selling soap or something," he said. "We don't look at it that way. We feel that Jesus Christ is the most exciting, best possible news in the world that has ever been, and that we have an obligation to use the best available methods to communicate the best message in the world."

He checked himself. "We don't expect everyone to agree with that," he said, "but there's no need for marketing to be *ipso facto* negatively perceived. Is it dishonoring to God or Christ to use secular methods, not for marketing ends but for spiritual ends?"

Here again, we saw the movement's tendency to reduce individual spiritual needs to the level of mass marketing techniques. As we turned this corner, Jones's higher musings gave way to a nuts-and-bolts discussion of the logistics of "Here's Life."

"It's a very carefully worked out global strategy factored in by the experience of our ministry and other ministries: how much advertising costs, how much materials, how much for tape recorders, motorcycles, portable screens . . ."

But we were concerned with the larger question.

"Would you say the goal of 'Here's Life' is not just to share the gospel but, in the end, to bring everyone in the world to Jesus Christ?" we asked.

Jones paused. He knew the implications.

"Sure, that's the goal," he confessed. "The goal of the Great Commission is to make disciples of all nations. But the *methods* are important, not to make Christians at the point of a sword."

Their methods were our concern too, and, in our view, far more disturbing than any blatant attempt to coerce. We asked Jones the same question we asked Roy Harrelson at Pat Robertson's place in Virginia Beach: "Might not other cultures react strongly to a crusade to convert every person on earth?" His answer was identical to Harrelson's.

"I don't think we can speak of cultures reacting. *People* react," he said. "Some people have reacted. There's been opposition to the proclamation of the gospel through 'Here's Life' in some countries around the world. There's nothing the matter with that. It's a free market of ideas. If you hold to one world view very strongly, Marxism or one of the other religions or whatever, and you find the Christian faith being prominently, persuasively and effectively presented in your backyard, it's not illogical for you to kick against that."

We asked Jones if "Here's Lifers" backed off when they encountered resistance in a target country.

"No," he said, "we just go ahead and try to make the proclamation in a loving and nonforcible way."

Apparently, those targeted for conversion did not always respond in an equally loving and nonforcible manner. Jones told us that in Mindanao, in the southern Philippines, a bomb was hurled into a showing of the *Jesus* film. "I think it hurt some people," he said. "I've got conflicting reports. Anyway, the film was started again and more people came back than were there before!" Jones described another incident in an unnamed "country in Asia" where it is illegal for a person to leave the religion of his father. "We have people working with 'Here's Life' there who are going around the country holding public meetings," said Jones. "At last count, about fourteen of them were in jail."

We asked why "Here's Life" didn't stay out of a country where it was officially unwelcome.

"Because we feel that God loves these people, too," he replied. "We accept the punishment. We don't go underground. It's done openly."

Later we were joined by Paul Eshleman, Campus Crusade's worldwide director of "Special Strategies." A fifteen-year veteran of Crusade, he had been director of U.S. Field Ministries, director of "Here's Life, America," and was now in charge of worldwide evangelical use of the *Jesus* film. Paul was the one, said Jones, to whom we should address any complaints we had heard in our travels. Eshleman listened as we relayed the charge of "open warfare" we had heard in college towns across the country. He seemed familiar with the stories we recounted of Crusade pressure tactics that ran counter to written orders. We asked if he had received similar complaints.

"Occasionally, we do," he acknowledged. "We'll get some feedback that our kids are too aggressive. You know, in most of the Christian world, nobody cares enough to share it, so if we err sometimes, we probably err in the direction of being too aggressive. I think it varies with the part of the country and what people are used to."

He described some of the group's less intrusive approaches. We asked if group leaders advised their people to identify themselves as Crusade members when they approached somebody to witness. He dodged the question.

"See, it's a little bit tough," he said, "because we're not trying to make *members* of Campus Crusade." Their goal was to make not members but Christians, he said. He described the group's guerrilla style of penetrating college campuses, an operation usually carried out by nonstudent "field staff members."

"Typically, they move into a community and get an apartment near campus," said Eshleman. "Then they would talk to a fraternity or sorority and find those kids who would be interested in sharing their faith. But you don't ever *join* Campus Crusade. You never get a card. You don't come to meetings. Nobody says you have to come to so many meetings."

We asked him about the "leadership sessions" one-time Crusaders had described to us. "Wouldn't it seem proper for a missionary group to identify itself as having a religious orientation?"

"I'm not sure about that particular situation," he said. "I know our people use a leadership survey and leadership forums . . . but I understand your point, that you ought to be up front about what you're doing."

The conversation turned to the international level. Again we asked Eshleman whether other cultures might react negatively to intrusions by aggressive evangelists. His answer was familiar.

"Cultures don't react," he said. "*People* react." Jones shuddered as Eshleman looked at him, confused.

"That was not a prearranged response," said Jones.

Eshleman elaborated on some problems of intercultural communication faced by "Here's Lifers" around the world. He recalled experiences with Masai tribesmen in Kenya, where he had visited recently.

"We had to start very simply at first, about who is God? You know, 'God is the one who made these cows. God made the moon.' They don't have a very long attention span. We had to show the movie one reel at a time. They'd say, 'Who is that man standing there? Who are those old people?' "

In places in the Arab world where it is illegal to hold Christian meetings or convert to Christianity, Eshleman told us guardedly, Crusade forces were working to distribute the *Jesus* film through the flourishing black market in videocassettes. He described other incidents in African villages where *Jesus* was the first motion picture some tribes had seen. In a remote section of India, he said, the film gave them a peculiar entrée.

"Somebody went in with a van and tried to hold an open-air evangelistic meeting and they drove him out," he told us. "They were going to burn the van. The next day our film team, all Indians, came in with a projector and they welcomed them. But there was no electricity in the town except in the bulb that burns in front of the temple to the Monkey God. It was the only electrical outlet in the city. The priest of the Monkey God temple went in and took the perpetual light out and stuck in a plug socket and we had two thousand people in the Monkey God temple watching a film about Jesus!"

THE GOSPEL ACCORDING TO BUNKER HUNT

Although already alert, we were stunned by these new tales of Crusade insensitivities and affronts to other cultures. Soon we climbed the next rung of the organization's hierarchy as we were joined by Stephen Douglass, vice-president for administration, who was, after Bright, perhaps the highest-ranking member of Crusade's headquarters staff. A tall, fair-haired man in his forties, Douglass accounted for much of the brainpower behind Crusade's management and marketing acumen. For his Harvard Business School dissertation in the mid-sixties, Douglass and a fellow student conducted a management study of Campus Crusade's staffing and organizational patterns. Bright accepted virtually all their recommendations and invited both men to work for the group.

Our conversation swung around to politics and "Washington for Jesus." Expectedly, all three men denied that the giant rally in the nation's capital was politically motivated. As we prodded, however, their façade began to crack. Jones, who had attended planning sessions for the rally with Bright, admitted that it had been conceived as a political event, but he claimed that Bright, who joined the committee late, insisted that the event be nonpolitical. We asked Jones how, given the tenor of events, the rally could be construed in that way.

"Okay, what you're talking about is *hardcore* politics," he said, "lobbying, advancing political issues, things like that. In terms of saying to people, look, conservative Christians in this country are aroused—and I'm speaking *theologically* conservative, not politically—and they want the people who pass the laws to be men of God, men whose values are biblical views, in that sense, it had indirect political implications. I think that is undeniable."

At last someone had admitted to us what we and many others had known all along. Remembering our talk with Frank Church, we asked Jones if Bright's motive was to send an indirect message to elected officials as well.

"That was something I never even heard him discuss," claimed Jones. "He feels that politics, while it has a place in a country's life, is too shallow to be the answer. The answer to man's dilemma is Jesus Christ."

At this point, Stephen Douglass stepped into the conversation. "Now, this is going to seem highly indirect to an audience out there who might ultimately get some of the distilled essence of this," he began, "but I want you to know that our first concern is as Christians—even if we had some ultimate political thought. It might seem unbelievable to you that here we were, right under the noses of the politicians, doing all these things. How could it not have some pretty direct link? Well, I'm sure it wasn't an accident as originally conceived, but if you look at the content that went down there . . ."

Again, as in Virginia Beach, we tried to explain to these encapsulated Christians that the secular world was growing increasingly concerned by their allegedly nonpolitical activities. Douglass admitted that he had heard about the mounting opposition.

"Sure, sure," he said, "but mind you, my interest is casual. We're a movement that's at the *front end* of Christians' lives. We preach the gospel. I know that at times a person's doctrine might exceed his love, but I think you've got to be careful not to characterize the entire movement this way. If people are offended, let them be offended, only at Jesus and his message. Some will be, because they feel personally convicted of sin, maybe, or something like that."

We reached a dead end. Unlike leading fundamentalist right PACs and lobbies, which admit to being openly political, Campus Crusade appeared to recast all things political in religious terms. We found their defense to be nearly impenetrable. We moved to change the subject away from politics to the group's finances. Mentioning the price of "Here's Life," we asked, "Why do you need a *billion* dollars?"

"You need some perspective on that," said Douglass. "There are over four billion people in the world. You're talking about twenty-five cents *per person* to communicate the gospel, to do what follow-up is necessary, and to create a structure that will facilitate, not just one exposure, but *multiple* exposures. All of a sudden, that twenty-five cents doesn't seem like a whole pile."

He elaborated on the material difficulties of translation, culturalization and what he called the "cost per person" of designing messages.

"I hope that isn't an offensive term to you," he said. "It's a sense of stewardship about the people out there. We need to get to them, and we need to get to them in the best possible way."

Eshleman covered the phrase, too. "Well, we're not into *souls per dollar* or that kind of thing."

Douglass parried quickly. "No, no. Our motive is that *one person is worth a billion dollars, okay?* Would God spend a billion dollars to reach a person? Yes, I believe he probably would. But would he like to see a hundred million reached for the same price? I think he would."

But hadn't they opened themselves to criticism by pursuing so many millionaires for contributions?

"Sure, it was a conscious effort," said Douglass, "to approach a group of people with a very stimulating thought: that they might make a significant dent on their world."

How did they find the millionaires they were inviting to their banquets?

"There are over five hundred and twenty-three thousand millionaires in the United States."

Did they have a list of them? "I wish we did," he moaned. Most of the names were acquired through "personal recommendations." Douglass said that, to date, they had received 146 commitments of a million dollars or more. We asked about Bunker Hunt's commitment. They repeated the figures that had been released in the press, but declined to reveal the amount by which he had exceeded his original $10 million pledge. We asked whether the secrecy surrounding Hunt's contribution wasn't out of character for Campus Crusade, which put so much emphasis on openness and full disclosure. Douglass stressed that individual contributions were kept strictly private, although all agreed that, considering the controversial nature of Hunt's financial dealings, it would probably be better to provide the facts. Why were the fund-raising meetings closed to the press? Jones said it was to protect the privacy of the "high-profile" people who were invited. He admitted that many of them had no idea what kind of meeting they were being called to attend. "They know that it is something of a religious type that is designed to make an impact on the world," he said.

Jones's second reason for closing the meetings was of greater interest to us. "There is an atmosphere of a kind of spiritual retreat," he said. "The main thrust, more than anything else, is ministerial. Our number one priority is to try to reach those people for Christ. A lot of people in that situation share things about themselves, their religious convictions, their experiences, which are very personal, very much to the quick, spontaneous." The ministering began on Friday, Jones said, requests for "Here's Life" funds didn't come until Saturday evening or toward the conclusion of the weekend, at noon Sunday. We hadn't realized that the fund-raising event was a closed weekend-long religious retreat.

"Maybe I'm making up questions," said Douglass, "but just to answer one that might be in your mind, it's not like we lock the doors or keep people from going out. There's not a lot of peer pressure. No, it really is not a fund-raising dynamic like that at all."

The thought hadn't occurred to us until that moment. We had spent many hours talking with people whose choices had been dramatically affected by similar retreats.

"There is no pressure of any *external* sort," Douglass repeated, adding, "Now, if God tugs at their heart, that's God's business, but they are not given an ultimatum that they have to decide."

With so many wealthy businessmen and industrialists in attendance, we asked, wasn't it logical to assume that many would be expecting some sort of return on their investments?

"I'm only guessing," said Douglass innocently, "but I would hope most of them would perceive their return as spiritual, since that's what we're in the business of doing."

"That's all we're going to do," repeated Eshleman. "If they expect something else, we'll disappoint them."

Again, Douglass picked up on our implication. "I do think the net impact of more spirituality would be a better land, and perhaps that is some part of their motivation." He revealed that one quarter of the money raised for "Here's Life, World" was earmarked for use in the United States. We asked again, "Could it be that these millionaire businessmen might be hoping to use Crusade for nonspiritual purposes?"

"Well, supposing it were true," said Eshleman. "I still have a pure motive as to why I'm doing what *I'm* doing."

Douglass echoed the thought. "We certainly aren't being used *on purpose,*" he said. "But supposing in the back of their minds they had some other motive. I'm still doing what I'm doing for the reason I'm doing it, and all I know is that people are being reached for Jesus Christ."

"How could somebody use us?" asked Eshleman, incredulous. Jones, too, was baffled. "Maybe I'm naïve," he said, "but I can't even imagine how." We prepared to drop the topic.

"Oh, I can conceive of ways," said Douglass for us. "If a country stays free and a man's business is in that country, I can imagine he would have an interest in keeping a stable economy. So, if you're asking, 'Does the presence of true biblical Christianity stabilize a society?' Yes, generally it does. And does a stable society contribute economically to a businessman who's got an investment? Possibly."

With only a slight qualification, he had confirmed for us the possible ulterior motives of the millionaire businessmen with domestic and international interests in countries within Crusade's domain. We asked about Hunt's role in the organization. How much influence did he have in shaping "Here's Life"?

"As he gave the first check," Eshleman answered solemnly, "he said to Bill, 'I hope you'll use this for evangelism.'"

Jones was not pleased with the question. "You've got to understand Bunker," he protested. "His mother was a strong Calvinist, a good religious woman. He is not above going witnessing himself with his wife, door to door. He's been involved with Campus Crusade for twenty years, and he's never brought political conditions into his giving."

His point was well taken. Clearly, if Hunt or any of Crusade's rich donors had hidden motives, we were not going to find out about them here. Winding up, we asked Eshleman for his view of Crusade's long-range impact on religion in America. As an upper-echelon insider who had spent many of his years in the trenches, he continued to arouse our suspicions.

"As to our impact on religion," he said, "our objective would be to help people who are investigating faith in Jesus Christ to know how to begin, if they want to, and hopefully to do it sensitively. If you find we're not in places, let us know, because we sure would want to know."

It wasn't much of an answer and Jones knew it. He was ingratiating.

"I was surprised when your call came through the other day," he said, "but I'm glad you came. Even when there are disagreements, it's good for people to have a chance to air them face to face. So I'm real glad you came. I'm not ashamed of Campus Crusade at all. I'm here just because of that crazy, inexplicable thing called a 'call' or something. But by no means would we say we're perfect or that people don't make mistakes or get out of line."

He walked us out, showing us past the chapel where the twenty-four-hour prayer chain was going on, by the curlicued mosaic swimming pool where Esther Williams once bathed in glory. We thanked him. He had been a polite adversary. Yet our meeting with these top-ranking Crusaders left us with the same feelings we felt as we left Roy Harrelson and Diane in Virginia Beach. To us, their common posture of naïveté could no longer be separated from the threat posed by the fundamentalist right and its strategies. Their movement's goals now opened onto new levels of big business and counterrevolution, raising the stakes of Holy Terror —along with serious questions about the future of religion in America.

Lamentations

Let us, then, fellow citizens, unite with one heart and one mind. Let us restore to social intercourse that harmony and affection without which liberty and even life itself are but dreary things. And let us reflect that having banished from our land that religious intolerance under which mankind so long bled and suffered, we have yet gained little if we countenance a political intolerance as despotic, as wicked, and capable of as bitter and bloody persecutions.

—THOMAS JEFFERSON—Inaugural Address, 1801

IT HAS BEEN SAID that the fundamentalist right crusade is nothing new, that religion and politics have always commingled in America, and that the current expression is only the latest in a long tradition of religion summoning moral values to the forefront of national debate. It is an argument we reject. Religion has always played a vital role in the lives of most Americans, in the development of our political system and in the social drama of our nation. But that role has not been a terrorist campaign. It has not proceeded by intimidation, manipulation and deception, nor by spreading intolerance and hatred of those with opposing beliefs. Rather, the course of religious freedom in the United States has been a testament to the strength and wisdom of the American experiment. Although it has deep roots in many faiths, the cause has advanced by reason, argument and honest debate.

In our travels, we were surprised to find that most people we talked to had no idea how our religious freedom has been won. Moreover, many seemed to have accepted a tremendous distortion of American history, much of it propagated by fundamentalist right claims that there is no such thing as the separation of church and state, and that the intent of the framers of the Constitution was to found a nation on a uniform set of biblical principles. In quoting selectively from the historical record, fundamentalist right leaders have twisted both the letter of our laws and the spirit in which they were written. And sadly, through their techniques and technology, their errors have been multiplied many times over.

A fairer reading of history refutes such claims. The infant Colonies were indeed settled by devout Christians, but they were not founded on a common platform of belief. The Pilgrims and Puritans who settled the Plymouth and Massachusetts Bay colonies were religious nonconformists who came to the New World after experiencing harsh persecution in England. In contrast, the Jamestown settlers were strict adherents to the Church of England, and among their first legislative acts was the establishment of the Anglican Church as the state church of Virginia. Other settlers brought diverse beliefs to neighboring colonies—Quakers to Pennsylvania, Roman Catholics to Maryland, Dutch Reformers and Jews to New Amsterdam—and bred sharp divisions among religious and civil authorities. In short time, it was obvious that new principles were needed if America was to avoid the persecution most colonists had come here to escape.

Ironically, it was the upstart Puritans who sparked the birth of religious liberty when they banished a young Englishman from their colony in the winter of 1636. Roger Williams objected to the oaths required by the ruling Puritan elders of Massachusetts, and he strongly criticized church domination of the new colonial government. Cast out for having "broached and divulged divers new and dangerous opinions against the authority of the magistrates," Williams traveled south, where he established a colony at Providence which he envisioned as a refuge for the "distressed in conscience." Williams's famous *The Bloudy Tenent of Persecution for Cause of Conscience,* published in 1644, was the first expression in the New World of the idea that "God requireth not an uniformity of Religion." As he welcomed into his community Catholics, Jews—even Indians, whom he considered as brothers—Williams developed his principle of "soul liberty," acknowledging the equal claims of religious freedom of "the most Paganish, Jewish, Turkish, or Antichristian consciences and worships." State-enforced uniformity of belief, he said, was "the greatest occasion of *civill Warre, ravishing of conscience, persecution of Christ* in his servants, and of the *hypocrisie and destruction of millions of souls.*"

Other colonies later met Williams at least partway. The Maryland assembly passed a Toleration Act in 1649. William Penn's "Great Law" of Pennsylvania was adopted in 1682. In these early years, colonial America was already abandoning the idea of a "Christian" republic. In fact, most colonists showed little interest in religion at all. Even in Puritan New England, by the early 1700s, fewer than one in twenty colonists belonged to any church.

Today, fundamentalist preachers point with pride to the Great Awakening of the 1740s, the religious revival that represented the first turnaround in the secularization of the Colonies. Spawned by the triumphant American tour of British evangelist George Whitefield, the Great Awakening began as a reaction to the stifling formality of most mainline denominations. Starting a tradition that many soon followed, Whitefield took his fiery style into the fields, preaching on repentance, the wrath of God and the glory of the "new birth" experience before audiences that swelled to 20,000 or more. He and certain young American preachers, such as Jonathan Edwards, railed against the "listlessness" and "spiritual sickness" of the day. In their revival meetings, sudden conversions would take place amid fervent praying, shouting, crying, fainting and fits of "enthusiasm." But the fever soon grew to excess. In Connecticut, reborn "New Lights" were condemned for "wild, frantick and extravagant Management." In Boston, one New Light preacher was declared "unbalanced" and convicted of disturbing the peace for staging book burnings and bonfires of "breeches and Petty Coats." Yet, even in its extremes, the Great Awakening did much to advance the cause of religious pluralism—by advocating opposition to established state churches and by bringing together people from distant colonies and disparate religious backgrounds.

It also made colonial leaders wary of the potential dangers of religious frenzy and fanaticism to a struggling democracy. With the success of the Revolution, the Framers rejected New Light Christianity, building on European Enlightenment ideals of reason and human progress to construct a balanced system of self-government. Within this rational mechanism, they sought to enshrine the

principle of freedom of belief. Ironically, the doctrine was born in
the state that today harbors the most active forces working to undermine it. In Virginia, there was widespread sympathy for a
move to disestablish the Episcopal Church, led primarily by
Baptists who were opposed to paying taxes for the support of
teachers in church schools. In 1779, under the leadership of James
Madison, a General Assessment Bill was defeated, paving the way
for Thomas Jefferson's landmark Bill for Establishing Religious
Freedom. Jefferson's fight for religious freedom was no act of
caprice or personal bravado. For him, it was the fulfillment of a
lifelong philosophical passion. Introduced in the legislature in
1779, but not enacted until 1786, the Virginia Statute was the first
formal expression in law of the concept of unrestricted religious
liberty. The full text is an eloquent expression by Jefferson of the
converging thinking of his day. The business end of the bill, however, is concise and comprehensive:

> *Be it therefore enacted by the General Assembly.* That no
> man shall be compelled to frequent or support any religious
> worship, place or ministry whatsoever, nor shall be enforced,
> restrained, molested or burthened in his body or goods, nor
> shall otherwise suffer on account of his religious opinions or
> belief; but that all men shall be free to profess, and by argu-
> ment to maintain, their opinions in matters of religion, and
> that the same shall in nowise diminish, enlarge or affect their
> civil capacities.

The battle in Virginia was not easy, even for the likes of Jefferson and Madison. But at the federal level it was even more contentious. Modern-day fundamentalists are quick to point out that
the first Continental Congress opened with a prayer, but slow to
recall that for the next ten years controversy over religion continued unabated. At the Constitutional Convention in Philadelphia,
when an aging Benjamin Franklin moved for daily prayers "imploring the assistance of Heaven, and its blessings on our deliber-
ations," the motion failed. When the final draft of the Constitution
was adopted, it contained no references to God—unlike the Declaration of Independence. Instead, by unanimous vote, it framed in

federal law one of the most important provisions of Jefferson's Virginia Statute, passed just two years earlier:

> Article Six: . . . no religious test shall ever be required as a qualification to any office or public trust under the United States.

In the spotlight of the First Amendment, Article Six of the Constitution is often overshadowed, yet it stands today as an unqualified injunction against most of the fundamentalist right's aims and tactics: from its practice of issuing "moral report cards" as measures of political fitness, to its demand that legislators and judges adhere to a single theological viewpoint on abortion, to the command of movement leaders that only born-again Christians or those committed to "biblical morality" are fit to hold public office. Article Six also negates all fundamentalist right claims about the First Amendment, particularly that its first provision;

> Congress shall make no law respecting an establishment of religion, or prohibiting the free exercise thereof;

was designed merely to protect religion from government persecution. The historical debate on the clause confirms that the delegates to the convention that drafted the Bill of Rights were concerned that the law might be used by one denomination to gain ascendancy over others. James Madison, who led the floor fight for the measure in Jefferson's absence overseas, expressed the concern that, apparently, was shared by many. The record notes:

> MR. MADISON thought if the word national was inserted before religion, it would satisfy the minds of honorable gentlemen. He believed that the people feared one sect might obtain a pre-eminence, or two combine together, and establish a religion to which they would compel others to conform.

In their final form, the laws did not prohibit clergy or religious groups from participating in the life of the young nation. If anything, they enhanced the freedom of many religions to contribute to the broad moral base of American society. The Second Great

Awakening was an early illustration. This repeat revival lasted only from 1798 to 1803 and gave rise to much of the same frenzy that accompanied the first explosion. This time, however, the evangelistic thrust was tempered by an equal commitment to good works. The Second Great Awakening was a leading force for human betterment and social progress. It was in large part responsible for civilizing life on the expanding frontier, for bringing democracy to church institutions and for laying the groundwork for the American system of public education. It also gave rise to moral outrage over slavery, a sentiment that smoldered for half a century before erupting in the Civil War.

In fact, throughout the nineteenth century and into the twentieth, most church-related social and political campaigns brought advancements, not reactions. They stimulated the building of schools, hospitals and orphanages. They nurtured the cause of women's suffrage. Some religious attempts at social reform got out of hand, such as the drive to combat the growing problem of alcoholism advanced by the Women's Christian Temperance Union, the Anti-Saloon League and other religious-based organizations. Yet the Prohibition era stands as an early parable of religion run amok. In 1919, when the crusade triumphed with passage of a constitutional amendment outlawing all traffic in alcohol, it touched off a nationwide wave of social chaos and a murderous outbreak of organized crime.

Over the years, in their successes and failures, America's religions have had to learn how to participate in the political process without overstepping the law or the wisdom of the founders. The nation's many faiths have had to learn to use the power of the pulpit and the privileges accorded to religion to guide their adherents without manipulating or exploiting them. Above all, they have had to learn how to distinguish moral principle from dogma in their public postures. It hasn't been all black and white. Time after time, the courts have been called on to intervene. And without major exception, they have upheld the founding spirit, reaffirming the notion first expressed by Jefferson in 1802 that there ought to be "a wall of separation between church and state." As the Supreme Court ruled explicitly in 1948:

> For the First Amendment rests upon the premise that both religion and government can best work to achieve their lofty

aims if each is left free from the other within its respective sphere. . . . The First Amendment has erected a wall between church and state which must be kept high and impregnable.

The judgment is only one of many Supreme Court rulings that have come under attack by the fundamentalist right. The new movement is a renegade in the ongoing process by which America's religions have learned to work constructively together to advance their sectarian interests in a manner consistent with the public good. For decades, the nation's mainline religions have moved freely in the political arena. Many have even established high-visibility bases in Washington from which to promote a variety of general and special-interest goals. The U.S. Catholic Conference opened offices in the nation's capital in 1917, and the move was soon followed by the Baptist Joint Committee on Public Affairs, the Lutheran Council's Office for Government Affairs, the Washington office of the National Council of Churches, the Friends Committee on National Legislation and the American Jewish Congress and American Jewish Committee. Since the days when the nation's fundamentalists were preaching noninvolvement and an apolitical approach to salvation, these groups have been mixing religion and politics with little public or governmental opposition, arguing successfully under the law for their rights to operate denominational schools, to retain their tax-exempt status, and to insure that their adherents were not penalized for practicing their beliefs in good faith. They have also worked tirelessly toward common goals that transcend any single scriptural position, advancing the causes of world peace and nuclear arms control and promoting domestic and international programs to provide food, housing, education and health care for the needy.

Through the sixties, mainline denominations worked hard to fulfill the "social gospel," to advance the cause of civil rights and to end the Vietnam war. Yet, in the seventies, when their fundamentalist counterparts dived into politics, leaders of America's other religions were taken aback. Many sensed that the new fundamentalist groups were not striving for the common good, but rather to violate the basic tenet of pluralism by moving to enact their scriptural interpretations into law. Representatives of many faiths perceived in fundamentalist right goals and tactics a threat to their own integrity as religious institutions, a direct assault on their beliefs and, in some cases, an attempt to prey on their congregations. Yet few knew what, if anything, to do about it; and many clergy were intimidated. Although they felt that the fundamentalist right was wrong in most of its initiatives, many were left to question whether, on behalf of their own denominations, they might be doing some of the same things. As we traveled to Washington and around the country, listening to the lamentations of leaders of America's major religions, we began to see yet another side of Holy Terror.

Jews. Understandably, American Jewry has been quick to respond to the fundamentalist right. Historically victims of persecutions and pogroms, from ancient times to the modern horror of the Holocaust, Jews around the world have grown alert to any threat, not only to their own survival, but to every infringement on religious liberty and human freedom. Jews have learned that where intolerance flourishes—whether or not they are the immediate targets—their cultural integrity and, quite possibly, their very existence is endangered.

This is no doubt why American Jews are disturbed by the fundamentalist right. The movement's vocal attacks on minorities such as homosexuals; the racist undertones in its opposition to government aid to the poor; its antifeminist slant; its echoes of McCarthy era anti-Communist paranoia; the sweeping derision of its coded attacks on "liberals" and "secular humanists"—not to mention its expressed attempt to "Christianize" America—these judgments sound all too familiar. Yet the threat of the crusade escapes many Jews, large numbers of whom are second- or third-generation descendants of European immigrants. They have no experience of persecution. They know only that America has been more hospitable to the Jewish people than any nation in history, and that here Jews have found security and prosperity beyond their dreams in other lands.

But the Jews' distinguished place in America has been hardwon. In the 1630s, when Roger Williams first offered them "soul liberty," Jews from Spain and Portugal found refuge in Rhode Island, yet later laws discriminated against them. In 1655, they were granted a haven in New Amsterdam by Dutch governor Peter

Stuyvesant, but only after the West India Company turned down
his request "that the new territories should not be further invaded
by people of the Jewish race." In the 1700s, Jews were more
warmly accepted in Massachusetts and in South Carolina, where
the first Jew in the modern world was elected to public office in
1774. They fought honorably in the Revolution, but the number
of Jews in the Colonies was small, never more than a thousand altogether. By the end of the Civil War, following the first influx of
German Jewish immigrants in the 1820s, the American Jewish
community numbered only about 200,000.

They came in great waves in the late 1800s, as Jewish immigrants in large numbers fled poverty and persecution in Russia
and eastern Europe, settling for the most part in northern cities
crowded with other ethnic groups and afflicted with the growing
pains of industrialization. Only then did historic anti-Semitism find
its way to the surface of American life. Its roots reached back
through centuries of social ostracism and deep-rooted animosities,
caused in large part by the historic blame placed on the Jews for
the crucifixion of Christ and for their rejection of his claim to be
the Messiah. In the 1920s, these age-old enmities were unleashed
anew as white Christian America, marching to the beat of a revived Ku Klux Klan, nurtured many of the same hatreds that were
reverberating through Germany and the rest of Europe.

Yet the American movement was not confined to the rural,
racist South. In 1920, industrialist Henry Ford fanned anti-Jewish
feeling with his publication of the *Protocols of the Elders of Zion*,
a faked document purporting to reveal a detailed Jewish plan for
global conquest. Hostilities flourished for seven years before Ford
finally retracted his anti-Jewish charges, but the onset of the Great
Depression and the rise of Marxist communism led to continued
allegations that the Jews were in league with "godless devils" to
seize control of the western world. In the thirties, radio preacher
Father Charles Coughlin's anti-Semitic ravings were broadcast nationwide, providing a platform for the militantly anti-Semitic
views of "The Christian Front" and allied hate campaigns. Even
after World War II and the exposed atrocities of the Nazis, Cold
War tensions kept anti-Jewish feeling alive on the far right.

And into the eighties, the same tired old hatreds rebound along
the fringes of the fundamentalist right. The Christian Nationalist

Crusade, founded in the thirties by Rev. Gerald L. K. Smith, continued as late as February 1977 to publish its monthly magazine, *The Cross and the Flag,* and to sell copies of the discredited *Protocols,* Ford's *The International Jew* and other equally distasteful titles. Less slick but more vituperous is the surviving *Winrod Letter,* launched decades ago by Rev. Gerald B. Winrod, which still claims "The god of the Jews is the devil" and describes Judaism as "the synagogue of Satan." Its December 1979 issue denounced the Jew as "a liar," "a murderer, destroyer of the earth," "the witting and willing child of Satan" and a member of "a secret, conspiratorial, international Sect" who "exists for the single purpose of the destruction of Christianity."

Today, the still swift traffic in such fabrication continues to worry many American Jewish leaders. Although they assume that hardcore anti-Semitism retains only a minor presence on the extremist fringe, they are concerned that such sentiments will find fertile ground in the ignorance and naïveté of newly aroused Christians. And in large measure, their fears have been well founded. Blatant outbursts of anti-Semitism are rare on the fundamentalist right, but when they come they are spectacular. No remark in recent times caused such a furor as that of Rev. Bailey Smith, president of the Southern Baptist Convention, who stated at the Religious Roundtable's 1980 national affairs briefing in Dallas that "God Almighty does not hear the prayer of a Jew." Smith only partially retracted the remark. "I am pro-Jew," he said later. "I believe they are God's special people, but without Jesus Christ, they are lost." Subsequent meetings between Smith and national Jewish leaders did little more than bandage the laceration.

Of even greater concern to Jewish leaders, in the light of history, is the almost obsessive preoccupation with Jews, Judaism and the state of Israel displayed by many spokesmen for the fundamentalist right. Jerry Falwell personifies this perplexing attitude. Like many fundamentalists, he claims to have great love for the Jews, and publicly, at least, he has long since renounced his earlier vows to Christianize America. Falwell has even declared himself a staunch "Zionist" supporter and defender of Israel, and in late 1980 Israeli Prime Minister Menachem Begin presented him with a medal honoring his efforts on behalf of the Jewish state. But this new phenomenon of Christian "pro-Semitism" bears close scrutiny, for it has little to do with human affection. Most fundamentalist love for the Jews and support for Israel takes its lead from the closing chapters of the New Testament, where the prophecies of Revelation set down the conditions that must be met before Christ's Second Coming and the end of the world. These include the "ingathering" of the dispersed tribes of Israel in the holy land, and the fighting of a great war between two nations fundamentalists currently interpret to be Israel, on one side and, on the other, Russia, acting through its military client states in the Arab world.

Most American Jews dismiss these dark prophecies and their undertones, preferring instead simply to accept fundamentalist pro-Semitism at face value. But that estimation may be inflated. Jerry Falwell's own statements and those made by other fundamentalist activists are laced with anti-Semitic connotations. In *Listen, America!* Falwell lauds "that miracle called Israel," yet he deems the Jews as a people "spiritually blind and desperately in need of their Messiah and Savior." His public pronouncements have been even more derogatory. At a rally in Virginia, Falwell said, "A few of you here today don't like the Jews. And I know why. He can make more money accidently than you can on purpose."

We spoke with a broad sampling of Jewish leaders across the country, rabbis and representatives of national Jewish organizations, and with local Jewish community leaders. Few were serene about the fundamentalist right. They condemned its political ambitions, its social goals and, above all, its expressed aim of elevating the Scriptures to the level of law and foreign policy. Yet many feared to speak out publicly. In late 1980, when Rabbi Alexander Schindler, president of the Union of American Hebrew Congregations, declared in a highly publicized address that it was "no coincidence that the rise of right-wing Christian fundamentalism has been accompanied by the most serious outbreak of anti-Semitism in America since the outbreak of World War II," his comments drew fire both from the fundamentalist right and from American Jewish leaders, many of whom were unwilling to challenge the movement because of its vocal support for Israel. Throughout 1980, Falwell's militant Zionism allayed Jewish fears while his new right allies won broad Jewish support for candidates whose positions ran counter to nearly every goal of Jewish activism for more than a century. On Election Day, Jews voted for conservative candidates in greater numbers than ever before. In his remarks made after the election, Schindler denounced Jewish "flirtation" with fundamentalist right forces bent on the "political assassination" of Israel's staunchest allies in the U.S. Senate as "madness—and suicidal." Months later, during the heated public battle in which the new administration and Congress moved to sell advanced AWACS radar plans to Israel's declared enemy, Saudi Arabia, Senate leaders reported an alarming "resurgence" of anti-Semitism among their constituents and in the climate of debate in Washington.

Another Jewish leader who has sparked controversy on both sides is Rabbi Balfour Brickner, head of the Stephen Wise Free Synagogue on Manhattan's Upper West Side in New York. In his mid-fifties, Brickner is a veteran activist and spokesman on behalf of liberal social and political causes, standing on more than two decades of front-line organizational and grass-roots experience. In the sixties, he marched alongside priests, ministers and civil rights workers in the South. During Vietnam, he played a prominent role in the clerical wing of the anti-war movement, and he has since broadened his activities as a member of the executive board of the National Abortion Rights Action League, as founder of the New York-based Religious Leaders for Free Choice, and as chairman of the Mass Media Committee of Religion in American Life and of the Interreligious Coalition for Health Care.

With the rise of the fundamentalist right, Brickner stepped into a new combative role, denouncing national Jewish organizations that "diminish their integrity" by presenting awards to TV evangelists and sidling up to pro-Semitic fundamentalist right politicians. By catering to figures such as Falwell and Robertson to raise funds, wrote Brickner in a 1981 article, such organizations "insult the Jewish community socially and intellectually." He underscored his warning, noting that "a polarized society, an economically unstable society, a society where the gap grows increasingly wider between 'haves' and 'have nots,' a non-democratic society, an irrational society, has never been good for the Jews or the larger community."

We talked with Rabbi Brickner in his New York office. A youthful, lanky figure, and something of a wildcat, he was quick to support the right of fundamentalist preachers to become political activists.

"I'm absolutely convinced, I've always been convinced that religious groups have an obligation to become involved in the political process," he said, pulling on his pipe. "The church dare not stay out of politics. I've been doing it myself for twenty years and I'm not going to change my position now."

Yet he contrasted his own public efforts over the years with those of the emerging fundamentalist bloc. "Political lobbying and legislative pressure was always the domain of the liberal churches," he said. "We were the guys who did the work and the evangelicals were the pie-in-the-sky types who sat back and waited for Jesus to come. Now all of a sudden, there is a reversal of roles. We discover that we have been pre-empted. I don't object to their activism, but I do object to their use of religion and religiously raised funds for *partisan* purposes. I never use my pulpit to endorse candidates. I never use my congregation to press for an overtly political issue. I urge people to become involved, but I would never say that a person has to pass a certain kind of moral or religious test to be an acceptable candidate."

Brickner traced for us the liberal battles he fought in coalition with many religious and minority groups. The victories they won, on civil rights and social programs, against official prayer in schools and for other issues of church-state separation, bred much of the blue-collar resentment and conservative frustration which, he said, converged to form a "river of reaction" in the seventies. He scoffed at those Jews who embraced that reaction in the hope that it might somehow benefit Israel.

"I think it is a disastrous and stupid mistake to believe that, and Jews will reap the whirlwind of it, too," he said. "The fundamentalists' love for Israel is not a love for Zion. They are not interested in seeing the Jewish people survive in Israel. On the contrary, their ultimate goal is to see the triumph of good over evil in the battle of Armageddon, after which all men will be one in Christ. The moment that happens, good-bye Jews. We're out of business."

We asked Brickner why he thought so many Jewish leaders and organizations were vulnerable to the courtship of the new right.

"Because they feel so insecure," he said. "They'll take support for Israel from whatever corner they can get it. And besides, most Jews don't take fundamentalist theology seriously. They figure, as long as it means a lot of letters to congressmen and pressure on Washington to give Israel more aid, they'll let it run on, and they won't confront the fundamentalist right on those issues where they really are the enemy: abortion, ERA, civil rights, censorship, defense spending."

Brickner agreed that if the fundamentalist right were seeking one soft spot to press that would assuage Jewish fears and win support for their other programs, they found it in Israel. But like other Jewish leaders we spoke with, Brickner viewed the threat as one facing not only Jews but all Americans. "The alarm signals are ringing like crazy, but the American people learn things very slowly," he said. He placed much of the blame on the shoulders of religion itself, which he saw as long overdue for reform.

"When it comes to religion, Americans have been kept *spiritually infantile* by their leaders," said Brickner. "For too long, it has been feeding them pablum. Religion needs to change drastically. It needs to start being tough, hard, analytical and philosophical. We need to demythologize the Bible and rerationalize the religious approach to life. There are a lot of people struggling to do that, but they aren't making headlines because rational approaches to life are always more difficult to convey than simplistic ones."

His counterpunch to the new right coincided with his approach to other social problems. "The key to beating this thing back is *coalition*," he said. "Jews are going to have to forge new coalitions with the same groups they were allied with in the sixties: blacks, Hispanics, women, young people. We also have to link up with the mainline Protestant denominations. They are just as scared about the Moral Majority as we are. We need to reach out to *all* Americans. There are a lot of nice middle-aged folk out there who know that if they don't do something, all this is liable to do them in, too."

A die-hard organizer and fighter, Brickner was confident that, once mobilized, clerical leaders could help reassert the proper role of religion in the social and political process. He looked back to the early civil rights era, when he marched with the same ministers Jerry Falwell once condemned for becoming politically involved.

"We spent the better part of our lives in the sixties sliding up and down Mississippi and Alabama and Georgia," he recalled. "We lived down there. We sat in the Senate gallery in '65 when they passed the Voting Rights Act. We were up there with Martin Luther King and Andy Young and priests and nuns, sitting so close somehow we must have rubbed off on one another. If it hadn't been for those damn religious types, we wouldn't have had that law. When the vote was taken, we all stood up and screamed and cheered and they threw us out of the gallery!"

The same tactics, he suggested, might have to be used against the fundamentalist right. "We have to take them to court and challenge them at every single opportunity," he said. "We should be shouting like hell, before people reach a point where they can be drugged."

He rocked back in his chair, poking the bowl of his pipe.

"In the short run, we may lose a lot of our freedoms," said Brickner. "We can't beat them at their game. But we can neutralize them, and in the long run, I think people will come to their senses. They aren't going to win. But they are going to give us fits."

The Anti-Missionary Institute.   American Jews have yet another dilemma on their hands in fundamentalist right pro-Semitism. That is the massive thrust on the part of major evangelical organizations to convert Jews to Christianity. Many Jewish leaders are reluctant to discuss the problem, yet recent decades have seen the rise of more than forty active nationwide "Hebrew-Christian" organizations and, according to some estimates, the conversion of thousands of Jews. Over the years, groups such as the American Messianic Fellowship, the American Board of Missions to the Jews, the Messianic Jewish Movement International and the International Board of Jewish Missions have engaged in a variety of low-key, low-profile conversion drives. And with the born-again boom of the seventies, many fundamentalist organizations have become bolder and more visible in their approaches.

The newest and best-known missions to the Jews are not known for their soft-sell marketing methods. Instead, they pioneered the use of hard-line confrontational tactics that have alienated and angered more Jews than they have converted and threatened repeatedly to disrupt tenuous interfaith relations. The notorious "Jews for Jesus" have been primary culprits. Since 1970, their flamboyant leader, Moishe Rosen, has led roving bands of converted Jews on campuses and into major Jewish communities waving inflammatory posters and handbills and, on occasion, staging arcane prayer vigils in white-face makeup and early Christian garb. Other missions have been less forthright, shaping their images in ways that tend to soften expected Jewish resistance, often substituting for "born-again Christians" terms such as "messianic Jews," "Jewish believers" and the more cryptic label "Completed Jews."

Although it is seldom talked about, most major fundamentalist organizations seem to approve of missionary activities aimed at Jews. At least four Hebrew-Christian missions are listed as members of the Evangelical Council for Financial Accountability. Some electronic church programs regularly present converted Jews as featured guests, and in our research, we heard numerous reports of shared college programs between Jews for Jesus and both Campus Crusade for Christ and InterVarsity Christian Fellowship.

Most Jews are strongly opposed to such efforts, yet there has been only scattered protest from the Jewish community. Some cities have organized loosely formed "Jews for Jews" groups, and on some campuses the orthodox Lubavitch-Chabad movement has urged Jewish students to find new meaning in the return to ancient customs and strict ritual observances. One California Chabad unit has started its own cult and missionary "counteraction program." None of these efforts, however, matches the scale and daring of an organization we came upon in New York. In its attempt to counter what many perceive to be a growing "missionary menace" to all faiths, the Anti-Missionary Institute may be laying the groundwork for a much broader defense against Holy Terror.

We met with three men: Hesh Morgan and Tvsi Kilstein, cofounders of the Anti-Missionary Institute, and an AMI undercover operative whom we will call "Mork."

"What manner of *institute* is this?" we asked. Morgan, a commanding figure of about forty, began.

"We are not like other organizations in that we do not particularly want to be in existence," he said. "We came into being in response to a particular challenge: the singling out of Jews for conversion. We don't hold meetings. We don't collect dues or stage fund-raising drives. We simply have a few hundred people around the country working on a volunteer basis to help counter the missionary threat."

Morgan explained how the anti-missionary effort came about. "For me, personally, it started around '72. I had a friend whose daughter became involved in a Hebrew-Christian group. I had never heard the term before. Hebrew or Christian—to me, you're either one or the other, you can't be both. Soon we realized that this was not just some isolated situation. It seemed to be a nationwide operation. So I started compiling information. Then about four years ago, I met Tvsi and we began to see how big this thing *really* was. We figured that, if nothing else, we had to make the Jewish community aware that they were being targeted."

Public education, he said, was the main function of the ragtag institute. Another focus was on an unlikely area of Jewish study: the New Testament. "Most Jews don't even own a Bible," said Morgan. "If they do, it's probably collecting dust on a shelf somewhere. When they are approached, they have no idea if the missionary is misquoting, mistranslating, misinterpreting. It's all the same to them. Even the rabbis can't argue with them or debate with them. They know the Old Testament very well, but most Hebrew scholars don't know anything about the New Testament. Well, we've spent hours and days and months studying the New Testament. We can blow them away with it."

Morgan emphasized that the AMI was not out to undermine Christians' faith in their own religion. "Our feeling has always been that we are not against Christians evangelizing," he said. "What we are against is the use of fraud and deception in the proselytization of Jews. Very often Hebrew-Christians present themselves as something they are not. Many claim to be rabbis, but they are not rabbis. They never have been rabbis, and they never *will* be rabbis. They are simply following what it says in the New Testament: 'To the Jew you come as a Jew that you might gain the Jews.' That's fraud and deception. They don't talk about Jesus, they talk about 'Messiah Yeshua.' They don't mention the cross, they refer to it as the 'tree.' They say that they are against organized religion, yet the first thing they do after they convert you is take you to a fundamentalist church."

He went on to describe AMI's second major function, which he called "counseling." "A sample case," he began. "I got a call last month from a Jewish family. Their sixteen-year-old son had been talking about nothing but Jesus for the past six months and was now going to become baptized. So I got him on the phone and I said, 'Will you do me a favor? Would you be willing to put it off a week and sit down with me before you do it?' He said, 'Sure.' So I went to his home that Sunday and as soon as he opened the door he said, 'I just want you to know that you're not going to change my mind.' I said, 'I *can't* change your mind. That's between you and God. I just want to know how you came to this decision.' Well, it turned out that he had been watching the '700 Club' and reading a few Christian books and he felt that it was definitely the answer. I asked him if he had ever read the Bible. He said he had read most of Matthew and parts of the Book of *Palms*. I said, 'The Book of *what*?' He said, '*Palms,* P-s-a-l-m-s, *Palms.*' I said, 'Oh boy, I've got one here who doesn't even know the *books* of the Bible!' The next week I met with him again and started reading him quotes. Obviously, they were things he had never seen. It threw him into total confusion."

To us, it sounded very much like a cult "deprogramming." Kilstein anticipated the comparison. "In most cases, Hebrew-Christian groups are not like cults, where the person undergoes a complete personality change, leaves home and all the rest," he said. "Most of these people live normal lives. Many of them still live with their parents or with their spouses and families, but they never tell anyone that they've become a Christian. They don't display Bibles or crosses in front of their families. They sneak off to prayer meetings. But they spend every spare minute reading the Bible, and when their families sit down to talk with them or argue with them, they listen but they don't hear. They look back at them, they give some response, but they're really not responding."

Morgan elaborated on the distinction between deprogramming and the AMI's counseling. "In a deprogramming, you look for the psychological keys that will bring them out of the mind control. Here you look instead for the *emotional* keys."

His distinction was in line with the picture of emotional control we had been forming. In addition to their public information and counseling work, Morgan and Kilstein described two other activities of their institute: intelligence gathering and harassment. Here the AMI's operating tactics assumed a guerrilla-style character—not very scholarly, but as it turned out, little different from those used by the opposition.

"We never did any infiltration until we learned that a number of missionary groups had been infiltrating Jewish organizations in order to seek out converts," said Morgan. "Then we got a copy of a confidential memo Moishe Rosen sent to his top people telling one of them to infiltrate Hadassah, the Jewish women's organization," he claimed. "And we got a call from B'nai B'rith—all the people on their mailing list were suddenly receiving mail from Jews for Jesus. So we contacted a few people and asked them to join messianic groups."

"That's when we began to see how all the bits and pieces fit together," said Kilstein. "How all the various leaders confer with one another, how they exchange information and materials, how they channel people in and out of various fundamentalist churches in the area."

Kilstein said he had been one of AMI's first infiltrators. He described a harrowing encounter. "One group invited me to a series of Friday night meetings. Then the head of the organization asked me up to his office. We were in there alone and he took out this little pamphlet on *The Five Jewish Laws* and started reading it out loud. He kept putting pressure on me and when he came to the end he said, 'Wouldn't you like to get down on your knees right now and accept the Messiah?' He really got to me. I was so completely shaken that I ran out to the first pay phone I could find and called my rabbi. He had to talk me down, the way you might talk someone down off a bad LSD trip. Everything was confused in my mind."

His description sounded familiar. So many times in our earlier research, we had heard first-hand reports of cult infiltrators and investigators who had been intensely affected by personal encounter techniques. Eventually, however, Kilstein regained his composure, never really making a commitment, but managing to move convincingly among members of the group for several months.

After he had brought back a wealth of information regarding the group's travel plans, witnessing initiatives, finances, etc., he moved to end his undercover role.

"I told them that my parents were after me and that they wanted me to come and talk to some people," he continued. "But the pastor of the church said to me, 'We haven't lost one yet and we don't have any intention of starting now.' The leader of the group was even more adamant. He said, 'Listen, we've got a place for you to live. If you need money, we'll give you money. If you need a girlfriend, we'll get you a girlfriend. Whatever you need, we'll give you. We have an apartment; you can have your own room.' They were all set up for it. It was streamlined."

Kilstein left anyway. Before long, AMI began putting its several infiltrators' finds to work. Morgan picked up.

"One year we got the itinerary for Jews for Jesus' entire summer campaign," he said. "When they pulled up at each location, we were waiting for them. They would walk up to people on the street, and we would walk up right alongside them, refuting everything they said point by point. At their rallies, we would stand up and shout, *Ladies and gentlemen, can you believe this? This person wants me to burn in hell because I don't believe in Jesus!* The missionaries would melt into the ground."

Other AMI counter-efforts were more intricate and required advance planning. "We planted one guy in an organization and waited eight months before we used him," said Morgan. "They invited him to speak at a gathering of five hundred young Jewish kids after a rock concert. Everyone else got up and gave the typical testimony about sex and drugs and how they met Jesus in a flash of light on the top of a hill. Then our man got up and said, 'I've been involved in Hebrew-Christianity for eight months. I've been to the prayer meetings. I've read the books. And I just want to let all of you know that I think it's the greatest fraud ever perpetrated on the Jewish people.' He went on for twenty minutes. No one knew what to do. When he finished, there were nine people left in the audience."

The combined impact of all these minor incidents had been to decimate Hebrew-Christian missionary activity in much of New York and elsewhere around the country. Said Morgan, "We haven't stopped them, but they never imagined there would be

infiltration on such a scale. Our success has been such that they
now have to start treating everybody as an infiltrator. That's what
we want. We want them to doubt every convert."

Needless to say, through their unconventional activities, the
"faculty" of AMI have alienated themselves, not only from the
Hebrew-Christian movement, but from much of the Jewish community as well. Morgan defended AMI's tactics.

"Look, we believe in mutual respect among religions," he said,
"but the Christians aren't respecting us. When it comes to missionary activity, the Jewish community has always put itself on the
defensive. For centuries we've had to defend Judaism and defend
our beliefs and react to what the other side was doing. Well, we
are no longer just reacting. We are taking the offensive. We study
their Bible. We read their books. We watch their TV shows. But
we don't want to go on television and debate Scriptures with them.
We just want them to know that whenever they move in on the
Jewish community, there is going to be opposition."

Mork spoke. He had been silent through most of the discussion.
"Don't forget," he said, "we only exist because they do. If the
missionaries stopped targeting Jews, we would disband the organization."

As we broke, Morgan said, "By the way, could you use a few
Bibles?" He motioned to the shelves stuffed with crisp new copies
of the Scriptures.

"We got those with a Luke 6:30," said Kilstein. The reference
escaped us. Morgan told the story.

"One day the Gideons came to Brooklyn College with seven
thousand Bibles in the back of a van," he said. "And we went
over and hit them with a Luke 6:30, that's 'Give to every man
that asketh of thee; and of him that taketh away thy goods ask
them not again.' Then we said, 'Do you really believe that?' And
they said, 'Of course.' And we said, 'Then can we have those
boxes?' And they said, 'Well, you know, we need them.' And I
said, 'Then you must not believe in the Bible, because if you did
you'd give them to us if we asked.' Then I just walked over to my
car and opened the trunk and said, 'Do you want to put them in,
or do I have to carry them?' And they loaded them into my trunk
and we drove away."

"Luke 6:30," Kilstein reminded us, "it may come in handy

sometime. Or try Matthew 5:40, 'If any man will sue thee and take away thy coat, let him have thy cloak also.' We've used that one to get suits, ties, leather jackets. . . ."

Mork, ever-vigilant, jumped in at defense. "We donated them to an old-age home," he said. "They were thrilled."

Catholics. More subtle than the biblical designs of pro-Semitism on the Jews, the fundamentalist right has taken advantage of deep divisions within the Roman Catholic Church to engineer decisive swings in religious and political loyalties. America's fifty million Catholics, already divided over Church positions on issues such as abortion, the role of women in the Church, and government support for parochial schools, have become prime targets of the fundamentalist right. In the religious arena, the charismatic movement, paralleling the explosive growth of evangelicalism, has barnstormed across America to become the fastest-growing segment of the Catholic Church. Although it has been criticized for its sharp deviations from traditional Catholicism, the charismatic revival has been officially praised by Pope John Paul II and other Catholic leaders as a Great Awakening of sorts for the Church.

At the same time, fundamentalist right political strategists have leaped upon this emotional tide in well-planned efforts to woo Catholics to fundamentalist causes and candidates. The strategy has been most successful in the furor over abortion. As a political tool, the abortion issue has been to American Catholics what fundamentalist right support for Israel has been to American Jews: a magnet, drawing many to support social, political and economic positions that run counter to nearly every stance the Catholic Church has taken in this century. Some prominent Catholic clergy and lay leaders have attempted to bring this point to wider attention. In magazine articles and personal statements, Monsignor George C. Higgins, for thirty-six years a member of the National Conference of Catholic Bishops before his retirement in 1980, has castigated the fundamentalist right for their "strangely selective and extremely simplistic" approach to complex issues. He also has broken with ecumenical tradition by condemning fundamentalist right activities on theological grounds, opposing their "uncritical use of biblical citations for partisan political purposes."

Concern over Catholics becoming pawns of the fundamentalist right has also penetrated Washington political circles, where elected officials have found themselves cornered on the abortion issue and forced to give in to pro-life intimidation or risk losing important Catholic votes in their home districts. All this, despite the fact that, according to most polls, the majority of Catholics oppose the rigid pro-life anti-abortion stand. U.S. Senator Patrick J. Leahy, Democrat from Vermont, a Catholic and a survivor of a 1980 new right targeting effort, has been bluntly outspoken on the subject. Writing in the Washington *Post* on the *"de facto* political alliance"* between the Catholic Church and the fundamentalist right, Leahy charged: "The Church we love is being used in a dangerous way." For the Church to undertake moral "instruction" on abortion is, Leahy said, its right and duty. But he criticized the Church-supported campaign for legal restrictions which, he said, had made the Church a "stalking-horse for the right." In their sincere belief, Leahy noted, "many Catholics have been manipulated by far-right political action groups," even taking positions opposite to those of official Catholic bodies on health care, civil rights, fair housing, worker safety, adequate wages, religious tolerance and other issues of "justice, compassion and human dignity."

The threat has not been ignored by the current Church hierarchy. As early as 1979, the U.S. Catholic Conference expressed its concern over single-issue abortion-determined voting, striving to walk a fair line without undermining the Church's own anti-abortion stand. Officially, Church leaders declared their priorities, even if in practice many Catholics remained unmoved by the plea. The U.S. Catholic Conference statement, "Political Responsibility: Choices for the 1980s," placed traditional Catholic concerns ahead of pro-life politics. "In order to be credible and faithful to the gospel," it said, "the Church's concern for human rights and social justice should be comprehensive and consistent . . . formulated with competence and an awareness of the complexity of issues . . . and respectful of the rights of all." The statement also pledged that "the Church will not confuse its mission with that of government":

We specifically do not seek the formation of a religious voting bloc; nor do we wish to instruct persons on how they should vote by endorsing candidates. We urge citizens to avoid choosing candidates simply on the personal basis of self-interest. Rather, we hope that voters will examine the positions of candidates on the full range of issues as well as the person's integrity, philosophy and performance.

To some degree, the Catholic Church has adhered to that position, taking varying positions on most other critical social issues. Even on the right to life issue, which it championed long before the fundamentalist right went into high gear, its official position remained a consistent one, in contrast to many fundamentalists, applying the sanctity of life principle beyond the womb to include strong stands against capital punishment and, in a new round of initiatives, advocating strict nuclear arms control and world disarmament.

However, the pro-life issue remained its most visible crusade, and in late 1981 the U.S. Church hierarchy seemed to violate its own promise not to "confuse its mission with that of government," taking its first official legislative stand in favor of a proposed constitutional amendment that would overturn the Supreme Court's 1973 decision legalizing abortion. Like so many positions dividing the modern-day Church, this new official stance defied the realities of modern life for most practicing Catholics, and threatened to do irreparable harm to the Church's broader social concerns, to its standing among its flock, and to its respected position among other mainline denominations.

As it strengthens, the *de facto* alliance between American Catholics and the fundamentalist right reflects the growing struggle within the Church worldwide over liberal-conservative issues such as women in the priesthood, the Church's long-standing tradition of critical scholarship and recent Church support for Third World liberation movements. In many ways, the outcome of the American debate will affect the course and cohesiveness of the larger Church, determining whether it edges closer to its own form of fundamentalism or continues to move forward in its historical commitments to social justice and human development.

The alliance is even more ironic in light of the long-standing enmity fundamentalists have shown toward the Catholic Church and Catholic faithful in America. Unlike the effusive mission to the

Jews, which has gone forward in a flood of love for God's "chosen people" and their prophetic homeland, the mission to the Catholics has been one of barely disguisable hostility. Fundamentalist Rev. Bob Jones's broadside slamming of Pope Paul VI as the "archpriest of Satan" and his attack on the "blood-drunk," "fornicating" "old harlot Church" of Rome is not an example of fundamentalist experimental journalism. These charges date back to the start of the Reformation in Germany and can be traced through northern Europe and England to the early Colonies, where anti-Catholic feeling was widespread.

Most Catholics today are unaware of the trials their immigrant ancestors suffered on their arrival in the New World. The Maryland Toleration Act of 1649, for example, was motivated by Lord Baltimore's desire to protect Catholics from the kind of persecution they had suffered as British subjects. In the drive for nationhood, many colonists continued to view incoming Catholics as spiritual infiltrators, agents of a "foreign prince"—the Pope—who many felt was trying to dominate the Colonies as he had come to influence Spanish Latin America and much of French Canada.

These fears were not fully flushed out until the Federalist period, when the new government enacted the Alien and Sedition Acts of 1798. Passed in anticipation of war with France, the laws' most appalling provision made the publication of malicious writings against the United States, the President or Congress a crime punishable by fine and imprisonment. But the hidden intent of the legislation was to protect the privileges of "Native Americans" from the first waves of Irish Catholic immigrants, raising the residency requirement for citizenship from five to fourteen years and giving the President the power to deport aliens considered dangerous to the public peace. Coming at the time of the Second Great Awakening, the Acts had obvious religious implications. They also evoked strong reaction. In fact, Jefferson's election to the presidency in 1800 and the subsequent demise of Alexander Hamilton's Federalist party were in large part due to public revulsion over the laws.

Yet the rancorous Nativist movement was far from dead. A generation later, it got a fresh start with the wave of Irish Catholic immigration that peaked during the Potato Famine of the late 1840s. The tide of foreigners—rising to 370,000 in 1850—accompanied the birth of the Industrial Age and caused violent up-heavals in America's still largely rural Protestant society. The poor Irish provided a ready supply of cheap labor for manufacturing and industry in the urban Northeast, but the Catholic Church was left to bear much of the burden of feeding, clothing, sheltering and educating the immigrants. In the process, the American Roman Catholic Church championed the nation's earliest battles for social welfare and improved labor conditions.

Even then, such liberal positions did not sit well with hard-line Christians. As early as 1827, they were expressing their dislike in thirty anti-Catholic periodicals. In the 1830s, opposition heightened with the rise of publications such as *Priestcraft Unmasked* and in public debates over questions such as "Is Popery Compatible with Civil Liberty?" In 1834, following the appearance of a nun's alleged "confessions," a Boston mob set fire to a convent in Charlestown. The attacks soon spread nationwide, prompting insurance companies to refuse to insure Catholic buildings unless they were made of fireproof materials. Also in 1834, nearly a century before Henry Ford launched his attack on American Jews, inventor-industrialist Samuel F. B. Morse led his own campaign against immigrant Catholics, accusing them of being participants in a plot by the Pope to subvert American democracy and pave the way for papal rule. Morse's paranoid vision, published in two articles, "A Foreign Conspiracy Against the Liberties of the United States" and "Imminent Dangers to the Free Institutions of the United States Through Foreign Immigration," was widely disseminated and debated.

The controversy grew worse with the founding in 1841 of the American Protestant Union, headed by Morse and officially opposed to the "subjugation of our country to the control of the Pope of Rome, and his adherents," and, in 1844, erupted in violence in Philadelphia. The Philadelphia riots began with the destruction of Irish homes and spread to the burning of two local churches and widespread mob violence in which several people were killed. Foreshadowing later court battles, the violence grew out of a conflict over Bible-reading in schools and was one of the major factors leading to the establishment of the Catholic parochial school system.

By the 1850s, the Nativist movement had grown into a full-fledged anti-Catholic "Know-Nothing" Party, a nationwide, semi-secret political organization open only to American-born Protestants who were not married to Roman Catholics. Named after its members' universal answer to questions from outsiders, "I don't know," the Know-Nothings had their own oaths, rituals, passwords and initiation ceremonies. The central plank of their platform, as stated in Article II of the Party constitution, affirmed the group's objective "to resist the insidious policy of the Church of Rome" by electing to office "none but native-born Protestant citizens." The *Know-Nothing Almanac* was even more obsessive, embracing "Anti-Romanism . . . Anti-Pope's Toe-ism, Anti-Nunneryism, Anti-Winking Virginism, Anti-Jesuitism and Anti-the-Whole-Sacerdotal-Hierarchism with all its humbugging mummeries."

In one of the darker chapters of American politics, during the decade before the Civil War, Know-Nothing mobs ran roughshod over America. They tarred and feathered a priest in Maine, wrecked a chapel in New Hampshire, touched off street fights in New York City, and ignited an election riot in Kentucky in which twenty-two people were killed. By 1855, the Know-Nothing party claimed a million members and elected forty-three loyalists to the U.S. House of Representatives and five to the Senate. But the Know-Nothings also turned out to be Do-Nothings, accomplishing nothing of lasting legislative merit and sinking into oblivion with the ascendance of the slavery issue after 1856. Even so, following the Civil War, anti-Catholic feelings remained strong and were further inflamed by official Church pronouncements such as the Vatican Decree of Papal Infallibility of 1870, which caused many Protestants to question anew the allegiance of Catholics to American law and government.

And into the twentieth century, along with anti-Semitism, anti-Catholic sentiment persisted through the revival of the Ku Klux Klan and in widespread opposition to the 1928 presidential candidacy of New York Governor Alfred E. Smith, a Catholic. Suspicion lasted through the successful campaign of another Catholic, John F. Kennedy, in 1960. Even at that late date, on the eve of the liberating reforms of the Vatican II Council, Protestants with little understanding of Catholicism still perceived its authoritarian Church government as a threat to the security of the United

States. In a bold inquisitional session that foreshadowed elements of later election campaigns, candidate Kennedy was called to Texas to address a gathering of ministers to assure them that he did indeed believe in the separation of church and state and that, if elected, he had no intention of surrendering his responsibilities to the command of Rome. Dutifully, Kennedy pledged that as President he would make decisions on issues such as birth control, divorce, censorship and gambling "without regard to outside religious pressures or dictates." But he bridled at the ministers' intimidation during follow-up questioning, saying, "For while this year, it may be a Catholic against whom the finger of suspicion is pointed, in other years it has been, and may someday be again, a Jew—or a Quaker—or a Unitarian—or a Baptist." Despite their suspicions, Kennedy said, he refused to disavow his religious beliefs in order to win the election, adding:

> If I should lose on the real issues, I shall return to my seat in the Senate satisfied that I tried my best and was fairly judged. But if this election is decided on the basis that forty million Americans lost their chance of being President on the day they were baptized, it is the whole nation that will be the loser in the eyes of Catholics and non-Catholics around the world, in the eyes of history and in the eyes of our people.

We talked with many Catholics around the country, with priests, nuns and laymen, with traditional churchgoers and newly inspired charismatics, with liberal social activists and conservative pro-lifers, with proper Irish clerics in the Northeast and radical Chicano organizers in the Southwest. Their Church is no longer a monolith. Officially, all roads still lead to Rome, but even under its globe-trotting, telegenic Pope John Paul II, there is political division, theological dispute and a general dispersion of the faith. Some Catholics we spoke with viewed this as a positive trend: the Church adapting itself to modern realities. Others saw it as a danger sign, evidence that the Church is losing its grip on its people, especially its younger clergy and laymen. Many Catholics we spoke with were torn in their response to the fundamentalist right. Despite its overtures toward Catholics, many in the movement continue to attack the Pope and condemn Catholics as less than true Christians—a position most Catholics could not comprehend. Yet many we spoke with seemed reluctant to air their views. Among Catholics, more than most, the spirit of ecumenism still runs strong.

Our most enlightening view of how the Catholic Church has been caught in the squeeze of Holy Terror came in conversation with Monsignor Francis J. Lally, secretary of the United States Catholic Conference's Department of Social Development and World Peace. A prominent spokesman on behalf of social welfare, human rights and other issues of concern to American Catholics, like most Washington-based clergy active in political affairs, Msgr. Lally was troubled by the manner in which the fundamentalist right had seized the momentum of change. In published statements, he had called the idea of morality ratings "radically divisive" and warned that the fundamentalist right drive "could develop into a right-wing movement that is completely un-Christian." Yet, as we sat together, Lally, a broad, stately man dressed in a simple black suit and traditional white collar, was quick to acknowledge the right of fundamentalist preachers to join other ministers, priests and rabbis in the social and political process.

"They have every right to say their piece if they are speaking from what they believe to be an authentic religious position," said Msgr. Lally, his opening remark echoing Rabbi Brickner's perfunctory nod to the movement. However, that seemed to be the extent of Lally's agreement with the fundamentalist right. He wasted no more time getting to his concerns over the scriptural approach to politics.

"My anxiety is principally this," he said. "They derive their social response from a fundamentalist interpretation of the Bible. A very straightforward quotation brings them to a very straightforward conclusion of what the Lord intends. For us this is simplistic and unsophisticated and in the long run damaging. The mainline churches, ourselves included, have for many years been social development operations. We study social questions in the light of the gospels, to be sure, in the light of the values of the Christian faith. But we are not conclusion-jumpers. We do not leap directly from the text into action. Ours is a long, drawn-out *rational* process, a process of linking the revealed faith to a realistic position. That is a studied, analytical business—and it should be. These things are not simple. There are no easy answers. If you persuade people that there are, you are deceiving them."

Politely, Lally contrasted the Catholic view to that of many fundamentalist right preachers and politicians who adhere to the Word without benefit of what he called "mediating rationalizations."

"Do they really believe that the Scriptures contain the answers to all our present-day problems, without the aid of the physical sciences, the social sciences, the political sciences or economics?" he asked rhetorically. "Our position would be that that is naïve, that that is not the way the Scriptures should be read. We need those intermediate structures in order to find the implications of the gospel for contemporary life. We are in agreement that the Scriptures are the revealed Word of God, but in our methods of operation and our ideology, we are miles apart. They believe, sincerely, that the Bible is a direct guide for life. We feel it provides a *value background* against which you derive a social position."

That process of shaping a value background, as Lally went on to explain, lies at the heart of Catholic social and political philosophy.

"In our political activities, we hope to bring religious values into the world, into the marketplace, into the halls of Congress or wherever. But we are not interested in holding rallies on the back steps of the Capitol. We are interested in providing food and housing and employment in ways that will touch people's lives and help them build families and become decent human beings. We think this is the most successful way to realize the Christian ideal. Give people good homes, help make them productive people, give them a world they can be free in. We put a good deal more emphasis on that than on Scripture reading in Congress or prayer in the classroom."

We asked Lally where he would draw the line on the proper role of religion in politics.

"I think you have to be very careful about drawing that line," he said, "because there is always going to be a gray area between the two. It's a healthy gray area, an area of discussion. But I would say there are certain things the Church should not do. It must not seek to infringe on the rights of others, it must not try to pass a law that deprives people of their social and constitutional rights."

Lally was referring to some of the more extreme proposals of the fundamentalist right, particularly their attacks on homosexuals and their coolness in the area of civil rights. To our ears, however, his position sounded surprisingly similar to that of many pro-choice activists on the subject of a woman's right to have an abortion. We questioned him on the matter of joint Catholic-fundamentalist efforts to ban abortion. Lally stepped gingerly along the tightrope.

"I think that some of our right to life people are so very concerned about the right to life issue that they almost cross over the boundaries of appropriate political action," he said.

The dilemma again. Where would he draw that boundary line on this issue?

"I don't think that the Church should knock down abortion clinics," he said. "I think some pro-life people, Catholics and fundamentalists, have been exaggerated in their approach. I wouldn't follow their techniques, either. I think their techniques betray their cause."

What about the Human Life Amendment? Did he feel that seeking legislation of such doubtful constitutionality was a proper course for religious groups to take? In a seeming display of church-state schizophrenia, Lally sided with the fundamentalist right.

"The Church has asked for a constitutional amendment on that, through the proper channels," he said.

But wasn't he concerned that maintaining such a position could make Catholics easy prey for other fundamentalist right crusades?

"There's no question about that," he said, flipping back to the other side of the argument. "There's a great danger of Catholic pro-lifers getting caught up in the Moral Majority crowd. Many pro-lifers are paying very little attention to other right-wing positions they may be taking that are contrary to Catholic teachings on civil rights, on human rights and especially in their Neanderthal approach to social service."

We asked Lally for his views on the many Catholic charismatics in the fundamentalist camp. Did he see their newly adopted fundamentalist rituals as similarly contrary to Catholic teaching?

"Oh, I think if you accused Catholic charismatics of being fundamentalists, they would be very unhappy," he said. "They would say, 'I'm nothing of the kind. I'm very proud that I am a Catholic and of the tradition I come out of.'"

Yet his view of the revival was mixed. "I think that some charismatics have come very close to fundamentalism in some of their liturgical prayers and so on," he admitted. "This is a real anxiety for us. We are pleased that they come to their experience from our tradition, but it's true, some Catholics have gone over the balance point, and when they move into that fundamentalist, simplistic experience without rationalization, it becomes dangerous."

As in the international issues we discussed with Rabbi Brickner, the larger subject we sought to take up with Lally was the general area of Christian evangelization. Catholic orders pioneered the spreading of the gospel to remote corners of the world, and we respectfully pointed out that, in days gone by, the Catholic Church had led the league in involuntary conversions. Did the Church have some hard-won wisdom to offer the brash new fundamentalist armies deploying around the world? Instead of backing away from the issue, as we thought he might, Lally reminded us that the Catholic Church had certainly not gone out of the missionary business.

"No church is going to turn its back on evangelization," he said. "The preaching of the gospel, the presentation of the Good News of salvation, the process of conversion is an essential part of the Christian message. Now we do not believe in imposing the faith through forced or fraudulent means, but we do maintain that the gospel must be preached and that people should be given an opportunity to accept it."

He contrasted the Catholic approach to that of fundamentalist missionaries. His view was directly opposite of the one we heard at Christian Broadcasting Network and Campus Crusade for Christ headquarters.

"We recognize that many cultures of the Third World react badly to missionary efforts, and we have very few missionaries in countries where they are not welcome, in Islamic nations, for example, or in parts of Africa. We seldom go where we are just tolerated or where there is tension. They would see us as bringing American values into a world that does not want to accept them.

We still have many missionaries in Latin American countries that are almost totally Catholic, but they are not down there to change people's religion. They are down there to help: to build schools and clinics, to assist people in changing their oppressive living conditions and institutions. The old-style Protestant and Methodist missionaries did these same practical things, helping people to help themselves, bringing in modern wells and irrigation. Today's straight fundamentalist missionary effort is more apt to be more of a mere recruitment and conversion operation than a broad attempt to raise the level of the people and improve the quality of life."

As Lally talked, we took note of striking similarities and differences among various Catholic and fundamentalist views. Yet, in this one conversation, we saw many signs of the intense conflict between liberal and conservative forces within the Church itself. In closing, Lally expressed satisfaction with how far the Church had come in recent years, along with his hope for where it may be heading in the future.

"The Church has learned to change with history," he said, "to respond with time to changes in culture and civilization, in technology and human understanding, in knowledge and science. We change with all of these, adapting the essential gospel to the period in which we live. Our confidence is that the Church and its message will adapt, will seek new truths and make them part of our ongoing faith. But we must keep the human person at the forefront of our thoughts. He is the one who must be served."

Protestants. Jewish opposition to the fundamentalist right and its political and religious proselytizing might be expected. Catholic collusion on the pro-life issue is also predictable. We ran into some of the biggest surprises of our investigation, however, while sampling the range of opinion within America's Protestant community. The nation's Protestants are too many and too diverse to be considered as a single religious bloc. Rather, they make up a collection of blocs so varied in their doctrines, social status and political outlooks that, as a group, they seem less like a close-knit family than a get-together of distant cousins. Like all relatives, they have their disagreements, but on one subject we found a remarkable degree of solidarity: most Protestant denominations oppose the goals and methods of the fundamentalist right.

Some of the protest comes from obvious critics. Spokesmen for the liberal National Council of Churches, an association of thirty-two Protestant denominations representing over 40 million churchgoers, have sharply denounced the Moral Majority and the political maneuverings of the new right. In New York, we spoke with William F. Fore, director of communications for the NCC, who wrote an early article deriding the electronic church for driving religious diversity off the air and, in the long run, misleading far more people than it helps or heals. In person, Fore was even more critical, accusing the fundamentalist right of exploiting the media and the public in its efforts to build a political power base. "It's not religion, for heaven's sake," he said, "it's the worst form of blasphemy to do all these terrible things to people in the name of God and Jesus and the Bible."

We heard similar responses from other Protestant leaders. In Boston, an Anglican minister we met on Beacon Hill saw the nation's politicized preachers as "self-deceivers" and their electronic ministry as "a truncated concept of a church." Of their approach to the Bible, he said, "It boggles the mind." Of their politics, he lamented, "We cannot use those tactics and be true to our calling as Christians. In the long run, they will destroy Christianity rather than protect it. The harm they are doing may never be undone."

Yet Moral Majority and other fundamentalist right groups feed on this kind of criticism from liberal churchmen in the Northeast. What they have been unable to cope with is the mounting backlash from closer Christian relations. Since 1980, the flow of criticism from broad-based moderate and conservative denominations has been constant. One statement, issued by spokesmen for thirteen Christian organizations, including the United Church of Christ, the Christian Church (Disciples of Christ), the United Presbyterian Church of the USA, the American Baptist Churches, the Lutheran Council USA, the United Methodist Church, the Christian Methodist Episcopal Church and the Evangelical Covenant Church, assailed the selection of issues by the new right as "theologically and ethically inadequate." Attacking the narrow range of fundamentalist right interests, their joint message declared that "an agenda identified by Christian believers ought to reflect God's concern for the whole world," adding:

There is no place in a Christian manner of political life for arrogance, manipulation, subterfuge or holding others' sin in contempt. There is no justification in a pluralistic and democratic society for demands for conformity along religious or ideological lines.

Even within the ranks of the nation's largest Protestant denomination, the Southern Baptist Convention, which is often linked to the independent Baptist ministers of the new right, there has been outspoken opposition. Rev. Jimmy Allen, past president of the 13-million-member group, called the political activities of the fundamentalist right "divisive and ultimately damaging to both religion and government." In a prepared comment, Allen railed against the "total capitulation of a segment of the evangelical Christian movement to right-wing politics and sword-rattling jingoism."

It was in these comments and others by conservative Baptists that we began to see just how lonely the fundamentalist right's position is in the larger Christian world. In its numbers games and media wars, the movement has convinced many Americans and, apparently, many politicians as well, that its brand of religious and political fundamentalism is broadly shared in the heartland. The real picture is quite the opposite. On nearly all grounds, the fundamentalist right seems to be an isolated minority. Traditionally, of course, America's born agains have been apolitical to a fault, and the fundamentalist right has been successful in mobilizing them only to the degree that they have exploited their deeper supernatural and other-worldly urges. But the limits of that exploitation are lower than generally presumed—and dwindling. For as many non-Christians may be surprised to learn, most evangelicals are not fundamentalists. Moreover, the alleged theological base of the political movement has virtually no grounding in Christian tradition. In fact, most Christians view fundamentalism as an aberration of their faith. As one prominent Southern Baptist Bible translator said of the fundamentalist approach to Scriptures: "Only willful ignorance or intellectual dishonesty can account for the claim that the Bible is inerrant and infallible. No truth-loving, God-respecting, Christ-honoring believer should be guilty of such heresy."

Americans United. The thought that even conservative Christians would denounce the fundamentalist right outlook never occurred to us until we began talking with Baptist ministers. Baptists, as it turns out, were America's first champions of religious liberty. Their commitment dates back to Roger Williams, the dissident Englishman who was tossed out of Massachusetts in 1636 and went on to found the first Baptist church in America. Williams was soon joined in Rhode Island by another Englishman, John Clarke, a Baptist preacher who, like Williams, had been appalled by the established intolerance of the Massachusetts Puritans. A century later, yet another Baptist minister, Isaac Backus, led the fight against taxation for the support of established churches, representing the New England Baptists at the Constitutional Convention in Philadelphia and at the Massachusetts ratifying convention, where he staunchly defended the article banning religious tests for public officials. "And let the history of all nations be searched, from that day to this," Backus declared, "and it will appear that the imposing of religious tests hath been the greatest single engine of tyranny in the world."

The Baptists fought for religious freedom on many fronts. In the late 1770s, Rev. John Leland, chairman of the general committee of Baptists in Virginia, spoke frequently before the state assembly, arguing for the overthrow of the established Church of England. Throughout the colonial period, Baptists had been widely discriminated against in Virginia by the dominant class-conscious Episcopalians who, among other injustices, prohibited Baptists from preaching in certain meetinghouses, from performing legally recognized marriages and from preaching to the troops during the Revolution. In 1785, joining Methodists, Presbyterians and other minority denominations, they defeated the state General Assessment Bill for the support of Christian teachers. Then finally, under Leland, they lobbied successfully for the disestablishment of the state church.

Mindful of those early discriminations and their hard fight for equality, Baptists remained firmly committed to the principle of church-state separation. Through stormy generations, including the North-South split over the slavery issue during the Civil War and the subsequent splintering and fragmentation of Baptist belief into varying conventions and independent churches, the commitment survived. And it was passed down to present-day groups such as the Baptist Joint Committee on Public Affairs, established in 1939, and other organizations which sometimes find themselves siding with groups whose beliefs are vastly at odds with their own, but with whom they share unwavering devotion to the principle of church-state separation.

Such is the case with Americans United for the Separation of Church and State, a nonprofit, nonpartisan, nonsectarian organization whose current executive director, Rev. R. G. Puckett, happens to be a Baptist minister. Americans United is no overnight sensation. It has been around thirty-five years and has more than 100,000 members of every persuasion—and some of no persuasion. Founded in 1947, the group was born of a joint effort by conservative Christians to resist what they saw as a threat to the separation principle in a campaign undertaken by the Catholic Church to obtain tax funds for aid to their parochial schools. In those days, before the rise of the fundamentalist schools movement, the Catholic effort was strongly opposed by nearly every other denomination, as was a similar proposal then under consideration by the Truman administration to send an official U.S. ambassador to the Vatican. The group's early days were marred by bad publicity, however, for in its original inception it had a faintly nativist ring, opposing Catholic initiatives under the name Protestants and Other Americans United for the Separation of Church and State.

"The lack of wisdom in the title soon became apparent," Rev. Puckett said diplomatically as we traced the history of the group over coffee in his office in Silver Spring, Maryland. A mild-mannered, pleasant-looking man, Puckett's involvement with Americans United is fairly recent (he has been director only since 1977). A Southern Baptist minister for more than thirty years, he was not around in the early days when some of the nation's most respected Protestants—including Baptists, Methodists, a U.S. senator and the president of the Princeton Seminary—formed the coalition whose name and initial activities gave the group an anti-Catholic image.

"It really was a terrible liability," said Puckett, "because the people who shared our views were not necessarily Protestants. The Catholic Church pounced on us immediately, but it wasn't until the late sixties that they changed the name, mainly because the Catholic Church began shifting its positions. Then, as it turned out, we found a lot of lay Catholics who agreed with us. There was Justice Brennan on the Supreme Court, a practicing Roman Catholic whose position was identical to ours. When Father Drinan, a Jesuit priest, was in Congress, his position and mine were identical."

Since coming to his job, Puckett told us, he had been "bending over backward" to soften the group's image and, in the process, gained support from both the Catholic and Jewish communities. Today, Americans United serves as a roving watchdog of religious liberty: initiating lawsuits and leading legal battles from local levels up to the Supreme Court, and disseminating a broad selection of materials supporting their view that government should not intrude in the internal affairs of churches or other religious groups, and that, in return, churches and religions should remain wholly nonpolitical. The group's tradition, Puckett pointed out, was not only in line with the Framers, but a reaffirmation of the historical Baptist "witness" of religious freedom. As our talk turned to the preachers of the fundamentalist right and their political ambitions, Puckett explained how, from his conservative standpoint, their platform was blasphemous.

"Now, I have said this publicly," he announced, eager to go on record, "the fact that the far right evangelical community went political is an admission that they have failed in the proclamation of the gospel! They won't admit it. But that is the case. You see, historically, the evangelical posture has been 'to believe the Bible literally, to preach the gospel enthusiastically, to convert people genuinely,' and only *then* to expect changed people to change society. That's the tradition of evangelicalism. It's as orthodox as you can get. Now suddenly, the fundamentalists have set all that in second place and gone out there to capture the political arena through congressional candidates and an executive branch which they hope will implement the legislation they want."

This turn, stressed Puckett, amounted to a confession that their fundamentalist vision was bankrupt. He restated the Americans United position.

"We believe in the absolute separation of church and state," he said. "We firmly believe that there must be a public morality, but that public morality must not be a Roman Catholic morality, or a Southern Baptist morality or a Jewish morality. It must be arrived at through a public forum to which all of us have a right to come."

Despite his traditional evangelical position, Puckett did not hold to the old idea that Christians should shun the political process. "I believe a good Christian also ought to be a good citizen," he said, "but let it be said, too, that if you are a believer and your faith means anything at all to you, you will bring your value system out of that faith to your political involvement. You won't bring it under a religious label. You'll bring it as an individual who has a value system—regardless of where it came from."

His argument was sound, virtually identical to Msgr. Lally's idea of a "value background" and to Rabbi Brickner's call to "rerationalize" the religious approach to life. The fundamentalist right position, however, seemed to us, by definition, to pose a barrier to that kind of larger dialogue. We asked Puckett how Christians wedded to a literalist interpretation of the Bible could extract a personal value system and then bring it to a larger, pluralistic arena.

"I don't think they can," said Puckett. "That's the problem. The adherence of the far right to the literal word of the Bible is so fundamental that they'll never pull away from it. If they did, it would shatter their whole position. They just don't think that way. The Bible to them is the supreme authority. Their security as Christians comes from their literal interpretation."

It was a revealing insight into the fundamentalist right mind-set. As Puckett talked, we came to see more clearly the role of the Bible in the movement's overall scheme of control.

"Of course, I, too, have a deep commitment to the Bible," said Puckett. "I, too, see it as the authoritative, inspired, revealed Word of God. But the problem with the fundamentalists—and most of them aren't even aware of it—is that they are really contradicting their own theology. They make the Bible more important than God! The common phrase is *bibliolatry*. Now, the average Christian believes very deeply in the Bible, but he hasn't made it into God. You see? That's what we're really talking about with the fundamentalists. They have not made the distinction. They are guilty of bibliolatry. They'll deny it, but they are."

Bibliolatry—a fundamental error, and an explanation for much of what we had observed. In describing the fundamentalist mindset, Puckett also drew a distinction for us between the character of the nationally organized, democratically governed Baptist conventions, within which heated debates over biblical inerrancy were raging, and the independent Baptist movement, a loose-knit network of nonaffiliated churches from which many fundamentalist right leaders had emerged.

"You have to understand the structure of a church like Falwell's," he said. "These are—this sounds like an ugly phrase and I don't mean it to be ugly—but they are personality cults. The church is centered in the pastor. He *is* the authority, the ruling force. Falwell, Robison, Robertson, all the rest—these are personality cults. People follow the person, the pastor, not Jesus Christ. He may say he is not telling anyone how to vote or how to live, but the very climate and mentality of the whole church says: what the pastor wants is what we do."

Puckett's words played in our minds as we reviewed our travels to Virginia Beach, where Pat Robertson's voice and image hung in the air like an apparition; to Lynchburg, where Jerry Falwell was grooming a "disciplined, charging army" of prayer warriors in his image; to San Diego, where Tim LaHaye's hatred of the secular world permeated his church, college and creationist institute; to the San Bernardino hills, where obliging Campus Crusade officials spoke reverently of their unordained minister and mimicked his businesslike, counterrevolutionary style. As we had asked others, we asked Puckett for his outlook on the future of religion in America.

"Well, now you have moved into an area of my greatest concern," he said. "I fear a sharp reaction to what's taking place. I fear it will end up harming legitimate, responsible religious groups. And I fear it will fuel an anti-church mentality across America."

Most endangered of all, said Puckett, was evangelical Christianity itself. By reducing the timeless Christian message to one of hardened bibliolatry and ruthless political action, the fundamentalist right now threatened to bring down the backlash so few of its leaders or followers could even envision. R. G. Puckett wanted no part of it.

"We must remember that Christians are a minority in the world," he said. "We don't like to think so, but we are. And we're just denying reality if we think we can impose our particular plan on all the nation and ultimately all the world. We're giving an open invitation to a sharp reaction, and I fear it will be forthcoming."

The only way to prevent it, according to Puckett, was to fight for another kind of literalness: to take the Founding Fathers at their word when they spoke of religious liberty for all Americans.

"That's all we're here for, to retain the pluralism of American society," said Puckett with a gentle smile. "I hope we're doing a service for people."

Despite R. G. Puckett's best intentions, despite the best intentions of everyone we spoke with on this emotionally exhausting tour, that structure of pluralism seemed to be crumbling. We listened respectfully to the lamentations of priests, rabbis and ministers. What we heard, in unison, was how much each faith valued pluralism and the root principles of American democracy. Their shared views on the proper role of religion in politics and American life painted a hopeful picture of mankind progressing through joint caring and commitment toward fulfillment.

Looking at this glowing picture, it was hard to imagine the fundamentalist right splitting these united ranks. But it had. We saw how, not in interviews with clergy but in informal talks with their followers. Across all faiths, Americans we talked with spoke of intense personal conflicts and struggles among their churches in undertones of disdain. Members of every religion still seemed to judge each other in old patterns of hostility and historical prejudice. Like the wall of church-state separation that guaranteed their religious freedom, the surviving barriers among Americans of different faiths seemed to be equally high and impregnable. In many places we visited, they made up the face of religion itself, standing as firm among clergy as in their congregations.

Despite our common vows of tolerance and pluralism, it seems, as Americans we don't much like one another's beliefs. Across all faiths, we share, not mutual acceptance, but religious prejudices that appear scarcely diminished after 200 years. In the end, this may be the secret source of power the fundamentalist right has

PART II

COVERT OPERATIONS

Covert Operations

Nothing is worse in times of danger than to live in a dream world. To warn a political system of the menace hanging over it does not imply an attack against it, but is the greatest service one can render the system. The same goes for man: to warn him of his weakness is not to attempt to destroy him, but rather to encourage him to strengthen himself.

—JACQUES ELLUL—*Propaganda*

WITH TEN THOUSAND MILES behind us, we sought refuge on a tiny island off the East Coast, where we began to decode the signs of Holy Terror we had brought back. Our talks with mainline clergy had put a stamp of currency on the mixing of religion and politics in America. Almost without exception, we found, religions that have shown concern for the development of this country have done so with a shared commitment to principles of individual growth and social progress. Indeed, those religions that have flourished in America have done so because, regardless of their separate origins or exclusive doctrines, they have built bridges to the larger world and stretched to meet the demands of change.

Traditionally, religion has offered people valuable instruction in how to conduct themselves as members of a society. Those religions whose beliefs were compatible with America's commitment to the common good came forward in mutual respect, if not in shared affection, while those religions with different values and priorities tended to withdraw from society and pursue their separate courses. The fundamentalist right, however, has chosen a third route. Although it stands opposed to so much that is

America, it has not withdrawn passively like its traditional forerunners. But rather, it has recoiled angrily, only to spring forth with zeal. The holy war it has declared on·society is something new, but in our view it is not a new turn in religion. It is a new wrinkle in an old strain buried deep within the American character.

In our months on the road, we saw many of its effects in the anguish and bewilderment of people and in the affairs of our country, which seemed to be succumbing to fundamentalist right intimidation as an inevitable and acceptable thing. We did not see it as either inevitable or acceptable. As we came to grasp the network—the linkup of ministries, missions, PACs and nonprofit foundations—we came to see the movement as a whole of interrelated tactics and technology, a full-fledged system of social and political terrorism.

Here was no cult or conspiracy as traditionally defined. Practically speaking, the fundamentalist right juggernaut was just too big, too complex and too sophisticated to fit either term. Its membership was too diverse and spread out. Its leadership had already penetrated the highest levels of society. Theirs was no underground network. On the contrary, it craved exposure. Yet behind all this up-front openness hung a larger curtain, a clandestine quality that we detected everywhere. Before long, we came to see the men and machinery of Holy Terror as engaged in one giant covert operation: most of them projecting on-camera, in person and through the mails a carefully crafted image of religiosity and morality, of public directness and personal candor; yet masking an arsenal of communication strategies that may mislead, distort, deceive, manipulate or coerce by *indirection*. As the movement's distinguishing quality, we found the use of indirect tactics and technology had spread to every level of fundamentalist right activity, private and public, social and political, affecting equally individuals, groups, mass audiences and the nation as a whole.

In this hierarchy of covert operations, we can begin to understand the system of Holy Terror. It is a system of *terrorism by communication,* a plan of social and political control using, not guns, bombs or other physical implements, but *information:* symbols, statements, images, myths, coded messages and other meanings. It works, not by violence, but in casual exchanges between individuals, in private encounters and in expressly public media, marketing and mass-communications campaigns. The instruments of Holy Terror may be as hard as copper wires and computer consoles, as remote as satellite parking spaces on the road to the moon. But their impact is as soft as a touch, as fleeting as a picture in the mind's eye, as intangible as a quiet suggestion slipping undetected through a barrage of noise.

By these means, in the eighties, the fundamentalist right has become an intrusion in all our lives. Its leaders have not confined their interests to religion, nor have they stayed within the historical framework of religious participation in politics. Instead, they have seized the flow of information, of everyday messages and meanings, in an orchestrated attempt to impose their beliefs on *all* Americans. But in many ways, their crusade has been ongoing. From the beginning of American fundamentalism, many fundamentalist groups and leaders have moved in this way to force themselves on the larger society. Early on, they embraced the confrontational style of evangelism most practice today. Since the dawn of the electronic age, they have breached the ethics of the nation's airwaves. These practices alone have removed fundamentalism from the domain of private belief and thrust it into the public sector. And with their latest incursions into the political arena, fundamentalist leaders have made their religion urgent public business. It is this threat to individual freedom and our system of self-government that leads us to examine the new fundamentalism, not as a mode of religious belief, but as a system of manipulation, and as a political movement with avowed authoritarian aspirations.

THE SYNDROME OF IDEOLOGICAL FUNDAMENTALISM

To begin, then, we consider the movement's seat of power in this variation on the theme of Christianity. Most people think of religious fundamentalism as a primitive social trait, a dying holdout from an earlier age. But fundamentalism is not an old-world tradition. For two thousand years, there have been contentious rifts, cleavages, rebellions and reformations within the Christian faith.

There has been endless argument over the origin and authority of the Bible, its divinely inspired nature and its meaning in the light of history and human progress. But only in recent times has there been a movement whose theological platform has only one plank: the elevation of the Scriptures to a position of supernatural authority over all matters of faith, knowledge and everyday life. It is in this unquestioning adoration of the Scriptures that fundamentalists part company with other Christians.

As it turns out, this knot in the line of Christianity has little to do with religion and much to do with modern society. Fundamentalism began as a reaction to the material, educational and social demands of an increasingly technological world, and it continues to thrive on the conflict. In principle, the reaction was conceived as a revolt against "modernism" in Christian theology, but in fact, then as today, it was largely a recoding of social and political disputes in religious terms. Jerry Falwell is more or less in agreement on this point. In his 1981 book *The Fundamentalist Phenomenon,* edited by Falwell but written by two faculty members of his Liberty Baptist College, the authors select earlier definitions of fundamentalism as a movement distinguished by its "militant opposition of liberalism"—viewed here in large part as modernist "accommodation to cultural change." With his own movement in mind, however, Falwell unflinchingly recasts fundamentalism as "reactionary evangelicalism," as he describes it, a revolt against the spread of "rationalism" and "secularism" in modern society.

The organized movement itself is quite young, a twentieth-century and almost exclusively American invention. Although Falwell and others have attempted to place their brand of fundamentalism in direct line with nonconformist European sects such as Mennonites, Baptists, Quakers and others, most old world breakaway groups were born of theological disputes (over ecclesiastical rules, infant baptism and other modes of worship) and today stand apart from fundamentalism in both their beliefs and politics. The American movement has followed an almost completely separate line of descent. Anti-modernist, anti-liberal and anti-scientific sentiments had been brewing in the United States through most of the latter nineteenth century, but the reaction itself was ignited only in 1909. That year two Christian laymen began publication of a series of twelve booklets, *The Fundamentals,* which were intended to "set forth the fundamentals of the Christian faith" as derived from a strict literal interpretation of the Bible. Over the next ten years, some three million copies of *The Fundamentals* were sent to ministers, evangelists, missionaries, scholars and "others engaged in aggressive Christian work," succeeding in their time, as fundamentalist right manifestos such as Tim LaHaye's *Battle for the Mind* have today, in fueling hostility between isolationist Christians and a bewildered secular world.

The actual fundamentals seemed traditional enough: belief in the deity of Christ, his virgin birth, the "substitutionary atonement" of his death, the notion of his resurrection from the dead, along with the forecast of his Second Coming. What made these beliefs unique, however, was the fundamentalist demand that Christians accept the Bible as "revealed, inspired, infallible and inerrant."

In their reaction to the modern world, the new fundamentalists not only embraced wholeheartedly the documented errors and contradictions of the Scriptures, but discarded more than two thousand years of biblical scholarship and painstaking efforts by theologians in every era to restate the wisdom of the Bible in terms sensible to their times. The new fundamentalists categorically opposed this time-honored tradition of interpretation, proclaiming their splinter movement to be a test of "true" Christian faith. Their five-fingered gauntlet dared Christians to accept the entire Bible as literal *fact:* to grant the literal existence of Jesus Christ as an eternal living being, to believe in the literal reality of heaven and hell, to fear the literal temptation of the person of Satan, to embrace the literal account of creation—and to await the literal end of the world. On every point, the fundamentalist command was for the true Christian to obey or be damned: to deny the weight of history, science, logic and the reality of everyday life.

As intended, the challenge pressed many Christians against a wall of inner conflict. Pushed to absolute limits, many rejected more moderate beliefs they had held their whole lives and took refuge from the onrushing complexities and anxieties of the twentieth century. In its condemnation of reason, its vivid appeal to the supernatural and its warlike attack on liberal churches and the modern world in general, the new fundamentalism quickly became an institutionalized force. Like all popular reactions, however, the movement was only as strong as its ability to confront and attack, to instill fear and fire dormant passions and thereby cause its numbers to swell. The new fundamentalists, of course, saw it from another angle. They took the position that it was their beliefs and values that were being assaulted. As Falwell described it: "It was the threat of a common enemy that caused Bible-believing Christians from every conceivable kind of denominational background to form a mutual alliance of self-defense."

And to some degree, they were right. Only the "common enemy" was no persecuting group or government but the growth in human understanding. In the beginning, it was evolution, the first single-issue cause of the fundamentalist right. Like the pro-life issue today, the controversy over Darwinian theory, at once scientific and theological, provided an ideal vehicle for recruiting grass-roots Christians with little understanding of the facts in the case. Highly emotional, as simple as the opening sentence of the Bible, the ruckus attracted many to fundamentalism and drew increasing public attention to the movement, culminating in the 1925 Scopes "monkey trial" in Dayton, Tennessee. The case itself was incidental—a local school teacher was charged with blasphemy—but the drama found an all-star cast in acclaimed trial lawyer Clarence Darrow and ardent fundamentalist, former presidential candidate William Jennings Bryan. The jury of twelve farmers convicted Scopes, but the court of public opinion decided for Darrow. His deft cross-examination of Bryan, conducted before a hundred reporters, impaled the flamboyant fundamentalist on his own biblical claims and brought nationwide humiliation to the crusade.

After the Scopes trial, most Americans assumed that the movement had been permanently repudiated and that fundamentalism as a religious position was a dying, if not long-dead, issue. In fact, the movement was not dead but merely thrown back, forced underground and, if anything, hardened in its reactionary stance. In the thirties, the movement began its formal split from the larger body of evangelical Christianity, establishing a small but fiercely independent network of churches, seminaries and foreign missions. Over the next two decades, the new fundamentalism began its love affair with the mass media, beginning with Rev. Charles E. Fuller's "Old-Fashioned Revival Hour" on radio, the weekly publication of John R. Rice's *Sword of the Lord* magazine, and the Moody Bible Institute's popular home correspondence school.

By the late forties, the movement had bounced back stronger than ever and was becoming openly political. No longer taken seriously in mainline religious circles, it had built up considerable grass-roots strength, which it began to channel into a renewed bid for social dominance. This first incarnation of the fundamentalist right as we know it today was born of modern postwar passions and delivered in the same bundle with the anti-Communist fever of the McCarthy era. The drive was led by ultrafundamentalists Rev. Carl McIntire, founder of the Faith Theological Seminary in Philadelphia and the International Council of Christian Churches (a fundamentalist foe of the liberal World Council of Churches), and by the notorious Rev. Billy James Hargis of Tulsa, Oklahoma, founder in 1948 of the Christian Crusade, a multimedia campaign to stamp out "godless Communists" and other religious "apostates." McIntire and Hargis, like a fifties' Falwell and Robison team, rode to national prominence atop more than a million six-foot helium balloons, which they launched to carry pages from the Bible into countries behind the Iron Curtain. Later, the duo took on the United Nations and the National Council of Churches, while Hargis opened a second front, attacking new trends in sex education. Throughout the sixties and into the early seventies, McIntire and Hargis nursed the fundamentalist right through its clamorous infancy. Hargis' best-selling book *Is the School House the Proper Place to Teach Raw Sex?* made him a favorite across the Bible Belt and in the Christian media, until his crusade went down amid allegations that he had had sexual relations with members of his All-American Kids chorus, and with both a young man and a young woman at whose marriage he later officiated.

Over the years, many accusations have been made against the fundamentalist crusade, but none strikes as close to home as those leveled at its religious pretenses. As Darrow did in the Scopes trial, numerous scholars, philosophers and theologians have exploded fundamentalist beliefs, puncturing them on points of reason, science, history and religion itself. The response of Christian scholars has been the most damaging. One of the foremost critics of fundamentalism has been Oxford professor James Barr, a theologian and Bible scholar who observed the movement firsthand when he lectured and taught at Princeton Theological Seminary, Union Theological Seminary, Princeton University and the University of Chicago. In his 1977 book, titled simply *Fundamentalism*, Barr excoriated the movement, calling it "a pathological condition of Christianity." While admitting that, to a large degree, fundamentalism and evangelicalism share the same conceptual base, Barr stressed the differences between the two and declared that "fundamentalism distorts and betrays the basic true religious concerns of evangelical Christianity." Instead of seeking the "warm, living gospel," said Barr, fundamentalism had become cold and hardened in its doctrines. In its reaction against the modern world, he said, it had unfairly rejected all outsiders as "carnal" Christians. Trapped by New Testament commands that a person can achieve salvation only by being born again, fundamentalists denied the larger Christian notion that, ultimately, men shall be judged by their good works. The fundamentalist alternative, said Barr, is no alternative at all, but a "fossilized," "fragmented," "inactive," "theology-less" body of doctrines maintained with unbending rigidity for fear that one tap at the foundation might cause the entire brittle framework to fall apart.

Yet, in Barr's view, that framework was ramshackle to begin with, a haphazard and arbitrary structure. Barr pointed out the selective nature of fundamentalist literalism. While other devout Christians shy away from the material world, he said, fundamentalists rush to embrace it, as we have seen, incorporating new technology and modern marketing strategies into their no-holds-barred crusades. At the same time, while fundamentalists reject the "social gospel" of good works, they exalt the political and economic gospels of nationalism, republicanism and free-enterprise capitalism. Following this trail of discrepancies, Barr was prompted to wonder:

> Does it [fundamentalism] really preach a gospel of salvation for men? Or does it use the gospel as a weapon in an ideological conquest of man?

Even Jerry Falwell, in his bid to establish himself as chief theorist and unifier of the movement, appears to view the entire history of fundamentalism in political terms. In his fundamentalist vision, Americans have been recast as God's "modern-day 'chosen people,' to be used as a vehicle for His purposes." Militarism is glorified as "the means of defending the peace so that law and order may prevail, allowing Christians the freedom to spread the message of Jesus Christ to the world." To these ends, says Falwell, fundamentalists have always been engaged in "infiltrating the grass roots of America," not to control the nation, he insists, but "to see freedom preserved so that the work of the gospel may go on unhindered in the generations ahead."

In the eighties, with this marriage of religion and politics fully consummated, the threat of the fundamentalist right has emerged full-blown, and its arrival on the national scene has coincided with the blossoming of similar fundamentalist hybrids around the world. In our view, the trend defines a broad *syndrome of ideological fundamentalism,* a movement of supernatural pretensions and real-world dangers that can be examined as a phenomenon per se: a comprehensive personal, social and political reaction to a modern world in the process of change.

The thrust of the reaction is not merely one of public *persuasion* but one of *control.* As we have observed it in the United States, the fundamentalist right does not want to influence beliefs and opinions by means of reason and argument. Its leaders want to *rule by indirection* and in the process convert the larger society to a mind-set beyond reason. Before considering their grand social and political designs, however, we must explore the manner in which movement leaders use practices from religion in ways that, we believe, describe a dangerous new form of personal manipulation.

The heart of the syndrome can be found in this program of indirect control at the individual level. Across the spectrum of the movement, we have found widespread use of covert communication techniques that, in our view, undermine vital human processes of thought and feeling. To better understand the syndrome and its implications for both religion and politics, we turn to a step-by-step examination of the fundamentalist program and its covert methods.

The Seeds of Suggestion. In recent years, leading fundamentalist groups in America have adapted techniques from the business of advertising for purposes of evangelization. In practice, these groups and their leaders seldom distinguish between advertising and evangelization, yet the two ventures are human enterprises of vastly different orders. Advertising, as it has been developed in this country, focuses on a person's buying choice. Simply stated, its goal is to make money in exchange for some material good or service. Fundamentalist evangelism, on the other hand, seeks more than mere money or consumer behavior. By definition, its aim is to effect a life-changing personal commitment.

Similarly, the means by which the two operations are carried out are altogether different. Advertising, for the most part, relies on direct methods: on the presentation of documented facts, claims and benefits. Even its emotional appeals are fairly simple and straightforward. In contrast, the fundamentalist endeavor is, by its nature, indirect. The spiritual facts, claims and benefits it makes cannot be documented. Its appeal to unquestioning faith confounds the process of informed decision-making, and its use of suggestion is almost always covert, mixed into supernatural terms, symbols, images and myths. These spiritual matters are heady stuff to treat like just another business, yet many fundamentalist enterprises have reduced these high matters to such mundane levels.

By these means, across most of America, the seeds of ideological fundamentalism are sown in personal contacts on a one-to-one basis. Like any good salesman, the fundamentalist "witness" begins his thrust in casual conversations that appear to be straightforward, but are often designed to disguise the intent of conversion. In many instances, the process is one of subtle deceptions and misrepresentations, methods in which popular guidebooks in evangelism appear to give explicit instruction. One leading paperback, *Disciples Are Made—Not Born,* which has sold more than 300,000 copies through Christian bookstores and other outlets, counsels witnesses in indirect methods of making contact and building rapport. As his first of many "Principles in Evangelism," the author advises readers to "Open the opportunity by asking a favor." He continues:

In making friends with people, there are many things we can do to make them feel important. On the ski slopes or on the golf course, you could say to someone, "Say, I noticed you are really proficient at this. I wonder if you could spare a few moments to give me some tips on how to improve my style." A housewife can use the same approach with her neighbor by asking to borrow a recipe or a cup of flour. . . . It is probably not the best approach to walk up to a stranger and say something to the effect, "Do you want to be saved?"

Similarly, a Campus Crusade for Christ training manual coaches recruiters in a variety of seemingly impromptu conversation starters, among them:

To a neighbor: "Hi, my name is _____. How long have you lived here?"
To a fellow traveler: "Hello. Where are you traveling to?"
Waitress, service station attendant or other sales person: "How do you like working here?"
Others: "Do you live in this city or area?"
"What do you do for a living?"
"How is the (name of activity—fishing, football game, etc.) coming along?"

After making a friendly approach, witnesses are advised to come to the point by circuitous means:

Through the use of simple transitions, you can easily turn the topic of conversation to Jesus Christ. . . . Talk about current world problems and ask them if they see any likely solutions. They will usually ask you the same questions, which will enable you to share the *Four Spiritual Laws* and your personal testimony.

Other transitions include personal and casual approaches common to advertising strategies, such as: "Would you help me by giving me your opinion of this little booklet?" and "Do you ever think about spiritual things?"

In contrast to these methodical operations, most groups in the Hebrew-Christian branch of the movement resort to greater subterfuges in the face of more formidable obstacles to conversion. For example, a booklet written by Moishe Rosen, head of Jews

for Jesus, cautions witnesses to be alert to "Jewish sensitivities"
and to avoid all terms that have "a negative emotional valence"
such as "Born again—Blood of the Lamb—Trinity—Cross—Church
—Christian—Convert—Saved." A Messianic Jewish Movement International training manual is even more explicit:

> AVOID DISPLAYING PICTURES OF JESUS OR STATUES . . .
> AVOID DISPLAYING CROSSES . . .
> AVOID JOKES ABOUT THE JEWISH PEOPLE (THEIR MONEY,
> ETC.) . . .
> AVOID ANTI-SEMITIC (ANTI-JEWISH) TERMS; SUCH AS . . .
> "CHRIST-KILLERS" . . . "DIRTY JEW" . . . "JEW BOY" . . .
> ETC.

A more positive approach, and one of the more creative ones we
came upon, avoided direct contact altogether in favor of the ultimate personal appeal. In one community, members of a small fundamentalist church distributed copies of this preprinted "letter"
from Jesus in local laundromats and other public places hoping
that "lost souls" would come upon them and take them to be of
divine origin:

> Dear Friend,
>   I just had to send a note to tell you how much I love you
> and care about you. . . . Today you looked so sad, so all
> alone. It makes my heart ache because I understand. My
> friends let me down and hurt me so many times, too. But I
> love you. Oh, if you would only listen to me. . . . If you
> only knew how much I want to help you. I want you to meet
> my Father. He wants to help you, too. My Father is that
> way, you know. Just call me, ask me, talk with me. I have so
> much to share with you. But, I won't hassle you. I'll wait be-
> cause I love you.
>
>   Your friend,
>   Jesus

"The Secret Is Surrender." The seeds of suggestion slip in
quietly and are cultivated in follow-up conversations. In the fun-

damentalist program, follow-up is not left to random happenstance. In the same training manuals, there are explicit instructions about how to arrange these further contacts. Campus Crusade advises: "Set a definite time and place. . . . To a service station operator, you might say, 'I'd like to get your opinion of this booklet. Would you read it and Thursday when I get the car serviced, I will get your opinion of it.' (Hand the person a *Four Spiritual Laws* booklet.)" Others: "To a friend, 'Here is a tape. Let's have lunch tomorrow.' To a person at work, 'Here is a letter. During the coffee break, let's get together.'"

Step by step, these methods and materials may lead an individual to the desired end: rebirth. In our years of research, we have heard hundreds of descriptions of the celebrated born-again moment, the instant of conversion when a person may experience a profound spiritual awakening. Some of these descriptions were truly exquisite, sensitive, breathtaking stories told to us by people whose lives had suddenly soared to new levels of feeling and understanding. Many others described intense moments of conversion that had been concocted: engineered group rituals and orchestrated ceremonies in which people were brought systematically to peaks of physical and emotional release.

Most fundamentalists, however, look with disdain on these feverish conversions. For them, being "saved" is not so much an emotional release as an act of will. Compared to more dramatic acts, fundamentalist conversion seems coldly clinical. Yet, among all forms of evangelism, it may be the most efficient, requiring little in the way of group dynamics or fiery rituals. In fact, the fundamentalist approach appears to have been the big breakthrough for modern evangelicalism, opening the door to salvation by remote control: to the quiet act of accepting Jesus by reading books or pamphlets, by listening to radio or tape cassettes, or by watching a TV preacher in the solitude of one's living room. From what we have seen, it may also be the key to fundamentalist right grassroots mobilization in the larger political sphere.

But what is the product these entrepreneurs are so methodically marketing?

Campus Crusade for Christ has perhaps the most comprehensive personal evangelism program in the new fundamentalism. In every other group we studied, we saw reflections of Crusade techniques and materials. Unlike other leading fundamentalist organizations that work mainly with those who have already been converted, Campus Crusade focuses primarily on recruitment, providing its tens of thousands of "lay evangelists" with a broad line of aids to effecting one-on-one conversions. One Crusade booklet, *Jesus and the Intellectual*, reveals to inquisitive skeptics what many in the movement see as the essence of being born again. "The secret is surrender," writes author Bill Bright. "Commitment to Christ involves the surrender of the intellect, the emotions and the will—the total person."

In our research, we have found virtually identical suggestions employed by cult leaders to induce ongoing states of suspended judgment in their followers, calls to "surrender," to "relinquish the will," to "let go" or merely to "let things float." The same call is basic to most forms of Eastern meditation and, in different contexts, to nearly all methods of hypnotic induction. In each instance, we have found, the simple call to surrender may have a profound effect: to serve as a triggering mechanism in the process of indirect control. In clinical hypnosis, for example, it may bring on a classic trance state in which subjects may be commanded to perform feats of uncanny recall or bizarre fantasy. In forms of meditation, it may lead to altered states. Similarly, in the fundamentalist program, we have found, the call to surrender may act as a form of covert or indirect induction, bringing about a sudden release of individual control, which the individual may be led to interpret as a "personal encounter" with some external force, and rendering him almost wholly vulnerable to further suggestions and commands. Through this head-on targeting of the "will," an individual may be brought to suspend his critical thinking and decision-making capacities and believe he has surrendered control of his life to the living spirit of Jesus Christ.

In our view, this principle of surrender is indeed the first secret of the syndrome of ideological fundamentalism.

Other Crusade materials repeat the call. One booklet portrays the "carnal" or "self-centered" Christian as having his "ego or finite self on the throne," depicting the true Christian as one who is "filled, controlled and empowered by the Holy Spirit." Author Bright writes, "Christ cannot be in control if I am on the throne. So I must abdicate . . . I surrender the throne of my life to Him."

not fancy. In lieu of sudden blinding conversions, it may swing people around slowly and subtly, transporting them from an everyday level of rationality and self-awareness into a nonrational, supernatural fundamentalist world. It may also contain a measure of intense indoctrination and ritual practice that in many ways resembles a process that has been recognized as mind control.

Fundamentalist mind control is not like bedrock cult methods that use nonsense mantras and empty chants to still the workings of the brain at neurophysiological levels. As we saw in our first conversation with Diane and later interviews, the fundamentalist program revolves almost exclusively around the repetition of verses from the Scriptures. Through this process, the Bible assumes an omnipotent position in the lives of many fundamentalists. In effect, the book becomes their secret policeman, an intimidating inner force of suggestion that acts as a constant test of their faith and everpresent check on their thoughts and feelings. This, in our view, is the second secret of the syndrome: the use of literal adherence to maintain unwavering obedience and subvert an individual's capacity to make reasoned, independent judgments. In this way, the Bible may also act as a barrier to interaction with the larger world, further isolating the individual and rendering him more vulnerable to manipulation by other indirect means, such as the suggestions and emotional appeals of fundamentalist right preachers and political leaders.

Yet "living by the Word" is not merely a matter of simple repetition. Nor is it an easy or natural process. For many, it requires constant reinforcement through a mode of special instruction and ritual procedure known in fundamentalist terms as "discipling."

Moral Majority co-founder Rev. Tim LaHaye describes discipling in his pamphlet, *How to Read the Bible*. The LaHaye method stresses consistency, aids to concentration and a positive attitude. "Begin your day fortified with God's promises and the instruction of His Word," he writes. Keeping a daily "devotional diary" and other study aids are recommended. "The best way to dial your brain into a vital attitude is to pick up a pencil and be ready to receive a message from God," LaHaye suggests. "The very act makes you more alert and expectant so that God will communicate something to you which you need to know." For

LaHaye, however, the Bible is more than a message. It is also "a command to keep":

> The Bible is filled with commands for God's people to obey. These commands are for our good. . . . As you come upon them in your reading, select the most important for your life at that moment and enter it into your diary.

Another approach is to "read it by need," a method that prescribes concentrated doses of Scripture for the general treatment of personal ills. LaHaye writes:

> Let your spiritual needs determine what you read. For instance, if you lack assurance of salvation, read 1 John every day for thirty days. So far I have yet to find one Christian plagued by feelings of insecurity after reading 1 John daily for a month.

LaHaye's approach to the Bible is methodical but relatively innocuous. His suggested minimum dosage is only fifteen minutes per day, and he cautions Bible-believers not to lift verses out of context. Other major instructors advise much less balanced methods.

Perhaps the most potent program of discipling is the *Topical Memory System* devised by the Navigators, the worldwide missionary organization based in Colorado Springs, Colorado. Following its beginnings in the U.S. military, Navigators developed after World War II into a broad-based "evangelization and discipleship" enterprise. Less aggressive in its recruiting efforts than Campus Crusade for Christ, and much less wealthy (1980 income: a mere $17 million), Navigators and its NavPress publishing arm produce materials that are widely distributed in fundamentalist churches and Christian bookstores.

The Navigator course begins with rote memorization. Its *Topical Memory System* (*TMS*) consists of a boxed set of three booklets, each containing a packet of small flashcards listing selected Bible verses, along with a vinyl wallet for carrying the cards bearing pep-talk slogans such as "REVIEW! REVIEW! REVIEW!" The accompanying guidebooks are unequivocal, claiming that the course will fulfill a host of spiritual and practical needs. The *TMS* says it will help "overcome reticence" in witnessing and reduce anxiety caused by "uncertainty of the future or remorse over the past." It also claims to help "overcome worry . . . by writing His Word on your heart and keeping your mind fixed on Him."

Although billed as nondenominational, we found the Navigator memory system to be a programming method in the strictest fundamentalist mode. Through its flashcards, weekly study plans and frequent "self-checking" quizzes, the *TMS* trains the newborn fundamentalist in the habit of unquestioning obedience. *Guidebook 2* goes further, offering an explicit plan of "meditation," a method of focusing one's thoughts by "revolving a phrase or verse of Scripture in the mind." Quoting a biblical commandment to "meditate day and night on the Word of God," the *TMS* suggests that Christians "make meditation a part of your life" and offers practical techniques, among them: emphasizing different words and phrases, paraphrasing, and using visualization techniques to form "mental pictures" of required verses. Unlike LaHaye or other instructors, the Navigators don't set minimum times for daily Bible study. Rather, they advise at least two separate times during the day for Scripture memory and imply that meditation should be an ongoing process. An advice column in a Navigator magazine describes the process as one of "subconscious meditation" which can be carried out while awake or asleep:

> Here is the secret of the consistent Christian life. . . . We can meditate on the Word of God while we sleep. . . . Read the passage intended for the next morning's quiet time just before you go to sleep. Take about three minutes to scan through the passage and ask God to give you a thought that will help you live for Him the next day. Take this thought with you to bed.
>
> Your subconscious mind will work on the thought while you sleep, and you will probably have the same thought in your mind the next morning. . . .

Navigators is not the only fundamentalist enterprise that teaches meditation techniques as an ongoing ritual for strict scriptural adherence. Campus Crusade for Christ has its own form called "spiritual breathing." As the final word in many Crusade instruction materials, the method is introduced as an almost casual practice. Yet the command is clear: it is to be employed whenever an individual finds himself slipping in his fundamentalist faith:

> If you retake the throne of your life through sin—a definite act of disobedience—breathe spiritually . . . (exhaling the impure and inhaling the pure). . . .
> 1. Exhale—confess your sin—agree with God concerning your sin and thank Him for His forgiveness for it.
> 2. Inhale—surrender control of your life to Christ. . . . Trust that He now directs and empowers you. . . .

A Crusade magazine suggests that, done properly, spiritual breathing may submerge to unconscious levels:

> Inhaling and exhaling is an ongoing process. . . . At first, [it] may seem a bit mechanical. I liken it to driving a car. At first, you feel a bit frustrated, and you are conscious of every move that you make. . . . However, after a while, every movement becomes automatic . . . and you move along smoothly with the traffic.
> So it is as you walk in the Spirit. You find yourself, without any conscious effort, exhaling and inhaling. You even forget the whole concept of spiritual breathing because it becomes so automatic.

Danny. One of the saddest stories we came upon in our research was that of a young man we will call Danny, an honors student and award-winning athlete from the Midwest who had embarked on a promising career in electrical engineering when he took his life at the age of twenty-five. He had been recruited by the Navigators at the start of his freshman year in college. "There are pages and pages of material our son wrote," his mother told us in a letter, "from all the lectures that were used to indoctrinate him. The time he used to do all this is unbelievable. It was too much for his mind to handle." After only a few months at college, Danny informed his parents that he planned to give up engineering to become a full-time staff leader for the Navigators. "He gave

up his former friends for these new ones, gave up baseball for
Bible study, gave up his Lutheran faith for this fundamentalist
version of religion," she continued. "He roomed with their choice
of roommates, gave them his car to use, lent them money. Then
they completely rejected him."

They said he wasn't good enough to be a staff leader. Danny's
mother believed the rejection threw her son into depression. During a visit to the college, Danny's Navigator staff leader suggested
to his parents that they take him to an emergency health center.
"One psychiatrist said he was so far gone he would never be able
to open a book again. He was labeled as paranoid schizophrenic."
The family was outraged by the diagnosis. "A second psychiatrist
told us to take all religious materials, including the Bible, away
from Danny for two weeks. That's all it took. His mind needed a
rest." He recovered quickly, returning to college and completing
his degree; he took a job as a teaching assistant at a university and
another at an engineering firm in Colorado, where he became involved with the Navigators once again. Two years later, he took
his life, sitting in his car in a church parking lot in Denver.

We spent a morning at Navigators' headquarters in Colorado
Springs. Their ranking officials were genuinely concerned when we
brought up the letter we had received about Danny's suicide. They
admitted that, at times, they had had "some problems" with particular staff leaders of Navigators' groups around the country,
but denied any responsibility for pressuring or traumatizing their
members. Other Christians who had been through their programs
reported positive results. Danny's suicide, however, remained an
indelible tragedy, only one of many reported breakdowns we came
upon in connection with fundamentalist evangelization and discipleship programs.

Danny's mother sent with her letter copies of some of the voluminous written records her son had kept during his years as a
fundamentalist Christian. His handwritten testimony revealed the
suggestions he was subjected to in a process of Bible study that
ripped away his sense of self, his ability to think rationally and his
grip on the world. Central to his demise in our opinion, and a recognized aspect of the process of mind control, was the stilling of
doubt, of the individual's natural inclination to question information, suggestions and commands he is given. One book we re-

ceived, *God Can Make It Happen,* written by a former Naviga-
tors' regional director, dwelled on this theme in a section called
"The Devil Is a Doubt-bringer." "Call doubt sin," it read, re-
peating, "The Bible says doubt is sin." At the back of the book,
Danny had written, *"Living on reason causes me to doubt faith in
God and the commands of God."*

Another aspect of the mind control process is the severing of
relationships with the outside world. In place of normal personal
interactions, like other fundamentalists we interviewed, Danny
was led to give up all outside interests for Jesus. Entries in his
devotional diary suggest that he was indeed subjected to overwhelming pressure—both from within and without—to make that
all-consuming commitment. He described how the Scriptures had
changed him:

> Must make a basic decision that the Bible is the Word of
> God and base my life on it. . . . Bible is my life, neglect ev-
> erything except the Word. . . . I am a seed available to be
> planted anywhere. The sower is Jesus . . . Power of the
> Scriptures . . . the book must be inside me.

Throughout the process, however, Danny remained torn by inner
conflict. Later entries quoting from various books of the Bible
reflected his growing preoccupation with self-destructive notions:
*"John . . . Self death." "Mark . . . Life is but a vapor. Day of
Lord will pass as thief in the night."* In time, the source of conflict
emerged on the page. Months before his death, Danny wrote this
entry in his diary:

> Big hassle over Lordship . . . I still have mind problems
> continually. It is hard to see Jesus, have joy in heart, and
> give myself to Him. . . . I am a little worried that I might
> overdo it. . . .

Kristy. In a southern California suburb, we spoke with a young
woman we will call Kristy, now an ex-born-again Christian, who
told us how a gift of the Bible brought her quickly and deeply into
the fundamentalist camp.

"One night I was out getting a Coke and I met these two peo-

ple, a guy and a girl," she told us. "They were reading and I said,
'Oh, what are you reading?' And they said, 'The Bible!' I said,
'The Bible? Really? I don't know anyone who would read the
Bible in public.' So we started talking. They told me about the
endtimes and said that Jesus had the power to give me eternal life.
I said, 'Wow!' It was really an overwhelming idea. Then all of a
sudden, it was midnight. The time went by just like that. I said,
'I'm so excited, I can't sleep. Can I borrow your Bible?' I wound
up staying up all night."

Even without explicit instruction, Kristy found herself meditat-
ing on the Word late into the night and beyond into sleep. Phrases
she had been given—one in particular, "To live is Christ, to die is
gain"—sank into her imagination. By the time she awoke, she told
us, she had made the decision to become born again.

"Something just clicked," she said, "I don't know what it was,
just something intangible I can't put my finger on. They had mentioned to me that the next night they were going to Bible study
and asked me if I wanted to come. But the next day, I just
crashed. About midafternoon they came knocking on my door. I
was sound asleep, but they woke me up. They had their hands
behind their backs. They asked me if I was going to Bible study
and I was about to say no, but they didn't give me a chance. They
said, 'Well, we brought you something to take along.' And they
pulled out this Bible. I just melted. I said, 'Oh my gosh. Well, of
course I'm going.'"

Kristy went with her new friends to Bible study.

"There were about ten people there," she remembered. "They
opened with a prayer, then we sang some Christian songs, then everyone talked about what happened to them during the week. Of
course, the big topic that night was that I had come to the Lord.
Everyone was really excited about that. Then they gave out these
little guides from the Navigator series. The topic that week was
women in the Bible and one of the girls in the group led. She
pulled a verse from here and a verse from there. It bothered me
that they were not in the context in which the Bible was written.
But no one ever pointed that out. They just used the verses to
make their points: that women in the Bible were submissive to
men; that it wasn't right for a woman to speak up and voice her
opinion."

At the conclusion of the Bible study, the group closed with a prayer and then remained together for "fellowshipping." Kristy described the evening's effect on her. "I came out of that Bible study with such a good feeling. I had made all these new friends who really cared about me. I went home and, again, read the Bible and stayed up all night."

In fact, she stayed up for the next seven nights, reading the Bible between midnight and 6 A.M. At the end of the time, she was high on inspiration and exhaustion.

"Believe me, I was on such a high," she remembered. "I had so much energy. I just felt great. I wanted to smile all the time. I felt all this love pouring through me. Nothing mattered. I just felt that I could take on the world. With each new insight, something else would click, like in Galatians, where it says, 'Do not be deceived. God cannot be mocked. A man reaps what he sows.' It was just common sense, but because it came from the Bible it seemed to mean something extra to me. Another verse that really got to me was in Proverbs, 'Trust in the Lord with all your heart and lean not on your own understanding.' That was a big thing, because I had no clear understanding of what all this was about."

By the end of the week, she was on the brink of physical collapse, but she managed to go to church with her friends on Sunday. Soon she became born again in a manner reminiscent of our earlier talk with Diane. "I read the Bible. I went to Bible studies and church groups. And when I had decisions to make, as I was told, I checked them out with the pastor or with 'older' Christians. 'You're too young to know the right Christian viewpoint,' they said. 'You're too young.' They kept playing it back."

Watching her transformation, however, Kristy's family grew increasingly concerned. They could not understand how this independent young woman who had been a top-ranking student and ardent California outdoorswoman could have become so indecisive and consumed by a brand of Christianity they hardly recognized. Eventually, mounting family conflicts and continuing exhaustion brought Kristy to a breaking point.

"It was on a Friday night," she recalled. "There was a Bible study dinner and I told them I wasn't going and I just sat down and had a really good cry. I cried hysterically for four hours. When my friends came by after dinner, I just broke down. I was

COVERT OPERATIONS

crying so hard I couldn't hear what they were saying. The next night one of my Christian friends came back and I told him I didn't think I could handle things anymore. I was losing my health, my family. I said, 'I just can't give up any more for the Lord.' And he said, 'Why don't you just let go and give in? What are you holding on to?' I said, 'My *life!* I'm holding on to my life!' He said, 'You've got to give your life to the Lord. You can't be a total Christian and be totally obedient unless you totally give your life to the Lord.' "

The tension grew worse. "I felt like I was treading water," she continued. "I was so tired. I wanted nothing more than to just let go, but I thought if I let go I would just sink, go right down. A couple days later, I did let go, only I found that I was floating. It was amazing!"

And for a time, Kristy remained a devout Bible-believer. Then, again, the pressures overwhelmed her. She looked back on the period just before she left the group in response to continuing pressures from her family—and from within.

"My Bible-reading time started to increase. Whenever I needed some rejuvenation, some strength, I would turn to the Bible. I'd be walking across the street and a new verse would hit my mind. When I talked to people, everything I did, everything I said, I would attribute to the Lord. But that was only on the outside. Inside I was like a pendulum, on a roller-coaster ride. Sometimes I would feel high, just on top of the world. Then I would find myself so depressed, I just felt worthless and hopeless. I didn't want to eat or sleep. The conflict was immense."

Fundamentalist Emotional Control. Prolonged, intense meditation on the literal Word of the Bible is only one part of a fundamentalist program that goes far beyond mind control. As we learned in our interviews, the syndrome rapidly develops into an all-encompassing system of emotional control. Why *emotional* control? Because as human beings, beyond all differences of faith and culture, our feelings are our most important resource, our most complex, fully integrated and universal communication capacity. They may also be our most accurate monitor of personal morality—of what is right and wrong for each of us as individuals

—and of the fairness of our conduct in relation to one another. When at that intimate level the wisdom of our feelings is stilled, distorted or thrown into confusion, our greatest strength may quickly be turned into our greatest vulnerability.

After the surrender of the will and the subversion of the intellect, fundamentalist emotional control—the reduction of individual response to basic emotions such as love, guilt, fear, anger, hatred, etc.—is the third and final secret of the syndrome. This crippling assault on human emotion is accomplished almost solely by means of suggestion, by the indirect use of cues, code words, symbols, images and myths. And, we found, it left many Christians reeling and vulnerable to larger designs.

As we have come to understand it, fundamentalist emotional control grows out of the movement's emphasis on the supernatural. Just as the literal Bible may act as a secret policeman, undermining a person's real-world capacities for critical thinking and decision-making, so, too, the rush of fundamentalist supernaturalism may shatter a person's faith in his own feelings. At the heart of the process are discipling instructions that target a person's natural emotional responses. A Navigator leaflet, for example, highlights the quote, "Alas! It is this that deceives you, for your heart is the worst part." Similarly, Campus Crusade's *Four Spiritual Laws* ends with the command: "DO NOT DEPEND ON FEELINGS." Following the suggestion to turn over "control of the throne" of one's life to Jesus, the message is driven home with a drawing of a three-car toy train with "Fact (the Bible)" as the engine, "Faith" as the tender and "Feeling" as the lowly caboose. "The train will run with or without the caboose," it says. "In the same way, we as Christians do not depend on feelings or emotions, but we place our faith (trust) in God and the promises of His Word."

As with the process of mind control, once the call for the surrender of feeling is heeded, the process of emotional control may proceed swiftly, much of it spurred by visualization techniques. Dr. Em Griffin, not an evangelist but a professor of speech-communication at Wheaton College, describes the use of visualization and other methods from his discipline in an academic work, *The Mind Changers,* which has become a popular guidebook to conversion. "Pictures in the mind move people," notes the author. He advises witnesses to:

> use words that help your listener call up in his mind the same image that you have in yours. . . . Talk about Christ stilling the waves as reported in Mark 4. Get him to visualize the small boat plunging down the backside of a twenty-foot wave. Get him to see the desperation on the disciples' faces as they scream. . . . Stimulate his other senses as well. Encourage him to hear the roar of a forty-mph gale. . . . Get him to feel the numbing ache of muscles straining against the oars—the sting of salt spray in the membrane of the eyes and nose. . . .

Similarly in discipling, simple terms and images from the Bible engage the imagination as the individual's own natural feelings may be short-circuited. And gradually, he may come to live in a separate, engulfing supernatural world, a universe of living supernatural beings, of human values personified as material evils and enemies, and of prophesied events foretold with certainty as if time itself did not exist. In this supernatural world, the range of personal emotion is bound to a variety of literal figures, foremost among them:

The Supernatural Jesus. The supernatural Jesus is the ruling figure of this universe and the source of many fundamentalists' perceived feelings of righteousness and omnipotence. Through this powerful image the individual projects himself into the fundamentalist world in moving pictures binding his "entire person"— intellect, emotions and will—to the literal story of Christ's magical birth, death and physical resurrection. Unlike the founders of other religions, as we learned in our talks, the supernatural Jesus is no mere inspired person from ancient times. For fundamentalists, he is alive and omnipresent. As one Navigator leaflet states, "The founders of all man-made religions are dead or will die, but the founder of Christianity, Jesus Christ, is alive today and forever." When fundamentalists report that they have been born again and established a "personal relationship" with Jesus Christ, very often they mean this living entity has come to physically inhabit their bodies, controlling them from within. A Campus Crusade pamphlet explains: "When He is within you, He wants to think with your mind, express Himself through your emotions, speak through your voice, though you may be unconscious of it."

The Supernatural Satan. In contrast, the supernatural Satan is Christ's counterpart on the outside, for fundamentalists, the ruling force of the nonfundamentalist world. For many, the image of the devil fuels feelings of fear and guilt over acts of disobedience, and of anger and hatred toward all things secular. The fundamentalist texts we studied, however, did not portray Satan as a cartoon figure with horns and pointed tail. Rather, they gave the impression that, like Jesus, Satan is a living being, all-powerful, ever-present and, if not indwelling, at least lurking around every corner. With the introduction of the supernatural Satan, fundamentalist polarization and separatism becomes complete. Jesus lives in the soul of every "true" Christian. Satan inhabits everyone and everything that is of "the world." Yet ironically, for many fundamentalists the figure of Satan often looms larger than that of Jesus himself, like the real world he represents, threatening to invade and overwhelm at every moment.

We gained further insight into the character of the supernatural Satan as he is taught to newborn Christians from the Navigators' *Studies in Christian Living*. Before his death, like many fundamentalists, the young man Danny seemed to be hounded by Satan. In his workbooks, he left these handwritten answers to questions about the "Archfiend":

What is his occupation?
  To work disobedience into mankind.
How is Satan described?
  He was a murderer from the beginning and he speaks lies by his own nature.
What does Satan want to see happen to Christians?
  To see our minds become corrupted from the simplicity that is in Christ.
How are we enabled to overcome the enemy and those he uses to deceive us?

By Jesus Christ, who is in me.
What does Ephesians 6:10–12 reveal about Satan?
He is crafty.
He has superhuman spiritual power.
He has other powers helping him.
He can be withstood with God's armor and strength.

Holy Warfare.   Together in their biblical roles, the supernatural figures of Jesus and Satan form an airtight lock on the mind and emotions, creating a counterfeit reality in which the everyday world becomes a battleground between warring forces of good and evil. This posture of holy warfare appears frequently in fundamentalist texts filled with words and images depicting God's armor and militant strength. The fundamentalist reaction was conceived in this spirit and has gone forward into battle armed with a handful of warlike images from the Bible. As in the secular armed forces, fundamentalists in basic training are drilled in the dress code of Christian soldiers. One Campus Crusade workbook displays a caricature of a fundamentalist gladiator standing in his visored "helmet of salvation," clad in his chain-mail "breastplate of righteousness" and his broad "belt of truth," and armed with his thick "shield of faith" and his lumbering "sword of the Spirit (Word of God)." Only his shoes are marked "to spread the gospel of peace." In Campus Crusade's Great Commission Army, however, as in Falwell's "disciplined charging army" with its paper "prayer warrior's" paraphernalia, fundamentalists are instructed to be on guard and poised at all times for close combat with the enemy. According to one workbook given to us already filled out by a newborn disciple, the breadth of that enemies list covers much of both the human and supernatural worlds:

Christians are engaged in warfare.
   a. Who are the enemies?
   Adulterers and adultresses [sic], *friends of the world, the devil.*
   b. How should we respond to these enemies?
   Do not conform to the world, be transformed by the renewing of your mind, walk in the Spirit and submit to God.
List four ways we can use God's Word in an offensive action:

Teaching, rebuking, correcting and training in righteousness.
The successful warrior is alert and is always:
Praying.
WE ARE MORE THAN CONQUERORS THROUGH CHRIST!

The Endtimes. Convinced of their own power and eternal life, many fundamentalists stand ready to sacrifice all in their temporal battles against the world. Win or lose, they rest assured that, ultimately, victory will be theirs. The specter of the endtimes is the grand finale in the fundamentalist program of emotional control. However, the endtimes image poses its own set of problems for fundamentalists. Despite their claims of literal truth and absolute certainty in the Word, many remain torn with feelings of doubt and inner conflict over the final book of the New Testament, Revelation, reported to be the prophetic vision received by the Apostle John during his imprisonment for being a Christian. In brief, the book foretells the imminent end of the physical world in a tumultuous seven-year period of "tribulation" or persecution ignited by the arrival on earth of a deceiving "Antichrist." The doom begins in a bloody battle of Armageddon (a biblical site purportedly located southeast of modern Haifa in Israel) and is followed by the "rapture" or physical removal of all true Christians to heaven. In the fundamentalist conception, however, all this, like all of human history, is simply prologue to the "millennium" or thousand-year blissful rule of Christ's Second Coming.

Filled with mystifying language and psychedelic imagery, Revelation has been both a boon and bane to fundamentalists. While many have been forced to admit that the forecast strains even the most "yielded" credulity, others are making real-world preparations for the end of time. Disconnected from reason, reality and human feeling, the kinetic imagery of Revelation tends to feed on itself. Fundamentalists caught in its vortex may be drawn into a kind of endtimes warp, perceiving figures in the news as potential antichrists, reading the beginning of the end into every natural disaster and climatic change and in their own inner conflict weaving intricate paranoid tapestries from the thread of everyday world events. On the electronic church, among fundamentalist right strategists and in the expression of endtimes sentiments by public officials, we heard this same twisted rationale which, unchecked, creates its own self-fulfilling prophecies. This excerpt from a rambling half-page advertisement in the New York *Times* shows how easily the mind-set gets out of hand:

DEADLINE 1981: MOCKERS BEWARE

Absolute proof—we are in the last days spoken of by the Bible. . . . You can't say you didn't have the chance to know.

[The Bible says] the Jewish people would be scattered all over the Earth, but in one single day, Israel would become a nation again. This happened May 14, 1948. . . . Add 40 years—May 14, 1988. Jesus may return before this date. . . .

The Bible describes the effects of the newly created neutron bomb. . . .

Impossible—that 11 straight predictions could be made 2,000 years ago and be perfect was 1 chance in 80 with 63 zeros. There is more. . . .

There would be a nation to the far east of Israel that spoke a strange language. How strange is Chinese to Hebrew? . . . This [the endtimes] will happen before the treaty is signed between Israel and the Antichrist who will head the EEC [European Economic Community]. . . . A one-world system under a new world leader is set up. . . . At the 3½ year point he is killed with a wound in the head. . . . China marches into Israel with 200 million troops across the dried-up Euphrates River; ⅓ of what remains of earth's population is killed . . . 144,000 Jews were protected in a fault that opened. The blood at Armageddon—several feet deep. . . .

The argument concludes:

Even the BIGGEST skeptic in the world can see we are in the endtimes. Ask Jesus to come into your life NOW. . . . The time for jokes and mocking is passed.

Jerry. In its unprecedented denial of the individual, his mind, his feelings and his bonds with society, the fundamentalist program may spin the Bible, Jesus, Satan and a person's misperceptions of the world around him into a debilitating system of indirect control. One young man we met put this destructive picture into perspective for us. Jerry lives in a rural California town with a heavy fundamentalist population. Years earlier, he became born again through the steady loving pressure of a personal acquaintance. His conversion was unemotional—"There were no flashy fireworks or anything"—and he was soon channeled into a local fundamentalist church called the Calvary Chapel. Later, he came in contact with members of the Campus Crusade for Christ, and he spent more than a year in their Bible study and evangelistic programs. After several years of Bible-reading, regular church attendance, witnessing in the faith and fellowshipping with other born agains, he was overcome by doubts and, through counseling with nonfundamentalist clergy, left his fundamentalist group. His experience described to us the way fundamentalist mind control and emotional control may come together in a viselike grip on the sincere Bible-believer.

"It's funny the way it gets into you," he told us as we sat around his small apartment. "They start giving you quotes from the Bible, then before you know it you start saying them to yourself. Then you're saying them out loud. Then you begin telling a couple of friends. Then you go to a fellowship and, bingo, you're in over your head. It's like a quicksand effect."

In his personal behavior, Jerry was not the most obedient Christian. He had disagreements with church leaders over fundamentalist practices he viewed as unreasonable, and he indulged in a forbidden beer or two on occasion. On matters of faith, however, he was unwavering.

"I was more scared than anything else," he said, describing the controlling effects of the supernatural creatures that had come into his life. "As soon as I became a Christian, they told me that the devil was after me. Before, they said, the devil left me alone because I was doing exactly what he wanted me to do—not having a relationship with God. But now that I had a relationship with God, I was going to have a lot of doubts and fears, they said. And where did they come from? The devil."

"Do you see how that works in somebody's head?" he continued. "They used the devil to get me to block doubts out of my
mind. Any time I had questions, it was the devil. If a member of
my family came to me and said, 'Hey, what do you think you're
doing?', it was actually the devil speaking to me, not my mother or
brother. They made sure I realized that the devil was as real as
God Himself."

Jerry recalled a harmless incident that convinced him that the
devil was hot on his tail.

"I used to have this little thing over my door," he said, "a cute
little plastic bullfrog that said PRAISE THE LORD. Well, one night
after Bible study, just before I went to sleep, all of a sudden it fell
to the ground and I thought, 'Oh no, it's the devil!' That was the
first thing that came to my mind. It wasn't that the building might
have settled. It wasn't that the tape fell off. It wasn't that someone
might have slammed a door somewhere. It was the devil, pure and
positive. I just sat there in bed, terrified. I couldn't go to sleep and
I was too scared to get up. I was afraid to even go out into the
hall and pick it up."

As Jerry described it, his born-again Christian life was defined
by this terrorizing power of Satan. He remembered another shaping incident.

"A lot of people at the Calvary Chapel would speak in tongues.
They told me I should be speaking in tongues, too, and I really
wanted to do it. But the first time I tried, I just went, 'Blah-blah-
blah,' and blabbered it all out. They said the devil was right there,
trying to stop me."

Fearful of Satan, Jerry told us, he began to shun every influence
in the real world. Over time, however, his isolated life containing
little but Bible study, fellowshipping, witnessing—and his constant
pursuer, Satan—began to affect him in disturbing ways. Foremost
among them was a feeling of withdrawal and detachment.

"I felt like I was seeing the world on a different plane," he said,
"like everyone else was down there and I was way up here looking
down on them. As I moved through the world every day, I'd
watch people and say to myself, 'Why are they doing that? Don't
they understand?' I was aloof, above it all. As it says in the New
Testament, I was *in* the world but not *of* it."

Toward the end, Jerry said, he even developed a different aura or look about him. He characterized it as "Christian eyes."

"You know how when some people get deeply involved in born-again Christianity, they get these loving, understanding eyes?" he asked. "And their voices get real *soft* and they have this kind of 'I understand' look about them all the time? I see them now and I want to shake them and say, 'Come on, cut the bull, be a *person*!' But they can't hear me. They're probably trying to figure out why the devil is making me say those things. Well, that's how I was."

Finally, plagued by fears and troubled by his progressing detachment, Jerry sought out an acquaintance he had made in another denomination. The friend brought him to a clergyman whose views were "180 degrees" from those of fundamentalism. The fresh angle sprang him from his confinement. His friends at the Calvary Chapel did not take his defection lightly.

"It took me a while to sort things out. My friends kept coming over and saying, 'Oh, let's pray for Jerry. The devil's really got ahold of him.' I said, 'Go ahead, pray for me. I'll even pray, too.' I said, 'Lord, if I'm doing something wrong, then stop me.' And I looked straight into their eyes and said, 'I'm sorry, Lord, but I think I've made a mistake.'"

TEA AND SYMPATHY WITH SISTER RUTH

In our review of the professional literature on persuasion, "attitude change" and "motivational research," we were surprised to find few insights in the area of mental and emotional manipulation by indirect means. Academic approaches to the subject dealt mostly with behavior and bore little resemblance to the stories we were hearing from people in all walks of life. Textbook treatments of methods of "influence" used in both mass-marketing and therapeutic contexts described powerful instruments of personal manipulation as neutral tools. We could see how fundamentalist right strategists could have come to view their techniques with such calculated cool. The underlying assumption of American research—that new knowledge will be used for positive ends in an open society—led away from, not toward, the prospect of covert control in the closed fundamentalist world. Yet we had seen it countless times, people who by choice or default had surrendered their wills to preachers, church leaders, to the imagery of the Bible, or to social and political crusades being mounted in the name of Jesus or in opposition to Satan. Soon we came to feel that even the mechanistic term "control" was a mild description for this new form of terror.

Our most enlightening conversation on the subject was with an evangelist, in fact, a world-renowned faith healer: Ruth Carter Stapleton, sister of Jimmy Carter and a hotly controversial figure in her own right. Before the fundamentalists took center stage, "Sister Ruth" was a symbol of the "new evangelicalism" of the seventies. Yet, when her brother ran for President, she was derided as a con artist and a potential embarrassment to a Carter White House, and with Jimmy Carter's fall from favor among conservative Christians, Ruth's star seemed to dim as well.

We spoke with her at her Christian healing center north of Dallas, Holavita Ranch, a thirty-acre complex comprising several buildings for healing and therapy sessions, a sculptured white concrete chapel, a small swimming and baptizing pool and Stapleton's two-story western home. As she poured fresh sun tea, we asked her if she could tell us something about the mind-set of the fundamentalist right forces that had seized the national spotlight.

"I don't have any idea how they think," she said. "I don't see how it relates to Christianity or Jesus in the least way." She traced her disagreements with the movement. "Some of these people are acquaintances of mine. I've had conversations with them where I've looked them in the eye and said, 'You know, you are the most religious people I've ever met—and the least Christlike!' That's the way I feel. They put so much emphasis on ritual. They think it's so holy to go to a Bible class. Well, I don't see that as holy. The way I see it, you go to a Bible class to learn how to come back and *be* holy! You don't become a Christian by going to all these meetings and seminars and other activities. The only way you can express the Christlike life is in your everyday relationships. Jesus didn't go around trying to convert everybody. He didn't hold these big crusades. That's not what he meant when he said *witness*. I think he meant: be that expression yourself."

Stapleton went on to explain her "holistic" approach to Christianity, an approach she had written about in her book, *The Experience of Inner Healing.* We were intrigued by her method of "faith imagination" as a healing tool in a process she called "emotional and spiritual reconstruction." Simply outlined, Stapleton's faith imagination method is one of picturing positive scenes and images, generally from the Scriptures, and recreating past experiences in ways that will give rise to positive feelings, which may have healing effects. Stapleton did not hesitate to admit the similarity of the technique to a therapeutic tool from humanistic psychology called "guided fantasy." In contrast to many of the destructive discipling programs we had studied, her method focused on the positive and, as she said, "on keeping the individual in control of the process." She spoke proudly of her professional credentials which included a master's degree and advanced study in holistic psychology. We asked if she had ever felt any conflict over her scholarly endeavors in a discipline many Christians characterized as satanic.

"I never had any conflict," she said confidently. "Everyone else had the conflict. Pat Robertson once said to me, 'Ruth, why are you such a controversial person?' And I said, 'There's nothing controversial about me. It's only small minds like you that find me controversial, because you want everyone to believe exactly as you do.' I've heard it all—psychology is of the devil and almost everything else is of the devil. But I have to maintain a state of consciousness that's above what my critics say or do."

As it turned out, however, she was not immune to the impact of the fundamentalists' charges.

"I have hurt," she confided. "I have suffered. I have gone through all the guilt trips that go on. But I'm beyond that now. I'm not trying to change my critics. I'm not trying to change anybody. And if anybody tries to do it to me, I shake the dust off my feet as fast as I can. I won't even have an argument with that kind of person. You can't change them. I see that as sickness, not as Christianity."

One of the more innovative faith healers in a field known for its quacks and rip-off artists, Stapleton claims to have produced positive results among Christian individuals and couples suffering from sexual problems, marital conflicts, teenage identity crises, adult traumas, as well as long-term illnesses and physical handicaps.

She was less prone than most to attribute her successes solely to divine intervention. Inner healing was, for her, more of a human process than a supernatural one. Yet, like other Christians, her writings laid heavy emphasis on the "power of surrender." To us, the call rang familiar alarms. We asked if she could distinguish between her kind of surrender and the fundamentalist "surrender of the will" we had seen ample reason to mistrust.

"As I use the term, you surrender to *yourself*," she said, "not to something out there. Jesus is not going to make you a whole person. Jesus is not going to make you a loving person. You have to will it. You have to do the job yourself. When I say, 'You've got to have will,' I mean *you've* got to make the decision. And when I say, 'You've got to surrender,' I mean you must surrender your lower self to your higher self. It's all an inside job. None of it is out there."

She compared her view to fundamentalist thinking, as she understood it.

"You see, in my opinion there's a confusion in their minds as to what is spiritual," she said. "To me, to be truly spiritual in the highest sense is to be totally free from bondage and prejudice of any kind, to purify the heart. And when you purify the heart, the outward circumstances of life begin to evolve in a positive way. It seems to me that the right-wing fundamentalists are more concerned with the outward expressions, the external manifestations. They're treating the symptoms rather than trying to get to the real problem, which is the heart of the person. The only way to do that, I feel, is to provide people with a cushion of love and acceptance—physically, mentally and emotionally. That to me is Christianity."

Like her view of inner healing, Stapleton's notion of spirituality was holistic. She explained how the "new age" perspective meshed with her evangelical views.

"As a Christian, you must look at the whole person," she said. "No matter how much faith you may have in God, no matter how hard you may try to be obedient to the Scriptures, if you have hostility and all these negative emotions within, you're going to be ill —physically and spiritually. You ask for that divine Holy Spirit to open your heart, but you have to will that Christ-consciousness from within. You have to will to love. You have to will to be healed. That's where psychology comes in, because you can't do that if you are filled with fear and frustration and guilt. The truly Christlike nature frees people to make their own choices—even if that means choosing whatever religion they desire. Jesus wasn't just trying to convert people. He was trying to bring out that highest potential in every person and break down the barriers between them. He was expanding all the time, broadening all the time."

She paused, her cheerfulness dropping away. "You know, the hardest thing I have to do right now is maintain my sense of who Jesus was in the light of what I'm told Christianity is." How did she do it? "By refusing to be in the presence of that judgmental type of Christian who would try to force my way of thinking. I just won't do it." These days, she admitted, that was easier said than done. "It's so hard," she continued, "you know, I woke up this morning and I thought to myself, 'Oh gosh, I wish there were just somebody really positive and wonderful that I could watch on television without being preached to and screamed at.' But there wasn't."

Since she brought it up, we asked if she would offer her opinions on the healing styles of preachers of the electronic church. She declined tactfully.

"I can't," she said, "because I really don't watch them. I don't know what they're doing."

However, she was not reluctant to talk about other fundamentalist preachers.

"You know, I've had to put up with so much over the last twenty years, and especially the last four," she began. "One minister heard me use the term 'transcend' in a meeting. I said that through prayer you could *transcend* negative thought patterns and turn them into positive ones. Well, he had heard the term 'transcendental meditation' somewhere, and he published this article saying that I was no longer a believer in Jesus Christ but was practicing eastern religions. Now, that's when you know you're dealing with fanatics!"

Stapleton described her own experiences as a victim of Holy Terror. Following her brother's election, she told us, a group of hard-line fundamentalist ministers began a coordinated campaign to discredit her.

"Right after Jimmy went in, five of them got together against me. If it hadn't been for the grace of God, I would have been totally wiped out. Each one took a different tactic. One used radio. One used direct mail. One used tapes—he called me not just a witch but the 'queen of the witches.' Another wrote a book about me and, two days after it came out, he had a heart attack. I sent him a telegram hoping he'd get well."

She declined to identify the ministers who were involved, saying "I'd rather not get into name-calling." But she acknowledged that the campaign achieved much of its desired impact.

"They really came after me. They were against inner healing. They were against women evangelists. Really, they were against women altogether. They said every woman had to be in total submission to the male." She paused. "And you know what happened? All the wives began to divorce the husbands. So many of these ministers' wives began to leave them. I'd go into my counseling meetings and all the wives would come to me, telling me what their husbands were forcing them to do—and what *not* to do. They couldn't teach Sunday schools. They couldn't attend certain meetings. They had to have certain hours of prayer life every day. They couldn't stand it! There is just something basic within the human being that has to be free. I told them, 'Unless you are your own person, you are going to get sick or have a breakdown. And if you really can't stand it, if you're strong enough, you'll just have to get out.' "

We asked Stapleton if any of those who had teamed up to discredit her years ago were the same fundamentalist right leaders who had become so active in the eighties. To our surprise, she didn't know the names of any of the political strategists we mentioned, and only a few preachers were familiar to her. She knew of front-line activists such as Falwell and Robison, but she seemed largely unaware of their political activities. Of the leading names on our list, only one rang a bell for Ruth Carter Stapleton.

"Bill Bright?" she asked, agape. "Bill Bright. Seven years ago, I knew him overseas. And I said then that he was the most dangerous man on this earth."

We asked twice, but she refused to give specific reasons for her opinion. "All I'll say is that I saw what he was doing overseas. I saw his followings over there. I saw what they were all about. And I saw how it was building," she said.

We prodded for details, but she refused to elaborate.

"They came to me," she said, speaking more broadly, "people on the planning force of Moral Majority and other groups. Oh, all those poor little unaware Christians, giving their last cents to these political groups in the name of Jesus. Let 'em learn. Let 'em go hungry. Then they'll say, 'If I had only known.' "

Her seeming callousness surprised us.

"I don't mind people having to suffer," she said, her own strict background showing through. "I've come up against conflict in my life, and I've become stronger for it. If Christians listen to these people and get confused, maybe the suffering will do them good. When they get the legislation they want, when they get the President they want and the government they want, when there's no longer a First Amendment, maybe they'll realize that they were wrong."

She seemed almost angry now. We wondered if her rancor was a response to her brother's election defeat. When we mentioned Jimmy Carter, however, her voice grew soft again.

"You know, he was so condemned. He was called the Antichrist by so many right-wing Christians. And why? Because he did not believe in legislating for prayer in schools or that Christian schools should be supported with tax money. These were just things he felt the government should not interfere with. But he was a good President. He was a *Christian* President. I'm not just saying that as his sister but as someone who was on the inside and who had many long, long discussions with him where he explained why he took the stands he felt he had to take. He was warned by his campaign people that the failure of his programs would lose many votes. But he said, 'I can't be concerned about the election.' "

We asked if there was truth to reports that the Carters had been deeply disturbed by fundamentalist right slurs on their faith.

"Heavens, no," she said. "The papers kept bringing that up, about how upset he was and how upset Rosalyn was. But it wasn't true. They're so happy to be out of there. And I don't feel sorry for him at all. I'm glad he's not President now."

In parting, we asked if, in the mounting turmoil, she worried for her own reputation as a Christian healer.

"No," she said, contrasting herself to fundamentalist right leaders. "I'm told they still don't know what to do with me, but I just want to make one thing known. I want every Christian to know that I'm not on their side. I couldn't speak out until the election, but I don't care if I'm on the front pages now. I don't care anymore, and that's great. I had to keep it inside for all those years."

Babes in Toyland

Most of the communication devices, which now play such an important part in our daily activities, have been with us but a brief moment if viewed within the extended span of man's social and cultural life. . . . It may seem strange to suggest that these devices, which have invaded our homes, represent a kind of *communications revolution,* a set of rapid technological changes unique in the history of mankind.

—MELVIN L. DE FLEUR—*Theories of Mass Communication*

AS WE LOOKED BEYOND BELIEF to patterns of ritual practice and technique, the syndrome of ideological fundamentalism grew in our perspective from one of mere "reactionary evangelicalism" to a comprehensive system of indirect control. Its methods, we found, could have profound effects on a person's basic capacity to make reasoned, independent choices, on his ability to interact with others, and on his perceptions of the world around him. We spoke with many Christians who, like Kristy, had come to view themselves as "babes" unable to make decisions without turning to church leaders for literal instruction. We met many more like Jerry, who had become separated from reality to the point of dissociation, passing through the world in a fog of supernaturalism, fearing unseen masters, both supreme and satanic.

Following this thread, we began to trace these same indirect techniques in their advance on the larger society. Here the question was no longer one of personal manipulation but of an outright drive for power: for unprecedented levels of social and political control over all Americans and our nation as a whole. To these ends, early on, the fundamentalist right expanded its operations beyond religion, applying its methods of personal evangelization and discipleship to the broad domain of social issues. In their crusades against abortion, pornography, sex education, the Equal Rights Amendment and other "anti-family" causes, fundamentalist right leaders gained access to bedrock emotions at every level of society. In their campaigns on sensitive political issues—military topics of defense preparedness and strategic superiority; economic matters of government spending, taxation, welfare and monetary policy; and ideological disputes such as those between free-enterprise capitalism and foreign models of communism and socialism—they resurrected their entire agenda of old right targets. With the rise of Holy Terror, public debate on many of these vital issues has given way to new forms of fundamentalist reaction: to biblical arguments and other forms of literalist rhetoric; to code words, suggestions, emotional cues and other indirect ploys; and to a dangerous new hybrid of religious, patriotic, free-enterprise zealotry. With this blurring of boundaries and fuzzing of distinctions between private belief, public morality and the political process, the syndrome explodes in all directions, emerging full-blown as "complete" ideological fundamentalism, at once both religious and political and throughout, indirect in its techniques and use of technology.

In fact, it is at these larger levels that the fundamentalist right carries out its most sweeping covert operations. Yet, as there has been little recognition of the movement's use of covert techniques to manipulate individuals in the arena of religion, so, too, there has been almost no public discussion of its even greater method of mass manipulation over public communication channels which have been developed, historically, for very different ends.

In many ways, fundamentalist right preachers and their allied strategists are babes in toyland, newcomers to the charmed circle of media power. Until recently, this powerful technology was almost exclusively the province of the secular media, private enterprises subject to rigorous public scrutiny and strict government regulation. However, by exercising the all-important tax breaks and other privileges accorded to them as religious or nonprofit institutions, the movement has created a protected class of unlicensed, unchecked media power brokers who now possess multiple means of entry into the privacy of people's living rooms, their minds and their daily lives.

In its use of the media, the fundamentalist right has changed the function of mass communication in the United States, from its recognized role of direct dissemination of information for purposes of public discussion and the formation of public opinion, to one of disseminating indirect messages to millions of Americans for ulterior religious and political ends. It is at this level of covert operations, in our view, that the movement commits its gravest violations of the ethics of communication in a free society. To understand how, we look first at its use of new communications technology, beginning with the most powerful mass medium of all time.

GOD THE SPONSOR, GOD THE PRODUCT

To date, no one has been able to pinpoint the real threat of the electronic church. In their stated purposes, religious broadcasters seek only to exercise their freedoms of speech and religion, to preach their faith, to reach out to the unchurched, and to provide a service to shut-ins and others who, for whatever reason, may be drawn to this unorthodox form of religious devotion. The common charges do not stick: there is no evidence that the electronic church is siphoning either money or members from local churches, and with only a few exceptions, TV preachers have been careful to use their enormous cash flows for approved religious purposes.

Yet, in all the quibbling over dollars and ratings, a larger infraction has been ignored: the movement's use of religion to legitimize a program of mass manipulation that is unparalleled in American media history. Never before have independent broadcast interests acted as God's chosen representatives to produce, sponsor and market programs of indirect control on a national scale. Yet, in the flashy world of paid religious broadcasting, fundamentalist right preachers and strategists use television to seed the culture for conversion, and to further the movement's social and political ambitions in covert ways.

In practice, TV evangelists use the same recruiting devices as tent-show holy rollers and street proselytizers everywhere, targeting thought and feeling by suggestion and indirect command. However, when these tactics are pumped through advanced technology to mass audiences worldwide, in our view, their supernatural promises, insupportable claims and other subtle frauds and deceptions breach new trusts in the ethics of communication.

Highly emotional revivalists like brother Jimmy Swaggart take the first steps in this direction. Swaggart's rendition of "The Destructive Power of the Gospel of Jesus Christ," for example, brings to television a program of submission no secular broadcaster or advertiser would dare to disseminate. Couched within each phrase, heavy on repetition and reminiscent of personal ploys used by Tim LaHaye, the Navigators and the Campus Crusade, his message contains all the seeds of suggestion, including the attack on thinking and reason, that, we have found, make up the preconditions of fundamentalist control. Even stripped of Swaggart's pounding delivery, these words retain much of their emotional impact:

> Casting down, He said, these imaginations . . . bringing into captivity every thought unto the obedience of Jesus Christ. Captivity, making captive every thought unto the obedience of Jesus Christ. Now, I want to tell you, you can't do that without God. It's impossible. Your mind is the gateway to your spirit. The mind is the place where the battleground is. That's where the fight is. That's where the roar takes place and it wrestles until you sometimes wonder what is going on. The mind . . . where your thought processes literally congregate. . . .

Here, as in all revivals, Swaggart rendered the traditional "altar call"—a call to surrender—adapted for television:

> O Jesus, how dependent we are on Thee . . . by television all over America, the Philippines, Australia and other parts of the world, many are sitting now under conviction. Would Thy Spirit move and touch them. Would Thy Spirit go into that home and that heart. . . . I want you to bow your heads, please, each one of you. I want you to close your eyes. I'm going to pray the sinner's prayer and I want you to

repeat it after me and believe it with all your heart. . . .
Dear God in heaven, I come to you in the name of
Jesus. . . . With my mouth, I confess Jesus Christ. In my
heart, I believe. . . . Right now, in front of all these people
and the God of heaven, I accept Jesus Christ as my personal
Savior. I will live for Him, trust Him, and accord to His
word. Right now. This very moment. According to God's
word. I'm washed. I'm cleansed. I'm redeemed. I'm saved.
Hallelujah! It's done!

Swaggart's mass ritual of surrender is only the beginning. As
star of "The Old-Time Gospel Hour" on radio and television,
Jerry Falwell uses his electronic pulpit, virtually without reserva-
tion, to advance the movement's plan of political ascension. In a
1981 broadcast, Falwell made this pitch to bring the nation under
command of the Scriptures:

God doesn't use dirty instruments. Not only must you be
saved by the new birth experience, trusting Christ as your
Savior, but day by day in your Christian life you need to use
God's detergent, the Word of God, as a cleansing agent.
Read it. Study it. Memorize it. Meditate upon it. Hide it
away in your heart. . . . I wish that for all of our congressmen and the leaders in government and our President and all
the pastors of the land, that we could learn so much Scripture, memorize so much Scripture, that in the great decisions
that face us in the leading of the nation and the leading of
our people, God will be able to bring to our mind, to our
memory, to our attention at the right moment, the right
Scripture, the right truth, to give us the wisdom and guidance
we need to perform our God-given task. . . .

Over television, Falwell hammered home the bottom line of
fundamentalism:

We must be obedient to the Word of God. Obedient.
Whatsoever He sayeth unto you, do it! That's all there is to
it! Find out what God is saying to you and obey Him. Obey
the Lord. Obedience! . . .

At the end of his televised Sunday service, Falwell's altar call linked the promise of salvation to the movement's hidden enemies and rising militancy:

> Help us, our Father, while the heat is on and we're being attacked from every side, help us to stand true. . . . Help us send out an army of champions one day to turn this nation around. . . . While our heads are bowed and our eyes are closed . . . come right now, would you? Those by your television set who need the Lord, just bow your head and say, "Come into my heart, Lord Jesus." Trust him right now. . . . If you have further questions about your salvation, give me your telephone number. . . . Our soul-winning pastor will call you at our expense and lead you to Christ. . . .

Breaking new ground in the indirect use of television is Pat Robertson of the Christian Broadcasting Network. In his claims on the "700 Club" of privileged communications with God, Robertson is often openly political, planting volatile suggestions and sowing strong emotions. But Robertson's greatest power may lie in his subtlety. Like the "700 Club," CBN's newly marketed Christian soap opera, "Another Life," the first in its expanded lineup of "wholesome family-oriented programs," works fundamentalist religious messages into a secular entertainment format. To unwitting viewers, the spread of fundamentalist beliefs may seem incidental, yet the familiar vehicle of the daytime drama may indeed be drawing them into another life. This scene involving a young woman and her doctor displays CBN's growing mastery of the medium:

> DOCTOR: He seemed like a nice young man. Pre-med, isn't he?
>
> WOMAN: Yeah. Before the accident, we were planning on getting married. Now it's all so different. Everything's changed. He's changed.
>
> DOCTOR: How?
>
> WOMAN: Before the accident, I thought we shared the same beliefs. We talked about it and prayed about it.

DOCTOR: And now?

WOMAN: Now I don't know. I think Russ wanted to share my faith just to avoid any problems.

DOCTOR: Laurie, I've been where you're at. I was engaged in med school. Pam and I went so far as to set a wedding date. And ten days before the wedding, we broke up. She couldn't understand why I chose to be a Christian.

WOMAN: How did you handle it?

DOCTOR: Simple reality. I told her if she wasn't willing to accept the Lord, the engagement was off.

WOMAN: That's pretty blunt.

DOCTOR: So's divorce. There may not be a painless answer. But there is a right answer. . . .

Two segments later in the same episode, following a CBN commercial for Bible-reading mixed in with ads for beauty cream and other products, two other characters, a husband and wife, delivered another fundamentalist message—with political shadings:

WIFE: Is that you? Scott! You're home two hours early. What's the occasion?

HUSBAND: Afraid you're going to have to get used to me around here. . . . I've been let go. . . .

WIFE: Scott, you are a very talented newscaster, and I'm sure you won't have any problems finding a new job.

HUSBAND: I don't know, honey. I don't know. I'm not as young as I used to be. Look, news broadcasting today is show business. It's the under-thirties gang, the twinkee-dos, the local open-collar, capped-teeth beautiful people.

WIFE: Don't worry. You've always found work. . . . "All things work together for good to them that love God."

HUSBAND: Yeah, Romans 8:28. I said it a hundred times on my way home today.

WIFE: Then relax. Let go.

HUSBAND: I will. I will. . . . Thanks for being here and not letting me sink into it.

WIFE: You're very welcome. And unemployed or not, Scott Davidson, you'll always be my anchorman.

Finally, there is Jim Bakker, the electronic church's master of naked emotionalism. Viewed from a distance, Bakker's pleas to his viewers stand as priceless examples of the movement's abuse of the power and prerogatives of television. The following fund-raising pitch on the "PTL Club" used stark personal appeals and supernatural hype to sell an expensive religious product:

> We are very close to disaster. We desperately need your support. The devil honestly tells people their gifts doesn't [sic] mean anything. . . . We need you to minister back to us with your love offerings. . . . With an extra hundred dollars, you could give this to a friend or Christian family or an unsaved family even . . . a five-volume home Bible study course from the Heritage School of Evangelism. . . . This course sells for over three hundred dollars. . . . The Bible says in the last days people will perish. Perish for what? For a lack of knowledge of the Word of God. And if you want to survive, you're going to survive through standing on the Word of God. This course can mean the difference between heaven and hell. You know, if you knew that famine and pestilences and horrible things were coming, if you knew a hurricane was coming, you'd prepare for it. You'd batten down the hatches. You'd put boards over your windows. You'd seal your house up. You'd put water away. And you'd prepare for that hurri-cane that was coming that might destroy you. Well, I want to tell you something. There is an onslaught coming. It's already here. It's already begun. And the only way you'll survive is if you're founded on the Word of God. And I'm talking about storm insurance right now. And that's called the Word of God! . . . I'm almost positive you'll be able to get one of the last remaining courses. I think I have about twenty thou-sand left. . . .

Watching these preachers unleash so many indirect messages on a trusting public, we were appalled by their wholesale exploitation of the medium, and, as we expanded our inquiry into the elec-tronic church, surprised to learn that most Americans had no idea of the kinds of claims and suggestions being spread across the na-tion's airwaves in the name of God. Few nonfundamentalists we spoke with had ever watched one of these programs in its entirety. Yet, as we watched regularly and critically, we found ourselves asking the same question over and over: *What are these programs doing on television in the first place?*

THE STRANGE CASE OF PETITION #RM-2493

America's airwaves have long been considered a "public trust," a precious national resource. Since the passage of the Federal Communications Act of 1934, the broadcast media, first radio and then television, have been tightly regulated by the federal government to insure that those exercising such profound reach and impact on large numbers of Americans do so responsibly and with respect for the rights of the audience over their own financial or other interests as broadcasters. In federal rulings and court decisions, the freedom of speech of broadcasters has always been of ultimate concern, but it has been weighed and in many cases restricted in recognition of the fact that the electronic media constitute a uniquely pervasive and very often intrusive force in the lives of their listeners and viewers.

Over the years, this mass-media fact of life has been recognized and accepted by both our government and the broadcasting community. Network broadcasters have complied with strict regulation by the Federal Communications Commission designed to prevent potential abuses and dangerous concentrations of power, and with even more stringent voluntary guidelines and codes adopted by industry-wide self-regulating bodies such as the National Association of Broadcasters. In the world of mass marketing, broadcast advertisers are tightly tied, at great expense, to still harsher restraints dictated not only by the FCC but by the Federal Trade Commission and other government agencies, and by numerous advertising councils and monitoring groups. On political matters as well, candidates and incumbents, including most Presidents, respect federal laws compelling networks and local stations to adhere to strict standards governing political programs, to follow equal time rules in election campaigns and to recognize their obligation under the fairness doctrine to present both sides of controversial social and political issues. Even in their own paid commercials, candidates generally conform to standards of direct communication. Local candidates who have attempted indirect or subliminal appeals have been pounced on, and few, if any, have tried it on a national scale. Even the U.S. Supreme Court has ruled, in its landmark 1969 "Red Lion" decision—a case involving a scathing attack on an author by Rev. Billy James Hargis of the anti-Communist Christian Crusade—that any citizen who comes under personal attack in the electronic media is entitled to time to reply.

Why then, in its overwhelming domination of the religious broadcast spectrum, in its proselytizing and fund-raising appeals, and in its increasingly political content, has the fundamentalist right's exploitation of radio and television gone largely unchallenged?

The answer is not surprising: Holy Terror. Over the years, the tough Federal Communications Commission has been the target of ferocious campaigns by fundamentalists unwilling to adhere to the same standards and guidelines accepted by all Americans who use the airwaves.

We inquired at the offices of the FCC on M Street in Washington about government supervision of religious enterprises using the public trust of the broadcast spectrum. The civil servants there were indeed civil, some were even friendly, although the jittery chief of the Complaints and Compliance Division refused to let us tape his remarks for our records. In that conversation, Stephen Sewell reiterated the official FCC position that it has no policy specifically governing religious broadcasting. The FCC treats the religious broadcaster like any other broadcaster, said Sewell, that is, exercising no authority whatsoever over program "content." The agency's primary function, he said, had little to do with regulating the programs of individual producers or even large networks, but consisted of granting broadcast licenses to operators of local radio and television stations. With that activity as its sole authority under law, said Sewell, the FCC could in no way concern itself with the content of religious broadcasts. However, he did acknowledge the agency's obligation to insure that local stations which aired religious programs—in certain instances, stations owned by religious enterprises—conformed with FCC standards for the maintenance and renewal of their licenses. In short, Sewell was saying that, for all practical purposes, religious broadcasters were only vulnerable to scrutiny through their local stations, and then almost solely on financial charges such as fraudulent solicitation or misuse of funds. Moreover, the FCC rarely initiated investigative action, responding only when an outside citizen filed a complaint or brought such allegations to its attention.

On those terms, predictably, there had been almost no government interference with the activities of religious broadcasters. Sewell told us of only a handful of cases in FCC annals where religious broadcasters had been held accountable for misdeeds. One, the "Red Lion" case, had led to a ringing affirmation in the Supreme Court of the FCC's long-standing fairness doctrine, a rule most broadcasters and the new FCC chairman were eager to see abolished in their efforts to deregulate the industry. Another case, then ongoing, was the FCC's investigation of reports that Jim Bakker's PTL television network had, through PTL-owned local stations, raised more than $337,000 under false pretenses and diverted it to pay off other debts of his ministry. This case had been the subject of repeated protests and court appeals by Bakker, including broadside attacks against the FCC on the "PTL Club" that had been followed by angry write-in and phone-in campaigns.

But the real weight of Holy Terror pressing on the FCC had little to do with Jim Bakker. It was, instead, the result of a decade-long onslaught directed at the commission from sources unknown.

After our talk with Sewell, we met with Zora Brown, a perky, vivacious young woman and FCC "consumer assistant specialist." Since coming to the agency in 1977, Zora Brown told us, her primary duty had been dealing with the strange case of FCC rule-making motion #2493. Since 1975, Petition #RM-2493 had been the object of a bizarre write-in campaign by fundamentalist Christians who believe it to be an attempt by atheist crusader Madalyn Murray O'Hair to ban all religious broadcasting from the air. In that time, we were told, the FCC had received more than 60 *million* pieces of mail urging it to reject the O'Hair petition. At one time, the volume of protest became so heavy that the agency had to hire two full-time staff assistants simply to open and sort the mail. Several years ago, the FCC made an emergency request to congressional authorization committees for an additional $500,000 to process the flood. It got half that amount, which it

immediately applied to stepping up staff efforts to reduce the
backlog, to installing computerized mail-sorting facilities—and to
media efforts aimed at rectifying a growing public misconception.

The misconception is that such a petition exists. According to
the FCC, Madalyn Murray O'Hair has never filed any petition
with the FCC. The case number in question, #RM-2493, concerned a 1974 request by two University of California professors
who wanted the FCC to freeze all applications by religious institutions for the use of educational broadcast channels. In 1975, the
FCC unanimously denied the request, declaring that the First
Amendment required government agencies to remain wholly neutral toward religious groups.

"I have no idea how the rumor began," said Zora Brown. "It's
still a mystery to me. The mail has subsided somewhat since we
launched our media campaign, but it's still coming in. We're still
getting about three hundred letters a month, but that's really down
drastically."

She handed us a stack of letters off the top of her desk. "These
came in just last week," she said. "They're almost all form letters.
They use the same wording. It's all very polite. The signatures are
handwritten, the envelopes are all marked the same way."

We flipped through the letters. Most were poorly photocopied
slips of paper, obviously torn off a longer form, bearing a simple
three-sentence message. One, a typewritten note from Pico Rivera,
California, seemed like a parody of the standard complaint:

TO WHOM IT MAY CONCERN:
  I personally apperciate [sic], wholeheartley [sic], support,
  the Sunday Worship service, plus many other religious programs, that are now broadcast over radio and television, to
  fulfill their worship needs. I urge you to see to it, that such
  programming continues.
  I also protest her interference, in the choice of the programs in our public schools.

Another typed letter, from Little Rock, Arkansas, conveyed the
same sentiment, slightly improvised:

  . . . Whenever God is eliminated from TV and radio
  broadcasting, and the words IN GOD WE TRUST from our

money, etc., we can only expect Hell's doors to open wide to accept us all. . . . Which way will you cast your vote? For the Madlyn Murray O'Hares [sic] of this world, or for God and His righteousness to prevail?

Zora Brown was almost as baffled as we were. "People here think it may all be a fund-raising ploy by some religious group," she said. "They figure most people are afraid that something like this might happen, and they link Madalyn Murray O'Hair to it because she was successful in getting prayer taken out of the schools. I can imagine someone saying, 'Give me a dollar to help me stop this terrible thing—and while you're at it, send this letter to the FCC.'"

The next letter she handed us gave credence to the theory. The sender had forgotten to detach the form from its carefully worded instructions:

FOR YOUR IMMEDIATE ATTENTION

Madalyn Murray O'Hair, an atheist whose efforts successfully eliminated the use of Bible-reading and prayer from all public schools . . . *has been granted* a federal hearing in Washington, D.C. . . . by the FCC. The petition (RM-2493) would ultimately pave the way to stop the reading of the gospel on the airways [sic] of America. She took her petition with 27,000 signatures to back her stand.

If her petition is successful, all Sunday worship services being broadcast either by radio or television will stop. Many elderly people and shut-ins, as well as those recuperating from hospitalization or illness, depend on radio or television to fulfill their worship needs every week.

Madalyn is *also* campaigning to remove all Christmas programs and Christmas songs and carols from the public schools.

WHAT ARE WE DOING TO STOP THIS WOMAN? YOU can help this time. We need 1,000,000 (one million) signed letters. . . . BE SURE TO PUT PETITION NUMBER ON OUTSIDE OF ENVELOPE WHEN MAILING YOUR LETTER. A letter has been prepared for you to use at the bottom of this form. *Please use it* and help defeat this

woman and her cause. REMEMBER, she does not stop
working for her beliefs and neither should we!!

Part of the mystery was beginning to unfold. As we looked at
the letters, checking signatures and origins, Zora Brown told us
how she had stumbled on another piece of the puzzle one Sunday
morning.

"It happened in my own church," she said, still amazed. "The
minister stood up and read the letter and told everyone to write to
the FCC. He gave the same instructions. I just sat there with my
mouth open. Finally, I approached him and said, 'Where did you
get that letter?' He said, 'One of the church members got it in the
mail. There was no return address.' Well, I immediately rose to
the occasion. I told everyone, *'Please, don't write to the FCC.'*
There were thirty-five hundred people there and I could see what
we were in for."

When she came to the FCC in 1977, Brown told us, she was
appalled to learn that no one at the agency was doing anything to
stem the inundation.

"It was unbelievable to me," she continued. "I said, 'But the
taxpayers are paying for all this wasted energy in the mailroom.'
The chairman at the time told me, 'You know, there's no way we
can deal with it. All we can do is hold the letters for thirty days,
then shred them and take them to the dump.' But to me, that was
such a waste of time and space and manpower. So we decided to
launch a little mass-mailing campaign of our own. We took six
hundred thousand letters—a three months' supply at the time—and
sent replies explaining the rumor and asking people to help spread
the word in their churches. And do you know what? A lot of people wrote back and said, 'We never wrote you to begin with.' "

There is more to the story of Petition #RM-2493. No one at
the FCC was eager to talk about it, but for several years there has
been a smoldering debate within government circles concerning
the very premise of religious broadcasting. No action has been
taken, nothing is likely to be done, yet it appears that the massive
$600-million-a-year religious broadcasting industry may be, in our
terms, not only another covert operation, but an illegal one as
well.

Linda Jo Lacey, an attorney and member of the District of Columbia Bar, raised this sticky prospect in a 1979 article in the *Federal Communications Law Journal,* "The Electric Church: An FCC-'Established' Institution?" Lacey's thesis was simple: after examining the federal agency's official policies and unofficial practices regarding religious broadcasting, she concluded, "a strong argument can be made that the FCC's actions do constitute establishment clause violations"—that is, that FCC policy and practice breached the First Amendment restriction that the government "shall make no law respecting an establishment of religion." Although the FCC had told us they maintained a policy of strict neutrality toward religion, Lacey's facts to the contrary were plentiful and convincing. Station licenses were granted to religious organizations, although, in Lacey's view, the First Amendment implied that they should not be treated simply as commercial enterprises, especially when they used their stations for "a substantial amount of proselytizing." Even in its policies toward secular stations, Lacey argued, the FCC had helped establish certain religious groups. By including "religion" as a special category for required program-logging purposes, said Lacey, the FCC had indicated that "religion could be ignored only at a station's peril," creating a kind of "halo effect" in which stations presented religious programming as evidence of good behavior.

Lacey went on to describe how FCC practices not only encourage the establishment of religion on the airwaves but discriminate *in favor* of religious broadcasters over other educational and commercial ones. For example, most charitable groups are forbidden to make fund-raising appeals on educational channels, yet the FCC regularly ignored religious broadcasters who sought funds on educational TV or used their programs to promote religious "products" such as Bibles—a commercial practice expressly forbidden by FCC educational TV rules. Although, of course, commercial stations may sell airtime for money-raising purposes, FCC policy states that it considers "program-length" commercials of ten minutes or longer to be "against the public interest." Yet, noted Lacey, "the commission has specifically stated that programs which solicit contributions to religious institutions are *not* program-length commercials"—despite the fact that many religious shows are little more than half-hour or hour-long appeals for funds!

Lacey lists further discrepancies in FCC policies: nonenforcement of equal opportunity employment rules "connected with the espousal of the licensee's religious views"; the monopolization of the field by fundamentalist forces which, Lacey argued, "represents the type of concentration of control by a single voice that the commission has tried to prevent in the past"; and the increasingly political nature of many religious broadcasts, which appear to violate still another FCC guideline: that broadcasters should refrain from taking advocacy positions or promoting "divisive political strife."

No one we spoke with at the FCC had much to say about Lacey's federal law journal article. Her facts and arguments were not in dispute, they told us, but political reality was another matter. The weight of $600 million a year in religious broadcast money seemed to act as a controlling lever on the agency, not in direct dollars but through the force of pressure groups like the National Religious Broadcasters and through powerful radio and television lobbies whose local station owners stood to gain giant revenues by selling time to syndicated fundamentalist preachers that might otherwise go free to local religions in fulfillment of FCC community service obligations. Compared to the entrenched power of fundamentalist broadcasters, the government's watchdog efforts seemed puny, as did their defense of neutrality.

Yet even inside the agency, it appeared, the matter was not so cut and dried. On our way through the Sun Belt, we stopped at the University of Texas at Austin, home of the largest communications research center in the nation. In Communications Building "A," we met Stephen Sewell's boss from a bygone administration, Arthur Ginsburg, recently resigned head of the FCC's Complaints and Compliance Division. Now out of civil service, he could speak freely on a subject that was of great concern to him during his years in government.

"I came away from the FCC convinced that they wanted to brush under the table the serious establishment questions regarding the use of public airtime by the electronic ministries," he told us. "There was a big problem there, and I was marching to a different drummer than some of the commissioners."

He talked candidly. "It is my personal opinion that the commission made a terrible error many years ago when they began licensing stations to religious entities," he said. "It was the worst thing they could have done. But having done it, they were hoist by their own petard. They have never been able to back up. They tried to reconsider on a few occasions, but the religious establishment is so strong, the religious broadcasting lobby is so strong, that it would be very hard for them to pull back. They had maybe one opportunity in the last ten years or so, and they went the other way, they began licensing almost anybody. They didn't enforce their own requirements. Licensees were supposed to provide the whole spectrum of religious programming, but it hardly ever worked out that way. Many denominations never got on the air. I know of cases when I was at the commission where some religions wouldn't go near certain stations. They were kept out, in fact. They had the feeling that their religious programs weren't welcome there. Most of those stations were operated by ultraright-wing fundamentalist Christians and they had a very limited audience. I used to chomp at the bit, but the commission really had itself in a very bad bind there."

Ginsburg told us that, while he was at the FCC, the religious broadcast lobby exerted tremendous pressure on the agency as a whole, on individual commissioners, and on congressional oversight committees.

"I've seen them in action," said Ginsburg. "They are an extraordinarily effective group. The really big problem, from my observation, is that the public doesn't know what the hell is going on, and the religious broadcasters are taking advantage of this."

Ginsburg assailed recent initiatives by new FCC commissioners to force the total deregulation of the industry. The drive, already largely achieved for radio, was now advancing toward television with broad commercial and special-interest group support.

"Let's face it," said Ginsburg, "the God business is good business. Most stations who air religious broadcasts make a great deal of money doing it." In addition, he said, when religious cases came before the commission, the agency got "very frightened," backing away from anything which might be construed as acts of censorship or impingements on religious freedom. It was during Ginsburg's tenure in the Complaints and Compliance Division that

James Robison was kicked off the air by a station in Fort Worth for making disparaging comments about homosexuals. Robison appealed to the FCC, holding public rallies and mustering big-money and big-gun support. His appeal was denied on the grounds that the FCC had no legal right to dictate to stations what they should and should not broadcast, but Robison's supporters had long since succeeded in pressuring the station to put him back on the air. In the interim, Ginsburg had to weather much of the storm.

"I took the brunt of that one," he recalled. "I spoke at a religious broadcasters' convention and all hell broke loose. A thousand people in the hall thought it was the worst thing in the world to throw Robison off the air. We got some hate mail, people wrote in saying, 'You're in favor of homosexuality.' The pressure was terrific."

We asked Ginsburg whether, in his view, the time-honored notion of the airwaves as a "public trust" was being overturned in favor of a free-market concept where the power of the media was delivered to the highest bidder.

"Now you've opened up a Pandora's box," he said. "In the old days, when air space was limited and the number of available channels was fairly small, the airwaves *were* viewed as a public trust, and the government had to oversee the orderly distribution of space in the broadcast spectrum. But now we're entering a whole new era. The growth of pay TV, low-power and independent satellite and cable networks is creating enormous regulatory problems. If they choose to deregulate, give up the fairness doctrine, equal time, everything, turning the decision-making back to the individual states or localities, we'll probably wind up with eighty channels of garbage instead of thirteen. Then, who knows, people may come back to Washington pleading for the government to get back *into* regulation!"

But Ginsburg was not optimistic. "I think the cat's out of the bag. I'm not sure there is any way to regulate it any longer. There might have been, if the commission had been more astute in its earlier procedures, but now the religious forces are riding high. The cable people are riding high. It's a powerful moment and there is no way you can control them."

Ginsburg recalled his entry into the FCC when the commission was headed by Newton Minow, the colorful Kennedy-era administrator who coined the image of television as a "vast wasteland."

"Things were different in those days," he mused, recalling bold initiatives by the FCC to encourage public broadcasting and other quality programming. "But by the late sixties, imperceptible changes began to occur. Then it was all downhill as far as regulation was concerned."

In his final years with the commission, Ginsburg said, he held out for continuing oversight, but he knew he was bucking an insurmountable tide.

"I could have stayed on and made some trouble, but they would have put me in a job where I would have just been pushing paper around. I saw it coming. I had an opportunity for early retirement and I took it. I could see nothing but unhappiness in that job."

Looking eastward out the window, Ginsburg reflected on the difference between the current administration and the ones he knew. He found the new mood of government, if not of the whole country, disturbing.

"I don't think I could have survived under this government," he said. "I came from the days of the New Frontier and the Great Society. I feel like a beached whale today."

THE BLACK MARKETPLACE OF IDEAS

Arthur Ginsburg's reflections on the sixties confirmed for us that, long before the fundamentalist right began to capitalize on events in that breakthrough decade, those who would go on to lead the reactionary movement were already working behind the scenes, securing the mass-communications base from which they would reach out to the disenfranchised at home and abroad. But television is only the most visible toy in the larger game of Holy Terror. As a tactical instrument, the electronic church functions mainly as a tease, seeking out new converts, providing the movement with an image of respectability and an impression of clout, and seeding the ground for further social and political reaction.

The real dirty work of the movement is carried on in yet an-

other covert operation, a vast undercover communications network that plays counterpoint to the high-toned theme of the
electronic church. The medium of direct mail provides the
fundamentalist right with a channel tailor-made for its ulterior
ends, a private line of transmission that carries ideological fundamentalism into broader reaches of American life. As an intimately personal medium, largely hidden from public view, the
network has proved well suited for trafficking in acts of distortion
and misrepresentation, for disseminating suggestions, code words
and emotional cues, and for marketing supernatural myths, un-
savory ideas and ingrained hostilities to an audience that may be
easily misinformed.

In fact, in direct mail, the fundamentalist right may have discovered the perfect mass medium for indirect control, a veritable
"black" marketplace of ideas, a closed network for practicing intellectual and emotional manipulation free of the accepted terms
of public discussion. In this channel, fundamentalist right strategists may shape their messages confident that, for the most part,
the opposition and the larger public will never know what is going
out—or going on. Even if the other side should sink a line into
their stream of computerized communication, they still have no
way to respond, to reach the same audience with their side of the
story, their version of the facts, or their opinions.

In this maelstrom, religion and politics merge at will. Richard
Viguerie, the fundamentalist right direct-mail czar, is probably
correct in his claim that, without direct mail, "certainly there
would be no New Right." Without direct mail, the pro-life movement might cease to exist, having no other way to disseminate
photographs of contorted fetuses matched with pictures of targeted U.S. senators. Without direct mail, rabid anti-communism—
combining ignorance, fear and fundamentalist hatred of "godless
atheists"—might lose its distemper through informed public airing.
Without direct mail, few Americans would ever encounter so
many scriptural views presented as modern-day political realities:
biblical obsessions with might, militancy and revenge; blind notions of the divine nature of American nationalism and free-
enterprise capitalism; literalist thinking on such varied issues as social welfare, taxation and gold-based monetary systems; and
ancient stereotypes of sex, marriage and family life. Many of these

fruits of complete fundamentalism have tried and failed in open forums, yet they flourish in the black marketplace of ideas.

This covert operation encompasses more than direct mail, incorporating a variety of fundamentalist right newsletters, magazines and other publications which go largely unadvertised in the secular world. In its entirety, the black marketplace of ideas is the technostructure of the fundamentalist right, a vast communications network that shoots straight from the big guns of the master strategists into the hearts and minds of their activist armies. Through direct mail and its connected organs, the fundamentalist right leaps still another barrier in its bid for control by establishing a closed channel for manipulating a broad segment of public opinion in America. Direct mail manipulates public *action* as well, using the black marketplace to mount stage-directed social crusades, orchestrated voting drives and campaigns of constituent response to elected officials. By these actions, the movement disrupts the natural flow of information and ideas which, historically, has shaped public opinion and, in turn, the American process of representative democracy.

In our research, we collected dozens of letters sent to Americans in all walks of life by organizations in the fundamentalist right network. On the surface, the intent to deceive the reader concerning the impersonal nature of the computerized letter seemed obvious. Even more blatant was the attempt to foment hostility. Almost every letter seemed written to solicit money or action through fear and anger.

Jerry Falwell's introductory letter for Moral Majority is a vivid example. In it, he plays to every instinct, lobs unsupported charges at will and mixes religious and political fundamentalism in their most intimate relation. Wrote Falwell:

> Our Grand Old Flag is going down the drain. Don't kid yourself. . . . Homosexual teachers have invaded the classrooms, and the pulpits of our churches. . . . One day the Russians may pick up the telephone and call Washington, D.C., and dictate the terms of our surrender to them. . . .
> Is God finished with America? I don't believe He is for these reasons:
> 1. America has more God-fearing citizens per capita than any other nation on earth.

2. America is the only hope for the Jews today. . . .

3. America is the last logical base for world evangelism, which is the ultimate goal of the gospel. . . .

And in his boldest claim, one that would be met skeptically at best in any other forum, Falwell declared: "God has been calling me to do more than just preach. He has called me to take action."

Invoking God's name is only one of many devices common to a fundamentalist right medium that might more suitably be called "indirect mail." Another widely used and apparently highly effective ploy is the urgent reader "survey" or "petition" that solicits information, opinions or other personal participation. Moral Majority used this device in a series of mailings, enclosing a petition "To the Congress of the United States of America" demanding that legislators "Pass Laws in Support of My Moral Opinions Listed Below" on such issues as abortion, pornography, equal rights for homosexuals, school prayer, Taiwan and arms limitation treaties. The message at the top of the form suggested the poll's true intent:

Dear Dr. Falwell:
Here is my Congressional Petition on Moral Issues. Please tabulate the results from my state and deliver the results to the office of my U.S. senators.
And here is my gift of: $_____
YOUR IMMEDIATE REPLY REQUESTED

Similarly, "God's Angry Man," Rev. James Robison, floods people with "Urgent-Grams," Congressional Opinion Polls with special questions "For Contributors Only," and "Dear Friend" letters with printed emphasis designed to look like furious scribbling. Over his closed channel, Robison cuts loose in ways he has long since ceased on his failing TV show. One letter charged:

This past summer, homosexual perverts consolidated their power by organizing to control the 97th Congress. . . . As a result, we Christians may lose our right to preach Christ in freedom; but gays will have won the right to seduce our children—perhaps even in their Christian schools.

Another appeal for his ministry was laced with ideological threats and a variety of Satans:

> America is now totally vulnerable to an attack from the atheists in the Kremlin. . . .
> Christian friend, OUR NEGLIGENCE AND FAILURE TO STAND FOR GODLINESS IN THE POLITICAL ARENA IS A SIN—it is sin and nothing else. . . . Because of our national sin, here's the grim prospect we will face within three years—unless we act now with one united Christian voice:
> . . . Churches closed by force in violation of the First Amendment . . .
> A new political dictatorship in America in which Christians will be persecuted—perhaps imprisoned or killed for their faith . . .
> without prayer warriors and spiritual leadership, our efforts will be sidetracked by Satan. . . .

The Religious Roundtable, co-chaired by Robison but founded by Paul Weyrich's man Ed McAteer, used similar tactics in a 1981 fund-raising drive. Its theme, boldly emblazoned inside and out, "Stop the Liberals from Rewriting the Bible," charged that "liberals" (whether religious and / or political was left vague) in the National Council of Churches were "rewriting the Bible to please radical feminists." The letter drew on fundamentalist fears as it built to a hysterical pitch:

> You and I know that this attack on the wording of the Bible is the same as attacking God Himself. . . .
> There is reason to believe the NCC's ultimate goal is to publish and promote a "feminist" Bible. . . .
> If the principles of a feminist version Bible were applied to the home, the whole Judeo-Christian concept of family life would be undermined . . . this evil scheme . . . this wicked project. . . .

The letter, signed by McAteer, included a Reply Form / Petition along with the endorsing names of fundamentalist right preachers and U.S. senators and congressmen, and instructions to turn to Revelation 22:18, 19—a prophesied threat of plagues.

The method varied little among fundamentalist right groups ostensibly formed around social issues. Predictably, anti-abortion groups ran some of the wildest bazaars in the marketplace. Like the pro-life activists we encountered in our travels, today most pro-life groups steer clear of open talk about God and Christ and sin and Satan. Instead, they have developed their own set of symbols, slogans, and images that substitute real-world objects for their other-worldly beliefs and provide live targets for their political crusade. In place of the supernatural Jesus, they deify the supernatural fetus. In place of the supernatural Satan, they substitute all-too-human demons: U.S. senators whose votes against anti-abortion measures have consigned them to the pro-life hall of shame. In place of born agains, they speak of the "preborn" and the "unborn." In place of sin, they talk of murder. Damning their enemies, pro-lifers have also replaced the historic epithet "Christ-killers" with their equivalent: "baby-killers." A direct-mail letter from STOP THE BABY-KILLERS, a political action project of Americans for LIFE (their emphasis), hurls the curse thirty-seven times in a four-page mailing, complete with ready-made constituent response materials. The black-market appeal might be appropriately retitled, after Jonathan Edwards, "Baby-Killers in the Hands of an Angry PAC":

Dear Friend:

. . . help me STOP THE BABY-KILLERS by signing and mailing the enclosed anti-abortion postcards to your U.S. senators—(You'll find a list of all U.S. senators on the back of that sickening Baby-Killer propaganda)—men who apparently think it's perfectly OK to slaughter unborn infants by abortion. . . .

Abortion means killing a living baby, a tiny human being with a beating heart and little fingers . . . killing a baby boy or baby girl with burning deadly chemicals or a powerful machine that sucks and tears the little infant from its mother's womb.

. . . you can bet McGovern is vulnerable and his Baby-Killing friends know it.

. . . Yes, I'm harsh when I call them Baby-Killers, but it's time we exposed them for what they are. If they want to talk about abortions, then let's unite and perform an abortion on their political lives. . . .

Less visible in the marketplace of the movement are groups opposed to the teaching of "anti-God, anti-family" sex education. Here the anti-sex stance merges with the movement's multipronged attack on American public education. This 1981 mailing by TAX-PAYERS AGAINST SEX EDUCATION, a project of Christian Family Renewal, Inc., contains all the old saws, along with the standard Parent Petition / Poll urging Congress and the President "to cut off all taxpayer funding of immoral organizations who are peddling their own pornographic atheistic view of sexual relations to school age children." The cover letter used titillating language likely to anger, arouse and lure donations:

Dear Friend,
. . . right now, your tax dollars are providing America's schoolchildren with some of the dirtiest, filthiest and perverted books and films on sex education you can imagine! . . . let me share with you some shocking, downright disgusting facts. For example, did you know your tax dollars are teaching school-age children to:
 • "French kiss" and masturbate?
 • enjoy the roles of being a homosexual or lesbian?
 • draw the sex organs of men and women and the act of intercourse. . . .
Dr. William A. Block's *Do It Yourself Illustrated Human Sexuality Book for Kids* . . . depicts a nude "Sex Family" . . . including gutter terms for sexual organs and the sex act.
 I wish I had more time to share with you all the horrible things American children are being taught about sex in the classroom. . . .
 P.S. Originally I had planned to enclose a sampling of the crude street language and drawings used in Dr. Block's sex book. . . . However, they are so disgustingly graphic that I decided not to send them unless requested to do so. If you want to see what our schoolchildren are being exposed to,

just enclose a self-addressed envelope along with your donation.

The pattern of ideological fundamentalism was predictable, even among groups that were purely political in their expressed intentions. Terry Dolan's letter for the National Conservative Political Action Committee, soliciting funds for NCPAC's "Target '80" campaign, ran the gamut of fundamentalist right negativity. In Dolan's "gut-cutting" attack style, his saved men are "conservatives," his Satans "liberals, radicals and extremists," their sins: support for the ERA, legalized abortion and "Big Labor." And NCPAC's battle of Armageddon is always the coming election.

Despite Dolan's denunciations of fundamentalist right moral and social issues, his organization relies heavily on religious appeals. In a 1980 letter signed by U.S. Representative Daniel B. Crane, NCPAC leveled unrestrained attacks on the defense voting records of its targeted senators:

> At every opportunity, they have used their Senate votes to run down America. . . . The liberals, especially these five senators, have stripped America of her defenses against Communist Russia. . . . Each of their Senate votes is like another nail in our nation's coffin.

Then it unleashed a fusillade of low blows around moral and social issues, ending on a strong fundamentalist theme:

> Our nation's moral fiber is weakened by the growing homosexual movement, by the fanatical ERA . . . pushers (many of whom publicly brag that they are lesbians), by leftist-produced movies and television programs that are often indecent and full of sex.
> Which side are these five liberals on, the side of decency, or the other side? . . .
> Because of the votes of these liberals, the ERA was given a new life—and fanatics like Bella Abzug were given a soapbox for another few years from which she can spew her poison on decent American housewives and mothers. . . .
> Over six million preborn babies will die in the next five years

. . . *unless* we can pass a Human Life Amendment. We will
have a very hard time saving these six million infants unless
we beat five of the biggest enemies of the pro-life movement. . . .

Yes, your prayers are *essential*. But it is also true that God
helps those who help themselves. Help yourself . . . to five
great victories.

We tried repeatedly, in writing and by phone, to procure an
interview with Richard Viguerie, whose organization conducts
direct-mail operations for NCPAC and other fundamentalist right
groups and politicians, and whose new right publications have
provided many fundamentalist right PACs and lobbies with rich
sources of funds and converts. Above all questions of his political
aims, we sought Viguerie's views on the unfolding mass medium.
We had questions about the uniquely intimate nature of direct
mail, about the inability of those targeted to reach his tightly controlled audience and about the manner in which personal passions
were converted into political action. When he declined to see us,
we were obliged to turn elsewhere.

We called the U.S. Postal Service, hoping to unearth specific
regulations for the use of the mails for religious and political purposes, but our calls to Postal Service headquarters in Washington
led us to no one who had even begun to consider the implications
of this emerging medium that was delivered to people's homes by
government couriers. One Postal Service spokesman advised us
only that, like the FCC, the service's oversight functions were
strictly limited to investigating charges of monetary fraud. Apparently, such acts as misuse of the mails in religious and political
campaigns of deception, distortion, suggestion or other forms of
manipulation were untouchable. And obviously, the medium
offered no opportunity for enforcing "fairness doctrine" or "equal
time" provisions.

Apparently, as social theorists warned more than a decade ago,
the dawn of the computer age had given rise to a potent new instrument of mass manipulation. Yet who but the manipulators was
giving a thought to the transformation of the mails, and who, if
anyone, was showing even the slightest concern over the new medium's potential for abuse?

We found one direct mailman who was. Tom Mathews is Richard Viguerie's counterpart on the left. As a founding partner of the direct-mail concern of Craver, Mathews & Smith of Arlington, Virginia, Mathews and his principal cohort, Roger Craver, have played kingmakers to a number of liberal causes. In 1970, they were instrumental in launching Common Cause, the Washington-based lobby that has enjoyed strong liberal and populist support. As Viguerie learned the trade working for Young Americans for Freedom, Mathews and Craver cut their teeth on Common Cause, learning the ins and outs of direct mail as they built the starting concept into a well-financed lobby. In 1973, with Common Cause at the peak of its support, Mathews and Craver left to start their own direct-mail firm. Within a few years they had taken under their wings a modest but impressive brood of liberal causes. By the late seventies the CM&S client list had become a fundamentalist right nightmare, with progressive clients that matched the reactionary effort almost one for one, including Planned Parenthood, NARAL (National Abortion Rights Action League), NOW (National Organization for Women) and Handgun Control, Inc. Mathews and Craver raised millions for the liberal senators Viguerie's groups were targeting. In 1980, it was Mathews who almost single-handedly convinced Illinois Republican John Anderson that he had potential as an independent presidential candidate. Then Mathews went out and raised an unprecedented $20 million for the doomed campaign. Following the 1980 election, CM&S found their services more in demand than ever, as worried liberals and moderates sought funds for newly established PACs and foundations formed with one purpose in mind: to counter the growing threat of the fundamentalist right machine.

We spent a few hours with Tom Mathews one afternoon in his office across the Potomac from the capital. He was sanguine, if not downright giddy in the face of the fundamentalist threat. A gnomish man with a quick smile, he explained to us that he and his firm had suddenly found themselves in the midst of a business boom of tidal proportions. We asked Mathews for his assessment of direct mail as a political tool, mass medium and growth industry.

"What industry?" he asked straight-faced. "There's only two of us." He was scarcely exaggerating. On the right and the left, the medium could be defined by Viguerie's company and his. Each had competitors, but most simply handled the overflow. And, contrary to public impressions, said Mathews, his firm was the larger and more effective fund-raiser.

"We raise a lot more money than Viguerie among a lot more people," said Mathews. "In 1980, we raised forty-five million dollars. Viguerie didn't come close to that. We have ten million active names to his four million. Our average contribution is almost twice as much as his—or at least it used to be."

If so, we asked, how come his issues and candidates got clobbered in 1980, while Viguerie's triumphed? According to Mathews, Viguerie's clout was a function of the times—and of his possessive approach to direct mail.

"Viguerie's prominence is due to his being the sole owner of his lists," Mathews explained. "He seems to think of them as his private property. We rent our lists off the market. We do not have a master computer. We look for known contributors to liberal causes, for subscribers to quality magazines and so on. Viguerie virtually controls the whole right side of the political aisle. He owns the lists. He creates his own appeals, his own organizations and his own movements. And within that universe of names, he has been extraordinarily successful."

Had Viguerie changed the rules of the direct-mail game?

"No, he didn't change them," said Mathews. "He simply adopted a method of operation we rejected. We don't believe that much power should reside in a single person."

Mathews expanded his view of the two-man medium, not as a private network for acquiring and consolidating power, but as a kind of privately held utility with public responsibilities.

"Yes, we're a private company," he said, "but we work on the basis of contracts and agreements that are not secret. We are completely open. You can look at any contracts we have with anybody."

Viguerie's operation, on the other hand, was "a little murky," according to Mathews. For example, he had no idea if Viguerie was swapping lists with TV preachers or collaborating with other undeclared fundamentalist right forces. We asked Mathews what he made of Viguerie's clandestine method of operation.

"I understand what he's got," said Mathews, referring to Viguerie's mother lode of four million proven contributors. "It makes you very wary of abusing the kind of trust those people have in you. It induces a strong sense of stewardship about what you're doing. We're like that, too. We're very fussy about who we'll raise money for."

Mathews was quick to disavow any implication that he was the altruist and Viguerie the villain.

"I do not want to obscure the fact that this is a profitable enterprise," he said. "Our power on the left may be as great as Viguerie's on the right. We believe in a much more diversified approach than he does, but I don't want to appear any holier than Dick Viguerie, because I'm not."

Mathews went on to describe the CM&S operation. In many ways, all direct-mail ventures followed the same procedure: names are procured, sample letters written; limited tests are run on small samplings of the audience, then a major mailing is sent out. After the flood, regardless of the client or cause, the return was surprisingly predictable: one to two percent was normal, three to four was considered outstanding, six to eight, said Mathews, was "like striking oil." In keeping with his public utility concept, Mathews contrasted his operation with the common fundamentalist right method.

"You see, we are really only a nexus between the mail and our client," he said. "Our client is the originator of the message and the appeal, not us. He writes the letter. It's his organization. Viguerie, very often, does everything. He'll even loan you the money to get started if you give him the names that result from the effort. That's how he builds his base."

Yet, Mathews admitted that his company had recently begun similar joint efforts.

"Let me make it clear that we did that in the Anderson campaign because that was a speculative political effort. Our deal with him was to share ownership of the lists after the campaign was over. So we do own that one list, but it only has two hundred thousand names on it."

Mathews showed concern about exploiting that base. He did not want his new technology to become an intrusive force in the lives of those on his lists. He acknowledged that some people opposed their very presence on a mass-mailing list as an invasion of privacy.

"It's small," he said. "I'd say maybe three or four percent resent getting all that mail. They think it's a waste and an affront and an offense. But we recognize that, and we do our best to get them out of the stream. We offer all our clients the opportunity, if they'll just drop us a card, to take their name off any list they feel they may be on. But those who exercise that option are very, very few."

Beyond the figures, we told Mathews, we were interested in the kinds of appeals he sent out. Did his firm go in for the same computerized emotionalism and other devices used by direct mailers on the fundamentalist right? He pulled out a stack of recent mailings for his clients. In the material he showed us, there was no computer typing, no insertion of the addressee's first name throughout the text, no imitation underlining and handwriting—and not one Petition / Poll to Congress, the President or anyone else! We asked, did Mathews object to the flashier methods, or did he just lack the technological capability?

"Look, our people are serious people," he said, comparing his lists to Viguerie's. "They're better educated, on the whole. They're in an *information flow*—they read the editorial pages and the news weeklies. They have many different interests and concerns and, in general, a level of income that allows them to give when someone touches those concerns. The right is more monolithic, less educated and less well off, on the whole. Their views are simpler, simplistic. Many seem caught in some mythical remembrance of the past, an intense desire to return to a time when life was secure, less uncertain and less fraught with danger. People will pay plenty for that and to anyone who promises it to them. But that's the only thing that will work for them. If I used that kind of appeal on our side, it wouldn't work at all."

Did he think people on the right were more vulnerable to emotional appeals than those on the left?

"Sure," he said, "but *all* direct mail is emotional. Our people give out of an emotional impulse, too, not an intellectual one. On both sides, people give out of fear and anger, not out of lofty principles."

If that was all it came down to, how was a Craver-Mathews letter any different from a Viguerie or Falwell letter?

"Well," he said slowly, "maybe their fear and anger is low and ours is lofty. Theirs is the devil's and ours is—*Kierkegaardian!*"

He was only half joking. "Look," he went on, "read their letters. They're very effective, very clever. They don't always come out and say it, but the devil's always implied. It's simply an imperative. It appalls me, but that's how their minds work."

Listening to Mathews, we began to get our own picture of the developing industry. As a medium of mass communication, direct mail seemed well suited to the hard edge of the fundamentalist right. Gone was the radiant happiness of the electronic church: for Falwell and Robison, as for NCPAC, the pro-lifers and the rest, direct mail served as an unseen channel for riling and arousing. Yet it seemed logical to us that the two media would complement each other, that, in the comprehensive fundamentalist right assault, there must be some connection between the pull of television and the prod of direct mail. We asked Mathews whether combined TV and direct-mail appeals enhanced the power of the letters to draw a response. To our surprise, he said one didn't affect the other at all.

"If you've ever contributed by mail, just ask yourself what went through your mind," he said. "What steps did you go through that led you to sit down and write a check? You'll see that it was an intensely private experience. You probably didn't call anybody up and ask whether or not you should give. No, what that letter did was catch you at a moment when, although you didn't know it, you were ready to do something about some cause you cared about. Now, we've found that television and other publicity don't really affect that kind of attitude, except maybe in a kind of slow, cumulative way over a period of years."

But didn't that describe almost exactly the role of the electronic church in the lives of many Americans? Mathews hadn't thought about it earlier, but the connection seemed to click with something else on his mind.

"I'll tell you a little technical secret that's just barely taking shape in my head," he confided. "In the Anderson campaign, we tried to raise money by television. We created some very effective five-minute spots that we were sure would do the job. Zilch! Absolutely nothing! But you know what we found? When you go to twenty-eight minutes, it happens! You can't get it in five, but in twenty-eight you get a contribution."

"Why?"

"I don't know," he said. "It's a psychological thing, I suppose. In twenty-eight minutes, you've got him roused to the point where he'll do it. It's no different in direct mail. It takes you fifteen minutes or so to read a letter, doesn't it? A shorter one won't work as well. So even there, it must be a function of the length of time your attention is focused on the subject. Now, look at Falwell and Pat Robertson. You know, they're both on for an hour at a shot. Now, I'm certain that one reason for their success over the others is the length of time they're on the air. That's what gets a person to call in or contribute, but I still don't think television has anything to do with the success of their direct mail. Not at all. They're whole different planets."

Or were they? Throughout our research, we had wondered about the interacting roles of various mass media. How did the electronic church affect its electronic flock? Maybe not at all on any immediate basis, but in all likelihood, over time, the dissemination of so much suggestion wrapped as religion and bathed in the glow of television gave immeasurable impact to fundamentalist forces. Inevitably, we felt, the cumulative barrage had to have some long-term effects on regular viewers: as they went about their daily lives, as they went to vote, as they opened their mail. Mathews didn't deny it, but as perhaps the only man in America with a machine to match Viguerie's, he was untroubled by our scenario.

"You and I could kick the hell out of the new right," he said impishly. "An intelligent, accelerated effort by the left could stop the right dead in its tracks. Technically, I could write it for you right now. If you'd just buy what I write blind, I could raise millions. I could re-create the left, but I wouldn't do it unless the responsibility were broadly shared."

That, to Mathews, was the problem. In contrast to the monolithic right, he saw the political left today as a fragmented force. In the sixties, he said, there was Vietnam, which tapped into "an enormous reservoir of national feeling." Mathews saw a resurgence of that reservoir of feeling as the far right threatened to become a governing force.

"Our readings show that the average decent, concerned citizen agrees that the government may have gotten a little bloated, but basically he thinks his government is OK, that it should help the poor and the needy and attend to other social concerns. People in our contributor base, *our* family, are becoming active again. They're starting to give like gangbusters—and I have no doubt the pendulum will soon swing the other way."

"So all the new right's money and machinery don't worry you?" we asked.

"They don't," said Mathews.

"Because you're confident of victory?"

"No," said Mathews, "because it's good for business."

Mathews was jubilant. Our talk had buoyed his spirits, even as it had dampened ours. In coming campaigns, we foresaw an escalation of gut-level warfare that was bound to affect millions of Americans on both sides, and which threatened to get uglier still. We liked Mathews. He showed a rare concern for his clients, his lists and his awesome technology. But as we left his office, we wondered whether he, too, might just be a bit too enamored of his direct-mail hardware. The fundamentalist right machine was already assembled and in high gear. The opposition remained diffuse, just reawakening, and possibly too tired and torn to regroup. Would he be able to revive and unite them?

Closing the Loops.   In the meantime, the fundamentalist right rolled on, over radio and television, through the mails, by cassette tape and through still another novel mass-communication channel, perhaps its most subtle and intimate yet: the telephone. The only electronic device more common to most Americans than their televisions, in the eighties the simple household telephone is rapidly being transformed into a remote command center for a variety of advanced communications functions: from full-service telephone shopping to space-age home computer tie-ins. Like the mails, the nation's vast prewired telephone system has become a mass medium in its own right, as homeowners and businessmen take ad-

vantage of new dialing features that promise to revolutionize the
field of personal communication.

The fundamentalist right, too, has been quick to realize the potential of the new improved telephone. Flashing numbers on their
electronic church screens, TV preachers prompt millions to contact their waiting banks of telephone operators. Using volunteer
troops, they ring up astronomical sums in marathon fund-raising
telethons, take floods of calls in response to TV offerings of free
pins, pamphlets and other Christian paraphernalia, and seal trans-
actions for books, Bibles and other religious products which the
FCC refuses to classify as commercial deals. Moreover, over their
long-distance lines and collect 800 numbers, fundamentalist right
Big Fathers have discovered a powerful new instrument for recruiting new converts and soliciting commitments to their broader
social and political campaigns. Here, with little doubt, the two
media work together.

Even more than direct mail, telephone contact between fundamentalist preachers and their followers is intimate and immediate,
establishing tight bonds that foster trust and openness to personal
appeals, new beliefs and opinions, and other indirect suggestions
or commands. Rev. James Robison, "a Man with a Message,"
uses both media together in his effort to lead "Bible-believing
Christians to stand firm on God's Word and reclaim America as
'one nation under God.'" In a soft-spoken introduction to one
fiery televised crusade, Robison urged viewers to help expand his
home audience:

> Would you take the time to pick up the telephone and call
> a family member or a neighbor, a relative, a friend, someone
> you've been praying for, and simply ask them [sic] to turn
> on the television? . . . I want to help you, and one of the
> ways I feel I can help you is by helping to reach those you
> love with the message of our Lord and our Savior, Jesus
> Christ. So please, very prayerfully, go to the telephone and
> call a friend and ask them to watch. . . . I hope you called
> one of your friends. If not, do so right now.

Like other TV preachers, Robison followed this request with
still another, asking viewers to call his ministry over a toll-free

hookup. This time, however, his message was less relaxed, more urgent and rhythmically repetitive:

> As you look at the screen, would you write that number down, that phone number, that 800 number? I'll pay for the call. Our ministry will pay for the call. People that love you, we'll pay for the call. . . . You dial the number. Write it down. . . . I want you to call until you get through and simply say, "I prayed along with Mr. Robison and I invited Jesus to come into my heart. . . ." I want to send you some material that will help you in the Word of God. So call the number in response and let us know you invited Jesus into your heart. . . . We want to bear your burden. . . . I hope you'll call.

Jerry Falwell has an active telephone hookup, too—he claims, one of the busiest 800 numbers on television—manned primarily by students at his Liberty Baptist College. For most of his "Old-Time Gospel Hour," Falwell solicits toll-free calls for a variety of purposes. Most seek cash donations, some offer free gifts, while others appear to serve as vehicles for larger fundamentalist right campaigns. One late-1981 program was a nonstop pitch for a multitude of Falwell enterprises:

> We desperately need to find "15,000 Club" members [donors to his college]. . . . We have purchased 50,000 [copies of Falwell's book] and as long as they last we are going to make them available to everyone who calls us on the toll-free number. . . . This decade, the 1980s, I believe will be known as the decade of destiny for this country, but it isn't going to happen by chance, so call us on our toll-free number and ask for a free copy of *Listen, America!* . . . then put it to work. Let's ask God to help us turn this nation around. . . . I'd like to urge all the pastors, Sunday school teachers, workers everywhere . . . call to attend superconference [a nationwide meeting] and learn how to capture your city for Christ through your superaggressive local New Testament church. . . . We'll be asking God to help you, to

lay upon your heart to pick up your telephone and call
today. . . . I'll be looking for your call.

But by far the most intriguing area of fundamentalist right telephone activity is its personal counseling services. Many TV
preachers maintain around-the-clock prayer and crisis "hotline"
centers. Falwell even has a teletype number for the deaf and dis-
abled. But as we saw in Virginia Beach, none matches the sophistication of Pat Robertson's nationwide network of eighty-three
phone counseling centers, with their multicolored counseling, crisis and prayer request forms. Unlike the targets and victims of
other fundamentalist right strategies, we found it almost impossible to locate people who had been drawn into the movement by
telephone. So, catching the current, we experimented, inserting
ourselves into the loop as any casual or innocent caller might.
And we saw how many counselors had been trained systematically
to turn any call into an opportunity to win new converts.

During one afternoon broadcast, Pat Robertson invited home
viewers to phone in their "personal problems" to "700 Club"
counselors. Jim took him at his word. A pleasant-sounding woman
answered the phone:

WOMAN: "700 Club."
JIM: "700 Club"? I was just watching the show and the man
    said you did counseling, and I wanted to know if you
    could give me some advice. I'm in this job that I really
    don't like and I'd like to know what I ought to do.
WOMAN: Well, uh, what's your name?
JIM: Jim.
WOMAN: Where are you calling from, Jim? What city?
JIM: New York. What do you advise people to do in cases
    like this?
WOMAN: I can't really advise you. There's only one person
    who can do that and that's the Lord. Do you know Jesus
    as your personal Savior?
JIM: No. I was just watching this show and it said you did
    counseling. Are you a psychologist?
WOMAN: No, I'm just one of the Christian counselors here. I
    can pray with you and I can ask the Lord to help you. But

before I do that, I would first ask you to give your heart to
Jesus, because that's where it all lies.

JIM: How would that help me get a new job?

WOMAN: Because He said, "If you seek, to take the Lord
into your heart . . . then all else will be added unto you."

JIM: Then do you think that if I would ask Jesus to take me
into his heart that he would—

WOMAN: No, you would take Him into *your* heart.

JIM: He doesn't take me into *his* heart?

WOMAN: No. He already wants you, but you would have to
invite Him to come into your life and be your Lord.

JIM: Do you think then he might help me get a new job?

WOMAN: Well, I don't know, but I definitely would not advise you to leave your job unless you had another one to
go to. . . .

Some months later, the "700 Club" aired a week of special
shows titled "Seven Days Ablaze," filled with more politics than
usual and stepped up talk of spiritual warfare. Pat Robertson's
usual wide-eyed cheer had given way to near-hysteria over family,
education and social issues that had changed little in the interim
months. In his panic-stricken charges of religious persecution, we
felt an attempted escalation of hostilities between Bible-believing
Christians and the secular world:

Ladies and gentlemen, there are two major elites who are
working in conjunction to take away the religious heritage of
our nation . . . the first is the educational elite. It is found in
the universities . . . they were the ones [who] declared there
is no God . . . that human beings should be allowed to engage in any sexual activity they feel is appropriate and [that]
the biblical ethic is based on superstition, it's outmoded and
should be done away with. In league with them are many
people in the judicial system, in the legal system, who . . .
believe there's got to be an elite who will control the masses.
The dumb masses who believe in God and believe in the
Bible have to be put under control. . . . This is a monstrous
evil. . . . What are we going to do? . . . We have some
telephones and I want you to call in.

Flo accepted the invitation. The lines were jammed. Robertson's frenzy appeared to be a powerful draw. But apparently it was just another ploy. After several tries, a young man answered:

MAN: "700 Club." May I help you?

FLO: Yes, I'm watching the "700 Club" and I'm very confused and frightened by what I'm hearing. Could you explain things to me?

MAN: Let me just ask you a couple of questions. Are you a Christian?

FLO: I'm not sure I understand what you mean by that.

MAN: Well, uh, have you accepted Jesus as your Savior?

FLO: What does that have to do with the things that are being talked about on the "700 Club," the problems with the educational elites and the family and the courts?

MAN: That's the heart of what is being broadcast. People that aren't saved, that are not Christians are of Satan and they are coming against the Christians trying to rule the world, trying to cast the Christians out because they do not believe in the Lord, they do not believe in Christ and they are putting us under persecution. They are trying to take over the world. It's all been prophesied in the Bible.

FLO: Aren't you frightened?

MAN: No, because I know that Jesus is my Savior and there is nothing Satan or the spirits can do to me. I've been a Christian for four years now and every day my walk with the Lord gets better and I'm strengthened.

FLO: Well, you have certainly given me something to think about.

MAN: I encourage you to watch the "700 Club" and hope that the Lord will lead you to Him and open your spirit up to receive His message.

In these conversations and others, we experienced yet another method by which fundamentalist right leaders sow the seeds of supernaturalism and political reaction. Over these separate media channels, they practice all the indirect methods of personal evangelism, along with far-reaching variations on the theme of emotional control. Through this network of closed loops, flexing out

COVERT OPERATIONS

and back, the movement has become an ominous force in mass communication. By twisting the heartstrings of communication into tight knots, we believe, it has gained a measure of control over mass audiences that, until now, has not existed in the free flow of information in America.

To us, it is more than ironic that this war of mass communication is being waged, not by overbearing government institutions or by profit-oriented commercial enterprises, but by ideological fundamentalists using religion to divert public awareness from their hidden social and political goals. What is it, then, that America is witnessing in the rise of the fundamentalist right? A spontaneous outburst of public enthusiasm? A cyclical wave of social reaction? Or does this potpourri of sales pitches and smorgasbord of high technology define a much larger whole? As we laid out the pieces before us, the picture of Holy Terror began to assume a different, distinctly foreign shape.

Total Propaganda Comes Home

We can no longer afford to take that which was good in the past and simply call it our heritage, to discard the bad and simply think of it as a dead load which by itself time will bury in oblivion. The subterranean stream of Western history has finally come to the surface and usurped the dignity of our tradition. This is the reality in which we live.

—HANNAH ARENDT—*The Origins of Totalitarianism*

CASUAL CONVERSATIONS that are not casual at all. Test-marketed emotional appeals. Seeded storms of public protest. Millions of letters to Washington—all written by the same computer. Surrender of the will on satellite TV.

What in God's name is going on in America?

So far in this book, we have referred repeatedly to a process known as "communication." We have spoken of "communication techniques" and "communication strategies," of the process of "mass communication" and of sophisticated "mass-communications technology." But Holy Terror really has little if anything to do with communication, that is with a genuine *exchange* of information, messages, thoughts, feelings and opinions among people. In the human sense, communication demands relationship and interaction. It *presumes* respect for individuals as something more than mere objects to be bombarded and manipulated. Above all, communication is a direct process, even when it takes place at nonverbal and emotional levels. When communication becomes covert, when it is designed to mislead, distort or deceive, when it sets out to subvert reason and individual decision-making in favor of suggestion and other forms of indirect control, then the won-

derful process we have been talking about becomes something else
again.

It becomes *propaganda*. Like the term terrorism, the notion of
propaganda seems to make Americans uncomfortable. The idea
seems foreign to us, undemocratic and sinister. It conjures up two
images—Nazi Germany and Soviet Russia—and other dark visions
of controlled societies. Yet the act of propaganda as the world has
come to know it in this century has its roots in the United States,
in Allied wartime efforts and in American inventions in the field of
mass-communications technology. Historically, however, Americans have always been reluctant propagandists, while other nations have embraced the process, refined it and deployed it enthusiastically against their own people and foreign populations.

In the eighties, that historical picture has begun to shift. With
the rise of Holy Terror, propaganda has come home in its most
potent form. To grasp the magnitude of this shift and its meaning
for America, we must understand how propaganda came to be
scorned as anathema to our way of life, and how it found fertile
ground in other cultures, only to return in a uniquely American
guise.

Most scholars mark the dawn of modern propaganda during
World War I, when governments first used psychological techniques to mobilize their people and prepare them for the sacrifices
of war. The challenge was immense. Soldiers had to be recruited.
Money had to be raised. Material comforts had to be given up.
Nationwide industrial efforts had to be mounted with great haste—
and all-out public cooperation was essential. People had to be rallied to fight for freedom, to hate and fear the enemy, and to forego
their own pleasures for the sake of the boys "over there." To accomplish these ends, Allied policy-makers in the United States
and England gave birth to the systematic practice of propaganda.
In speeches and other official pronouncements, in news stories,
photographs, films, phonograph records, books, circulars, handbills, billboards, posters, even in carefully planted rumors, governments developed new methods for disseminating information that
reaped windfall benefits in public attitudes and morale.

Suddenly, democratic governments found themselves in the
sticky business of information management. As details of the war
came in, authorities privy to the whole picture learned the value

and necessity of filtering the release of incoming reports to the public. News of key victories and losses not only had immediate effects on public spirits, but rebounded quickly to affect soldiers in battle. Moreover, they soon learned, deliberate false reports could wreak havoc on enemy combat plans and resolve. And there were new technologies to contend with. The demand for rapid wartime communications prompted crash programs for the development of "wireless" radio transmission. Almost instantly, governments around the world came to recognize the potential of broadcast communication, and the way the new medium could be used to shape public attitudes.

In the cold reality of the "war to end all wars," these practices proceeded with little concern for their enormous ramifications. Only after the war, in the early twenties, did the experts who were involved in the first flowering of propaganda begin to have second thoughts about the manipulations they had carried out and, in some cases, severe guilt feelings about the lies and deceptions they had spread. In the postmortem, American researchers came to dread this mysterious new power capable of welding "thousands and even millions into one amalgamated mass of hate and will and hope."

The prospects were unlimited and frightening—and repugnant to most Americans. With the first roar of the twenties, the government delivered control of the electronic medium into the hands of the new, publicly owned Radio Corporation of America (RCA). Almost overnight, radio burst forth with music and popular entertainment and became an indispensable household item. New stations sprang up willy-nilly. Nationwide networks were patched together, and the broadcast spectrum quickly became jammed with overlapping signals and competing interests. In 1927, President Coolidge asked Congress to help sort out the chaos, and legislation was enacted that declared unequivocally: *the airwaves belong to the people*. In 1934, this principle formed the basis of the Federal Communications Act, the pioneering law that, although outmoded in some technical aspects, continued to govern radio and television broadcasting to the start of the eighties, insuring for the most part that the public would be protected from manipulation and exploitation by either government or private interests.

But as the new media spread outward from America, other nations chose to pursue different routes in the development of mass communication. Some Western European governments maintained limited authority over the distribution of the technology and its programming. More insecure regimes assumed strict control over radio and soon extended their domains to include motion pictures and printed matter as well. In the volatile time between the wars, many world leaders found no conflict between the public's growing interest in news and entertainment and the government's interest in maximizing its power at home and abroad.

The most repressive of these foreign models, so alien to our American experience, launched many of the propaganda strategies we have come to recognize in Holy Terror.

THE GERMAN MODEL

In their most blatant instances, some fundamentalist right campaigns follow the historical lead of the propaganda machine assembled in Nazi Germany. Like the current movement, that dreaded regime aspired to power in a time of economic crisis and public reaction to social change. In the mid-twenties, while American researchers were busily adapting the lessons of wartime for use in commercial advertising, a youthful Adolf Hitler, imprisoned following the unsuccessful Nazi *Putsch* in Munich in 1923, distilled for posterity what he had learned from his experiences as a victim of propaganda during the Great War. In the study of propaganda, there may be no more ironic expression of its effects than this account of the impact on one unsuspecting target. Describing the inept ploys of Germany's wartime "enlightenment service" in *Mein Kampf,* Hitler wrote:

It was absolutely wrong to make the enemy ridiculous, as the Austrian and German comic papers did. . . . This falsification went so deep that people became convinced that in the Englishman they faced a businessman as shrewd as personally he was unbelievably cowardly. . . . I remember well my comrades' looks of astonishment when we faced the Tommies in person in Flanders. After the very first days of battle, the conviction dawned on each and every one of them that these Scotsmen did not exactly jibe with the pictures they had seen fit to give us in the comic magazines and press dispatches.

Hitler went on to express admiration for American and British propaganda efforts which, he said, were conducted "with amazing skill and really brilliant calculation":

> By contrast, the war propaganda of the English and Americans was psychologically sound. By representing the Germans to their own people as barbarians and Huns, they prepared the individual soldier for the terrors of war. . . . After this, the most terrible weapon that was used against him seemed only to confirm what his propagandists had told him; it likewise . . . increased his rage and hatred against the vile enemy.

Through such efforts, Hitler took his first lessons in propaganda from Allied leaflets dropped into the trenches in an attempt to convince German soldiers that their cause was hopeless. While those around him were being shattered in their resolve, Hitler was fascinated and strengthened:

> There was no end to what could be learned from the enemy by a man who kept his eyes open, refused to let his perceptions be ossified, and for four and a half years privately turned the stormflood of enemy propaganda over in his brain.

In the aftermath of Germany's humiliating defeat, Hitler entered politics and began to formulate a strategy he described as "spiritual terror." In 1920, he adopted the "hooked cross" or swastika as his emblem, coupling popular Aryan myths with the rampant anti-Semitism of the era. He condemned "democracy and humanism" and fumed over the moral decay of German society. In later writings, Hitler railed at length over the horrors of syphilis in tones foreshadowing modern-day fundamentalist right crusades:

> Particularly with regard to syphilis, the attitude of the leadership of the nation and the state can only be designated

as total capitulation. . . . What was done to combat the resulting syphilization of our people? . . . It was not permissible to take this question frivolously. . . . The fortune or misfortune of generations would depend on its solution. . . . The whole attention of the nation had to be concentrated on this terrible danger . . . Its injurious effects should have been hammered into people . . . by the use of all available means, until the entire nation arrived at the conviction that everything—future or ruin—depended upon the solution of this question.

As Hitler led his storm troopers into the streets and beer halls, he was laughed at by the public. Imprisoned for treason, he reconceived his plan to target the "emotional ideas" of the German people who had rejected him. Embittered, like later propagandists, he came to view his audience with contempt:

The receptivity of the great masses is very limited, their intelligence is small, but their power of forgetting is enormous. . . . All effective propaganda must be limited to a very few points and must harp on these in slogans until the last member of the public understands what you want him to understand.

Hitler locked onto this notion in his principle of the "big lie":

. . . the magnitude of a lie always contains a certain factor of credibility, since the great masses of the people . . . more easily fall a victim to a big lie than to a little one, since they themselves lie in little things, but would be ashamed of lies that were too big. Such a falsehood will never enter their heads, and they will not be able to believe in the possibility of such monstrous effrontery and infamous misrepresentations in others; yes, even when enlightened . . . they will long doubt and waver, and continue to accept. . . .

On his release from prison in 1925, Hitler began immediately to revive his plan of spiritual terror. Determined to seize power by constitutional means, he launched a broad campaign to sell his image and ideas to the German people. His first published statement was titled *A New Beginning*. This all-encompassing program was not his sole invention, however, but largely the work of his mastermind, Dr. Joseph Goebbels, the frail academician and political strategist who engineered the "Führer's" rise to power. A frustrated author, Goebbels was touched by Hitler's fiery rhetoric in 1922. "At the moment I was reborn," he said. In 1928, he was named propaganda chief of the Nazi party, and over the next four years, according to historian William L. Shirer, he and Hitler

> directed a propaganda campaign such as Germany had never seen. They plastered the walls of the cities and towns with a million screeching colored posters, distributed eight million pamphlets and twelve million extra copies of their Party newspapers . . . and for the first time in a German election made good use of films and gramophone records.

The campaign left the Nazis far short of the majority they needed to gain power, but it more than doubled the party's support and enhanced Hitler's image as a strong leader and champion of Aryan supremacy. In 1933, when Germany's senile President von Hindenburg named Hitler chancellor in the hope of rekindling the spirit of German unity, Hitler rewarded Goebbels for his efforts by appointing him the Third Reich's official "Minister of Propaganda." The position gave him unrivaled control over all information reaching the German people: not only official pronouncements but public events and mass media throughout Germany, including newspapers, radio and film.

The age of government by propaganda had begun.

In his wartime diaries, salvaged by American occupying authorities in Berlin in 1945, Propaganda Minister Goebbels laid out the principles of manipulation that governed information management in the Third Reich. Goebbels saw propaganda as the dominant activity of the state. "I believe," he told Hitler, "that when a propaganda ministry is created, all matters affecting propaganda, news and culture within the Reich and within occupied areas must be subordinated to it." Acting on this principle, he spread spiritual terror as government policy. One month after Hitler became chancellor, Goebbels arranged for the burning of the German Reichstag, which he blamed on Communist revolutionaries. Soon after, he led Germany's first book burnings. As the nation was cut off from outside sources of information, Hitler's rhetoric, now amplified by radio, brought the nation under near-hypnotic control. Symbols, emblems and rituals were used to evoke intense, automatic emotional responses. At the same time, terms that provoked undesirable images and emotions were filtered out of official pronouncements. "There are certain words from which we should shrink as the devil does from Holy Water," wrote Goebbels. He also learned to use negative means to his advantage by engaging in "wedge-driving" to foment suspicion and distrust among rival factions; by exploiting widespread anxieties and frustrations; and by stoking the fires of international aggression and the desire for revenge for Germany's wartime defeat.

As World War II began, Goebbels' ministry became an integral arm of the Nazi war effort. At home, he targeted every German for assault by newspaper, radio and motion pictures. Listening to foreign radio broadcasts was made a crime punishable by decapitation. Abroad, Goebbels relied heavily on propaganda to affect enemy policy, action and morale: by spreading doctored news in foreign-language broadcasts and by disseminating desired views through Nazi-controlled newspapers and theaters in occupied countries. He also experimented with different forms, alternating his efforts between "white" or official propaganda and "black" propaganda—rumors and unverifiable word-of-mouth reports.

Yet, for all Goebbels' rigor, Nazi propaganda had only limited impact on the German masses, and even less abroad. Although bold in theory, in practice it turned out to be a superficial force. By focusing his efforts almost exclusively on the manipulation of symbols and the management of news, Goebbels failed to achieve the control he sought over the minds of the German people. Instead, as the tide of war turned against Germany, he had to settle for simple control over public behavior, which with the failure of his machine the Nazis were forced to maintain by coercion. In the end, the Aryan myth succumbed to the reality of war, and Goebbels' acclaimed "strategy of terror" proved powerless to blunt the onrushing Allied drive. As early as 1943, Goebbels realized that his methods were failing. He wrote:

At the moment we cannot change very much through propaganda; we must once again gain a big victory somewhere.

Throughout this period America's energies were mobilized to defeat the Nazi threat and ward off any similar American reaction. In the thirties, scholars in a number of disciplines worked to redirect the discoveries of propaganda in constructive, enduring and ethical directions. Their early focus on "attitude change" in groups and small communities, and on "mass persuasion" over radio and in film, spurred the development of peaceful instruments of influence and the advance of knowledge in psychology and sociology. In these first studies in the science of communication, American theorists pointed to a new view of society as a living, interacting whole in which individuals were shaped by their relationships with one another, not merely by engineered mass-media messages. With the outbreak of war, however, most of this promising new research was curtailed, as experts in every field were diverted to strategic communication tasks: to the necessary management of news; to the gathering of intelligence on enemy strengths and weaknesses; and to the internal problems of national mobilization with their inevitable effects on public morale.

This time, however, the American propaganda effort was, at best, halfhearted. Deep ethical concerns continued to plague experts who found propaganda abhorrent to an open society. Some strategists even considered it unethical for use against the enemy. To the extent that the practice was seen as a way of saving lives, however, Allied propaganda continued, usually under strict cover and often without the knowledge of ranking government and military leaders.

Efforts aimed at the American public, however, were transparent. In patriotic appeals on radio, in film and in the press, the government made little use of deception on any appreciable scale, and almost no attempt to manipulate deep psychological processes in the American people. In one of the war's most memorable efforts, a series of nationwide fund-raising marathons over radio led by popular singer and entertainer Kate Smith, nearly every American tuned in to her eighteen-hour broadcasts for the sale of U.S. war bonds. Millions of dollars poured in, and advertising executives hailed the triumphant power of persuasion by mass media. But as an isolated media event, the celebrity spectacular did not warrant the praise that was heaped on it. Fewer than one percent of the audience actually bought victory bonds as a result of the broadcast—and nearly all turned out to be regular bond purchasers anyway. To analysts, the lesson of U.S. domestic wartime propaganda was reassuring: the direct approach over a single medium, regardless of its reach and popularity, had little or no lasting effect on public behavior or attitudes.

Only after the war, as the extent of enemy efforts became fully known, did American researchers fan out in interdisciplinary studies of propaganda, examining its effects on individuals, small groups and mass audiences in the hope of discovering ways to "inoculate" people against it. But with the start of the Cold War—a battle fought with words, threats and ideologies, not weapons—the positive direction of their efforts was again shaken to its core by news of encroaching Communist regimes in Russia and China. Leaders of these emerging monoliths were refining methods of control over their own people, over other nations and, some believed, over many Americans as well, into an elaborate mechanism of domination that anticipated western understanding by many decades. In the shadow of the "red menace" and the "yellow peril," Americans faced a new specter: total propaganda.

THE SOVIET MODEL

Ironically, despite their obsession with godless communism, fundamentalist right leaders have adopted major elements of the three-step strategy for the seizure of power first used by the small group of Russian revolutionaries who called themselves the "Bolsheviki" or "Majority."

At once predating and surviving the Nazi machine, the Soviet model is the prototype for all systems of total propaganda. Dr. Harold D. Lasswell, who pioneered the study of propaganda in the United States, performed one of the first dissections of the Soviet model in a 1951 article, "The Strategy of Soviet Propaganda." In examining the historical "zigzags" of Russian policy—from Lenin's early Communist ideology, to Stalin's totalitarian reign, through wartime alliances, to the Cold War vilification of the West —Lasswell perceived the unity of Russian propaganda goals: *to economize the material costs of maintaining power at home and abroad*. Propaganda was an instrument of "total policy" in the Soviet Union. Through it, Lasswell noted, the ruling elite reduced the material costs of domination, reaping broad economies in the use of coercion, in the need to divert material goods for military aggressions, and in decreased dissension among the masses whose needs, historically, came second to those of the all-powerful state.

The Soviet model was conceived with far more depth than Goebbels' lurching Nazi machine. In place of primitive symbols and nationalistic myths, Nikolai Lenin, chief architect of the 1917 revolution, built on the grandiose economic theories of Karl Marx and on sweeping themes of international class struggle, world revolution and the inevitable triumph of communism over a capitalist system he portrayed as inherently corrupt and morally destitute. Lenin's appeal to overarching values and global principles held mystical sway over starving Russian peasants, exploited factory workers and other laboring classes. In his renowned chronicle of the Russian revolution, *Ten Days That Shook the World*, American journalist John Reed gave a rare firsthand description of the Russian people, pure at heart, caught at this crossroads of history:

> Never have I seen men trying so hard to understand, to decide . . . their brows wrinkled with the effort of thought, sweat standing out on their foreheads; great giants of men with the innocent clear eyes of children . . . lifted out of the ordinary run of common thoughts, thinking in terms of Russia . . . as if it depended on them.

Yet, like his counterparts in every era, Lenin viewed the masses with contempt. He saw the Russian people historically as lazy, stubborn and stupid. And, unlike Hitler, he saw no hope of winning them to his cause by constitutional means. In the chaos that followed the first Russian revolt of 1905, more than a decade before his final seizure of power, Lenin devised his great covert scheme for transforming his own tiny political minority into a ruling elite. Central to his plan was the task of transforming the downtrodden masses into an uprising throng by means of propaganda.

Stage one in Lenin's strategy was: *the formation of "primary nuclei" capable of further expansion.* In Lenin's vision, these nuclear cells were essential to provide revolutionary leaders with a solid core of loyal followers and full-time labor for performing endless man-hours of propaganda work. This, in turn, would attract new followers and, in the process of Soviet multiplication, lead to the formation of new nuclei and successive generations of leadership. At the core of his nuclei were Russia's youth. Lenin commanded: "Form hundreds of circles . . . among the youth and encourage them to work at full blast." During this stage, new recruits were won over by means of "direct personal propaganda." Students, teachers and genteel women "broken away from their class" went door-to-door in citywide campaigns designed to win over the working classes. In many instances, direct recruiting was preceded by "the output of the party presses." In others, raw recruits were brought to informal "study groups" devoted to the writings of Marx, Engels, Lenin and other early luminaries of socialist thought. In these days before radio in Russia, the study group provided an ideal forum for the dissemination of Lenin's political and economic ideas. The potent dynamics of the group served well for indoctrination purposes. As Lasswell pointed out, their effectiveness remains undiminished in later times and more sophisticated cultures:

> In these intellectual "speakeasies" the doctrinal system is expounded in a pious atmosphere free of the critical deflating effect of vigorous evaluation on a comparative basis. Study groups are an important example of the tactical principle that it is possible to move toward effective power in an indifferent or hostile society by limited concentrations of superiority of books and man-hours of propaganda work.

Stage two in Lenin's program was: *cooperating with allies in the arenas of power accessible to the nuclei, who are by this time sufficiently strong to act as "parties," "unions" and the like.* Lenin's problem in stage two was to make alliances without losing independence. To accomplish this, he sought to collaborate with other groups and movements, at the same time, like Hitler and Goebbels, preying on the natural tensions between competing factions. Lenin's strategy, wrote Lasswell, "was to keep alive an attitude of suspicion toward allies, while at the same time lulling the ally into complacency, or diverting his attention to a common enemy."

Stage three represented the culmination of the revolutionary drive: *the seizure of power*. By this stage, the power of the core movement and its allies was great enough to effect, in 1917, a *coup d'état* or takeover of the state by a ruling elite. Once this final stage was reached, however, the need for propaganda did not diminish. On the contrary, in the Soviet model, the consolidation of power hinged on the success of an ongoing propaganda effort conducted with one aim in mind: *to demoralize the potential opposition, and to gain support, by creating an impression that all further opposition, or noncooperation, is both useless and immoral*. "The third stage is less subtle and far more ruthless," wrote Lasswell, "since it involves the spreading of terror." Although much of this terror consisted of acts of violence, much of it was psychological, designed to sow fear and hopelessness and to "impress all with the 'inevitable' triumph of Soviet power." Using this model, Lasswell noted, successive generations of rulers in the Kremlin abandoned all other ethical considerations in furtherance of "a world-encompassing goal that is treated as beyond the reach of discussion or inquiry."

The Soviet model worked well abroad. In the United States in the twenties and thirties, Communist ideologues used personal propaganda techniques to penetrate middle-class communities and organize sympathetic Americans into required cells. Later, in Canada, government authorities traced the discovery of a Russian spy ring to a network of privately organized study groups. In Hungary and Czechoslovakia in the fifties, similar tactics were used to penetrate trade unions and other private associations. And today, in Africa and throughout the Third World, Lenin's program for recruiting the young and the disenfranchised still provides a workable basis for Soviet expansionism. In every context, as they did in the beginning, Communist organizers follow the principle of *dual organization,* using open channels of communication—"white" propaganda—whenever possible, but maintaining closed, secret channels and shadowy front groups—"black" propaganda—as Lasswell put it:

> to permeate every national community . . . to reach the armed forces, the police, the foreign service, business, the professions, trade unions, cooperatives, schools, publishing houses, radio-television, films and the like. . . . Through these organizational networks, a great number of special environments are made available for the restamping of minds.

But the Soviet machine is no clockwork stamper. History has demonstrated that by Soviet methods the seizure of power may be systematically achieved, but holding on to that power requires extraordinary coercive measures and military strength. Like Goebbels' Germany, post-Leninist Russia quickly became a nightmare world of suffering, deprivation and punishment—both physical and psychological. Far from basking in the fulfillment of their promised workers' paradise, the Russian people were soon forced to resign themselves to lives of unending bleakness in service to the state. Soviet propaganda failed in its aim to economize the cost of world dominance. Indeed, like the German model, it barely succeeded in keeping its own citizens in line. In Russia, at least, the repeated failure of national political and economic programs, not to mention the insecurity of the ruling elite, may be due in large part to the legacy and net effect of Soviet propaganda: the systematic demoralization of an entire people.

THE CHINESE MODEL

The late fifties saw the breakup of American propaganda research into insular, compartmentalized endeavors. The bulk of the Holocaust had been digested. Government intelligence on Communist societies remained largely classified. In the chill of the McCarthy era, researchers stepped gingerly around the unsettling question of how so many bright, independent-minded Americans could have been swept up in a wave of mass hysteria unleashed primarily through the new medium of television. And as the witch hunts receded, social theorists retreated as well, into labyrinths of statistical and experimental detail in "safe" fields of marketing and motivation research.

But there were new propaganda puzzles to be solved. With the return of American prisoners of war from North Korean prison camps, the specter of "brainwashing" caught American researchers, once again, by surprise. Quick defense projects were launched in an effort to understand the mystifying transformations that had prompted downed American airmen to make seemingly "voluntary" confessions and defections. By the late fifties, the focus of government-funded research closed in on the sudden conversion of individuals by precision weapons of psychological warfare: brainwashing, encounter group dynamics, new forms of hypnosis and mind-altering drugs. Yet the American reluctance to confront total propaganda on its own terms led researchers away from, not toward, a unifying view. It also left the nation more vulnerable than ever in its complacency, and in its confidence that the wasting force of propaganda could never strike here.

It took a farsighted Frenchman, Jacques Ellul, a respected social philosopher and veteran of the wartime French underground, to put the phenomenon into perspective. His book, *Propaganda: The Formation of Men's Attitudes,* published in the United States in 1965, leaped over scattered statistical studies and test-group findings to view propaganda in its real-life effects. Unlike earlier piecemeal efforts, Ellul's inquiry treated propaganda not merely as a body of techniques deployed for political ends but as a sweeping long-range social process. This larger view we found to be rich with insights into Holy Terror.

Ellul defined propaganda as a covert operation or "secret action" having goals of which "the listener is not conscious." In his view, propaganda is an inevitable outgrowth of technological developments that tend to reduce society to a homogenous mass that may be easily manipulated. In that sense, Ellul saw propaganda in every form as "a direct attack against man." And for Ellul, all modern propaganda that is effective is *total propaganda.* His description struck us as remarkably similar to Jerry Falwell's concept of "saturation evangelism":

Propaganda must be total. The propagandist must utilize all of the technical means at his disposal—the press, radio,

TV, movies, posters, meetings, door-to-door canvassing.
. . . Each usable medium has its own particular way of
penetration. . . . To draw the individual into the net of propaganda, each technique must be utilized . . . and fused with
all the other media, each of them reaching the individual in a
specific fashion and making him react anew to the same
theme—in the same direction, but *differently*.

But the key to total propaganda requires more than a multimedia blitz. As Goebbels and Lenin grasped, but incompletely,
to command individuals and whole nations, total propaganda must
claim to reach for something higher, appeal to some larger purpose, to broad principles or values or, better yet, to the indis-
putable attraction of the mystical. It is in myth and mysticism, this
deep-rooted area of feeling and belief, Ellul argued, that the techniques and technologies of total propaganda find their firmest anchor:

> We are here in the presence of an organized myth that
> tries to take hold of the entire person. Through the myth it
> creates, propaganda imposes a complete range of intuitive
> knowledge, susceptible of only one interpretation, unique and
> one-sided, and precluding any divergence. This myth be-
> comes so powerful that it invades every area of consciousness
> . . . controls the whole of the individual, who becomes im-
> mune to any other influence.

Here, for the first time, Ellul connected the controlling power
of myth with the concrete act of propaganda. In Germany, the
Nazi Aryan mythology, its notion of the "master race" and use of
other primitive symbols and rituals, fulfilled this requirement. In
Russia, it was met by elevating to mystical heights abstract entities
such as the "State" and the "Proletariat." From these all-encompassing visions rooted in deep emotions and national feelings,
total propaganda branches freely into a multitude of forms. There
is *overt propaganda,* direct attempts to modify attitudes and pro-
voke action, which can be accomplished either by *propaganda of
the word* (oral or written presentations) or by *propaganda of the
deed* (political acts carried out for purposes of terror, intimi-

dation, etc.). But according to Ellul, direct propaganda can only be effective if it is preceded by *pre-propaganda,* long-range social initiatives designed to create a favorable climate for later campaigns. Pre-propaganda is subtle. Very often, Ellul noted, it consists of simply "creating ambiguities, reducing prejudices and spreading images, apparently without purpose." Complementing these overt measures, however, is what Ellul called *covert propaganda*—Lenin's "black" propaganda. In contrast to overt propaganda, practiced openly by governments and political groups for the benefit of their own forces and to influence others, covert propaganda "tends to hide its aims, identity, significance and source." Used separately, the two methods, black and white, provide the propagandist with a flexible range of alternative techniques. Together, they expand his options and open still more possibilities of indirect control.

Through this slow, constant impregnation, said Ellul, "propaganda tends to make the individual live in a separate world." He develops "unfailing responses" to specific words, signs and symbols. The myth harnesses his "sense of the sacred . . . takes possession of a man's mind so completely that his life is consecrated to it." At that point, the myth and the machine become one, and the individual is little more than a cog in the larger propaganda complex:

> Even in the actual contact of human relations, at meetings, in door-to-door visits, the propagandist is . . . nothing else and nothing more than the representative of the organization. . . . He remains a manipulator, in the shadow of the machine. . . . His words are no longer human words but technically calculated words; they no longer express a feeling or a spontaneous idea. . . . But this human contact is false and merely simulated. . . . In the very act of pretending to speak as man to man, the propagandist is reaching the summit of mendacity and falsifications, even when he is not conscious of it.

To us, Ellul's words described the strategists and foot soldiers of the fundamentalist right, but the people who were drawing his attention were not Americans nor Europeans, but Asians. In his later research, Ellul became particularly interested in developments taking place in Communist China under Mao Tse-tung. Although patterned largely on the Soviet model, the Chinese revolution took place under unique circumstances and posed enormous propaganda problems: masses of unprecedented size spread over great distances, nearly illiterate, speaking a multitude of different languages and dialects, living in abject poverty and squalor—and with virtually no mass media. Radios and newspapers were nonexistent. Even wall posters, the closest thing in China to a mass medium, were rare. To meet the challenge, Mao devised a comprehensive system for inculcating belief and action with two major components: education and organization.

Ellul distinguished Chinese propaganda from "brainwashing," which he understood, correctly, to be a form of coercion practiced primarily on prisoners of war and political dissidents and incorporating extensive use of physical punishment and deprivations. He also distinguished Chinese education from public education in the West, which generally confined itself to instruction in basic skills. In contrast, education under Mao was a vehicle for political indoctrination and motivating myth, and with the success of his campaign he established a nationwide network of "re-education" centers to fuel hatred of the "running dogs and lackeys of Imperialism" and plant visions of the "new man" who would emerge in his glorified "People's Republic." Building on the Soviet model, as Mao's forces occupied new territories they were deployed at three levels of organization: official "Peasant Unions" in which people were enlisted for education and official "discussion"; his clandestine "parallel hierarchy," a covert propaganda network established in areas still controlled by the ruling government; and the Red Army, his insurgent people's military force. At every level, the goal was to mobilize the masses to "make propaganda in every instance." Even the Red Army was ordered to "function among the people like a fish in water." Mao said:

> The Red Army does not make war for war's sake: this war is a war for propaganda in the midst of the masses.

Like Lenin, after the revolution, Mao continued to rely heavily on propaganda. His network of education centers and discussion groups had one remaining goal: "to drain the opponents of their energy and their convictions . . . to 'work over' every member of the group until, fully and of his own free will, he adheres to a proposition declared to be the absolute truth by the leader." In the Chinese model, the goal of propaganda was not merely to influence morale or behavior, as Goebbels tried, not simply to enlist the masses in service to the state, as Lenin did, but to fully "remold" the "new man" of China into an ideal prototype. In Mao's China no one, not even Mao himself, escaped the "mold." He wrote:

> . . . every person must be placed in the mold, the exploiters as well as the workers. . . . We ourselves are being placed in the mold every year. . . . I have gone through the remolding of my own thoughts . . . and I must continue.

With the birth of Mao's "new man" and his ritual of remolding, China took total propaganda one step further, beyond Hitler's "master race" and Lenin's mythical "State" to the ideal of a perfect nation of perfect people. Yet the socialist vision had built-in limits. Its mythical engine was driven by material goals and expressed in real-world terms, and in the end, like Hitler and Lenin, Mao was forced to resort to coercion and violence to seize and maintain power. It took the American dream and the syndrome of ideological fundamentalism to transmute total propaganda into its ultimate form.

THE FUNDAMENTALIST RIGHT MODEL

As we assembled the parts of the fundamentalist right model, its driving myths, controlling techniques and almost magical dependence on new media technology, we had no trouble drawing parallels to major propaganda systems of the twentieth century. But those parallels soon ran askew. For decades, Americans have been subjected to sophisticated methods of mass persuasion: in commercial advertising, election campaigns and various social and cultural crusades. Yet, in their limited aims and relative directness, these methods have been rightly distinguished from more distasteful and frightening forms. In our society, with its built-in checks and balances, its broad individual freedoms and its diversity of competing voices, not one of these accepted practices, nor all of them taken together, comprise anything close to a system of total propaganda, that is, a comprehensive attack on the thoughts, feelings, beliefs, values and guiding vision of a people and their culture—culminating in the outright seizure of power. In that sense, Americans have never experienced total propaganda the way people have in Germany, Russia, China and other nations.

In our view, the assault on secular society by the fundamentalist right constitutes such a threat. It is the first instance of total propaganda brought home to the United States. And it is propaganda in its cruelest form to date: politics masquerading as religion. Religion is the only avenue through which total propaganda could strike America. It is our only institution with no checks and balances, and the last place most Americans would expect to find an attack on their freedoms. Yet, throughout this century, religion has served as a haven for far right reaction in America. And in the last decade, it has become the base for an orchestrated attack on our culture with the expressed aim of seizing control of the government.

The fundamentalist right model may be the most comprehensive of all, comprising the classic elements of total propaganda: a mammoth mass-communications network, a tightly coordinated political machine, a fiercely independent education system—all predicated, for the first time, on the deep structure of religion and suffused to grass-roots levels through a coalescence of separatist churches, Bible studies, parachurch and missionary organizations. Its expressed objectives, as fundamentalist right spokesmen have described them in this book: to Christianize the nation, to fill all government positions with "Bible-believing" Christians, to gain ascendancy over the national media, to have fundamentalist beliefs taught as science in public schools, to dictate the meaning of human life and, ultimately, to convert every person on earth.

No totalitarian regime has ever aspired to do more. Of graver concern, in our view, is that atop it all sits no single maniacal leader, no lone rebel, visionary or even a formal ruling clique, but the syndrome of ideological fundamentalism. Leaders of this movement claim to be literally empowered by God. Many believe they have surrendered their wills to a supernatural force that controls their every thought, feeling and action. The government and nation they envision would be similarly yielded to supernatural beings and revealed books, in effect, run in its entirety by disembodied indirect control. With this mythical program, the fundamentalist right has vaulted over all earlier obstacles of propaganda into the free domain of religious terrorism. Through religion, it has already brought a segment of America under control, and through religion—one way or another—it will fail or succeed on the national scene.

Jacques Ellul was well aware of the inherent dangers of mixing religion and propaganda. He gave great credit to the insight of totalitarian propagandists who appealed to man's "sense of the sacred." Yet, as a political weapon, Ellul dismissed religious propaganda as "not very successful." Writing in the late fifties and early sixties, he concluded that "society as a whole is no longer interested in religious problems." Apparently, even Ellul underestimated the power of propaganda. Less worried about its threat to governments or societies, he was more concerned about the corrupting effects of propaganda on religion itself. His crisp warning is pregnant with insight for today:

> Christians often claim they can separate material devices from propaganda techniques. . . . They think they can use press and radio without . . . having to appeal to conditioned reflexes, myths, and so on. . . . If a church wants to use propaganda to be effective, just as all the others, it must use the entire system with all its resources. . . . Propaganda is a total system that one must accept or reject in its entirety. . . . [Yet] Christianity disseminated in this way is not Christianity. In such moments . . . Christianity ceases to be an overwhelming power and spiritual adventure and becomes institutionalized in all its expressions and compromised in all its actions. It serves everybody as an ideology with the greatest of ease, and tends to be a hoax. . . . It reaches the masses, influences collective opinions, leads sociological movements, and even makes many people accept what seems

to be Christianity. But in doing that the church becomes a false church.

Ellul's indictments map onto the fundamentalist right in its campaign of Holy Terror. In its use of the "big lie"—in some NCPAC campaign ads, in Tim LaHaye's definition of humanism, in several of Jerry Falwell's public statements and media presentations, in Pat Robertson's more preposterous television claims—the movement undermines its every pretension of morality. In their attacks on homosexuals, feminists, Communists, liberals and members of minority religions, like Hitler and Goebbels, fundamentalist right leaders fuel hatred and prejudice. In their use of symbols and code words such as "pro-life," "conservative" and "secular humanism," in their adoption of fetus emblems and attempts to usurp the banner of the American flag, they play on intense and automatic emotional responses. In their annual mass "March for Life" and election-year "Washington for Jesus" rallies, they employ, in Ellul's terms, *shock propaganda,* "intense but temporary, leading to immediate action." And in their myth of the all-powerful Superchristian, they ordain the "saved" fundamentalist as a being beyond sin, possessing eternal life, inerrant truth, magically at one with the indwelling supernatural Jesus—and now singularly qualified to hold elected office.

Playing as it does on profound currents in religion and American history, the myth of the fundamentalist Superchristian may be the most potent mythical image of modern time. Going beyond Aryan mythology and socialist abstraction, fundamentalist right supernaturalism is uniquely compelling. It appeals, not only to the ancient religious images that continue to hold sway over most Americans, but to modern themes of morality and patriotism, to the urge to surrender in the face of overwhelming change and complexity, and to untapped spiritual and psychic potentials many Americans are reaching to explore.

Yet, as simply another technique in the rush for power, as Ellul noted, the religion is a hoax. The whole package has become propaganda. In the electronic church, *pre-propaganda:* the use of mass media to bring about slow, general changes in public attitudes. On television and throughout the fundamentalist church, parachurch and missionary network, *covert propaganda:* the use of indirect methods to recruit new followers and train them in strict obedience to movement leaders. And finally, in the new right, *overt propaganda:* direct attempts to change beliefs and opinions through the black marketplace of ideas, and through its ideological PACs, lobbies and grass-roots organizations, to mobilize followers for political action.

In operation, the structure conforms almost exactly to the Soviet model. Stage one, *formation of primary nuclei:* through the Great Commission Army, local church Bible study groups and Christian schools, colleges and missionary organizations. Much of this first-stage activity is indirect, covert or openly deceptive, carried out in manipulated conversations, surveys and petition drives, in seemingly nonreligious training seminars, and in private invitations mailed to multimillionaires inviting them to help "change the course of history." In the political arena, the new right performs its own Soviet-style functions. Following the defeat of their champion, Barry Goldwater, in 1964, the hardened ideologues of the Young Americans for Freedom and other far right groups committed themselves to the long haul, like earlier thwarted revolutionaries. Laughed off by nearly everyone in that decade, they found positions in conservative media, as aides in government and as fringe organizers. Through the seventies, they developed their technical capacities, cultivated lucrative connections and, in general, moved forward in line with stage two of the Soviet model: *cooperation with allies* and *formation of "parties," "unions" and the like.* As their one-man operations grew into PACs, lobbies and foundations, fundamentalist right leaders began to talk openly of their goal, as Terry Dolan said, to "seize control of the U.S. Senate," or as others vowed, to take over the Republican party, the Congress and the White House by waging a new kind of war. Master strategist Paul Weyrich described that war:

It may not be with bullets, and it may not be with rockets and missiles, but it is a war nevertheless. It is a war of ideology, it's a war of ideas, it's a war about our way of life. And it has to be fought with the same intensity, I think, and dedication as you would fight a shooting war.

The propaganda poured out: pro-life, pro-God, pro-America, pro-free enterprise, pro-family and pro-morality movements of every stripe, each seemingly designed to form alliances without sacrificing independence. Falwell's Moral Majority played a tricky game of *integration propaganda,* keeping alive an "attitude of suspicion toward allies" while at the same time lulling them into complacency. Tim LaHaye and James Robison made *agitation propaganda* or *agitprop* in their incendiary writings and television specials, appealing to "simple elementary sentiments requiring no refinement" and to "key words of magical import." By 1980, the network was in place: the foot soldiers, the indirect techniques, the closed-loop technology.

The only problem was that the propaganda had taken over. If fundamentalist right leaders had any sincere intention of furthering the course of American values, morality or the Judeo-Christian ethic, their literal adherence, supernaturalism, intolerance and contempt for the knowledge they were using soon pushed their engine off the track. In their first bid to seize power, the machine ran amok. With the broadening of fundamentalism from religion to ideology, it had become unethical in its methods, un-American in its aims, fat with pride and prejudice—and anything but Christian. Twenty years ago, Jacques Ellul saw it coming in the inevitable end of any attempt to mix religion and politics by propaganda:

> At the end of this brief analysis, we can conclude that propaganda is one of the most powerful factors of de-Christianization in the world, through the psychological modifications that it effects, through the ideological morass with which it has flooded the consciousness of the masses, through the reduction of Christianity to the level of an ideology . . . all this is the creation of a mental universe foreign to Christianity. And this de-Christianization through the effects of one instrument—propaganda—is much greater than through all the non-Christian doctrines.

The Seizure of Power

We do not have a separate social agenda, a separate economic agenda, and a separate foreign agenda. We have one agenda. Just as surely as we seek to put our financial house in order and rebuild our nation's defenses, so too we seek to protect the unborn, to end the manipulation of schoolchildren by utopian planners and permit the acknowledgment of a Supreme Being in our classrooms. . . . The Marxist vision of man without God must be seen as an empty and false faith. . . . This is the real task before us: to reassert our commitment as a nation to a law higher than our own. . . .

Fellow citizens . . . our time is now, our moment has arrived.

—RONALD REAGAN—March 20, 1981

STAGE THREE: *the seizure of power.*   Through the early years, from 1974 to 1978, Richard Viguerie, Paul Weyrich and Terry Dolan, aided by Joseph Coors and other prime benefactors, assembled a virtual parallel hierarchy in the network of new right PACs, lobbies, foundations and think tanks which, in their vision, would supersede the institutional structures liberal politicians had used to maintain power for more than a generation. They even set up a "shadow cabinet," a schoolboys' parody (Viguerie was "secretary of commerce").

At the same time, like-minded senators and congressmen were making their way to Washington. Many were beneficiaries of the new money and political muscle of the surging Sun Belt and mountain West: hard-line Republicans such as Senators Jake Garn and Orrin Hatch from Mormon-dominated Utah; gentlemanly Paul Laxalt from Nevada; studious James McClure from

Idaho; millionaire rancher Malcolm Wallop from Wyoming. In the House as well, new right talent was blooming: Philip Crane of Illinois, Robert Dornan of California, Mickey Edwards of Oklahoma, Larry McDonald of Georgia.

But it was not until the mid-term elections of 1978 that the movement began to rumble in unison. The PACs began throwing hardballs, cranking out their first attack-style campaigns, pumping up their grass-roots organizations and fielding their initial slate of hand-picked candidates. Their first success in the Senate, former airline pilot Gordon Humphrey of New Hampshire, was elected largely on the strength of Dolan's NCPAC media strategy. Their second, Roger Jepsen from Iowa, proved the effectiveness of the movement's first working coalition of central organizing PACs and pro-life, pro-gun, pro-defense, pro-family and anti-big government forces. More limited efforts in 1978 helped other candidates to victory: William Armstrong, Colorado Republican who made the leap from the House to the Senate; John Warner, former Undersecretary of the Navy who won his first political campaign for the Senate from Virginia; Phil Gramm, a former Texas A&M economics professor who became one of the first Democratic congressmen in the fundamentalist right camp. Weyrich's Committee for the Survival of a Free Congress claimed thirteen winners in 1978.

By 1979, movement loyalists had found key positions on Senate committees such as Budget, Banking, and Labor and Human Resources, and established a strong presence in a number of equally powerful House committees and subcommittees. Many met regularly with new right strategists and maintained active lines of communication with coalitions and working circles with names like the Kingston and Library Court groups. By late 1979, when Paul Laxalt introduced the all-encompassing Family Protection Act in the Senate, grass-roots organizers were claiming the ability to deliver 25,000 letters to members of Congress on seventy-two-hour notice—and Weyrich was only beginning to mobilize and train his league of fundamentalist preachers.

With the advent of Moral Majority and the Religious Roundtable in 1979, religion became the magnet for fundamentalists of every stripe. Closing ranks around the "social" issues—abortion, school prayer, homosexuality, pornography, the ERA—they

formed a driving wedge of hardened belief and emotion that
pushed deep into the heartland. Early in 1980, the drumbeat of
"morality" began to throb. In Alaska, Moral Majority members
sprang up at winter Republican party caucuses and elected an
overwhelming majority of delegates to the state convention, in
effect seizing control of the Alaska GOP. In Alabama, Moral Majority forces threw their support behind another retired admiral,
Jeremiah Denton, a tough-talking superpatriot and ex-prisoner of
war in North Vietnam who had come home to found the anti-pornography, anti-adultery Coalition for Decency. In Oklahoma, they
backed Don Nickles, a young state senator who, according to a
Tulsa newspaper, advocated "the virtual dismemberment of the
national government."

By summer, the trickle-down effect of "Washington for Jesus"
was beginning to soak the grass roots. In our research, we were
hearing of numerous reports of fundamentalists active in the electronic church and lay ministries who were quietly shifting the
focus of their participation from religion to state party politics.
When the Republican National Convention opened in July, fundamentalist forces counted for more than a third of the delegates
and virtually dictated the party platform, overturning long-standing Republican positions in favor of fundamentalist right planks
reflecting scriptural stands on "the sanctity of innocent human
life," "the traditional role and values of the family" and "the importance of support for the mother and homemaker in maintaining
the values of this country." With the exception of a victory for
moderates in the GOP vice-presidential nominee, within the Republican party, for all practical purposes, the seizure of power was
complete.

But the GOP was merely a waystation on the fundamentalist
path to glory. With their PACs oiled and grinding, their foot soldiers roused for God and Country, and their multiple special interests flanking them on all sides, the movement made its triumphant
run on Washington, coasting to victory in dozens of races and riding the coattails of the presidential landslide in others. With the
dawn of the 97th Congress, a new burst of fundamentalist right
firepower exploded in Congress: in the Senate, Moral Majority's
Denton and Nickles; NCPAC's Dan Quayle of Indiana, Charles
Grassley of Iowa, Steven Symms of Idaho and James Abdnor of

South Dakota; Bob Kasten of Wisconsin and Paula Hawkins of Florida, two more beneficiaries of the Viguerie-Dolan-Weyrich machine; and in the House, dozens of freshman congressmen who had graduated from new right "training schools" or taken advantage of its PAC money, polling data and grass-roots support.

The new majority was studded with fundamentalist right superstars, ideologically pure and openly eager to perform for the movement. Symms, the Idaho Republican who unseated Frank Church, was quickly nominated by syndicated columnist Jack Anderson as odds-on favorite for "Worst Senator" and charged with "suspicious ties" to Nelson Bunker Hunt and his giant silver interests. Iowa's Grassley was lauded by Weyrich as an "exemplary Christian." Colorado's Bill Armstrong was showcased at executive dinner parties where, according to printed invitations, he would give testimony on how his "life-changing encounter with Jesus Christ . . . enabled him to be a more effective legislator."

However, the major action of the movement was taking place not at social gatherings but in social legislation, as its staunchest allies in Congress moved speedily to introduce bills that would turn fundamentalist beliefs into national policy. Early in the session, as Congress and the public were being bombarded by the new administration's emergency economic program, Senators Laxalt and Jepsen introduced a revived Family Protection Act of 1981. Among its thirty-one provisions, the bill proposed to withhold federal money for school books "that denigrate the role of women as it has been historically understood"; to exempt private and church schools from all federal regulations, including "actions designed to overcome racial imbalance"; to give parents a greater role in textbook selection and local schools final authority over "sex-intermingling in sports and other school activities"; to revise the definition of "child abuse" to exclude corporal punishment; and to restrict federal interference with state laws pertaining to spouse abuse or domestic relations. When asked if the bill embodied a single view of morality, Jepsen replied illogically, "Not at all. We acknowledge there is a God. We do have certain laws and rules, which as Christians we follow." A spokeswoman for Moral Majority said the bill "represented everything" her group stood for.

Or almost everything. Even before Laxalt and Jepsen filed

their reborn Family Protection Act, freshman Senator Denton unleashed another fundamentalist right salvo. His "teen chastity bill," introduced with support from Senator Orrin Hatch, chairman of the Senate Committee on Human Resources, allocated $30 million of a shrinking budget to redirect the activities of twenty-seven adolescent counseling centers around the country, away from providing information on pregnancy, birth control and abortion and toward a "pro-family emphasis" that would "promote self-discipline, chastity and other positive family-centered approaches" to reducing the number of teenage pregnancies. Following the public outcry that greeted news of the bill, some of its more pointed language was altered, and eventually it was cleared through committee. Meanwhile, Denton was quoted in an Alabama newspaper as saying, of his campaign against teen sex, "I don't care if they tickle where it itches. I'm talking about screwing." An aide said he thought the remark would be paraphrased.

But beneath all the codes and catchphrases, a larger transformation was taking place. Reveling in their first majority in a generation, ranking Republicans stepped into the chairmanships of the Senate's ruling committees: Garn at Budget, Hatch at Labor and Human Resources, South Carolina's Strom Thurmond at Judiciary. As the new administration rolled out its heavy artillery, all agreed to let matters of the economy and national defense take precedence over social and moral issues. Except for one man. Waiting not so patiently in the wings, nudging the movement's pet bills toward early floor votes, was the rowdiest Republican of them all.

Birth of a Shadow Government. No one noticed when Jesse Helms blew into Washington in 1972. Helms washed ashore in the first wave of reaction to liberalism, riding the coattails of Richard Nixon's landslide defeat of George McGovern. Yet, long before he tumbled into the Senate, Helms was aiming for something higher. By the end of his first term, he had laid the foundation for a fundamentalist right shadow government.

So unlikely a figure is Jesse Helms that the media ignored him in 1980 when he addressed the Republican Convention in Detroit and pulled the levers of power that transformed the party platform into a fundamentalist right manifesto. Only in the summer of

1981, long after the new Congress was called to order, did it come
to light that the courtly, bespectacled, "owlish" Helms, as he was
invariably described, was not only the granddaddy of the entire
fundamentalist right network, but that he had his own private propaganda machine that was on the verge of achieving a strangle-
hold on the new government. A sudden flurry of press reports
treated him with deference, yet his rise to power signaled the revival of a sordid strain in American government, an element of extremist zealotry that was presumed to have died out with the
McCarthy era. In the soft-spoken Helms's unvarnished ideological
fundamentalism, much of the intolerance of America's past was
born anew, and for the first time with no ready and effective counterforce to hold it in check.

Jesse Helms has spent more than half of his sixty years sharp-
ening his propaganda skills, first as a small-town reporter, next
as a writer of wartime press releases for the navy, then as city editor for a Raleigh, North Carolina, newspaper. From the beginning,
Helms recognized the potential of the electronic media as a political tool. In 1950, he used his position as the one-man news department of Raleigh's WRAL radio station to further the Senate
candidacy of Willis Smith, a Raleigh lawyer whose campaign
smear tactics made history as he attacked as a Communist his opponent, a university professor who had become a state symbol of
interracial progress. During the campaign, Smith's forces circulated handbills that read, "WHITE PEOPLE WAKE UP." They ran
newspaper ads headlined "The South Under Attack," and circulated retouched photographs depicting the incumbent senator's
wife dancing with a black partner. Helms denied having anything
to do with the underside of the campaign, but he trumpeted the
candidate on radio, and when Smith won, Helms moved with him
to Washington and became his administrative assistant.

Three years later, Helms was back in North Carolina, where he
soon launched his own political career, serving two terms on the
Raleigh City Council. In 1960, he returned to WRAL, which had
grown into a regional broadcasting empire. Named vice-president,
director of public-affairs programming and on-camera editorialist
for its flagship television station—known as "The Voice of Free
Enterprise"—Helms became famous throughout the state for his
tough-talking commentaries, which were also aired on the seventy-

station Tobacco Radio Network. Over the next dozen years, he broadcast more than 2,700 daily five-minute editorials, cultivating a large and loyal following.

And he became practiced in the use of the media for purposes of social and political agitation. In 1963, Helms slammed the civil rights movement led by Dr. Martin Luther King, Jr. "Dr. King's outfit," he charged in one attack, "is heavily laden at the top with leaders of proven records of communism, socialism and sex perversion." In 1965, he claimed to have "evidence that the Negroes and whites participating in the march to Montgomery engaged in sex orgies of the rawest sort." As Helms's political ambitions ripened, his targets expanded to encompass the entire old right menu: labor unions, the UN, U.S. immigration policy and Richard Nixon's moves toward "appeasing" Red China. In 1972, he used similar tactics in his Senate campaign against a liberal Democratic congressman who was the son of Greek immigrants. His winning slogan: "Jesse Helms: He's One of Us" made him the first Republican senator from North Carolina since Reconstruction.

Helms's return to Washington under his own steam in 1973 marks the beginning of the fundamentalist right's breakthrough to the circles of power. As a freshman senator and an outsider, he had little regard for the protocols of Washington society, and he proceeded to surround himself with bright young loyalists who shared his penchant for ruthless politics and his desire to rewrite the rules of the legislative game. Helms and his aides quickly mastered the rules of Senate procedure and developed a few new wrinkles of their own, pioneering a novel political subterfuge: the act of propaganda by crackpot legislative amendment. In a nerveless stream of proposed attachments to bills pending before the Senate, Helms brought his own pet issues to the floor, forcing his colleagues into required votes on sensitive social issues such as busing, abortion, school prayer, sex education and capital punishment. None stood a chance of passage. Most were defeated by twenty or fifty to one.

But according to many in Washington, Helms was not introducing his amendments with any real hope for their enactment. Rather, he was using them for purposes of propaganda and political intimidation. By stacking his own legislative record with hard-charging, far-right initiatives, he won loud praise and solid support from his fundamentalist constituency, at the same time acting as a beacon for sympathetic legislators. In the last Nixon years, Helms refined his obstructionist game, exploiting Senate rules to stall confirmation of executive appointees he considered too liberal. In 1974, he opposed Gerald Ford's nomination of Nelson Rockefeller to serve as his interim vice-president, condemning the once-divorced Republican stalwart on the grounds that "he stole another man's wife." Although few senators rallied around him, Helms's beacon lit the way for distant legions.

His pivotal role in the founding of the new right began the moment he arrived in Washington. Following his 1972 victory, Helms enlisted the aid of Richard Viguerie to raise money to pay off his campaign debts. With the help of Viguerie's direct-mail machine, he retired his debts and added hundreds of thousands of names to the mailing list of his own Congressional Club of North Carolina. Formed during his initial Senate run, Helms's Congressional Club flourished during his first term, providing him with a nationwide following of more than 300,000 contributors who gave over $7.5 million to his 1978 reelection campaign. But the state organization was soon obscured by the steam from larger efforts brewing in Helms's kitchen. In the mid-seventies, Helms acted as inspiration and chief instigator for the new right's central PACs. In 1975, following a meeting with Terry Dolan and longtime Helms aide Charles Black, Helms sent a confidential memo to a few key people on the right and NCPAC was born. About the same time, Helms acted on another memo from his top political adviser, John Carbaugh, and the Conservative Caucus came into being, headed by Howard Phillips, who was working in Helms's office at the time. Helms's direct-mail efforts for his infant PACs became legendary. His most famous, for NCPAC, ranted on about "cannibalism, wife-swapping and the murder of infants and the elderly." Others, for groups like the National Right to Work Committee and the conservative Public Service Research Council were less shocking but effective enough.

By 1980, following his Carter-era crusades against abortion, school prayer and administration foreign policy toward Taiwan, Rhodesia and right-wing dictators worldwide, fundamentalist right forces were singing hosannahs to Jesse Helms. Viguerie's *Conservative Digest* hailed him as "Mr. Integrity" and "the conscience of the conservative movement." As fundamentalist preachers entered the political arena, Helms emerged as their spiritual leader. On the last night of the 1980 Republican Convention, Helms took the podium to deliver his own sermon and clarion call:

> As Americans, we may give our votes to candidates and parties, but we give our loyalty only to God, family and country. . . . Let us live each day mindful that the Lord may be giving us just one more chance to save America. With a genuine spiritual rebirth, we can do it.

1980 also marked the year of Helms's emergence as a national power. That year, his Congressional Club began its own nationwide political efforts that complemented with minimal overlap those of NCPAC, Conservative Caucus and the rest. Helms's group donated money and other resources to thirty new right candidates and worked closely with Dolan on media campaigns against NCPAC's "Target '80" senators. It was Helms, along with Jerry Falwell, who recruited Jeremiah Denton to run in Alabama. And Helms's club waged its own winning battles on behalf of two more fundamentalist right Senate candidates: John East, an unknown North Carolina college professor and Helms protégé, and Alfonse D'Amato, who claimed a narrow victory in a bitterly divided contest in New York against aging liberal Senator Jacob Javits. When the final tallies were filed with federal election authorities, it turned out that Helms's machine had raised an astronomical $7.8 million dollars for the 1980 campaign, and spent a hefty $4.5 million of it on independent efforts on behalf of Ronald Reagan. Those figures put Jesse at the helm of the second-richest PAC in the nation—neck and neck with its prodigal spin-off NCPAC!

It took all that before people began to take note of Jesse Helms, his high-rolling PACs and his propaganda machine that was turning out ten to twenty million letters a year. Alone among U.S. senators, Helms had the strategic capability to unleash a blizzard of constituent mail in any direction he chose at the touch of a button. But there was still more to Helms's empire than propaganda. In Washington, it turned out, he was constructing his own independent fundamentalist right political establishment, a net-

work of PACs, institutes and allied power bases with national and
international levels of operation. One group, the tax-exempt Institute of Money and Inflation, founded in 1976, was dedicated to
returning America to the gold standard. Another, the American
Family Institute, boosted Helms's pro-life, pro-family, pro-God initiatives—its staff helped draft the Human Life Statute, introduced
by Helms to skirt the Supreme Court's *Roe* v. *Wade* decision.
Two more Helms spin-offs, the Institute of American Relations,
founded in 1974, and the Foreign Affairs Council, established in
1979, funded research, newsletters and more cantankerous diplomatic initiatives by Helms's aides, who traveled frequently to
South America and South Africa. In 1979, they caused a serious
foreign affairs blowup when Britain's Lord Carrington complained
to the U.S. State Department that they were trying to sabotage
delicate negotiations over the future of Rhodesia. Helms, too,
traveled abroad at institute expense, to Chile, Argentina and Uru-
guay, bringing back firsthand ammunition that added to his clout
in Senate foreign policy debates. In the 97th Congress, his personal power structure was extended into the inner workings of the
Senate itself, as he became chairman of the influential Senate Agriculture Committee, assumed a prominent role on the Senate Foreign Relations Committee, headed up the Senate Subcommittee
for Hemispheric Affairs, and became chairman of the secretive
Senate Steering Committee, a conservative planning group that
met weekly to coordinate legislative strategy.

Although the fundamentalist right hails him as a "political
saint," there are many people in and out of government who think
that in his far-reaching exercise of official and unofficial power,
Jesse Helms may be the most dangerous legislator to come down
the pike since Joe McCarthy. Throughout 1981, as Helms pressed
forward with his personal agenda, the press struggled to bring his
tactics to light. In an article in *The New Yorker,* respected Washington reporter Elizabeth Drew accused Helms of trying to establish a "government-within-a-government." In the foreign affairs
arena, she claimed, Helms's aide John Carbaugh "had astonished
people on Capitol Hill and within the bureaucracy with his knack
for acquiring information—sometimes highly sensitive information."
She cited claims that Helms had stacked thirty U.S. foreign policy
posts, run opponents out of their jobs, delayed appointments and,

in general, caused "carnage" in the State Department. Senator William Proxmire put it bluntly: "Jesse's got his own foreign policy."

But it was on the social issues that Helms's shadow government was most effective. As he gained Senate approval for restrictions on abortion funding, won a ban on federal intervention in busing suits and succeeded in positioning fundamentalist right legislation ahead of vital matters on the Senate calendar, some lawmakers grew reluctant to comment publicly on Helms's tactics. Said one first-term senator: "Every person in the Senate knows Jesse could unloose that barrage of letters. It makes them think twice." A nameless Democratic senator was livid: "This guy really does play a double-dealing game," he said. "He'll tell you he has nothing to do with the campaign against you and then go out and slit your throat, using third parties to do it." Other senators spoke for attribution. Democrat Dale Bumpers of Arkansas charged Helms with launching "a dangerous broadside attack on the Constitution." Alan Cranston of California, lone survivor of NCPAC's "Target '80" crusade, accused Helms of waging "warfare" against his opponents and blackening the traditional conservative image of the opposition. "He's reaching out," said Cranston, "building a subspecies of Republicans."

The wide-eyed Helms, however, seemed to play innocent, calling his bloodthirsty aides "delightful young people" and claiming, "I know almost nothing about the Congressional Club in terms of its day-to-day activities." Into early 1982, he battled inexorably on, converting his beliefs into floor confrontations and flexing his newfound muscle as the most powerful individual in the history of the United States Congress; while his aides taxed their minds to give Helms's fundamentalist crusade a rationale. James Lucier, his chief legislative assistant, told *The New Yorker* Helms's people do not see themselves as engaged in traditional right-wing politics. Rather, he said, they see their thrust as "pre-political," based on underlying emotions and akin to historical movements predicated "less on the mind than on the will . . . on acting rather than thinking." Lucier's discourse aimed to give intellectual credibility to the folk wisdom Helms is said to grasp intuitively. Instead, it provided a rare peek into the shadows of fundamentalist emo-

cial programs for the poor, a massive military buildup. But the fairy tale didn't last long. By the fall of his first year in office, the public was beginning to awaken from the Reagan spell. Wall Street blanched in the face of a "Reagan Revolution" that bore little relation to economic reality. Jolted Democrats, labor unions, elderly and minority groups began to rise up in protest. And many Americans began asking themselves how they had come to vote for this man who seemed intent on tearing down decades of social progress and generations of government.

It's not hard to see why. In our view, like Jesse Helms only more so, Ronald Reagan's political career has been a triumph of propaganda over democratic process. Indeed, by the time he took up residency in the White House, he didn't seem to know the difference between the two.

Long before Ronald Reagan was ever taken seriously as a presidential candidate, he was the darling of the fundamentalist right and the spotlight figure in its propaganda machine. From his first entry into politics in the mid-sixties at the urging of wealthy southern California businessmen who were looking for someone who could deliver their views to the public in a convincing way, former New Deal Democrat Reagan has sounded nearly every social, political and religious theme of the movement. Yet, from then until now, it has been impossible to see beneath the makeup and determine whether Ronald Reagan, born to an Irish Catholic father, a Scottish Protestant mother and steeped in small-town midwestern Americana, really believes all the fundamentalist proclamations he has been making over the years.

There is little doubt that fundamentalist preachers have played a heavy hand in his political career. His first gubernatorial campaign theme, the "Creative Society," was coined in 1965 by Rev. W. S. McBirnie, a hard-line anti-Communist crusader and California radio minister who was a leading figure in Reagan's first circle of advisers. In two modestly successful terms as California governor, he captured the hopes of the far right that had been shattered by Goldwater's defeat. In Reagan, they found a believable new outlet for their frustrated ideology, their abundant wealth and their developing organizing skills. His first presidential campaign and fundraising efforts were manned by ex-Young Americans for Freedom, who helped him assemble a solid core of grass-roots constituents. In 1976, while still short on credibility and support within his own party, Senator Jesse Helms's political machine gave Reagan his first primary victory in North Carolina. Yet, the campaign fizzled, leaving him with a brimming war chest and a standing army—but no war to fight.

So he began scrapping, first joining movement leaders and his friend and ex-campaign manager, Senator Paul Laxalt, in the new right's kamikaze mission to save the Panama Canal. Later, he became a headliner at new right political rallies and lent his name and image to a slew of fund-raising appeals. In a widely reprinted endorsement, Reagan hailed Dolan's NCPAC as "our best bet to keep the liberals from seizing total control of Congress." Mailings for other PACs and lobbies reprinted his photograph and signature *ad nauseam*. According to Richard Viguerie, prior to his 1980 campaign, Reagan helped "raise millions" for NCPAC, the YAF, the American Legislative Exchange Council and other right-wing groups.

That was only the beginning of Reagan's romance with the new right. In 1977, with nearly $1 million left over from his presidential bid, Reagan formed his own PAC, Citizens for the Republic (CFTR), and, a full two years before the 1980 election, hit the campaign trail, all expenses paid. Stumping on behalf of new right congressional candidates, to whom CFTR donated more than $500,000, Reagan taped radio endorsements, filmed television commercials and issued a biweekly newsletter, all of which helped spread his image nationwide. From the beginning, however, CFTR disclaimed any connection with a future Reagan campaign. "The fact is," said an early fund-raising letter, "CFTR is in no way a Reagan campaign organization. Under federal law, it cannot be."

By 1979, however, CFTR was taking dead aim at the presidency. While Viguerie's PACs and magazines were decimating Jimmy Carter's image and support among conservatives, Reagan's PAC was homing in on feared Democratic challenger Senator Edward Kennedy. A November 1979 letter, bearing Reagan's picture and signed by CFTR chairman Lyn Nofziger, Reagan's number-one loyalist from Sacramento days, showed all the warmth and goodwill of a NCPAC harpoon:

TEDDY KENNEDY IS RUNNING FOR PRESIDENT AND IF YOU
DON'T THINK THAT'S A DISASTER IN ITSELF, LOOK AT THE PEO-
PLE HE HOPES TO CARRY INTO OFFICE WITH HIM. . . .
All over our nation, he'll help re-elect the most radical
members of the U.S. Senate. . . . There are a dozen—a dirty
dozen—who vote and think like . . . Teddy and . . . his
socialist-leaning colleagues. . . .
1980 is the year they've been waiting for. The year they'll
turn on the tears and tell us we have to elect Ted Kennedy
because of his brothers. . . .

The appeal hit deep into CFTR's direct-mail constituency of
300,000. In 1980, the PAC checked in as the nation's fifth-richest.
At the start of the campaign, however, relations were decidedly
cool between Reagan and the new right. There were lingering tensions from 1976, when Reagan committed the cardinal sin of
reaching out to moderates and mainstream Republicans. In 1978,
CFTR refused to campaign against GOP incumbents. Worse yet,
Reagan seemed to be courting the support of the Eastern establishment. In the early months, *Conservative Digest* tilted first in
favor of Congressman Philip Crane, a core new right zealot, then
toward John Connally, former Texas governor with multiple ties
to the movement. Only after Connally failed in the primaries, and
with the entry of religious forces into the campaign, did movement
kingpins swing wholeheartedly behind Reagan.
And without missing a beat, Reagan donned the mantle of the
proverbial "Man on the White Horse," the political messiah
awaited historically by disaffected masses. As the party nominee,
walking a political tightrope between the surging force of fundamentalist right ideologues and the strain of moderate Republicans
seeking to broaden his support, Reagan stepped decisively toward
his fundamentalist supporters.
In truth, he had been in their camp for years. As far back as
1969, during his first term as governor, he gave the biblical creationist movement its first victory, when the California State Board
of Education declared creationism to be a valid alternative to evolution. Now, a decade later, it seemed there was nothing candidate
Reagan wouldn't say in his all-out quest for the Christian vote.
Like every other contender, he courted the nation's major reli-

gious blocs, but by the time of the GOP Convention, his campaign had become a stream of telegraphic messages to the fundamentalist right. In his convention suite in Detroit, he conferred with Jesse Helms, Jerry Falwell, Phyllis Schlafly and Howard Phillips (Paul Weyrich, who got stuck in traffic, missed the meeting). All were outraged when Reagan picked moderate George Bush as his running mate, but a month later he redeemed himself, giving a tremendous boost to the movement when he became the only presidential contender to appear at the Religious Roundtable's national affairs briefing in Dallas.

Reagan's Dallas remarks, widely reprinted in fundamentalist right circles, formed the centerpiece of his religious strategy. Playing directly to his devout audience, he tore into the First Amendment's separation of church and state; decried "government tyranny" over religion; attacked the Federal Communications Commission's inquiries into religious broadcasters and the Internal Revenue Service's "vendetta" against Christian schools; praised the Ten Commandments, St. Augustine's "shining city upon a hill," lawmakers who sought "divine guidance" in government, the audience's "rendezvous with destiny"; and noted "serious flaws" in Darwin's theory of evolution. His prepared text ended with a line that brought down the house:

> I can only add to that, my friends, that I continue to look to the Scriptures today for fulfillment and for guidance. Indeed, it is an incontrovertible fact that all the complex and horrendous questions confronting us at home and worldwide have their answers in that single book.

Did he really believe that? It was an astonishing comment by a man who, at the time, was aspiring to world leadership in an age of nuclear warfare, space travel, trillion-dollar economies and sensitive international relations. But as with other new right political leaders, Reagan's fundamentalist vows appeared to be sincere. Through the end of the campaign, he kept up a breathless flow of fundamentalist patter. Stopping in Lynchburg, he promised a group of religious broadcasters convened by Falwell that he would use the presidency as a "bully pulpit" and force for "moral suasion," then spurned the national press, taking questions only from

"the religious news media." A month later, in an interview in Jim
Bakker's "PTL Club" *Action* magazine, he condemned the ERA
and atheism ("which in fact is a religion") and reassured Bakker
that "I will personally be most comfortable to be surrounded by
advisers who believe in God." After the landslide, he continued to
speak in double meanings about his great "crusade" and the coming "era of national renewal." Two weeks after his inauguration,
in a segment of the "700 Club," host Pat Robertson touted the arrival of the Man on the White Horse, recalling another of his
famous private communiqués with God:

> ROBERTSON: I had been several times praying . . . God told
> me that Ronald Reagan was going to win the election and
> I was very happy to see that happen. Afterward, as I was
> praying at year end, He said that He was going to bless
> him, that we were not to criticize him. . . .

Then Robertson introduced Rev. Harald Bredesen, a member
of the board of directors of CBN, who told the audience about a
spiritual encounter he had with Reagan toward the end of his first
term as governor of California. The incident was revealing—if not
exactly inerrant:

> BREDESEN: Actually, it was right at the height of the cam-
> paign that he invited us to come. . . . I can still re-
> member his face as it was framed in the door receiving us.
> It had such a boyish, carefree expression. . . . He showed
> us around his private home. . . . And then Governor
> Reagan, to my great joy, began to tick off the prophecies
> that have been fulfilled. Now, I'd been in his home . . .
> when he was an actor and to see the difference that had al-
> ready taken place in his character and in his closeness to
> the Lord really impressed me very much, because he
> seemed to be amazingly consonant with the Scrip-
> tures. . . .
> ROBERTSON: I understand after the discussion of Bible things
> [you] began to pray. Did you join hands, you and Pat
> Boone, George Otis [another fundamentalist broadcaster]
> and Ronald Reagan?

BREDESEN: Yeah, that's right. . . . George had his left hand,
I had his right hand as we prayed, and George let out in
prayer and suddenly his prayer changed into prophecy. I'm
sure you've seen this happen. And in it God was saying
that if he would walk in His ways, He said, "I will put you
in 1700 Pennsylvania Avenue," which is the address of the
White House.

ROBERTSON: Whoa! Wait! That's 1970 and George Otis,
speaking in prophecy as unto the Lord said, "I will put
you in 1700?" Whew! That's electrifying.

BREDESEN: Well, I'll tell you—was *Reagan* electrified! I
had his right hand and, Pat, it was wobbling like this.
Honestly, I've never seen an arm wave so under the
anointing of God!

ROBERTSON: It's incredible!

BREDESEN: Interestingly enough, Pat Boone tells me that he
called him right after the election and said, "Mr. President, do you remember that day?" and he said, "Do I
ever!"

ROBERTSON: Somebody just said, by the way . . . it's *1600*
Pennsylvania Avenue. That was my fault. It's 1600 Pennsylvania. . . .

And it came to pass, as his administration unfolded, President
Reagan marched in step with the fundamentalist right. He relied
heavily upon movement resources, adopting wholesale recommendations from the 3,000-page study prepared for him by Coors
and Weyrich's Heritage Foundation. Yet, within weeks of the election, he began losing points with hard-liners. New right leaders
berated him for selecting Cabinet members they considered too
moderate. The Gang of Three warned Vice-President Bush to toe
the line—to which Bush responded, "Hell with them." They denounced other Reagan appointees as "Nixon-Ford retreads" and
"country-club, silk-stocking Republicans," and declared publicly,
"Something has gone very wrong." One month after he took
office, Reagan met in the White House with virtually every important figure in the movement: Viguerie, Dolan, Phillips, Schlafly,
representatives of Weyrich's PACs and foundations, of Helms's

Congressional Club, of the YAF and of pro-life, pro-defense, pro-gun, anti-labor and anti-tax groups.

Within another month, his administration took a sudden turn to extremes. The national media, which had praised him for first-round appointments that were for the most part nonideological, reported a massive infusion of fundamentalist right ideologues into key administration positions. At the Department of Health and Human Services, Reagan nominated for surgeon general controversial Philadelphian Dr. C. Everett Koop, an ardent fundamentalist and nationally prominent anti-abortion crusader. As director of the Office of Adolescent Pregnancy Programs, Reagan named Marjory Mecklenburg, president of one of the nation's largest anti-abortion committees. Fundamentalist right kingpin Rev. Robert Billings—formerly president of the National Christian Action Coalition and a deputy to Weyrich, then executive director of Moral Majority, then "religious liaison" for the Reagan campaign —was named a "consultant and assistant" to the Secretary of Education. Several months later, it was revealed, Billings had been promoted to a $50,000-a-year post as director of the Education Department's ten regional offices and as special "Christian school liaison officer," a newly created position with no counterpart for other religious denominations. Soon after, Reagan, who had expressed earlier intentions of abolishing the traditional post of White House religious affairs adviser, named Morton C. Blackwell to the post. Blackwell, former editor of Viguerie's *New Right Report* and former chairman of the Committee for Responsible Youth Politics, a PAC with financial ties to Viguerie, drew immediate fire from mainline religious leaders.

After the President, the man responsible for most of these appointments was Lyn Nofziger, at the time, the powerful White House assistant for political affairs. Nofziger, former chairman of CFTR and Reagan's campaign press secretary, was given the power of "political clearance" over all sub-Cabinet jobs in the administration, and total control over lower-level appointments. Most of those appointments were made on the basis of "ideological purity" and in an undisguised political attempt to expunge from federal agencies all evidence of liberalism, moderation and the Democratic party. "We've got to clean out the Democrats and get our own people taken care of," Nofziger admitted. Yet, one

White House aide noted, even "good, solid Republicans are getting screwed." Another staff member declared helplessly: "The revolution is happening and nobody is noticing."

And behind the smoke of Reagan's emergency budget initiatives, in 1981 America's fundamentalist right shadow government was quietly installed in federal policy-making posts affecting vital areas of our national life. For a time, the movement stood on the brink of taking over the whole of the executive branch. Budget cuts were made along the lines of fundamentalist right social and educational concerns. At the National Science Foundation, for example, project funding was slashed in apparent retaliation for NSF science texts opposed by fundamentalist censors. Throughout the Department of Health and Human Services, welfare programs were reduced in sync with the President's stated goal of making churches and charities bear the burden of social responsibility. At the same time, the department began an unpublicized series of "priority audits" of Planned Parenthood affiliates around the country, checking to see if federal funds were being used illegally to promote abortion. The audit went beyond bookkeeping, peering into confidential personal records, but no violations were found.

The fervor seemed to be contagious. Even Secretary of State Alexander M. Haig, Jr., often criticized but seldom accused of being a fundamentalist ideologue, stunned members of the House Foreign Affairs Committee during a closed meeting in which he justified United States support for the brutal right-wing military government of Argentina by citing the two nations' shared values of "a belief in God." In later Senate hearings, Haig made other references to the Bible and spoke of "the dramatic and God-given warning" he perceived in world events.

Then there was Secretary of the Interior James G. Watt. At the time of his appointment, no Cabinet member in modern times had unleashed such a hurricane of praise and protest. An avowed advocate of private development in the resource-rich West and former head of a "public-interest" law foundation started by Joseph Coors and fueled by grants from Chevron, Shell, Exxon and other energy interests, Watt drew heavy fire as the administration's most highly placed and ardent fundamentalist. A member of the 1.4-million-member Assemblies of God, the largest pentecostal denomination in the United States, Watt's statements to congressional committees became legend. In one early confrontation with committee members who questioned the role of his beliefs in the shaping of long-range environmental policy, Watt replied, "I don't know how many future generations we can count on until the Lord returns." Watt espoused the fundamentalist view that man has been divinely ordained to act as "steward" over the earth and its resources, yet he denied his critics' charges that he sought to despoil the environment. In a later interview, he defended his religious approach to his government job:

> I believe there is a life hereafter, and we are to be here to follow the teachings of Jesus Christ. One of the charges He's given us is to occupy the land until He returns. We don't know when He is coming, so we have a stewardship responsibility . . . to see that people are provided for until He does come and a new order is put in place.

And for Watt, apparently, that new order required opening federal parklands and protected seashores for oil and mineral exploration and turning over great tracts of wilderness land and government-owned properties to private developers. Environmentalists bewailed his tenure at Interior as "a disaster a day" and delivered more than a million signatures on petitions calling for his ouster. But Watt remained unrepentant. More candid than most, he boldly stated the principle of ideological fundamentalism that the Reagan administration seemed to have made its oath of office:

> I am a fundamentalist in economic, social, spiritual and political matters.

Beyond the realm of policy and appointments, however, the Reagan presidency raises larger questions about the fundamentalist right's seizure of power, questions about the degree to which the President and his protective ring of White House advisers have adopted strategies of mass manipulation and indirect control as central instruments in the conduct of government.

Since the Depression era when Franklin D. Roosevelt held his first radio "fireside chats," American Presidents have come to have increasing regard for the power of mass media to influence public opinion and voting behavior. With the election of John F. Kennedy in 1960, television came of age as a formidable campaign tool, and more and more, the success or failure of candidates came to depend on the skill and imagination of their image-makers. In the rapid evolution of the medium, increasingly scientific polling and public opinion research efforts went into political packaging efforts. Yet, in the end, for Presidents Johnson, Nixon, Ford and Carter alike, television contributed less to their successes than to their successive downfalls.

Then came Ronald Reagan, and television at last smiled on one of its own. Unlike any President before him, Ronald Reagan appears as a pure and simple media creation. The same traits that made him a leading man in Hollywood make him a viable political personality: his rugged looks, his sandpapery voice, his folksy manner and polished smile. Yet, despite his natural strengths, Reagan's political success has not been naturally won. On the contrary, from the start he has relied heavily on principles of psychological manipulation to win votes and support for his programs. Reagan's 1966 race for governor was said to be the first time in American history that a major political candidate had hired behavioral scientists to plot strategy and design his presentation. On every campaign stop, and later, throughout his term as governor, information was prepared for public delivery following a plan first laid out in the "black books" compiled for him by two Ph.D.s in psychology working for the Behavior Science Corporation. By the time he reached national office, his backup crew had grown into "the most sophisticated team of pollsters, media masters and tacticians" ever to work in the White House. And soon after, his program of social and economic reaction claimed high ratings in the polls and sailed through an intimidated and baffled Congress.

Much has been made of Ronald Reagan's prodigious "powers of persuasion" and his presidential image as the "Great Communicator." But by thoughtful standards, Ronald Reagan is no communicator. Like the stars of the electronic church and the strategists of the fundamentalist right, Reagan's fine-tooled exploitation of the media has little to do with the process of communication and everything to do with the act of propaganda. In fact, if any grand title is to be handed out, Reagan should more appropriately be labeled the "Great Propagandist." For in his own

way and from within the nation's highest office, working in concert
with the entire fundamentalist right network, President Reagan
has conducted an ongoing campaign of Holy Terror against the
American public.

From this perspective, in his role as chief executive, Ronald
Reagan has not used the nation's media solely for purposes of
public information, nor for accepted presidential prerogatives of
eliciting support for administration programs. Rather, in his first
year in office, he repeatedly took advantage of his unique access to
the media, mounting broad-based propaganda offensives which
relied heavily on indirect means of manipulating public opinion,
congressional legislation and other integral functions of the democratic process. As we came to understand it, the Reagan strategy
combined, for the first time by an American President, the bold
use of overt political propaganda carried out in unofficial cooperation with extragovernmental forces. Foremost among those forces
was the vast propaganda network of the fundamentalist right, including leading elements of the electronic church and the new
right's direct-mail, direct-phone and other high-technology channels. As formulated and directed by the White House, this integrated strategy, at once direct and indirect, overt and covert, has
been used repeatedly by the Reagan team.

We first became alert to the Reagan strategy during his 1980
campaign, as we watched what appeared to be a meshing of fundamentalist right forces with pollsters and strategists on the Reagan team. We noted the sympathetic seeding of the ground by TV
preachers, the coy "nonendorsements" of fundamentalist right
preachers and independent PAC leaders, and the streamlining of
special-interest and grass-roots support. When Reagan finally took
office, his longtime core of media strategists and public-opinion
analysts were given top-ranking status in his administration. They
played key roles in setting the agenda of White House activity,
using sophisticated methods of polling and analysis to orchestrate
presidential appearances and actions, televised speeches and press
conferences, and the release of legislative proposals. On a daily
basis, they oversaw the broad propagation of the President's ideology in concurrence with their best assessment of relevant "open
windows" of public opinion, "targets of opportunity" of issues and
events, "resistance ratios" of public acceptance and necessary "se-

quencing" or timing factors. They also determined that the President ought to be—as they called it—"proactive" in the formation of policy and public opinion.

Reagan's efforts to manipulate public opinion may be the most deliberate and ambitious of any President. His proactive "emergency economic recovery program," introduced to remedy what he called "the worst economic mess since the Depression," grew out of findings by his pollsters that the economy constituted the single most important issue around which he could rally public support for his overall agenda. As events demonstrated, the initial "emergency" provided an ideal cover behind which to advance fundamentalist right social and political goals to which the majority of the public was opposed. And the resulting changes in national economic policy quickly threw the nation deep into recession. As conditions worsened, memories faded, but the public record did not.

The assault began in April 1981, during the opening battle over the federal budget in Congress, in a series of televised addresses and administration publicity events designed to generate a flood of constituent mail to legislators. The overt White House effort was matched by an unannounced campaign led by Lyn Nofziger consisting of a "political blitz" designed to drum up constituent pressure in the home districts of fifty-one Democratic congressmen whose swing votes were needed by the administration. Nofziger coordinated his efforts with fundamentalist right umbrella groups such as NCPAC and Moral Majority, and with wealthy business and professional PACs, local civic organizations and other special-interest groups. In addition to local advertising and media appearances by administration speakers, the unit fielded a special team of workers to man direct-mail and direct-phone efforts. Lee Atwater, Nofziger's deputy in the effort, explained the thinking behind the blitz: "The way we operate, within forty-eight hours any congressman will know he has had a major strike in his district. All of a sudden . . . [the vice-president and congressman] in your district, ten of your top contributors are calling you, the head of the local AMA, the head of the local realtors' group, local officials. . . . Within forty-eight hours, you're hit by paid media, free media, mail, phone calls, all asking you to support the President."

The overall assault infuriated members of Congress, few of whom were pleased to lie down beneath the wheels of what was being termed the "Reagan juggernaut." Once-powerful Speaker of the House Thomas P. "Tip" O'Neill, Jr., rendered impotent by the sustained attack, protested publicly against the President's "propaganda machine" which, he claimed, had set off "a telephone blitz like this nation has never seen." He also railed personally against Reagan, who hit back hard, accusing O'Neill of "sheer demagoguery." As the battle wore on, other members of Congress became even more enraged at the President's tactics. "We are tired of being manipulated by the White House," said a Georgia Democrat. The chairman of the House Rules Committee accused Reagan of seeking "totalitarian" rule over Congress. "This is incipient tyranny," said Missouri Democrat Richard Bolling. "A popular President is attempting to tyrannize a whole Congress, a whole people. I'm using harsh words on purpose, so that people look at the fact that we're dealing with a very fundamental aspect of the way the country governs itself." Meanwhile, across the Capitol, Senator Daniel P. Moynihan of New York, commenting on administration tactics being used to gain approval for cuts in Social Security benefits, charged the administration with conducting "a campaign of political terrorism."

When the lightning raid was over, many congressmen awoke to find that they were unaware of major provisions they had just voted on. "Did any of you dream, were any of you told, was any hint given any member of this House that this bill would grant to [budget director] Mr. Stockman the power to determine poverty levels, the power to demolish the programs so carefully constructed by the Congress?" asked House Majority Leader Jim Wright of Texas the day after the vote. "I simply wonder how many more jokers are in this bill." Oklahoma Democrat James R. Jones, chairman of the House Budget Committee, put it more succinctly in a House follow-up session: "We're here today to complete a shameless charade of the legislative process gone mad."

With the President's stunning victory in the "battle of the budget," acclaim for the Reagan Revolution and the chief executive's "mastery" over both houses of Congress threatened to reduce the legislative branch to a rubber stamp. Several months later, the vote was closer in his upset victory over a resolute Sen-

ate in voting on the sale of sophisticated AWACS radar planes
and other military hardware to Saudi Arabia, yet the President
was hailed anew as the "Great Persuader," even though his arguments treaded on veiled prejudices and fundamentalist prophecy.
In one closed door White House meeting, the President plied a
wavering southern senator with an endtimes pitch about the approaching battle of Armageddon in the Mideast—which presumably would be hastened by the Senate's failure to ratify his weapons
deal.

But the heat of the President's scorched-earth AWACS maneu-
ver took its toll. Soon members of Congress and the media began
to pick up on patterns of White House manipulation. Reports surfaced that the administration's Capitol Hill team had prepared detailed intelligence reports on each legislator that included analysis
of his weaknesses and strengths and ways in which he could be
"threatened or seduced or suckered." As the mask cracked, the
ideological fundamentalism of the Reagan Revolution began to
show through. A New York *Times* editorial pierced the smokescreen of the President's economic plan: "What is no longer in
doubt is that his economic remedies mask an assault on the very
idea that free people can solve their collective problems through
representative government." By late 1981, the complexities of
real-world economics, along with rising domestic protest and international tensions, began to boggle the White House staff of experienced campaigners but ill-equipped national leaders. And his
juggernaut began to lurch, rooting for alternatives to its simplistic
solutions; breaking out in alleged scandals, embarrassing revelations and interdepartmental back-stabbing; raising alarms in Europe over nuclear proliferation and at home over its wars on
organized labor, the elderly and the poor. At the same time, the
President and his flankers rushed to reverse themselves on key
policy pronouncements and political maneuvers, in one instance
amid cries of racism raised by the sudden granting of tax exemp-
tions to the segregationist Bob Jones University and other fundamentalist schools and colleges, the fulfillment of an earlier Reagan
campaign pledge to end the IRS "vendetta" against Christian
schools.

So it went, into a second year. Charged with responsibilities beyond its image-making capacities, the Reagan Revolution became

encumbered in reality, and the Man on the White Horse began to resemble an aimless knight errant on a lumbering white elephant: dodging politically dangerous religious and social issues, launching a new blitz to sell the "New Federalism" and becoming increasingly combative in relation to administration critics. Yet, with his public approval rating eroding steadily, the President's men fought hard to keep his name and face separate from all bad news; and he stayed personally popular with the majority of Americans. As predicted, the larger public remained fixated on the nation's rapidly worsening economy, and few seemed concerned or even aware that, despite rising protests from its hard-line supporters, on nearly every count the Reagan government was following the blueprint of the fundamentalist right attack on American society.

SLOUCHING TOWARD 1984

At midterm, as Reaganomics slid into recession, bread-and-butter issues of soaring unemployment and skyrocketing budget deficits came to eclipse the fundamentalist right agenda in nearly every poll. In Washington, newly emboldened lawmakers rallied around the crisis in an effort to hasten economic recovery, and as a lever to wrest the nation's priorities away from new right ideologues in Congress and the White House.

On many fronts their efforts succeeded. In bitter floor battles over school prayer, tuition tax credits and the unquenchable furor over abortion, proposed statutes and constitutional amendments supported by the White House went down to bipartisan defeat in the Republican-controlled Senate or were summarily tabled in Democratic-run House committees. Hard-liners lost similar disputes over school busing, consumer tax hikes and a grandstand "Balanced Budget Amendment." Countering forces benefited heavily from fresh outpourings of public support and prevailed largely through the revival of traditional activist coalitions of minorities, women's groups, organized labor and concerned clergy of all denominations.

And stung by defeat, the Reagan-fundamentalist right coalition began to rattle and unravel. Initial embarrassment grew into humiliation and anger compounded by public squabbling between the White House and the new right. In the House, a strengthened Democratic leadership took steps to tighten party discipline among dissident "Boll Weevils." Senators and congressmen of both parties facing reelection moved quickly to cover themselves with newly aroused constituencies and secure their voting records on economic issues. As the election approached, the fundamentalist right smelled disaster. Heavy losses could not only diminish the movement's newfound power in Congress but expose once and for all the myth that its agenda was broadly supported by the majority of Americans.

On the surface, the 1982 election appeared to vindicate the pendulum-swingers. Bearing the brunt of the blame for the battered economy, Republicans lost 26 seats in the House and went down to defeat in 20 of 33 Senate races. But by most counts, the biggest losers in '82 were the new right's kingpin political action committees: Helms's Congressional Club and Dolan's National Conservative Political Action Committee. Helms, whose fearsome image had been badly blunted by his recent legislative failures, suffered anew when all six candidates backed by his PAC lost in his home state—despite the group's record haul of nearly $10 million!

Still flushed with success from 1980, NCPAC took aim at twenty-one new targets for '82, including some of the heaviest hitters in the liberal Northeast and blue-collar Midwest, such as Senators Edward Kennedy of Massachusetts, Daniel P. Moynihan of New York, Howard Metzenbaum of Ohio and Paul Sarbanes of Maryland. Also, for the first time, NCPAC singled out moderate and liberal eastern Republicans, including Vermont's Robert Stafford, Rhode Island's John Chafee and Connecticut's Lowell Weicker. The scattershot approach gave the PAC's targets more than a year to rally public sympathy and build their own campaign war chests.

By early '82, NCPAC was already in retreat. Facing possible equal time challenges, broadcasters in six states refused to air its negative commercials. Returning NCPAC's volleys, outraged Senators Sarbanes, Robert Byrd of West Virginia, John Melcher of Montana and others launched their own campaigns assailing the PAC for pouring outside money and ill-motivated propaganda upon the fair-minded citizens of their states. The backlash took hold. On the morning after Election Day '82, in contrast to its flush of victory two years earlier, NCPAC claimed only one scalp: that of Senator Howard Cannon of Nevada, a vulnerable Democrat who had been surrounded by scandal in his conservative Western state.

Viewing the overall results, new right strategist Paul Weyrich called the outcome "a disaster, a rout . . . worse even than a lot of people think." He tarred anti-Reagan moderates in the White House for betraying the administration's declared mandate, and for "letting the other side completely frame the issues" around unemployment and the economy. But like other chastened new right leaders, Weyrich was also quick to shoulder much of the blame, not for his side's negative tactics but, on the contrary, for its having played "the Washington game." As Weyrich saw it, the failures of 1982 resulted from the movement's deferring to White House strategists and Congressional moderates when they should have been out "in the trenches . . . creating the issues." "I've had enough of the Washington game," wrote Weyrich in the postelection *Conservative Digest*. "We've tried it and the rules are stacked against us."

Despite its setbacks, the fundamentalist right fared far better in 1982 than its opponents were prone to acknowledge. Running against the tide of Reaganomics and, in many races, against its own tarnished reputation, the movement was instrumental in electing three new Republican senators—Paul Trible in Virginia, Chic Hecht in Nevada and Pete Wilson in California—all considered to be more conservative than their predecessors. In California, a heavily funded campaign against a state gun control initiative drew a large turnout of hard-line voters and was credited with the election to governor of Attorney General George Deukmejian over Los Angeles Mayor Tom Bradley (an admitted racial element went against Bradley as well). In Michigan and New York, GOP "renegades" Richard Headlee and multimillionaire businessman Lewis Lehrman came surprisingly close to gubernatorial victories in states hard-hit by the recession. And by more than one objective view, even NCPAC came out ahead—*Congressional Quarterly* measured NCPAC's score in both Senate and House races, and found sixty-nine wins against only nineteen losses!

The movement's score in "the Washington game" was not all

goose eggs either. After more than a year of deferring to Republican moderates in the 97th Congress, as the election approached, Senator Jesse Helms and his core group of Senate allies came out with guns blazing on the fundamentalist right's agenda. Through months of heated floor fights and filibusters, Helms won an exhausting victory over school busing. He lost broader crusades on school prayer and abortion, but no longer by fifty-to-one ratios. Now he fell short by only one or two votes, losses nonetheless but signs of his growing ability to dominate the Senate's time and legislative business.

And despite mounting evidence of broad public rejection of the new right's goals, through 1982, the Reagan administration continued to stock key federal agencies with movement ideologues and insiders. While largely going its own way on economic and foreign policy matters, the White House seemed to turn over to the fundamentalist right the nation's domestic policy-making apparatus—to the limits that public opposition would tolerate politically. At the Department of Health and Human Services, for example, the post of deputy assistant secretary went to *Conservative Digest* columnist JoAnn Gasper, described in the magazine as the pro-family movement's "early warning system" in Washington. For years, Gasper had railed against the "social Gestapo" in the nation's capital. Now she was put in charge of reviewing government regulations on domestic violence. On an equally sensitive issue, one of her first actions was to approve a nationwide regulation requiring parental notification for minors given contraceptives by clinics receiving federal funds. But implementation of the measure, dubbed the "squeal rule" by critics, was quickly blocked by federal court action, pending appeal by the administration.

The real target of the right in Washington, however, remained the Department of Education. Under assistant secretary Rev. Robert Billings, a flood of new appointments brought even sterner hard-liners into the besieged agency the administration had once vowed to abolish. Dozens of fundamentalist educators were invited to screen research grant proposals. Richard Leiter, dean of the business school at racially discriminatory Bob Jones University, was appointed to read grant applications for programs aimed at bringing minorities into graduate institutions. Another Bob Jones faculty member was made an evaluator of grants for women's educational programs. Another was made a special department assistant, and still another was named to a presidential advisory panel on education matters. Susan Phillips, former researcher for the Conservative Caucus, was hired as a $52,000-a-year consultant. Rosemary Thomson of Phyllis Schlafly's Eagle Forum was named director of the department's Women's Equity Action Council. And officers of the Heritage Foundation were named directors of the National Institute of Education and the National Council on Educational Research.

The tide ebbed and flowed, through setbacks and around obstacles, while the media and much of the public took comfort in the movement's highly publicized misfortunes. Many new right organizers and grass-roots groups, downplaying their gains and expressing frustration with the Reagan White House, defiantly sat out the election. Instead of firing up their flocks in 1982, Moral Majority's national and state leaders staged a symbolic show of displeasure, convening in the Bahamas the weekend before the vote.

But the movement wasn't retiring, only regrouping in anticipation of bigger stakes in 1984. From their separate empires, Rev. Pat Robertson and Bill Bright, co-chairmen of the giant 1980 "Washington for Jesus" rally, geared up a larger effort for April 1984, sounding the drumbeat in a nationwide series of 250 local "America for Jesus" rallies. Not to be upstaged, Rev. Jerry Falwell announced plans for his own fundamentalist convocation in Washington the same month: Baptist Fundamentalism '84, touted in advance in Falwell's new *Fundamentalist Journal* as "The Event of the Century." The fundamentalist right was far from defeated. Its coffers were fatter than ever, its forces well entrenched in high places, its foot soldiers harkening for the call to fling themselves into new battles.

Meanwhile, back in the trenches, a new kettle of foment was brewing. In a calculated effort to hold on to their gains and, at the same time, claim new ground in their advance, movement leaders began slowly to change their tune and refine their sales pitch among select audiences of women, blacks and blue-collar workers. Hurting from negative exposure, the ailing new right launched a systematic search for a new name and image for their high-tech operation, latching on to the slogan of a "new populism" centered around anti-crime, anti-government and "anti-elitist" themes that rated high in their grass-roots polls. Again recoding their ideological goals in emotional terms, Viguerie, Weyrich, Dolan, Phillips et al. prepared for a new round of offensives aimed at rousing working class antipathy: toward foreign manufacturers and illegal immigrants; toward federal judges whom they dubbed "soft on crime"; toward the United Nations "forum for communists, revolutionaries, radicals, terrorists and their fellow travelers"; and last but not least, toward the insidious designs of "government schools" (as opposed to private and Christian schools). With economic concerns overriding all others, however, whether the new slogans and issues would set fire to the grass roots remained to be seen.

Through it all, a nagging question was that of the Republican party's complicity in the overall scheme. After the 1980 landslide, few party regulars were eager to examine the charge that the Grand Old Party had been taken over by the fundamentalist right. Yet for the next two years, party leaders seemed to slouch along agreeably behind the beast of Holy Terror, adopting many fundamentalist right tactics as their own and admitting leading movement strategists into high offices within the party.

Most notable among the new breed of Republicans was Richard DeVos, Amway Corporation president and ardent supporter of Campus Crusade, the Christian Freedom Foundation and other fundamentalist political efforts. In 1981, DeVos was named GOP finance chairman and soon began to rail openly at executive committee meetings against administration critics; he labeled them a "raunchy bunch" with a "limited mentality" who were out to "destroy our country" through socialism. Later, he publicly acclaimed the worsening recession as "a beneficial thing and a cleansing thing." A growing embarrassment to party leaders, he was abruptly dismissed three months before the election, after proposing to use Amway-style sales techniques to woo new GOP contributors. Soon after, DeVos and his Amway partner Jay Van Andel were indicted by the Canadian government on charges of defrauding Canada of $28 million in undervalued customs declarations on Amway products.

But DeVos's departure didn't signal any large-scale fundamentalist right housecleaning inside the GOP. Through its sagging fortunes in 1982, and looking ahead nervously to its 1984 convention in Dallas, the Republicans seemed to be locked in internal struggle between new right ideologues and mainline moderates. Repeatedly, behind-the-scenes battles broke into the open over questions of taste and truthfulness in GOP television and direct-mail campaigns. As a 1982 election day disaster loomed, however, party leaders closed ranks and the struggle submerged to silent depths.

The field of battle grew wider still. The mushrooming PAC explosion upped the ante for politicians in both parties, with many incumbents taking more than half their reelection funds from influence-seeking special interests. Complicating matters even more was a counterassault by liberal PACs established to challenge new right attack groups. Defeated Senator George McGovern formed Americans for Common Sense. Presidential hopefuls Senator Edward Kennedy and former Vice-President Walter Mondale founded, respectively, the Fund for a Democratic Majority and the Committee for America's Future. And a hard-hitting PROPAC, the Progressive Political Action Committee, denounced NCPAC's attack-style campaigns, then launched several of its own against vulnerable GOP incumbents, taking partial credit for the defeat of moderate Republican Senator Harrison Schmitt of New Mexico.

The emerging picture was not an inspiring one. Perhaps even more serious than its broad infusion into the centers of power, the fundamentalist right's drive on the political process was now threatening to consume both parties in a snowballing pattern of sky-high PAC money and attack-style negativity, reducing the campaign process to little more than high-tech, low-blow politicking. Voter sympathies in 1982 categorically rejected these sullying campaign trends, but the new strategies and technologies took hold. Before long, battle lines became increasingly blurred. And growing numbers on both sides were getting caught in the crossfire.

Senator Weicker. One senator who narrowly survived that crossfire was Republican Lowell Weicker of Connecticut. Fired on from both left and right, and by snipers within his own party, Weicker faced the toughest contest of his political life in 1982.

The fundamentalist right wasted no time going after him: one week after the 1980 election, Weicker was on NCPAC's hit list for '82. By late 1981, as the Republican senator with the worst voting record in support of the Reagan agenda, he had incurred the wrath of party forces who seemed to want him defeated more than almost any Democrat.

It was not the senator's first family feud. As a freshman senator in 1973, Weicker rose to national prominence as the most outspoken Republican on the Senate Watergate Committee. His scathing criticism of Richard Nixon and his unwavering stand on constitutional principles drew the enmity of Republican leaders and earned him a reputation on the Senate floor as a maverick. But it won him the respect of the nation and, more importantly, of his home state. In 1976, Weicker was reelected with one of the largest margins of any Republican in Connecticut history.

He went on to play the role of an obstreperous northern liberal in heated Senate floor fights over civil rights and school prayer. Through most of 1981, Weicker stood toe-to-toe against Jesse Helms, staging a one-man filibuster to keep alive federal school busing and integration efforts. The oratorical effort ran on and off for eight months as Weicker waved the Constitution high through the Senate chamber, but eventually the conservative body worked its will and voted down his filibuster. In 1982, when Senate Republican leaders made good on their political debts to Helms for yielding to Reagan's economic initiatives, a run of proposed laws, amendments and appropriations measures on school prayer, abortion and tuition tax credits brought Weicker to his feet again. This time, however, he won support from Democrats and Republicans alike who had grown furious at Helms, mounting marathon filibusters that blocked each bill—if only by one- or two-vote margins.

The showdown strengthened Weicker's standing back home, even while GOP leaders were marking him for extinction. Already under attack by NCPAC, and facing a strong grass-roots challenge from popular Democratic Congressman Toby Moffett, through much of 1982 Weicker was forced to divert precious campaign resources to win his party's endorsement for a third Senate term. His pursuer was the flower of Republican knighthood: Prescott S. Bush, Jr., son of a former Republican Senator from Connecticut and brother of the vice-president. Bush emerged with a well-oiled campaign machine linked to key presidential aides, but he denied charges that the White House was masterminding the drive against Weicker. Then, with Reaganomics on the skids and party loyalists falling into disfavor nationwide, Bush abruptly dropped out of the race before the primary, handing Weicker the GOP mantle. Weicker squeaked past Moffett with 51 percent of the vote—his margin nearly erased by a little known third-party challenger backed by NCPAC and other hard-line forces.

Before the drawn-out battle began, on the eve of his first Senate filibuster, we met with Senator Weicker in his office in the Russell Building across from the Capitol. The attacks had already started, but he seemed cool and casual, like his famed Watergate image.

"Well, how does it feel to be on a NCPAC hit list?" we asked.

"It doesn't bother me at all, really it doesn't," said Weicker. "I would say the practical effect as far as NCPAC is concerned has been just a great big minus in Connecticut. I only wish they had delayed their announcement for a year, because then I would have the whole state steamed up to work in my campaign."

Weicker mused over the irony of the targeting effort launched against him by NCPAC's Dolan.

"I gave Dolan his start in politics, you know," he told us. "He worked in my campaign for the House back in 1968, handing out materials at shopping centers. Needless to say, he never expressed himself then as he is expressing himself now."

Weicker turned from NCPAC to address the rising tide of religion in politics and government.

"I've been watching this whole thing for a long time," he said. "I was appalled in '76 when both Ford and Carter went down to address the fundamentalists in Texas or wherever. And Christ, Richard Nixon held more prayer breakfasts than any other President in history—literally, that's a fact. I've always tried to manifest the religious beliefs that I was taught in my concerns and conduct as a U.S. senator, but it's not the type of thing you wear on your sleeve. I can't tell you how strongly I feel that my obligation as a U.S. senator is simply this: to make certain that anybody in this country can believe anything he wants, can worship in any way he wants, and that's the extent of it. My job is to make policy that supports the laws of this country. So if I am on some NCPAC or anti-abortion hit list—and if I'm not mistaken I'm on that one, too —I will fight them tooth and nail on the Senate floor."

At that moment, however, Weicker seemed less concerned about NCPAC or the pro-life movement than about his own party.

"I haven't seen much criticism of Dolan by the Republican party of Connecticut," he said. "I wouldn't be surprised if this bunch here is actually glad he's raising a little bit of Cain."

Weicker revealed the real bone of contention between himself and party leaders: his manifest rejection of the notion of ideological purity within the party.

"The problem with the Republican party is that they don't look to elect a U.S. senator," he said. "They want to elect a *pope,* in the sense of the purity of what you espouse. I've told them, as I testified before the platform committee, you know, we live in an age when the credibility is strained between the American people and their politicians. And I think the best thing we can do as a party is have no platform at all. Let each candidate speak his own heart and mind on the issues, and at least we won't have to go through the embarrassing performance of having a platform that everyone runs away from once they're elected. Well, when I said that, with one exception, the platform committee kept absolutely quiet. They wanted me to get offstage as fast as I could."

We asked him how it felt to be seen as a troublemaker within his own party. "I'll tell you, it's tough," he said. "But I suppose I should expect it. You can't have both worlds. If you want to be a superpartisan, you're going to get the adoration of the organization. If you want to be an independent, you've got to give that up. But I'll tell you this, whatever I don't get in the way of encouragement within my own party, I get as I walk down the streets of Connecticut. People come up to me and say 'Give'em hell, Senator,' or 'Senator, I sure don't agree with you on every issue, but you just keep telling it like it is.' "

Weicker was quick to point out that, in discussing the rift between himself and party leaders, he was by no means speaking about Republicans in general.

"There are a lot of good people in the Republican party," he said. "I think the Republican rank and file is a good bunch. But I would hope we could be a moderate party and a truly effective force, rather than simply relying on some aberration every twenty years to give us a few moments of power. We ought to be more consistent than that. But the results certainly indicate that there is something wrong with our political tactics."

Although confident from the outset, Weicker was realistic about the scope of the threat facing him.

"I know what confronts me," he said. "And all I can say is that I'm ready to go ahead and do battle. But remember, it's my home turf. If the conservative majority thinks their time has arrived and it's now time to press home, they're going to be sorely disappointed. That's my view, and I'm going to go back there and deliver it personally."

With the Democratic party in disarray nationwide, Weicker seemed sure that he would triumph on his record and on the strength of the constitutional principles that had served him well throughout his time in office.

"I'm looking forward to the fight, absolutely," he said. "They have every right to bring my record out there and plaster it all over the place. It's going to be a very clear-cut choice as to what Lowell Weicker has stood for." He looked at us intensely. "But I have to ask this: Where were all those people who are now preaching about principles and morals ten years ago, when the Constitution and the institutions of this country were being decimated, were being *buried*? I never heard from any of them. And I don't want to hear from them now about who's moral and who stands up for what is right. *Where the hell were they?*"

Weicker was punching now, as he would soon be pummeling the far right on the Senate floor. As he evoked the memory of Watergate, which had been for many Americans first a trauma, then a reaffirmation of the system, we saw behind the loose, scrapping style of this independent-minded Republican a deep-rooted commitment to the American experiment. After suffering through so much cynicism and claptrap, we were at last surprised and inspired to hear a United States senator blasting out for the common good and the spirit of the Founders.

"Maybe we've drawn away from understanding our own origins," Weicker reflected as we pulled back from talk of political dogfighting. "Maybe we have to learn the lesson the hard way. But I'll tell you this. History is not an illusion. The very issue we're talking about is the issue this country was founded on: the principle of human freedom and equality as embodied in the Constitution of the United States. Maybe as we've come further along in time we've come to think it's unimportant. People read those words today, and if they aren't told it's the Constitution, more often than not they reject it as sounding 'communistic.' Well, shoot, it's the same damn language that was originally written, so why is it communistic? Because our standard of living has improved so much. People look at these concepts and they can't believe that we are where we are because of them. They see them as being against what is now called our 'self-interest.' But what everyone forgets is that the men who wrote those ideas wrote ideas that were against *their* self-interest! They were. Those men were the rich and powerful and educated of this country, and the principles of equality they embodied were against their self-interest. That's what has changed now. Today we're not just talking about twenty Virginia planters. There are millions of people out there that enjoy a quality of life that is fully the equal of Jefferson and Madison or any of our Founding Fathers. But are they willing today to go ahead and show the same courage to vote against *their* self-interest on behalf of somebody else? That's the issue for this generation."

＿＿＿ 13 ＿＿＿

Spiritual Imperialism

Democracy is essentially a matter of ethics, and in a democracy
we must stand ready for a daily test of ethics.

—ANWAR EL-SADAT—August 1981

HOLY TERROR IS NOT UNIQUE to America. Since the mid-
seventies, the syndrome of ideological fundamentalism has rum-
bled around the globe. Concurrent with the rise of Holy Terror
here, cultures far removed from ours have been gripped by similar
reactions to modernization and social change. In these distant examples, we can observe the larger syndrome in various stages of
growth and decay. We can also see a forecast of what may lie
ahead for the United States.

Twice now, we have witnessed the fever of destruction that has
overtaken whole sections of the Persian Gulf and Middle East in
the guise of militant Islamic fundamentalism. On the surface, it
might seem, nothing could be more contrary to America's plight
than the fanatical Shi'ite Moslem insurrection that deposed
America's imperial ally, the late Shah of Iran. Yet, the Islamic
fundamentalism of the Ayatollah Khomeini and his surviving
clerics parallels the current U.S. reaction in many ways. Like the
angry uprising of disaffected fundamentalists in America, the
stormy "Islamic Republic" was born of alienation and discontent.
There as here, the accelerating influences of a secular world
threatened the traditional underpinnings of a large segment of the
nation. As a remedy, the ruling Shah imposed a hasty and inequi-
table plan of modernization that produced few real material gains
and left most people feeling confused, afraid and powerless—a vol-

atile mixture of emotion which the Shah presumed to quench with torture and political repression. As events unfolded, it took only a spark from the charismatic Khomeini, operating freely in exile, to ignite a blazing popular reaction.

Yet, ironically, as in America, the insurgent movement that rejected everything modern and called for the revival of old rituals and customs was itself a child of advanced technology. Prior to his seizure of power, Iran's Ayatollah had his own "electronic mosque." Among poor Iranians, after the state-controlled radio, cheap cassette recorders were the prevailing medium of entertainment and mass communication; and it was primarily through black-market traffic in cassette tapes that the mystical fundamentalist leader propagated his militant ideology.

Since the fall of Iran, Islamic fundamentalism has spread rapidly through the Mideast, contrary to American diplomatic views, superseding the "Communist menace" as the driving myth and ultimate threat to stability in the region. Despite their own strict Islamic beliefs and policies, ruling elites in Saudi Arabia and other Gulf oil states have come under siege by Moslem fundamentalist sects; and it has been mainly through a broader distribution of wealth, education and opportunity that other Arab sheikhdoms have so far managed to contain the militant fervor. Some governing families, such as the House of Saud, have stemmed the buildup of revolutionary sentiment by granting recognition or official stature to fundamentalist forces. Yet, in the Mideast, as here, fundamentalist groups have used religion as a pretense for larger social movements and political power plays, and governments that court the syndrome have found themselves among its first and most bitter victims.

In October 1981, a shocked world recoiled at the assassination of Egyptian President Anwar el-Sadat, himself a devout Moslem, by a small band of fundamentalist zealots. Sadat had faced the threat of Holy Terror head-on. Just weeks before, he suffered the censure of world opinion when he moved swiftly and, many felt, mercilessly against an incipient fundamentalist revolt in his country. That September, in a wave of mass arrests, he swept down on 1,500 religious dissidents and political opponents, accusing Moslem fundamentalists of "sectarian sedition" and of attempting to foment a *jihad* or holy war against his regime. "No politics in religion and no religion in politics," said a fuming Sadat as he summarily dissolved the militant Moslem Brotherhood and other fundamentalist Islamic associations in Egyptian towns and universities. But the crackdown came too late. As Sadat labored boldly but with meager results to bring peace and prosperity to his struggling nation, fundamentalist forces overtook him in a sworn campaign of "sacred terror."

Only later did it emerge that Sadat had helped unleash the movement that destroyed him. When he came to power in 1970, Sadat had reached out to Egypt's fundamentalist fringe as allies in his bid to build a popular power base, increasing religious programming on radio and television and permitting fundamentalist publications to flourish in the closely monitored society. For three years, his government quietly funneled money into the nationwide network of neighborhood prayer groups and university Islamic associations with aggressive recruiting programs. Unlike his predecessor, President Nasser, who had outlawed the associations, Sadat encouraged them as a counterforce to pro-Soviet groups still active within Egypt; and by the mid-seventies they had taken control of nearly every student union in the country.

At the same time, however, Sadat also supported growing Western interests and influences, spurring fundamentalist reaction and demands for establishment of a social and political system based on strict Islamic law. In 1979, Sadat perceived the threat to his regime and tried to ban the organizations, but by then they had joined forces with older, more militant and fanatic groups. In 1981, the coalition mobilized grass-roots protests of 200,000 Egyptians. Dozens of hard-core cells were training for the violent overthrow of the government. The group that killed Sadat was a spin-off of the underground group whose leaders he had released from prison a decade earlier.

Surprisingly, in the end, Sadat's death was greeted with much official mourning but with little grief. After a year of assassination attempts around the world, people seemed numbed to the outrage, and in a growing international climate of religious terrorism, the free world seemed unable and unwilling to engage the threat of fundamentalist fanaticism on its own terms.

But Islamic fundamentalism was not the only troubling reaction in the region. In Israel, birthplace of three historic religions, a small but powerful coalition of orthodox sects had given rise to an unprecedented form of fundamentalist Judaism that raised internal tensions to new heights in the war-torn Jewish state. There, as in the United States, Iran and Egypt, traditional underpinnings had given way to a generation of rapid modernization and secularization, prompting many Jews, both young and old, to seek refuge in the simplicity of ancient tradition. Through successive wars and mounting internal strife fueled by runaway inflation, hard-line religion and politics merged in a sudden flowering of militant ultraorthodox sects and political parties that declared Hebrew Scriptures to be the sole authority for modern-day political, military and diplomatic action. The dominant group, the Agudat Israel Party, repudiated the existence of the Israeli state itself, taking an anti-Zionist position that precluded the creation of a Jewish state before the appearance of the long-awaited Jewish Messiah. In close parliamentary elections in 1981, the tiny Agudat minority and two allied religious parties won major concessions from Israeli Prime Minister Begin. The resulting coalition agreement contained eighty-three clauses, with the weakened Begin government agreeing in principle: to increase financial aid to students in religious schools, to abolish university dormitories occupied jointly by men and women, and to ban a variety of activities on the Jewish Sabbath, including popular soccer games, government-owned rail and oil drilling operations, the docking of cruise ships in Israeli ports and, eventually, all flights by Israel's national airline, El Al—a move that by itself threatened to cost the financially beleaguered nation up to $50 million a year.

Israel's crisis mirrored America's in many ways and linked up directly in others. To most Israelis, the concession agreement was viewed as an outrageous buckling under to the "tyranny of the minority," yet it was cast as merely expedient by Begin, whose personal beliefs were generally in sympathy with those of the fundamentalist sects. In the United States, where Begin's fundamentalist leanings were viewed with growing alarm by many American Jews, he actively courted the support of Christian fundamentalists whose New Testament views served his political and diplomatic ends. In 1980, Begin presented Jerry Falwell with a coveted Israeli freedom award for his ardent expression of pro-Zionist and pro-Semitic views. In 1981, following Israel's air attack on an

Iraqi nuclear reactor, Begin telephoned Falwell from Israel and asked for his aid in defending the condemned Israeli action before the American public. Falwell agreed, and Begin bragged at an Israeli rally that he had the support of "a Christian leader . . . who represents 20 million Christians in America." During later trips, Begin met with Falwell in the United States and his government hosted delegations of American fundamentalists in Israel who issued further statements of political support.

Events in other countries fanned still more hotbeds of fundamentalism. In India, a small minority of Moslem fundamentalists took steps to overthrow the ruling Hindu elite using religion as a means of recruiting members of India's downtrodden untouchable caste to their political cause. In some cases, upper-caste Hindus claimed that untouchables were being enticed into the movement with promises of money from oil-rich Persian Gulf countries. At the other end of the social spectrum, members of India's elite Sikh minority, adherents to a blend of Islam and Hinduism, formed a fundamentalist separatist movement of their own. Gajender Singh, leader of the 1,500-member "Society of the Pure," claimed his group was reaching out to allied Moslem fundamentalists in Pakistan and Kashmir, but opponents charged that the movement was created by the American Central Intelligence Agency. Even Indian Prime Minister Indira Gandhi claimed that Sikh supporters "in the United States and Canada" were behind the movement, but Gajender Singh denied any links to the West, describing his insurgent drive along the lines of the Soviet model. "We are maturing," he said. "We have finished with the organizational stage and are now involved in propagation. Next will come direct action. . . . At home we are prepared to use terror, the political language of the twentieth century." As he described them, the movement's religious, political and cultural goals were fused. "Even if we had industries and even if every member of the Indian Cabinet was a Sikh, we would still want independence because what we are fighting for is our cultural integrity," he said. "The Indians say they have a secular state, but it is really a Hindu state and it advances Hindu imperialism."

Spiritual imperialism. It may be Islamic, Hebrew, Hindu, Sikh— or Christian. In South Africa, the extremist Afrikaner Resistance Movement, led by a former policeman, used cassette tapes and

home videotape showings to advance its militant platform calling
for the abolition of all political parties in order to defeat the
forces of the "Antichrist" and preserve the country as a white,
Christian nation. The movement's magazine claimed that "the Antichrist . . . has grabbed the mineral resources and energy re-
serves of our Fatherland." The group's emblem, a red banner with
three interlocking sevens (drawn from the Book of Revelation),
resembled a bent swastika.

So into the eighties the syndrome spreads. As Holy Terror leaps
to other troubled regions, we can perceive the larger threat of the
worldwide phenomenon. That threat is not one of old-style political nationalism, not even one of what used to be called "imperialism" in the military or economic sense. Spiritual imperialism is a
new affront to personal freedom and national sovereignty. At the
local level, it seeks to impose a supreme set of religious beliefs
and social values on every individual. Internationally, it targets
other faiths and cultures for subjugation. America's fundamentalist right is integrally linked to this new imperialist thrust. In
fact, abroad as at home, the movement's indirect techniques and
advanced technology have transformed the historic missionary endeavor into a modern guerrilla operation.

THE MULTINATIONALS

Missionary zeal has come a long way since the days of the Holy
Roman Empire and the Spanish Inquisition. Sheathed for now is
the point of the sword. With the fall of Rome and Spain, the seizure of international wealth and power grew separate from the
propagation of the Christian faith. By the late-eighteenth century,
English missionaries began a more civilized deployment. Baptists
were already in India, Wesleyans had reached Africa, and in
1795, under the auspices of the newly founded London Missionary Society to the Islands, Congregationalists and Presbyterians
set sail for the far-off South Seas.

To the ruling classes of the British Empire, nothing seemed
more natural than the twin urge to claim the world "for Christ
and Commerce." Unfortunately, not every distant subject became
the perfect choirboy. In Africa, where jungle missionaries went

eagerly to shower upon "savage" tribes the saving grace of Christ and European civilization, many did in fact wind up in the legendary cannibal's pot. In the South Seas, where L.M.S. ships ferried pastors to the Polynesians and ministers to the Marquesans, more than one native tribe emphatically rejected the White Man's gospel with its baffling sexual mores and suffocating clothing. In preference, less grateful tribes indulged their hunger not for the Word but for the flesh, rendering tough-minded missionaries into tender *bokolo* (man-meat) and "long-pig." In some corners, apparently, the drive for cultural integrity was well under way.

From the beginning, the American experience was different. Our rebel forefathers, themselves victims of the colonial system, disestablished spiritual tyranny along with imperial rule. But the urges of Christian evangelism and national imperialism remained inseparable. By the mid-1800s, as Americans rolled westward in the spirit of the Second Great Awakening and "Manifest Destiny," America's first missionary alliances were organized to seek converts in foreign lands. Then, for almost a generation in the aftershocks of the Civil War, the nation withdrew into itself, healing its internal wounds, taking in the huddled masses of other countries, and gearing up for the period of rapid industrialization to come.

Toward the end of the century, however, with the first bursts of modern naval warfare, the need to protect American borders and trade lanes gave vent to a new expression of imperialist passion, a militant mood with distinctly religious overtones. The note was first struck by Rev. Josiah Strong, a Cincinnati pastor and former general secretary of the Evangelical Alliance for the United States. Throughout the 1890s, Strong's best-selling book *Our Country* was widely read in high government and military circles. Strong, whose personal inclinations have been described as "anti-Catholic, anti-Mormon, anti-immigrant, anti-liquor and anti-socialist," called upon America's white Anglo-Saxon Protestant majority to bring "the highest Christian civilization" to all mankind:

> . . . it is to the English and American people that we must look for the evangelization of the world. . . . It seems to me that God, with infinite wisdom and skill, is training the Anglo-Saxon race for an hour sure to come. . . . This pow-

erful race will move down upon Mexico, down upon Central
America and South America, out upon the islands of the sea,
over upon Africa and beyond. . . . God has two hands. Not
only is he preparing in our civilization the die with which to
stamp the nations . . . he is preparing mankind to receive
our impress.

And for the next half century, American missionaries went
forth for God and Country into remote places, performing the
time-honored tasks that characterize the missionary endeavor.
They preached the gospel, baptized the pagans, built churches,
schools and hospitals, and in the process helped in tangible ways
to bring to underdeveloped peoples the first lights of literacy, medical care, improved agricultural methods and modern living conditions. In the dawning age, many also brought with them the first
trappings of Western culture via newspapers, magazines, radios,
phonographs and other utensils, appliances and everyday conve-
niences. In this way, countless cultures were prepared for the
impress—and for the onslaught of Westernization that was to
come.

For close behind the missionaries, if not right alongside, were
the active agents of the growing American empire. First came soldiers and sailors, broadening the nation's military reach. Then
came procurers and prospectors, searching for raw materials to
meet American industrial needs. And last but not least, roving
American salesmen were set loose on the world, long before the
rise of the multinational conglomerates, already seeking out the
untapped foreign markets that would soon become indispensable
to the relentless growth of the American economy. With World
War II, the spirit of Josiah Strong was born anew. In his 1941
book *The American Century,* Henry R. Luce, founder of the
Time-Life publishing giant, called upon Americans:

> to accept wholeheartedly our duty and our opportunity as the
> most powerful and vital nation in the world and in conse-
> quence to exert upon the world the full impact of our
> influence, for such purposes as we see fit and by such means
> as we see fit.

Before long, the American Century found its fullest expression, not in military adventurism nor in mere economic exploitation, but in the specter of what a growing number of resentful populations were coming to see as American *cultural imperialism*. Much of the problem grew out of the postwar image of the "good life" and other visions of material splendor that were disseminated worldwide through American books, magazines, motion pictures, radio and television. This wholesale infusion of American language, values and images of material fulfillment made many around the world envious and hungry for more, but it was seen as a new form of aggression by developing cultures with their own native beliefs and national life-styles, many of which were clamoring for recognition and respect in the family of man.

The missionary efforts of U.S. religious groups have played an integral role in these proceedings. Yet, as American freedom and material plenty have become all-powerful images in the developing world, many American Christians have been deeply troubled by the fact that, despite more than a century and a half of their most ardent efforts, three quarters of the world's population remains non-Christian. While many place the blame on the spread of "atheistic" communism, in fact much of the failure of the missionary endeavor in recent years has been due to the reaction against Western influences by Third World cultures. As the latest upheavals in the Moslem and Hindu worlds suggest, many fundamentalist religious and political movements have arisen, not so much from Communist penetration, but in response to the heedless intrusion of American business and military interests, and to the flood of American culture in news, entertainment, fashion and modern life-styles filled with myths, images and promises that many shaky governments and fragile economies cannot keep.

In the face of this mounting frustration and hostility, American missionaries have suffered great losses. Since the mid-sixties, when the reaction began to take hold in the developing world (and in Europe, too, for that matter), nearly every denomination of U.S. Christians has witnessed a marked decline in its useful numbers abroad. The Lutherans have lost fifty percent of their missionary force, Methodists and Episcopals sixty, the Presbyterians roughly two thirds. American Baptists are down to only a quarter of their peak strength in the 1920s. Even the Catholic Church, which has a U.S. missionary force of priests and nuns more than four times the size of the combined groups listed above (in 1980, almost 6,400 compared to just over 1,500 for the rest), has lost more than a third of its strength since 1968.

Not surprisingly, the only missionary force on the rise is that of conservative evangelicals and fundamentalists. The Southern Baptists are up nearly a quarter, with more than 3,000 missionaries in 94 countries. Their forces alone outnumber all other mainline Protestant denominations. And independent Christian groups are growing fastest of all. Using modern business methods and communications strategies, many have grown into vast multinational operations. The international Youth for a Mission, for example, started only in 1961 by a California Assemblies of God minister, now claims 2,500 long-term and 10,000 short-term missionaries. The Navigators now count more than 1,500 full-time workers of 27 different nationalities. And the giant Campus Crusade, which had only 100 staff members and two foreign missions in 1960, now claims several thousand workers in more than 130 countries. In all, the North American missionary army is estimated to number more than 50,000.

But in a growing number of nations, the multinationals have been less than warmly received, a reality most groups we spoke with denied. Across more than two thirds of the world's land area, their activities have been severely restricted, not only by Communist and totalitarian nations but by democratic governments as well. In 1978, the Israeli Knesset enacted strict "anti-missionary laws." A person convicted of offering "material inducement" to an Israeli to change his religion would be liable to a $3,200 fine and five years in prison, and anyone found guilty of converting to another faith for nonspiritual benefit might spend three years in jail. Government officials denied that the laws were aimed at Christian missionaries, but Israeli anti-missionary organizations singled out U.S. Baptists and fundamentalists, whom they charged with "discreet and covert" proselytizing by distributing "extensive written propaganda," canvassing non-Christian neighborhoods and settlements, and by means of direct mail, deceptive advertising and broadcasting in Hebrew over foreign short-wave stations. Soon after, in New Delhi, the Indian Parliament introduced a bill—again denying that it was aimed at Christians—to ban the use of "force or inducement" to bring about conversion throughout the nation. Other countries have not been quite so formal. In Indonesia, one hundred Christian missionaries were notified that their visas would not be renewed after six months. In Central African Burundi in 1980, fifty-two missionaries were deported for "antigovernmental activities." Sometime later, Morris Cerrullo, an American evangelist who had been cited by Israeli groups, was refused entry into strife-torn Nicaragua when he promised "to annul the work of the devil so evident in the country today."

Meanwhile, a number of American evangelists became engaged in overt campaigns of spiritual warfare. Rev. Paul Voronaeff, a sixty-nine-year-old Russian refugee who became an American citizen, beamed his Russian-language short-wave gospel behind the Iron Curtain. He also smuggled Bibles into Russia by hiding them in grain and farm machinery shipments leaving Texas ports. Another California group, Open Doors, floated ashore one million Bibles—232 tons' worth!—in a secret late-night mission off the coast of China. In Southern Lebanon, site of fierce guerrilla fighting among Moslem, Christian and Israeli forces, an outlet of the Voice of Hope Radio, a country and gospel station sponsored by southern California evangelist George Otis's High Adventure Ministries, interspersed American music with Bible verses on the quarter hour in broadcasts aimed at warring factions and United Nations peace-keeping troops in the region. Over the objections of both the Lebanese government and the U.S. State Department, Otis's radio gave weekly airtime to the Christian militia leader, Major Saad Haddad, which he used to rail against his Arab enemies. In retaliation, Palestinian guerrillas shelled the station's powerful 25,000-watt transmitter four times with mortars. There were no casualties.

Not everyone has been so lucky. Amid rising international tensions, a number of American missionaries from across the religious spectrum have met with untimely death in recent years, not by accident, but at the hands of both insurgent guerrilla forces and avenging government troops. In 1980, four American Catholic missionaries were raped and murdered while working with refugees in El Salvador. Two were nuns in the respected Maryknoll order, the oldest Catholic missionary society in the United States, who were apparently murdered by Salvadoran national guardsmen

for their efforts in pursuit of social justice. In contrast, in nearby
Colombia in 1981, members of the "M-19" guerrilla group kid-
napped and later killed an American linguist, Chester A. Bitterman of the Summer Institute of Linguistics, a subsidiary of
Wycliffe Bible Translators of Huntington Beach, California. Offering no proof, guerrilla leaders accused Bitterman of being a CIA
spy and claimed that Wycliffe and the Summer Institute were CIA
counterinsurgency fronts working to destroy indigenous cultures
and promote American capitalism in the guise of fundamentalist
Christianity. Wycliffe officials denied any connection to the CIA—
and indeed no link has been established—but acknowledged that
the group did have a contract with the Colombian government to
transcribe Indian languages and prepare written materials of a
"high moral character." It also reported receiving grants from the
U.S. Agency for International Development and taking money
from other Latin American, Canadian and European interests to
finance projects in thirty-six countries.

As important as unproven allegations of CIA ties is the mere
perception by groups within host countries that America's multinational missionary organizations are not simply engaging in religious work but conducting political activities on behalf of U.S.
government agencies. Missionaries, whose good works depend on
their ability to move easily among native populations and gain
their trust—the same requirements of a good CIA agent—have
found the success of their missions and, at times, their physical
survival at stake over intangibles of rumor and native suspicion.
Yet, as past CIA covers around the world have been "blown,"
successive heads of American intelligence have adamantly refused
to exempt American missionaries from undercover activities—leaving them more suspect in both foreign and domestic eyes of activities that can only be dimly imagined.

The other side of spiritual imperialism probably has nothing to
do with government agencies, that is the attempt by multinational
fundamentalist missionary enterprises to impose their religious beliefs and political platforms on lesser-developed, often innocent
cultures. Throughout our research we raised this issue among fundamentalist right groups to no avail. None even acknowledged the
possibility that there might be something presumptuous in their
drive to "make disciples of all nations," and none saw anything

improper in their unrestrained use of mass communications. Yet like their foot-weary counterparts, many fundamentalist right broadcasters are running into international opposition. Cultures that have for years rebelled against the imposition of American myths and values through movies and television are now taking steps to limit the expansion of multinational religious broadcast enterprises. Mexico, for example, recently banned all evangelical broadcasting in that country, citing as its reason the nation's strict doctrine of church-state separation. Tough little South Korea has been even more direct: in 1980, it placed the nation's Christian Broadcasting System under severe governmental restrictions, allowing it to continue operating only so long as it refrained from social comment.

With the advent of satellite broadcasting, however, national action may soon be futile, as U.S. religious broadcasters attain the capability to leap across oceans and national boundaries without regard for the communications sovereignty of countries in the "footprint" of their transponders. At the moment, like most commercial satellite endeavors, direct religious broadcasting remains the exclusive province of American entrepreneurs. Yet, the global plans of the largest and most enterprising, Pat Robertson's Christian Broadcasting Network, are sufficient, all by themselves, to make American spiritual imperialism a critical international concern.

Programs to Change the World. "The scope of the attack is overwhelming," reads a CBN brochure headlined (echoing Campus Crusade) *Programs to Change the World.* "This is not just another skirmish with the enemy. This is a major confrontation, perhaps one of the last, great, strategic battles on earth for the souls and minds of men." Through multinational broadcasting, CBN head Robertson plans "to shake the very gates of hell to bring in the Kingdom of God." And one of the first gates to be rattled is Japan's, a nation with a population of 116 million—less than one percent of whom are Christian. Following World War II, wrote Robertson, "we revitalized that nation. We gave them American know-how and our Western life-style. We gave them everything we had—but Jesus." His current plans call for a mass communications assault on the island nation. "For the first time in the

history of world evangelization CBN will launch a multimedia
blitz, totally saturating an entire nation with the love of
Jesus. . . . CBN will bombard the nation with the Good News in
newspapers and magazines, on billboards and on radio and television." Already on the air is a lavishly animated and orchestrated
cartoon depicting magical tales from the Bible as childlike fan-
tasies—which Robertson claims may be readily translated into simple terms for every nation. Eventually, a Japanese version of the
"700 Club" is planned, with native hosts, guests and music.
Added Robertson, "In the next five years, if Jesus tarries, we expect to see thirty percent of the Japanese population won to the
Lord through this massive campaign. That's 34.8 million people!"

The next nation to be subdued is China, the once-dreaded
Communist monolith that is now being hailed as yet another vast
untapped market for American products and preachers. For
Chairman Mao, mass communication was a formidable task. For
Pat Robertson and his technicians, however, the giant country
poses only minor obstacles to salvation. With television still to be
developed, Robertson will use radio and "whatever it takes to tell
the Chinese about Jesus, to get them to listen and tune in for
more." The brochure outlines his strategy:

> In Hong Kong, Taiwan and into Mainland China, where
> almost one quarter of the earth's population hovers in spiri-
> tual darkness, CBN is preparing to launch thirty hours
> of exciting, innovative radio programming to reach the
> masses. . . . Virtually free of language barriers and with the
> government no longer jamming radio transmissions, today
> China offers the greatest potential for evangelization of any
> nation in the history of the world. What's more, almost half
> of China's population is under the age of eighteen.

But undoubtedly the most ambitious targeting effort of CBN's
"intensified ministry" is its "Latin American Strategy." CBN
claims that dubbed "700 Club" broadcasts are already "an established presence" in much of Central and South America. Eventually, Robertson plans to mount a Spanish edition of the "700
Club" (with a separate Portuguese version for Brazil), which will
serve as the centerpiece for an entire Latin network that will air

multilingual daytime dramas and other loaded CBN programming fare. According to Robertson, Latin CBN has begun reaping huge benefits, not only in fundamentalist terms but toward his ever-implied political ends. In ways no mere missionary or counterinsurgency team could equal, the magic of television has already won over whole guerrilla uprisings. The brochure boasts that

> CBN crews traveling with members of the Full Gospel Businessmen's Association to film in Nicaragua were recognized and joyously received by guerrilla forces there. Professing Jesus as Lord and Savior, the guerrilla band vowed to place a Bible in the hands of every man, woman and child in that war-torn country. . . . While Castro subversives are fanning the flames of revolution throughout Latin America, CBN is pioneering new Christian TV concepts to wrench lives from the present state of turmoil and confusion—and point them to Jesus.

The more we learned, the more startled we were at the scope of the assault by fundamentalist multinationals on foreign peoples and their native faiths and cultures. To us, it was ironic that so many fundamentalists, who condemned secular humanist plots to form a "one-world government," seemed dedicated to that purpose themselves: to bringing down a supernatural fundamentalist reign around the globe. This, to us, was spiritual imperialism at its height. No other sect appeared so openly contemptuous of other faiths, so hell-bent on spiritual warfare.

To find out how other countries felt about the crusade, we sought a sampling of international opinion, but as in the United States, we found there was virtually no awareness in official circles that their countries were being targeted for attack. In New York and Washington, we spoke with press attachés and consuls general of more than a dozen countries, including the Philippines, Mexico, India, Israel and a number of emerging African nations. Few spokesmen were willing to discuss reports of controversies involving American missionaries in their homelands. And no one anywhere seemed even faintly aware of the expansionist plans of the electronic church.

After drawing so many blanks, we turned to the United Nations. Since the mid-seventies, UNESCO—the international United Nations Educational, Scientific and Cultural Organization—had been debating sensitive questions of international broadcasting and cross-border "data flows." In the face of worldwide domination by the United States and other Western countries of news and entertainment in the developing world, many Third World nations were calling for the establishment of a "New International Information Order." The hotly debated proposal sought a rebalancing of resources and priorities that might give developing nations a fighting chance in the battle against cultural domination by outside influences. It was also a plea for understanding in the industrialized West of the unique social, political and economic problems confronting much of the Third World as it makes the transition from agricultural, tribal and even nomadic life into the age of modern technology and mass communications.

UNESCO was busy with these large questions, also busy defending itself against charges that the demand for a new information order was being instigated by the Soviet Union and its allies in a bid to tighten censorship over the world press. But no one we contacted, including officials based in New York, Toronto and UNESCO headquarters in Geneva, had considered the question of how America's fundamentalist media superpowers might affect the delicately balanced world information and cultural order. The prospect of electronic world evangelization seemed like science fiction to representatives of nations struggling to climb up from preindustrial poverty and squalor. To them, our concern lay beyond the frontier of international awareness. Yet American missionary groups and religious broadcasters had crossed that frontier years ago.

One man who has been ahead of them all is Dr. Herbert I. Schiller, professor of communications at the University of California at San Diego and the foremost international authority on the effects of mass media on developing economies and cultures. More than a decade ago, Schiller employed the concept of "cultural imperialism," and ever since he has been a central figure in the growing world debate over the cultural domination of emerging nations by the West. His books, *Mass Communications and American Empire* (1969), *The Mind Managers* (1973) and *Communication and Cultural Domination* (1976) are classics in the field of international communications, and his work has been widely studied abroad by government and media policy-makers.

When we set out for southern California, we had more in mind than simply checking out Rev. Tim LaHaye, the creationists and the Campus Crusade. Most of all, we wanted to see Herbert Schiller. For years, almost alone, he had been asking many of the sensitive questions about the long-range international impact of American business and culture that we were now confronting in American religion. As we wound our way through grassy canyons to the U.C.-San Diego campus, we wondered if Schiller would back away from religious controversy like so many "cultural attachés" we had interviewed. He did not. A tall, lean figure in his early sixties, Dr. Schiller listened intently as we described some of the things we had found among fundamentalist multinationals: CBN's direct broadcast empire with its satellite capabilities; Campus Crusade's films dubbed in native languages and played in remote villages using portable generators, its bullhorns blaring jingles and its picture booklets bearing primitive symbols and images; Rex Humbard's carload of television sets donated to a leper colony in the Philippines. Schiller was interested and concerned.

"This sounds to me like a very *special* special-interest group," he began. He admitted that in his studies of international big business, mass culture and high technology, the related spread of religion was one area he hadn't considered. He started making connections from his earlier research.

"You know, Christian broadcasting into Africa is a long-standing business in radio," he said. "In some places, it has been *the* major broadcasting activity. It's not only saturating whole countries but going beyond national boundaries. Ethiopia, for example, was a major center of religious broadcasting for decades, and its activities made neighboring power centers very unhappy." He edged forward. "From what you've said, it seems that what's coming along is expanding tremendously upon that base, fantastically widening and deepening the penetration."

Schiller's first question to us was: "Who is paying for all this?" Aware of the massive logistics and expense involved in establishing multinational broadcast enterprises, he found it hard to believe that charitable groups could generate the huge amounts of capital required for such ventures. We tossed out a few of the sky-high sums we had come upon in our research, noting some organizations' links to wealthy entrepreneurs with apparent political ambitions. It made perfect sense to him.

"I can only imagine that these things would merge into each other," he said, "that a certain amount of religion would spill over into the commercial side and that the commercial side would feed the religious. But more important than the commercial element, I think, is the political side, not that it would be spelled out specifically, but to the extent that this type of media and these kinds of messages would be thrust upon a society. I imagine that would be regarded by people in government as a huge plus and an activity to be supported. I would think these programs could be a very strong element in certain types of foreign policy."

As a former government economist, Schiller saw obvious benefits to be derived by both business and government from the activities of multinational religious groups. For him, they fell under the heading of cultural domination.

"This question of cultural domination, the imposition of values, has become a tremendously hot issue today," he said. "Twelve years ago, when I first wrote about it, it was not a big issue. Now it has become a central question. If you read the business newspapers and statements made by many of our business and governmental leaders, you'll see that they are finally being forced to acknowledge that there seems to be a lot of hostility toward America on a cultural basis."

Were American interests beginning to accept responsibility for some of the anger and resentment that has arisen?

"No," said Schiller, "all they're trying to do is figure out how to overcome it. Now, religion might just be a very useful avenue for this, because whether it is deliberate or just happening on its own, it feeds the overall penetration of American culture. And it's not nearly as open to the same charges that commercial business and government are. In other words, all this religious activity serves to prepare the ground in a general way for the commercial and political side of things."

A longtime defender of the right of other nations to maintain their own cultural identities, Schiller viewed the religious outreach with alarm. He simply assumed its larger interconnections and ramifications.

"It seems to me that this might be an effort to take a very justified opposition and rising resistance to certain forms of American domination—economic, essentially, but also political, social and cultural—and divert attention or transfer these questions from the very practical, observable levels at which a nation might be able to deal with them to some celestial plane that is quite clearly outside of the here and now. It seems to me that the existing powers would rather have people listening to this stuff and pondering these abstract messages than discussing scarce mineral resources or the new branch plant coming into their country. I don't mean to make this all sound too pat, but I don't think you can deny that these types of relationships exist."

Even as a casual observer, Schiller was well aware of the heavy political content of most fundamentalist right multinational activities, especially their strong-worded anti-Communist and pro-free-enterprise themes. Combined with religion, he speculated, these overt propaganda tactics could foster even more hostility toward American business and diplomacy abroad.

"The trouble comes when these spiritual messages take on a strong political character, when they say, 'Well, you people don't want to follow a certain kind of economic and political course because that would be incompatible with this religious message.' At that point, this is going to breed contention. As these missionary groups become closely connected with prevailing economic systems, they will be identified with other forms of oppression, and it could spark all kinds of unexpected opposition."

With so much potential for trouble, but with aims so attractive to American interests, Schiller assumed that, whether it wanted to or not, the U.S. government would eventually be drawn into the fray.

"All of this would need to be constantly supported at the governmental level," he said. "When you get into areas of direct satellite broadcasting and the free flow of information, it is really America against most of the rest of the world. How many groups have access to direct satellite capacities? Almost nobody. This has become the terrain of battle between the United States and the Third World. We control the instrumentation and expertise to bring these messages down. We have the resources to absolutely undermine any national sovereignty. Whether a nation wants it or not, we can beam it right in. Now begin to funnel this flow of American information and imagery through the loop of religion, and you have the makings for some really tremendously explosive situations."

As our talk turned to the penetration of foreign cultures by outside influences, in Schiller's view, it was a foregone conclusion that surreptitious governmental interests would become involved.

"There is no doubt about it," he said, "these activities will be infiltrated by the CIA. That goes without saying, but it's just one more consideration and to that extent it will be just another element of provocation. But again, none of this goes on by itself. We must see the religious factor and the commercial factor and the political factor and other material factors altogether. It seems to me that this movement is occurring, not as part of any elaborate design but as an outgrowth of different forces flowing in the same direction. And of course, what is going on over there is tied very closely to the domestic scene."

Moreover, he said, with hostility over cultural imperialism coming from overseas, most Americans were ignorant of the fact that some of the loudest voices of protest were coming from our closest neighbors. The Canadian response was a growing sore spot.

"Really," Schiller continued, "you should see the report that was produced there just recently. It stated in words stronger than I am saying that Canada is threatened with its existence by the domination of the U.S. electronic media. In most Canadian cities, fifty to eighty percent of the television audience is watching U.S. programming in prime time. In some cities, only fifteen percent of the people are watching their own national programming! Do you know the effect on Canadian advertisers? On Canadian business and broadcasting? Do you realize what this means when you talk about cultural domination?"

The Canadian example hit close to home. In our travels, we had experienced the cross-cultural hostility ourselves. We also knew that most American religious broadcasters, including Jerry Falwell and Pat Robertson, had established separate operations and specific channels for their Canadian viewers. Looking south,

Schiller likened the case of our other great neighbor, Mexico, to growing anti-American sentiment in the Third World. He explained how U.S. cultural imperialism had become a major source of tension in Latin America.

"I was in Mexico City several years ago, twelve hundred miles south of the Rio Grande, and I turned on the TV in my hotel and I was getting Texas stations brought in by cable without even the commercials taken out. Do you realize that the population down there is continuously treated to images of the alleged good life in America, to certain types of housing, certain types of clothing, automobiles and entertainment? What this means is that the Mexican population is constantly subjected to an outlook that does not correspond to their existing possibilities. The people are taken out of their own community and pushed along certain paths by all these visual images. They are given a different set of ideas, different values, interests and expectations which do not grow out of their own cultural reality. It creates all kinds of demands that cannot be met, all kinds of frustrations, all kinds of thwarted desires."

To better understand how cultural imperialism might affect a native population, Schiller suggested that we consider the United States itself as a target of outside economic, cultural and political forces.

"You see it all the time," he said, "when something comes in here that we don't like, we are very quick to react. When the Japanese buy up a couple of banks, we scream about them taking over the banking industry. When the number of imported cars cuts into domestic sales, it is regarded with great hostility. Even on this campus, to give you another example, there have been several clashes in the last few days with members of the Moonies religious group. They were parading with posters that said, 'Get Soviet and Cuban Death Squads out of El Salvador.' Other students were protesting and trying to stop it. They didn't want these reactionary forces from another country interfering with U.S. foreign policy. So it is not only the Third World that is being drenched with this stuff. It's not just the Kenyans and the Costa Ricans. We're getting it, too, and maybe even more than many countries."

The case of the Moonies was one we knew well. Over the years, we had studied the ample documentation suggesting that Rev. Moon's Unification Church was linked to the South Korean government and the Korean CIA in several attempts to influence American politics and foreign policy. But we also knew how small and isolated this single cult was compared to the mushrooming force of well-connected fundamentalist multinationals. Again, Schiller drew our attention to the domestic scene, focusing on the fundamentalist right as a kind of foreign power engaged in cultural imperialism on the home front.

"The United States' population is a target area as much as Africa or Latin America or any other target," he said. "And like any target, it is important to identify who it is that is targeting us and how they are doing it. These forces have special abilities and resources that we are vulnerable to. It's not quite the same as some other country where there may be no other messages coming in, but we are only talking about degrees of difference."

As our conversation neared its end, Schiller sounded a variation on a plea he had made many times before.

"Other countries have at last begun to recognize the problem of cultural domination, and they have begun to raise important questions. But the money and the leadership and the technology all flow from here. And here the whole issue as it is discussed—when it gets discussed at all—is in such an unbalanced way as to make alternative voices appear as rabble-rousers, without justification. No, this is a common question with both domestic and international components. And the battle is going to be fought here."

RELIGION RUN AMOK

After our talk with Herbert Schiller, we looked deeper into Holy Terror as an international phenomenon and at its lengthening American shadow. The domestic scene remained central, but surrounded now by widening circles of fundamentalist multinational imperialism. And the possibility of government involvement seemed more real than ever. We had little hard evidence, but as American citizens we had available to us legal means of ascertaining, at least to some degree, whether our government had become entangled in the affairs of American religious groups, either at home or abroad. So in early 1981, we filed a request with the Central Intelligence Agency under the Freedom of Information Act seeking access to any materials relating to CIA and U.S. governmental involvement with clergy or religious organizations, specifically, requesting information suggesting that American clergy or religious groups might be engaged in government-sponsored information-gathering, dissemination or other intelligence operations anywhere in the world. Under the law, the agency was obligated to respond to us within ten working days. Two weeks later, we received a reply from the CIA's information and privacy coordinator claiming that the agency had an enormous backlog and asking additional time to process our request. We agreed, asking only that the agency get back to us as soon as possible.

A year later, we were still waiting. In the interim, a number of related developments had taken place. The new administration, reacting to reported breakdowns in both performance and morale within the intelligence community, took steps to exempt the CIA from its legal obligations under the FOIA. In early 1981, revised guidelines were reportedly issued that, for all practical purposes, made such formal requests futile exercises. In addition, in response to earlier public disclosures of the names of U.S. intelligence agents around the world, Congress at the urging of the administration had taken steps to make any future disclosures criminal activities, regardless of whether they involved government agents or employees, or even if the information was legally obtained through unclassified sources. We had no desire to jeopardize vital U.S. security interests abroad, and faced with a chilling new law and an even chillier political climate at home, we chose not to pursue that avenue of inquiry. However, we did feel compelled to follow our concerns about the increasingly political appearances of many U.S. missionary ventures.

The case of Wycliffe Bible Translators and the Summer Institute of Linguistics is a vivid example. The death of twenty-eight-year-old linguist Chester Bitterman at the hands of guerrilla forces in Colombia has left many questions unanswered about the possible connection between Wycliffe, its subsidiary—the Summer Institute—and the CIA. In Colombia, where at the time of Bitterman's death Wycliffe had three hundred missionaries, there were frequent reports in the nation's leading newspaper about mysterious goings-on at the Summer Institute's large complex in the Colombian jungle. There were rumors that the radio network used by the institute to communicate with its translators was also used to supply information to the U.S. government. There were also charges that another Wycliffe subsidiary—JAARs, the Jungle Aviation and Radio Service—had been involved in illegal smuggling operations involving "strange people" and "secret landing strips" in the region. Although none of the allegations has been proven—and some have been explicitly *dis*proven—suspicions persist, as do other complaints that, at best, the institute unfairly uses its linguists and anthropologists for missionary purposes. And indeed, according to Wycliffe's own literature, conversion appears to be a major motive behind their Bible-translating efforts. One pamphlet states:

> Wycliffe Bible Translators believes that to accomplish Christ's commission the Gospel must be given to every man in the language he understands best. . . . The Scriptures are a means of evangelization and translation is essential to a Church-planting ministry. In the translation process, people become believers.

Other countries appear to be equally concerned. Shortly after Bitterman's death in Colombia, a communiqué was issued by the office of the president of nearby Ecuador banning the Summer Institute from carrying out any further activities in that country. The decision was made without explanation or elaboration, stating only: "Wide sections of Ecuador's society have noted problems in how the institute conducted its affairs . . . regarding matters of national sovereignty and the preservation of aboriginal groups." Commenting on the institute's operation in Ecuador's Amazon jungle, the government stated only that "it was necessary to regain control of that area." The U.S. government's acknowledged involvement in Wycliffe activities only complicated matters: Wycliffe had received two grants from the U.S. Agency for International Development (AID), a federal agency that, beyond its official projects and activities, has reportedly provided cover for some CIA operations in Latin America.

But beyond any question of government complicity, the further adventures of Wycliffe Bible Translators raise other sensitive questions. The Summer 1981 issue of Wycliffe's *In Other Words* magazine (the same issue that eulogized "Chet" Bitterman as

"God's special envoy to Colombia, sent there on a secret, short-term mission"), describes one Wycliffe project in Bolivia that, in our view, constitutes unparalleled interference by an American-based religious group in the internal affairs of another country.

An article excerpted from a speech by Luis Palau, an internationally acclaimed Argentine evangelist and president of Overseas Crusades, Inc., of Santa Clara, California, reports on the activities of David Farah, a Wycliffe translator who had been stationed in Bolivia since 1956. After being transferred from his remote jungle assignment translating the Bible for a tiny native tribe, Farah was asked by his "director" to move to La Paz, the administrative capital of the country, for reassignment in "government relations." There, according to the article, Farah carried out his instructions to establish relations with the government officer for Indian affairs, a colonel in the army who later became Minister of Education and liaison between the Bolivian government and the Summer Institute.

Then a revolution swept the country and the colonel disappeared, showing up eventually in the Argentinean embassy. Somehow Farah learned of his whereabouts and went to the embassy, where he gave the guard a copy of the New Testament to be delivered to the colonel. "Seven months later," Palau continued, "another revolution swept the country; the colonel's side won and he became President of Bolivia. David got in to see him right away." The friendship between the two thickened, along with the colonel's interest in the Bible, and sometime later he expressed concern over the moral condition of Bolivia. Palau continued: "David saw the opening. 'Mr. President,' he said, 'if Bolivia could have a spiritual and moral revival, things would change. Why not have a campaign to improve the moral tone of the land?'" The President agreed, and plans were made to include "the moralization of Bolivia" in the national budget.

As part of the campaign, Farah invited Palau to deliver the prayer at a presidential breakfast. Afterward, the President gave Palau five nights of prime-time exposure on Bolivia's national television network during which he conducted an evangelistic crusade and telephone call-in. Next Farah contacted the Minister of Education and proposed the placing of Bibles in the nation's schools. Palau continued: "The minister, knowing of the Presi-

dent's interest in the entire moralization of the nation, signed a
law making the New Testament the official text for the teaching of
religion in all of Bolivia's schools, both public and private." Over
the next few years, 850,000 Bibles were sent to Bolivia for use in
the nation's schools. An order from the Minister of Education to
the World Home Bible League read:

> Besides these for the school system, His Excellency the
> President has also requested the provision of 100,000 copies
> of the New Testament for use in military barracks, homes for
> the aged, orphanages, hospitals and other government depen-
> dencies. We appreciate your contribution to the moralization
> of our nation, and we anticipate a better Bolivia tomorrow
> because of your investment today.

In many ways, Bolivia's nationwide moralization effort resembles the drive by the fundamentalist right in the United States,
working through the media and the nation's educational system to
establish the Bible as a universal code of belief. It also resembles
other overseas crusades that appear to have similar long-range
goals. Although their declared purpose is evangelization, many
fundamentalist multinationals are inherently social and political in
their aims and, in our view, surreptitious in their manner of propagation. The Campus Crusade for Christ, for example, which dis-
tributes Wycliffe Bible Translators' recruiting materials at its regional conventions and, according to Crusade officials we talked
with, works cooperatively with Wycliffe on some foreign projects,
conducts its own extensive low-profile penetration efforts among
native populations, primarily through its Agape professional and
occupational missionary movement. One booklet displayed at a
Crusade convention detailed the entire organization's "international personnel needs" for that period. As we read, the following
excerpts described to us an astonishingly sophisticated covert operation:

LOCATION &   JOB DESCRIPTION
Europe   Staff men to study at the university . . . make in-
               roads into the culture and be involved with a few
               disciples and leaders to train and equip. . . .

Philippines	Work with Far East Broadcasting Co. . . . Develop ministries where radio transmitters are located. . . .
Sweden	. . . Develop spiritual multipliers. . . .
Mmabatho, Bophuthatswana	Work with lay leadership in capital. Oversee and disciple nationals. . . .
Manila, Philippines	Disciple top business / financial execu- [sic] including top government officals [sic]. . . .
Buenos Aires, Argentina	Executive ministry with English-speaking businessmen. [Also in Sao Paulo, Brazil; San Juan, Puerto Rico; and Mexico City, Mexico.]
Philippines	One man to work with key Filipino Military leadership, one to work with U.S. Military leadership. Develop outreach to Philippine Armed Forces. Mass outreaches among military. . . .
Paynesward, Liberia	Work for government: Ministry of Action for Development and Progress
Bahrain	General manager of . . . Construction (a Christian firm). . . .
Jos, Nigeria	Work with Plateau State Water Board. 1 staff will control water supply for large urban area. . . .
Mmabatho, Bophuthatswana	Work for government Department of Works, in charge of roads, heavy equipment, etc. Minister to government leaders and executives. . . .
Ganta, Liberia	Agricultural-vocational instructor . . . re-evangelize liberal Christianity. On the border of a Communist country dominated by Muslims.

Endtimes and endtimes. And the syndrome spreads. But the ultimate specter of spiritual imperialism may not lie hidden in the wilds of the Philippines, Liberia or Bophuthatswana. Rather, it may be encamped at home and abroad in perhaps the most sensitive area of government activity: the U.S. military.

Over the years, we've received many queries and complaints about the free rein given to many fundamentalist missionary groups operating within the Armed Forces community. One group, the Navigators, has become ubiquitous throughout the military, maintaining active ministries on more than one hundred U.S.

Army, Navy, Air Force and Marine Corps bases, with additional overseas ministries including five on military bases in Japan and forty in West Germany. Entirely separate is the Campus Crusade for Christ's special "Military Ministry," which engages in personal evangelism and follow-up, conducts Bible studies and "Training Institutes in Military Evangelism," hosts informal evangelistic meals and meetings and works cooperatively with base chaplains ministering to both active and retired military personnel. Such ministries give obvious reasons for singling out the military for special targeting, among them: the large number of single young men, the increasing numbers of single women and the many young couples raising families. But some appear to have deeper motives.

Bill Bright, head of the Campus Crusade, has been explicit about his group's intentions. This excerpt from his book, *Come Help Change Our World,* suggests that the American military is considered to be an integral operation in his plan of global evangelism and, in our view, raises serious questions of church-state separation:

> Besides living in a diverse and challenging community, Christians in the military have a unique opportunity to reach beyond their bases to the world. The United States has military installations throughout the world which allow a trained man or woman to become an overseas missionary for the Lord at the expense of the government.

Even at the military level, the threat of Holy Terror remains a personal one, a matter of individual mental and emotional problems with the gravest real-world dangers for governments and nations. In recent years, there have been growing complaints about the performance of fundamentalist Christians in the military. On one Air Force base in Idaho, a young airman who insisted on reading the Bible while on sentry duty was scheduled for court-martial for refusing to comply with military regulations that prohibit any kind of reading while on watch. At other bases, there have been bitter disputes between fundamentalist servicemen and base commanders over reported distractions from their official duties and over attempts to proselytize on government premises.

We tried repeatedly to find someone in the military who would speak frankly with us about these reports. We called chaplains in the Pentagon and local base commanders. Invariably, they referred us to government public relations officers. One chaplain declined to discuss the issue with a cryptic, "Obviously you recognize that it is a very sensitive issue." Another said, "I know what you're talking about," but refused to speak outside official channels. At an Air Force base in Colorado Springs, the assistant to the head of the Office of Media and Public Affairs told us, "There are no problems. They [base fundamentalist groups] only enhance morale." This view, he said, was based on his seven years of participation in the Navigators, the Officers' Christian Fellowship and the Fellowship of Christian Athletes. Yet, his blanket endorsement did not alter the unspoken reality that some ardent fundamentalists in the military are causing a new kind of morale problem. They may also be posing serious security risks.

"Captain X." In our research, we strived to distinguish between the personal and political consequences of Holy Terror, but no story we came upon so vividly dramatized the link between the two as the real-life scenario that unfolded in conversation with a committed military officer. The man we will call "Captain X" was only one of more than a dozen U.S. servicemen we talked to who expressed deep reservations about the activities of some missionary groups in the military. An officer who has served for nearly a decade in high-priority positions in the nation's strategic and tactical warning systems, in recent years Captain X has been stationed around the world supplying strategic information to various military and government command centers. He has also served extensively in the area of military security and personnel management. He agreed to speak with us, he said, out of a growing personal concern for the integrity and security of American military and strategic forces, and only after encountering what he saw as official reluctance to address the problem. Emphasizing that he was speaking unofficially and only as one concerned serviceman, he asked that we withhold his identity.

A strapping military figure, Captain X began our interview somewhat nervously. He hesitated to speak out, he said, but he was deeply alarmed by things he had observed. He first became aware of the problem while on assignment overseas supervising security and personnel on what he said he could describe to us only as a "high-priority warning mission."

"A case came up involving a major who was a fundamentalist Christian," he began. "He had been through the Navigators' training program and was very active in the base Christian community. In the course of a routine conversation, I asked him, 'Suppose you found yourself in a situation where you were confronted with a potential global nuclear confrontation, and you were under extraordinary pressure and critical time requirements. How would you respond?' And he smiled at me and said, 'Well, if that ever came to pass, I would simply put my faith in the hands of the Lord.'"

After years of systematic training and rigorous drills designed to insure reflexlike response to strategic indicators, Captain X assured us, that was not the answer the major should have given to a hypothetical situation of national survival.

"I asked him again," he continued, "I said, 'You know, to be an officer you have to be a leader. You have to make very fast judgments, important decisions based on a limited amount of information.' I said, 'As an officer, how do you feel about that sort of thing?' And he said, 'Well, I feel that basically I'm here because God wants me to be here. And whatever moves I make, that's basically all in God's design. It's all in God's will, and whatever happens is what Jesus has put in the Holy Spirit for me to enact.'"

Captain X let out a deep sigh. He was struggling to distinguish for us between his military responsibilities and his personal response. He went on slowly.

"My concern here is over the stability of military personnel who operate high-priority weapons systems or intelligence systems or any kind of defense management systems, who are no longer first and foremost dedicated to the requirements of their jobs or duty positions," he said with military precision. "Most of the fundamentalists I have spoken to in the Air Force have stated that they no longer make decisions for themselves, not in their careers nor when they are on duty. They say their decisions come from something else within them. They say at critical times it's not their decision anymore but God's will. That concerns me, not as a religious matter, but as a fundamental question of military leader-

ship and discipline. Whether it's on the battlefield in the Army, in
weapons development for the Air Force or in stress-endurance positions in the Navy, it's very serious when an individual puts the
Bible and biblical Scripture between himself and his military training, when he begins filtering his decisions through a biblical
decision-maker."

Captain X described a number of incidents in which devout
fundamentalists had let their religious devotion interfere with military duties. He recalled one incident when, during a classified
communication with a national military command center, Air
Force duty officers sending coded messages halfway around the
world punctuated their high-level strategic exchanges with born-
again banter.

"We'd get messages coming over the telex such as 'PRAISE THE
LORD' and 'ARE YOU BORN AGAIN?' and 'HOW MANY OTHER FOLKS
THERE SHARE A FELLOWSHIP?' We've had cases where men would
hold group Bible studies while on duty. In others, they would sit
at their consoles reading the Bible or typing out Scriptures and
sermons for hours on end without paying attention to the display
screens they were supposed to be monitoring."

To Captain X, the dereliction of duty seemed obvious. He recalled one of the more serious incidents involving the major and
another officer who was also a professed fundamentalist.

"In the course of performing their normal duties, these two
individuals committed certain errors in the processing of
data," he said, being purposefully vague. "It did not have an
overwhelming impact on the defense system, but it was certainly
noticeable to people at higher levels. Unfortunately, I can't give
you too much detail, except to say that they had to handle a certain incident somewhere in the world. They were responsible for
accurately processing this information and disseminating it to forward users. Well, they misinterpreted the data and basically sent
out an erroneous piece of information."

Among the recipients of the erroneous data, he told us, were
the highest offices in both the military preparedness and civilian
intelligence networks in Washington.

"When we asked them how the mistake had happened," he continued, "they said simply, 'Well, it must have been God's plan.'
They said, 'It certainly was a mistake, but at a higher level, who

knows what God had in mind? He probably meant for this to happen. Maybe He was trying to send a message to somebody about something.'"

He went on to describe how the case of the major was resolved. "He committed a number of errors and made the same kind of response. After a while, people didn't bother to try and correct his job performance. They knew what his answer was going to be. So they just humored him and always put him with somebody who was far more competent. He was a problem child, so to speak, although he had no idea he was being looked at that way. They just let his tour of duty run out and then transferred him out as fast as they could."

The captain told us of his attempts to discuss such problems with military top brass.

"On my last assignment, I brought to the attention of my superiors the case of an officer who spent his time reading Scriptures and typing out sermons on the job. I discussed his emotional detachment. Their reaction to this was to say, 'Yes, we're very well aware of what's happening.' But they said there was nothing they could do except restrict his job responsibilities and terminate his tour of duty as quickly as possible."

Part of the problem, he explained, was in the highest levels of the military itself. In his various training and performance assignments, he had repeatedly encountered instances in which high-ranking military commanders gave their full endorsement to base missionary activities, in some cases, becoming active participants themselves in military missionary groups.

"Recently I was attending an officers' development and leadership school at an Air Force base in Alabama, and during the course of our training they set aside a two-hour block for a Colonel Bottomly, who wrote this book, *Prodigal Father,* to appear before the students. He related his combat experiences. He talked about his weaknesses as a leader and officer. Then he told us, 'Don't neglect Christ.' He said, 'Christ is the most important thing you can discover in your life.'"

We were familiar with Colonel Heath Bottomly's book. First published in 1975, it described the colonel as a veteran command pilot who had flown more than 300 combat missions, a highly decorated officer who had flown with Charles Lindbergh, participated in the first transatlantic jet flight and served as assistant secretary to the Joint Chiefs of Staff. In the sixties, following a traumatic mission in Vietnam, he became a born-again Christian. Now he and his wife were listed as associate staff members of Campus Crusade's Military Ministry.

"After his speech, there was a discussion period with the students and the Colonel and the faculty. They mentioned Campus Crusade by name. They even threw in a plug for his book, which was in the bookstore. They advised us to buy it and read it."

Captain X paused, shaking his head. "I worry about the priorities of Air Force leadership when a representative of an independent military ministry is given two hours of official time to witness to an entire school of Air Force officers. Pilots, doctors, finance officers, lawyers—everyone was exposed to it. I understand what they were trying to do. They were trying to say to us, 'At all times, men, remember your humanity. Don't get so gung-ho about the job that you lose sight of what you're doing.' But I don't think they understand the overall commitment that is being asked for or the kinds of problems these people are creating on the job."

According to the captain, in part due to the encouragement of military leaders who, he said, often cited attendance at Bible studies and fellowshipping sessions as positive factors in performance reports, the fundamentalist segment of the Armed Services was developing into a separate subculture within the military community. His description sounded like our earlier sense of the fundamentalist right shadow government in Washington.

"It's almost like an air force within the Air Force," he said, grasping for an analogy. "The fundamentalist network is becoming parallel to the 'good old boy' drinking network. You always had sergeants or colonels who would drink together and reminisce over old times, bloody battles in World War II or shared bombing raids over Hanoi. Now there's this different network of people who attend Bible studies together. They form allegiances, little social and political groups within special working situations. And you feel the subtle pressure to join. During shift changes, they'll intentionally leave behind Christian materials at their duty stations. You'll be going through your in-basket and this little piece of Christian literature will come out of nowhere, and people at other work centers will discover the same kind of thing waiting for them. A lot of people don't like it. They may bring it up in private, but they'd never say so out loud. No one wants to come out against the Bible, which is what these fundamentalists would throw at them."

Captain X emphasized that the fundamentalist subculture in the military seemed to be stronger in leadership positions than at the enlisted men's level.

"And that's what worries me," he continued. "This group is creating its own distinct personality type. On the surface, they seem to be highly stable individuals. They have good positive temperaments at all times. But I'd have to say that they do not have the normal depth of response that most people would have. They never display anger or other intense emotions. They internalize everything. They interpret any situation that comes up in relation to the Bible. And very often, they respond in a kind of laid-back monotone."

We asked Captain X if the term "emotional control" might be an apt description.

"Yes, exactly," he said, picking up immediately. "As a commanding officer, I place my trust in full-blooded men and women who can experience a full range of emotions, and personally I have a lot more confidence in a guy who is willing to haul off and kick a table or utter a few profanities in a tough situation than in someone who just sits back and smiles and says, 'This is all God's will.' I can't deal with that. I work with devoutly religious men and women of every faith. They make good family types. They have strong values. But they never introduce their religious beliefs into a duty situation. When you ask them, 'If a critical situation arises, how will you respond?' they give you a standard Air Force answer. They don't say, 'I will respond in accordance with Matthew 4:23' or something. This blurring of the line between the religious and the military is a dangerous thing. I would not like to see the U.S. military become a branch of religion. I would like to see it remain a branch of the government."

The captain stopped again, retrenching. "This is really difficult," he said, looking somewhat pained. "Of course, when you send men into combat situations, you automatically worry over their morale. You want them to have some kind of faith. Before he goes off into battle, you want a man to have made his peace with God. But these people are playing on that. The military uses faith as a base and these fundamentalists come in and try to turn people into Christian *supersoldiers*. But I have to ask myself, 'Do these people really know what they are doing when they say that they no longer call their own shots, that somebody else, some Holy Spirit, is making their decisions for them?' I have to ask, 'Say there was a nuclear confrontation with the Soviet Union. Could we count on these people to respond the way they have been trained to, or would they have a different biblical interpretation of what's happening? Would God's will strike them into a different mode?'"

Reflections:
On Faith, Fanaticism and the American Way

We live in a technical age of plenty and are frightened because
we try to control this abundance by a morality which shuts its
eyes to the consequences of our acts. We are simply not thinking
through to the end the implications of the changes that we are
making in our lives and in the lives of other nations.

—JACOB BRONOWSKI, *A Moral for an Age of Plenty*

UPDATE. IN THE YEAR SINCE we completed the first edition
of this book, there were these developments:

Despite persistent reports of its decline, the electronic church
continued to expand and increase its concentrations of power. According to Arbitron, its viewing audience grew by almost 2 million, reversing a four-year slide. Jerry Falwell's ratings, although
still far smaller than he claimed, were up almost 25 percent. Another winner appeared to be Pat Robertson, who pledged to seek
commercial sponsorship to expand his Christian Broadcasting
Network into a full-fledged fourth network. In late 1981, Robertson announced the formation of the Virginia Beach-based Freedom Council, a nationwide network of fundamentalists organized
to "work closely with state and federal officials to . . . safeguard
the heritage of our people." And abroad, CBN began regular
broadcasts from southern Lebanon in English, Arabic and Hebrew, aired over what was said to be the most powerful transmitter
in the Middle East.

And after years of legal wrangling, FCC fraud charges pending
against Rev. Jim Bakker were quietly turned over to the Justice

Department, which promptly dismissed them as unfounded. Elsewhere, however, some Big Fathers who were having troubles found themselves with even bigger troubles: Rev. Robert H. Schuller lost the religious tax exemption on his Crystal Cathedral for holding pop concerts and other profit-making programs, and Oral Roberts laid off 100 employees of his City of Faith hospital for lack of patients.

Meanwhile, in Washington, more than fifty leading fundamentalist right activists joined together to form an umbrella Council for National Policy. Among its founding members: new right leaders Richard A. Viguerie; Paul Weyrich; Howard Phillips; anti-Equal Rights Amendment crusader Phyllis Schlafly; Moral Majority's Rev. Tim LaHaye; Reagan administration officials Morton C. Blackwell and Rev. Robert Billings; and movement financiers Joseph Coors and brothers William Herbert and Nelson Bunker Hunt.

Months later, many of the same figures gathered for Schlafly's "Over the Rainbow" party celebrating the defeat of the ERA. Ten years after it was passed by Congress, the proposed amendment still had the support of three quarters of the American public. But due to a ferocious campaign waged by Schlafly's Eagle Forum, with support from fundamentalists, the Mormon Church, the John Birch Society and powerful special-interest lobbies, the law fell three states short of ratification.

New right activists also took aim at the swelling nuclear freeze movement, echoing White House claims that the worldwide campaign was a Soviet front aimed at unilateral United States disarmament. With clergy from dozens of denominations, along with many others, actively working for a verifiable bilateral freeze, Schlafly appealed to her conservative constituency sounding this biblical charge: "The atomic bomb is a marvelous gift that was given to our country by a wise God." The Religious Roundtable's Ed McAteer waxed apocalyptic, offering a view that was gaining hard currency in high places: "Nuclear warfare just might be the prophetic fulfillment of prophecy. God has raised up Russia because man has rebelled against God." Escalating his crusade against the freeze, President Reagan issued his own religious call in an unprecedented attack on the Soviet Union, which he dubbed "the focus of evil in the modern world." In a speech to a national gathering of evangelicals, Reagan declared, "There is sin and evil in the world, and we are enjoined by Scripture and the Lord Jesus to oppose it with all our might."

At the same time, across nearly every segment of the executive branch, high-ranking Reagan administration officials moved boldly to convert United States government information organs into propaganda weapons. At the International Communication Agency, now renamed the U.S. Information Agency, Director Charles Z. Wick, a former advertising executive and long-time personal friend of the President, unveiled Project Truth, a joint effort with the State and Defense departments and the CIA to distribute a monthly *Soviet Propaganda Alert* abroad. (Under laws passed to protect Americans from propaganda by their own government, the *Alert* was not made public in the United States.) Closer to home, Wick lobbied Congress for special funding for a superpowered radio channel aimed at Cuba. After months of wrangling, Congress put a stall on Radio Marti—named for Cuban national hero José Marti—concerned about the project's ideological bent and the prospect of a hemispheric broadcast war that threatened to disrupt United States radio frequencies across half the country.

However, the first casualty of the new propaganda war was not a foreign power but a respected United States institution. At the Voice of America, the overseas broadcast network that struggled for two decades following the McCarthy era to regain its credibility with foreign audiences and its independence from political influence, a stream of ideological appointments brought public protests and waves of resignations by longtime Voice professionals. One notorious memorandum by newly appointed deputy program director Philip Nicolaides, a former *Conservative Digest* writer, called for the VOA to function as "a propaganda agency." It went on to declare: "We must strive to 'destabilize' the Soviet Union and its satellites by promoting disaffection between people and rulers." Several months later, Nicolaides and new VOA director, James B. Conkling, resigned abruptly. In less than two years under Wick, the VOA went through five full or acting heads and began carrying editorials containing harsh anti-Soviet language. In an unofficial VOA newsletter, demoralized Voice staffers complained of "a difficult psychological atmosphere" within the agency. One wave of high-level resignations included the head of the current affairs division and news division chief Bernard Kamenske, who said he "quit in disgust," claiming: "The administration is compromising the credibility and fate of the VOA to feed the political appetites of people with extreme points of view. Their appetites are insatiable."

And from the White House, the President launched his own propaganda initiatives. Abroad, he began a campaign of "public diplomacy" aimed at circumventing negative foreign government and press opinion to win popular support for his weapons policies, particularly in Western Europe. Domestically, his administration undertook a peacetime program of official information management unprecedented in past administrations. At every level of government, official efforts to curb the flow of news and information took on a frantic intensity. Embarrassed by unauthorized leaks, Reagan administration officials took steps to increase government authority to classify documents as "secret"—reversing a twenty-five-year trend of greater public access to information. They ordered many executive branch employees not to speak with the press; announced a plan to administer lie detector tests to military personnel; issued restrictive guidelines covering fees to be charged under the Freedom of Information Act; and citing cost-cutting measures, broadly slashed government data-gathering and publication budgets. Critics charged the moves were politically motivated to squelch internal dissent, cover up questionable government actions and impair the public's ability to measure the impact of administration cuts in federal programs. With few exceptions, the suppression continued unabated.

Yet through the first years of the Reagan administration, most fundamentalist right attempts to alter American law in defiance of public consensus were unsuccessful. As always, no single issue dramatized their frustration as vividly as abortion. The subject of so many fervent hopes and solemn promises, in the early eighties the abortion debate was marked by successive fundamentalist right defeats in Congress and the courts—and by a marked upsurge in violence nationwide surrounding anti-abortion efforts. Despite administration moves to separate abortion-related activities from family planning services that received federal funds, and despite Justice Department pro-life advocacy in abortion cases pending before the United States Supreme Court, overall, the movement lost ground in its efforts to reverse the historic precedent of *Roe* v. *Wade*. The defeats coincided with a string of acts of vigilantism, including the harassment of clients and employees of abortion clinics, legal intimidation of minor-age women seeking abortions, and incidents of violence and vandalism; at least fifty-two abortion clinics were vandalized and more than twenty-seven others were targets of bomb threats, fire-bombings or arson fires.

The most notorious group of attackers was the short-lived Army of God, a trio of ardent abortion foes who claimed responsibility for acts against clinics in Florida and Virginia. In late 1982, the three were arrested and subsequently convicted of kidnapping an Illinois physician, Dr. Hector Zevallos, and his wife, holding them captive in an abandoned ammunition bunker for more than a week and threatening them with death unless the doctor promised to abandon his abortion practice in their small midwestern town. Through the course of the kidnapping, Army of God members sent a series of "epistles" to nearby newspapers discoursing on abortion and government, on man's inherent "evil," and at one point demanding that President Reagan make a public statement denouncing abortion. Instead, Zevallos promised to stop performing abortions, whereupon the couple was released.

Lawlessness erupted on other fronts as well. In Oklahoma, a mother who sued a rural school board to stop weekly prayer sessions was assaulted on school grounds and threatened repeatedly with arson before her home was destroyed by fire. In Alabama, after being denied a hearing by the Supreme Court, Governor Fob James called on state teachers and students to defy a federal injunction against a new school prayer law based on a prayer written by his son. In Nebraska, a fundamentalist pastor who refused to comply with state education laws was jailed repeatedly and his church padlocked. Rev. Everett Sileven rallied more than 500 supporters, including TV preachers and members of other nationwide fundamentalist groups, at one point forcing a district court judge to back down in the face of threatened violence between police and out-of-state protesters.

And in tragic incidents around the country, shootouts between police and members of fanatical fundamentalist sects resulted in death, injury and ongoing hostilities. In an Arizona border town, two sect members died in a drawn-out gun battle in which nine deputy sheriffs were wounded. In Memphis, Tennessee, nine sect members were killed in a massive police assault after holding an officer hostage for thirty hours and then beating him to death. The day before, the wife of the slain sect leader was rebuffed in her request to have her husband—who had proclaimed that the world would soon end and that policemen were agents of the devil—committed to a mental hospital.

And there were other indications that extremist fundamentalist groups were edging closer to violence, vigilantism and outright terrorism. Across the country, a growing list of fundamentalist paramilitary units were training their members in survival methods and guerrilla warfare. In northern California, the Legion of Zion Army, a "Christian preparedness" group, instructed its followers to "outfit and train ourselves in a military fashion" in anticipation of "mob rule . . . general insurrection or foreign attack upon our soil." At a "freedom festival" in southern Illinois, members of the Christian Patriots Defense League drilled in "identity Christianity," a fundamentalist offshoot which claims that only the white race is descended from Adam and that God commands true believers to slay their enemies. In Kansas City, Missouri, the ultra-right-wing Committee of 10 Million held a conference in preparation for a Communist invasion that included training in firearms, counterpropaganda and nighttime paramilitary operations. And in rural North Dakota, Gordon Kahl, a heavily armed member of the nationwide Posse Comitatus, a militant anti-tax group reportedly open only to "male, Christian property owners," was hunted by 100 officers using an armored personnel carrier after he allegedly murdered two federal marshals who had tried to arrest him. He died in Arkansas after killing a local sheriff in a shoot-out at an ammunition-filled bunker suspected to be part of a loose-knit network of identity Christian paramilitary forces across the country.

But the most ominous development to date in the militant spread of ideological fundamentalism took place not in the United States but in Latin America, where in one troubled nation the historical rule of right-wing dictatorship gave way to a ruthless new form of fundamentalist right terror. In March 1982 in Guatemala, Central America's largest, richest country and the nation with the most United States business interests in the region, a swift, blood-less coup by young military officers brought to power Guatemalan General José Efraín Ríos Montt. Ríos Montt, a devout born-again Christian, was reported to have been in church at the time and un-aware that the government was being deposed until the small group of junior officers seized a radio station and made a public call for him to lead their new ruling junta. According to initial re-ports, when he heard the call, Ríos Montt, his wife and church elders decided that it was the will of God that he should leave the church school where he was academic director and help guide the new government until new elections could be held. Within weeks, however, he had fired the other two members of the junta and proclaimed himself President and sole ruler of the country.

Soon the world began to witness a new face of dictatorship in Latin America. Declaring an end to immorality and corruption, Ríos Montt appeared on television each Sunday evening to share his religious beliefs with the nation, preaching about love, ab-stinence from alcohol and other moral issues. But the spiritual thrust of Ríos Montt's born-again regime soon took a dark—and bloody—turn. Over the years, as in many Latin American socie-ties, profound inequities separating Guatemala's wealthy elite from its impoverished masses had bred vicious insurgency throughout the country, and by the late seventies government ac-tions and counteractions had earned Guatemala a reputation as one of Latin America's most repressive states. However, instead of initiating needed land distribution or other social and economic reforms, Ríos Montt cracked down even harder. In July 1982, proclaiming, "it is time to do what God orders," Ríos Montt an-nounced what he called the "final battle" against leftist guerrillas in the country. He declared a state of siege throughout the coun-try, suspended laws governing individual liberties, property owner-ship, religious practice, press freedom and the right to trial and or-dered the death penalty for Guatemalans found guilty of murder, sabotage, terrorism or treason.

The crackdown turned even uglier. Within weeks, reports began to surface of brutal killings and large-scale massacres of Gua-temalan citizens by government forces. In Guatemala's cities, cen-ters of upper-class and middle-class life, random violence and death had in fact diminished dramatically over previous regimes.

REFLECTIONS 423

But in the remote villages of the countryside where most of Guatemala's peasants live—including nearly 4 million descendants of the region's ancient Mayan culture, who comprise almost 60 percent of the country's population—the counterinsurgency program quickly turned into a broad campaign of genocide. In one incident, 300 men, women and children were killed by Guatemalan soldiers for allegedly collaborating with Communist guerrillas. International human rights organizations monitoring the situation reported 2,600 killings committed by government forces, including 112 separate actions involving torture, mutilation and mass executions. Fleeing the terror, more than 40,000 Guatemalans crossed border areas into neighboring Mexico. In total, the army's scorched-earth policy uprooted an estimated 500,000.

Government officials acknowledged the reports but showed little distress at the civilian killings. "The guerrillas won over many Indian collaborators. Therefore, the Indians were subversives," said Ríos Montt's press secretary. "Clearly you had to kill Indians because they were collaborating with subversion." The general himself seemed unrepentant: "We have no scorched-earth policy," he said. "We have a policy of scorched Communists."

But the most disturbing element in Guatemala's brutal regime was the ubiquitous presence of United States fundamentalists at nearly every turn in the new government's rise to power. Raised Roman Catholic, like most of Latin America's population, fifty-nine-year-old Ríos Montt had only recently become born-again through the fundamentalist Christian Church of the Word, an offshoot of the Gospel Outreach of Eureka, California. Following the devastating earthquake in Guatemala in 1976, members of the United States group came down to aid in the recovery operation and begin missionary efforts among the native population. For two years prior to the coup, Ríos Montt had been closely associated with the church, and upon assuming power in 1982 he installed Guatemalan elders of the church in his government: one as public relations director and another as his private secretary. The head elder of the church in Guatemala, a United States citizen who claimed to have been a hippie in Haight-Ashbury before being "saved," became the general's personal spiritual adviser, drawing up lists of Scripture readings to guide Ríos Montt in his newly ordained role—a role that, from the beginning, had the support of major United States fundamentalist right organizations and high-ranking officials in the Reagan administration.

The links between Ríos Montt and leading United States fundamentalists came to light almost inadvertently. In a press conference shortly after assuming power, Ríos Montt told a gathering of foreign reporters that he no longer desired the United States helicopters, weapons and other military aid that had been denied Guatemala because of human rights violations by previous regimes. "The only solution is love," said the general, beside a table in his office in the presidential palace piled high with copies of the New Testament in Spanish and five of the country's numerous Indian dialects. According to Ríos Montt, CBN President Pat Robertson had offered to send to Guatemala missionaries and "more than a billion dollars" in aid from American fundamentalists. Within days following the coup, Ríos Montt had granted his first interview as president to Robertson, who promptly aired it on his "700 Club" along with high praise for the new regime. Later, however, Robertson appeared to back off, claiming only that he hoped to match his earlier $350,000 in earthquake relief and send "a small team of medical and agricultural experts" to the country.

Soon the United States government surfaced in the fundamentalist right support plan. A month before the declared state of siege and the first reports of widespread killings among the Indian population, Ríos Montt sent his top deputy and Church of the Word elder Francisco Bianchi to Washington for a series of meetings with United States officials. One gathering, at the home of United States ambassador to the Organization of American States William Middendorf, was attended by the Reagan administration's most outspoken fundamentalist, Interior Secretary James G. Watt, and top presidential adviser Ed Meese, another devout born again. Also present were Revs. Jerry Falwell and Pat Robertson and the United States ambassador to Guatemala. On other trips to the United States Bianchi met with Rev. Billy Graham and Bill Bright of Campus Crusade. Through the height of the terror campaign, with Guatemalan refugees flooding into Mexico and Indian women begging for non-Indian "Ladino" clothes to wear instead of their readily identifiable native embroideries, the American media made few inquiries into the situation—perhaps due in part to a reported "public relations campaign" in the United States paid for by "a group of concerned Guatemalan businessmen." Only after the worst atrocities had been committed and a fearful quiet began to fall over the countryside did leading human rights organizations succeed in bringing the Guatemalan massacres to public attention.

By this time, however, Guatemala was being depicted as a model of effective counterinsurgency by the Reagan administration. On a trip to Central America in late 1982, President Reagan met with Ríos Montt and pledged to restore military aid to Guatemala, telling reporters, "Frankly, I'm inclined to believe they've been getting a bum rap." Claiming human rights improvements, the State Department recommended United States support for an $18 million international loan to the new government. As worldwide concern mounted, evidence emerged that Ríos Montt had participated in advance planning of the coup, and captured documents released by insurgent forces indicated that United States authorities were already providing military aid and equipment to Guatemalan forces in violation of congressional human rights restraints.

The evidence seemed to suggest that, at the very least, United States fundamentalists and high-ranking government officials were working together in support of Ríos Montt's regime: to further fundamentalist right missionary efforts; to advance the Reagan administration's ideological goals in the region; and in all likelihood, to improve the climate for United States business interests as well. If true, it would not be the first instance of United States government involvement in Guatemalan affairs—the CIA was a known sponsor of a 1954 coup. But it would be the most visible sign to date that United States actions aimed at influencing political events in foreign countries were beginning to turn toward United States-based fundamentalist groups and, possibly, toward other religion-oriented covert operations.

Then, in early 1983, despite promised reforms by Ríos Montt, a wave of sudden disappearances, secret tribunals and summary executions raised a renewed world outcry that even the United States found cause to join, at one point, recalling its ambassador to that country. Apparently, Ríos Montt's mix of political repression and public proselytizing was proving an unstable combination. In August 1983, after several attempted coups, a swift move by

senior Army officers overthrew Ríos Montt, installing in his place
Guatemalan Defense Minister Brigadier General Oscar Humberto
Mejia Victores, a more fervent, although less pious anti-Communist with political views even more closely aligned with the Reagan
administration. Reports of possible United States involvement
abounded: the day before the coup, Victores had made a visit,
described as a "courtesy call," to a United States aircraft carrier
conducting exercises in the region, in which he met with military
officials of the United States Southern Command. During the coup,
a deputy military attaché from the United States Embassy in
Guatemala was inside the national palace with a walkie-talkie.
But United States officials denied any prior knowledge of the
coup.

The United States role remained murky, but the Guatemalan
army's motives were explicit: the nation's military, business and
social elites had had enough of Ríos Montt and the Church of the
Word. In a communiqué broadcast over national radio, the army
high command declared:

> We have proved that a fanatic and aggressive religious
> group, taking advantage of the positions of power of its high-
> est members, has used and abused the Government for its
> own benefit, disregarding the fundamental principle of sepa-
> ration of church and state.

Holy Terror. We have come full circle, from the subtlety of
fundamentalist mental and emotional control, to the use of technology for political intimidation, to the mounting threat of violence,
to total propaganda on a worldwide scale. In our view, the distance from center to fringe is not great. And the potential for tragedy is almost limitless.

Historical parallels are insufficient. The rise of ideological fundamentalism in the eighties may be likened to the spread of fas-
cism in the thirties, only today the guise of religion has introduced
new elements of fanaticism, supernaturalism and indirect control.
Already in Europe there have been charges of racial and religious
bigotry, media distortions and other manipulative tactics made
against the French *nouvelle droite*—new right. In Spain, Portugal,
Canada, Brazil, Argentina, Venezuela and elsewhere in Latin

America, the interconnected Societies for the Defense of Tradition, Family and Property have begun international propaganda
efforts condemning programs of "state secularism" as promoters
of atheism, "evolutionism" and "self-management."

The patterns are familiar. Unlike earlier fascist campaigns with
their coercive behavioral codes and primarily political ends, the
holy war of fundamentalism targets the whole of culture, beginning with the heart and mind of every individual and reaching
outward for absolute control over governments, churches, mass
media and every aspect of communication and relationship that
shapes our lives. In this world climate, the spread of Holy Terror
will depend heavily on the success or failure of the fundamentalist
right in the United States, and on the degree to which its commanding lead in tactics and technology is met and countered by
other forces.

In closing this expanded inquiry, therefore, we turn to assess
the long-range outlook for Holy Terror in America. Despite recent
setbacks, in many ways the fundamentalist right still stands poised
to realize its dream. In only a few years, the United States has
taken dramatic steps toward becoming a fundamentalist nation.
Major branches of our government, including Congress, the military and key federal agencies, are now staffed with individuals
who claim to have surrendered control of their lives to a living,
supernatural being. Many of our national taxation, education and
social service policies have been restructured in ways that adhere
closely to scriptural doctrine. Other economic, natural resource,
foreign policy and defense programs have been infused with a similar ideology. The same mind-set in the White House has produced an animated paradox of fundamentalism: a President who
projects a newfound "realism" but who nevertheless stands removed from reality, and an executive branch that at its core rejects the very notion of self-government.

At the same time, across state, local and national levels, the authority of our courts and legislatures has been challenged by coordinated drives for fundamentalist right control. School prayer has
become law in several states. Publishers have buckled in response
to textbook challenges. And 80 percent of prime time television
sponsors have reportedly made "commitments of intent" to promote programs that are agreeable to fundamentalists.

There have been counterbalancing forces, to be sure. Fortified by mounting public concern, elected officials have begun to stand firm in the face of fundamentalist right intimidation. Our federal courts, on the whole, have shown laudable courage and clarity of vision. And rallying to meet fundamentalist right onslaughts, a heartening diversity of public interest lobbies, interfaith coalitions and concerned citizens groups have risen in defense of basic liberties. Indeed, on some fronts where the fundamentalist right had gained ground, the pendulum has begun to swing back.

But in our view, the greatest challenges still lie ahead. Each turn of events and twist of the economy provides new opportunities for exploitation and manipulation. Should the fundamentalist right crusade crest again, as in 1980, or triumph in its full magnitude, we may soon find ourselves living in an America reborn of surrender to the supernatural, a nation that rejects reason and science, caring and compassion and, despite claims to the contrary, the basic principles of human freedom on which this country was founded. Yet win or lose, the movement has already had profound impact on our national life. In the domain of religion it has distressed countless numbers and brought rancorous divisions to every denomination. In politics, it has unleashed the omnivorous power of PACs and the plague of attack-style campaigns. Above all, the fundamentalist right has poisoned the air of public debate with propaganda. In our travels across the country, we have felt its creeping impact, not in overt repression or outright censorship but in the chill of *self*-censorship; in the reluctance of many in government, in the media and in the field of religion to meet the fundamentalist right drive head-on; and in their failure to address the larger issues that have been raised and, in many cases, monopolized by the fundamentalist right for its own advantage. These issues lie at the heart of people's vulnerabilities: they raise legitimate questions of the personal and social values of the American people and of the directions we are pursuing as a nation.

At home, the damage can be measured. Abroad it is harder to calculate, and the implications are even more ominous. In the grip of Holy Terror, what image is the United States projecting as a superpower and world leader? Can nations whose economies and national security depend largely on American military might and diplomatic cool take comfort in the propaganda being aimed at them by American religious broadcasters and government agencies alike? How must our western allies feel when our leaders give the impression that they see the fight against communism as a holy war? Can leaders of nations that have seen havoc wreaked on millions in brutal reaction to the historical role of religion in affairs of state respond otherwise than in sheer horror at the outpourings of hatred being beamed at them by so many fundamentalist preachers and national figures? And finally, in this tinderbox of world affairs, how can we as a nation hope to merit the respect and friendship of developing peoples when we display a greater interest in capturing their souls than in helping them become truly free?

How then are we to face the threat? Obviously, there is little to be gained by attempting to beat the fundamentalist right at its own game. A counterattack in the same vein would only widen the communications battleground and lead to escalating media wars that will inevitably see similar arsenals of manipulation used by both sides. Already, on some issues, that escalation has begun, with many special interests resorting to rampant emotionalism and looseness with facts. In the end, the resulting public confusion and cynicism may be overwhelming and only increase popular support for the fundamentalist right.

Propaganda is propaganda, by whatever name it is called and for whatever party or cause it is enlisted to serve. We don't need it in America, and we don't need to use it to conquer other nations. As a people, we have more pressing business to attend to.

Before anyone can go forward, however, the instruments of Holy Terror in America must be disarmed. As a nation, we must act to straighten out the current entanglement of religion in politics and to develop new ethical standards for the use of our developing mass communications technology. To begin, we feel, our government should dismantle its own propaganda machinery now operating in both domestic politics and international affairs. It should also take steps to dissolve its propaganda partnership with the fundamentalist right by enforcing the laws that already exist in the area of church-state separation. Here precedent would seem to compel the disestablishment of the electronic church, a paid religious broadcasting monopoly that has strayed beyond any reason-

able notion of community service and far beyond its obligation to
remain a positive and politically neutral public voice. At the very
least, in our view, the tax-exempt status of competitive religious
broadcast enterprises should be rescinded. A more constructive
course, in our opinion, would be to end the business of paid
religious broadcasting altogether and, as the FCC originally intended, encourage stations to give airtime to local religions on a
free and equitably distributed basis.

In the same spirit, building on the precedent in the Arkansas
creationism trial in which fundamentalist beliefs disguised as science were barred from public education, we feel, political action
committees that have in fact cobbled their platforms from scriptural, supernatural, sectarian or other religious dogma should be
excluded from the political process for breaching the wall of separation between church and state and, explicitly, for violating the
ban on religious tests in Article Six of the United States Constitution.

The black marketplace of ideas is another information channel
in urgent need of public attention. In its private functions, the
United States mail serves a variety of interests including, quite
properly, religion. However, when computer technology is used to
transform the mail into a closed mass communications system run
by government employees, offering bulk mailing discounts and, for
many religious and nonprofit groups, taxpayer subsidized preferred rates, we believe that individuals or groups who are attacked or maligned by mail should have recourse to remedies
beyond prosecution for mere financial fraud. In our view,
mass-mailers who capitalize on areas of social and political controversy should be required to put copies of their letters on public
file and, if requested, make available to those they have targeted,
for purposes of response, copies of names and addresses to whom
letters were sent.

In the current climate, pressing for these enforcements and reforms may be futile, but it is important to make these efforts and
test these principles sooner rather than later. Yet, as important as
official action, we feel, is discussion in larger terms and broader
forums of the ethics of communication in public dialogue and
campaigns of mass communication.

This subject is not a new one. In fact, only recently has talk of ethics in communication vanished from public view. For half a century following the initial explosion of modern mass communications, like the subject of propaganda, the ethics of communication was a vital area of scholarly inquiry. In the thirties, drawing on examples from Allied wartime propaganda and their later outgrowths in politics and public relations, the Institute for Propaganda Analysis labeled a number of "allegedly spurious modes of persuasion" as *propaganda devices*. The IPA's descriptive terms, which have since become common usage, include the use of *name-calling* and *glittering generalities* in public campaigns; the technique of *card-stacking* in one-sided debates; and the avoidance of argument by innocent "We're just *plain folks*" appeals and simplistic calls to "climb aboard the *bandwagon*" in complex matters of public concern. Long before World War II and the Cold War, these tactics were cited as manipulative and deceiving, techniques that, according to Clyde R. Miller of the IPA, "make us believe or do something we would not believe or do if we thought about it calmly, dispassionately." Building on this base, later proponents of the "rational school" tagged as unethical emotional devices that defied the definition of persuasion as reason and argument. In the early fifties, Franklyn S. Haiman, chief spokesman for the rational view, declared that

> the deliberate use of nonrational motive appeals are inherently unethical because they short-circuit the listener's critical thinking process.

Yet simply identifying such devices was only the beginning. Later critics protested that, in certain instances, "rousing the emotions" might be a valid tactic, depending on how it is done and for what purposes, as in wartime uses. Dr. Wayne Minnick of Florida State University held that only the tactics included in the following list should be rejected as categorically unethical:

IT IS UNETHICAL TO FALSIFY OR FABRICATE.

IT IS UNETHICAL TO DISTORT SO THAT A PIECE OF EVIDENCE DOES NOT CONVEY ITS TRUE INTENT.

IT IS UNETHICAL TO MAKE CONSCIOUS USE OF SPECIOUS REASONING.

IT IS UNETHICAL TO DECEIVE THE AUDIENCE ABOUT THE SPEAKER'S INTENT.

Other thinkers of the day turned from general principles to specific communication techniques used in the political arena. One early report, singling out methods "PR and ad men . . . used in the selling of ideas and candidates," now reads like a primer for the fundamentalist right. The following political tactics were cited as unethical:

> Concentration on "issues" chosen "for their impact value, and by no means necessarily because they are the real or significant issues in the campaign."
> The emphasis on "attack" used "not just to give one's side of the question but to *define* the political situation."
> The "appeal beyond politics," in which "the indifferent voter is moved by being confronted with an imminent evil, something threatening to things as they are, against which he himself must fight."
> The elimination of debate . . . "providing almost endless repetition of the so-called issue and virtually crowding out competing ideas."

And the debate has gone on from there. Commenting in 1958 on the first uses of such techniques in the political arena, Thomas Nilsen, an associate speech professor at the University of Washington, recognized that modern political forces with vast financial and media bases threatened to disturb the delicate balance of power between competing voices in a free society. His eloquent defense linked the ethics of communication with the process of democracy itself:

> The persuasive techniques we have discussed are inconsistent with the fundamental democratic view that the human being is inviolable, that he is not to be treated as a thing, as a means, but as a person, as an end. This right seems to be respected for the physical person, but the persuasive methods

of the professional public relations man in political campaigns reveal a dramatic failure to respect the personality in the same way. The more the reader or listener can be made to respond to suggestion, the less he makes use of his critical faculties, the less he is induced to inform himself. . . . And the worse for democracy, which is based on the assumption that citizens can and will make informed and rational choices.

These violations of communication ethics are widespread in the crusades and campaigns of the fundamentalist right. Yet, to us, in its covert operations in both religion and politics the movement is guilty of a far more grievous act: of turning the range of mass communications technology into instruments of religious terror. Here the rupture of ethics breaks upon both the individual and democracy: in the use of fundamentalist methods of indirect control; in deceptive efforts to enact Scripture into law; in orchestrated attempts to fabricate public opinion and constituent response; and at every level, in sweeping uses of propaganda, beginning in the basic education programs of fundamentalist schools; continuing through nationwide proselytizing and recruiting efforts, politicized Bible study and "counseling" services; and beyond into programs of world evangelization with explicit ideological goals.

These larger aspects of the fundamentalist right system of total propaganda raise new levels of ethical concerns that demand public airing. For example, as a nation, how are we to confront the long-range threat of the gigantic fundamentalist schools movement, not only to America's system of public education, but to so many fundamentalist students whose minds are being shaped in their formative years by a lesson plan that appears to teach contempt for reason and science, and condemnation of those who do not share the same religious beliefs or political views? What kind of adults are these young people going to become? Are they being adequately prepared to live in an age of high technology and rapid change?

A larger question concerns the syndrome of ideological fundamentalism itself, not only in its American form but in its reflections in other faiths and cultures. How can any group, in the complexity of our time, counsel its adherents in the act of surrendering the intellect, the emotions and the will—to anyone or anything? In our view, this is an inexcusable abdication of responsibility and, as we have seen in countless personal interviews, one that may cause serious mental health problems that our society has yet to acknowledge: problems of crippling fear, guilt, anger, hatred, confusion, anxiety, depression, delusions and emotional detachment that, in extreme instances, may lead to violent or self-destructive responses. An increasing number of tragic headlines have demonstrated that these are problems that can no longer be ignored. Rather, as a growing personal, social and international concern, we believe, the symptoms of ideological fundamentalism must be recognized and understood in clinical terms.

Our final question in this area may be the most challenging of all, for it concerns not just ideological fundamentalism but the evangelical imperative in its largest sense. In the world of the eighties, how can any missionary group, church or faith defend the principle of global conversion? Tensions are already too strained among American religions and world cultures for any single faith or many in competition to wage guerrilla warfare for the minds of whole nations. In an age when the methods and technology of "saturation evangelism" can no longer be distinguished from those of total propaganda, we feel, the evangelical imperative must be questioned, not only in its denial of basic principles of pluralism and tolerance, but in its increasing uses of deception, both explicit and tacit, and in its ulterior social and political designs. In our earlier work, we have called upon every denomination to reevaluate its evangelistic aims and methods, and we do so again now with more urgency, for above all our concerns we believe that, in practice and principle, world evangelism by any group must be retired as a priority.

We raise these sensitive issues because, in our view, the new ethics so desperately needed to guide us into the future, not only in religion but in politics and our mass culture, must be based on broader imperatives than conversion and control. They must be based on the imperatives of communication, on genuine relationship and direct, open interaction, and on respect for our shared humanity over our separate sects.

As we stare at the picture of Holy Terror that has unfolded in this inquiry we are left to ask: What is the fundamentalist right's vision for America? What would they have us all become? For some years now, we have listened to their sermons. We've watched them in action. We've sat with their targets and victims. And we've looked to the movement's leaders for some sign of feeling, for a little love of their fellow man. As we have come to understand it, the fundamentalist right has no vision for America, not in its churches, not in its campaigns, not in the policies of its men who now run much of our government. In place of real vision, the movement offers only myths: a mythical view of America's past and purpose; a supernatural claim that they have been empowered to act for God; a preposterous insistence that the common good means nothing more than unquestioning obedience.

Time after time, as we came away from the preachers and politicians, the strategists and technicians, the pro-lifers, the creationists and the missionaries, we were left with the same overriding question: *What does the fundamentalist right have against human beings?* What grudge do they hold against the human mind, human feeling and our capacity to choose? In their escape from humanity through high technology, would they turn us all into machines programmed by Scriptures?

We cannot live as machines surrendered to Christ and computers. Nor would the United States long endure as a fundamentalist nation. But neither can we survive as two nations—one fundamentalist, one secular. If the leaders of the fundamentalist right really cared about this country, if they really cared about their children, as they say they do, then they would read history with an open eye and consider their goals and methods in the light of other tragic reactions in this century. And they would see the inevitable end of what they wish for America. Their whole grand mythical scheme will not stop this complex age from rushing down on them, nor will it stop their children from rushing to meet the world.

They can continue to divide us as Americans. They can play upon our panic in the face of complexity. They can create fear and turmoil in every corner of the culture. They may even bring down a second civil war. If that happens, it will not be because we have abandoned God, but because we have abandoned one another. As a nation, we can join together and reject the fundamentalist right plan. In coming elections, in our religions and in our daily lives, we can declare what we stand for as individuals and recommit ourselves to the founding principles of this country. This is the lesson we have learned from Holy Terror: that if we hold fast to America's freedoms, we don't have to be afraid. We don't have to live in terror. We don't have to be intimidated or manipulated. And we don't need propaganda juggernauts to make us a more moral people or a more perfect union.

What we do need is each other. If we come together, we can break free of fear and hostility and of those who would be masters of our souls. We can set new guidelines for our social relationships, our political interactions and the use of our developing communications technology.

Who knows? In the process we may even come to like one another, and in each other discover a new sense of ourselves as Americans. If we are not prepared to live the spirit of that shared commitment, then we might as well surrender. For as a nation we will fade in the face of Holy Terror.

Acknowledgments

AT THEIR REQUEST, some of the most important people whose information and experiences have contributed to the writing of this book will not be acknowledged here. We thank them for their time and help and for sharing their insights with us.

To others who aided us in our research we offer our gratitude for their invaluable support: John and Dorothy Baker, Robert Baker, Mimi Barker, Terri Barr, Lawrence Bernstein, Eleanor Bradshaw, Rabbi Balfour Brickner, Zora Brown, Dr. Gene Byrd, Fr. James Carroll, Morris Casuto, Sarah Cavanaugh, Senator Frank Church, Dr. Saul Colbi, George Cunningham, Dr. Martin Dann, Stephen B. Douglass, Paul A. Eshelman, William Fore, Georgia Fuller, Pat Gavett, Arthur I. Ginsburg, Sallie T. Gouverneur, Kathy Hand, Dr. Raymond J. Hannapel, W. LeRoy Harrelson, Edythe C. Harrison, Jim Hayden, John M. Jones, Jr., Tvsi Kilstein, Jackie Koch, Rabbi Bentzion Kravitz, Linda Jo Lacey, Msgr. Francis J. Lally, Norman Lear, Jim McElveen, Fr. James McGuire, Diane Marshall, Tom Mathews, Francie Meyer, Marty Moore, Hesh Morgan, Dr. John Murphy, Robert Nusbaum, Ted Patrick, Rev. Walter Pragnell, Rev. R. G. Puckett, S. Eric Rayman, Don Ross, Sondra Sacks, Dr. Bruce Schiffman, Dr. Herbert I. Schiller, Rabbi Alexander Schindler, Stephen Sewell, B. F. Skinner, Betty Lee Skinner, Ruth Carter Stapleton, Representative Michael J. Synar, Stuart Tower, Faye Wattleton, Senator Lowell P. Weicker, Dr. John Whitehead, Rachel Wilson, Ron Wolf, Leonard and Margaret Zola.

To those who hosted us in our travels and assisted us in important ways in our writing, we give our thanks for their warm hospitality and friendship: Amy, Bob and Eugenia, Diane, Don and Rene, Jay, Kurt, Scott, Stan, Stefanie, Dan and Daisy; Vickey Bear, Elly Bedol Bishop, Karl Brussel, Holly Conway, Kacey Conway, Patricia Conway, Bob DiPietro, Paul Grazda, Patrick Green, Subie Green, John and Carol

Hallman, George and Nancy Hickey, Dave La Camera, Joe Marcella, Bob and Esther Mezey, Paul Morantz, Doris Peck, Maria Piro, Diana Rowsom, Terrence Sheehan, Charna Sherman, Aaron Smith, Kris Tripp, Mike Wsiaki.

Special thanks to our friend and mentor in communication, Dr. Alfred G. Smith, for his generosity of mind and breadth of vision.

Our deepest gratitude to Tema, Mickey Miller and Ruth Pragnell for their tireless research efforts and their vigilant concern for our subject.

Much appreciation to Cleo Thompson, Mark Hurst and Cathy Fowler at Doubleday, and to our editor, Susan Schwartz, for her confidence in this project and her steady hand. And sincere thanks to Melvin L. Wulf for his patience and wise counsel.

Above all, we acknowledge the guidance and unfaltering support of Sterling Lord and Philippa Brophy, who have helped us immeasurably to grow in our work.

And finally, we thank our parents and families for handling special assignments, for reaching to be with us and for sustaining us with their spirit and love.

FLO CONWAY and JIM SIEGELMAN
New York, New York
January 4, 1982

Notes

Bracketed numbers refer to works listed in the accompanying bibliography.

PART I—HOLY TERROR

CHAPTER 1: HOLY TERROR

Page

5   *Snapping:* Conway and Siegelman [4].

6   First nationwide survey of long-term effects of cult ritual techniques: Conway and Siegelman [5].

CHAPTER 2: SLAIN IN THE SPIRIT

14   Epigraph: New York *Times,* July 13, 1979.

CHAPTER 3: POTOMAC FERVOR

33   Coalition of PACs against Church: New York *Times,* March 24, 1980.

NCPAC link to Anybody But Church: ibid.

NCPAC charges against Church as "radical" and destroyer of CIA: undated NCPAC fund-raising letter.

Church claims accusers used "big lie technique": New York *Times,* May 11, 1980.

34   Idaho newspapers on attacks against Church: ibid.

Documentation on Titan missile silo commercials: New York *Times,* October 27, 1980.

35   NCPAC admits error re Church's vote on pay raise: New York *Times,* March 24, 1980.

37   Quote from Christian Voice: Church's address to The Harmonie Club, New York City, March 5, 1981.

39   New York *Times* article on Synar: January 11, 1980.

CHAPTER 4: BIG FATHERS

49   Epigraph: in Lewis [52], p. 416, NAL edition.

50   Statistics on electronic church as colossal structure: New
     York Times, December 2, 1979, and Time, February 4, 1980.
     Statistics on weekly electronic church viewers versus weekly
     churchgoers: Fore, William F., "There Is No Such Thing as
     a TV Pastor," TV Guide, July 19, 1980.

     Findings of Dr. William Martin on electronic church audi-
     ence: Philadelphia Bulletin, June 15, 1981.

     Statistics on electronic church growth and decline in the
     seventies: compiled by Professor Jeffrey Hadden of the Uni-
     versity of Virginia and Charles E. Swann, of radio station
     WRFK-FM in Richmond, Virginia; see the New York Times,
     May 20, 1981.

51   Statistics on growing monopoly of paid fundamentalist broad-
     casters since 1959: New York Times, December 2, 1979.

52   Roberts's estimated $60 million annual revenues: in Sholes
     [87], p. 136.

53   Details of City of Faith complex: in TWA Ambassador,
     August 1978.

     ORU Law School charged with religious bias: by an Ameri-
     can Bar Association accrediting committee. ORU sued the
     ABA and a federal judge ordered the bar group not to deny
     accreditation on religious grounds: the New York Times, July
     19, 1981.

     Roberts sees 900-foot Jesus: Philadelphia Daily News, March
     26, 1981.

     Excerpts from Roberts's TV show: broadcast February 8,
     1981, in New York City.

     Roberts's declining ratings: New York Times, May 20, 1981.

54   Sholes on Roberts's direct-mail methods: [87], pp. 1–6.

     Sholes on Roberts's expensive trappings: [87], p. 95.

55   Statistics on Humbard and ministry: People, May 11, 1981.

     Humbard's estimated $25 million annual revenues: Time,
     February 4, 1980.

     Humbard's claims of debt and $650,000 home purchase:
     New York Daily News, June 3, 1980.

     "Financial lion" claim: Philadelphia Inquirer, June 4, 1980.

     "My people don't give a hoot . . .": Cleveland Press article
     cited in Philadelphia Inquirer, September 17, 1980.

     Humbard's declining ratings: New York Times, May 20,
     1981.

Excerpt from Humbard's TV show: broadcast February 8, 1981, in New York City.

56 Humbard on Jesus in politics and TV sets to leper colony: *People*, op. cit.

Schuller's claims of largest Sunday audience: New York *Times*, May 15, 1980.

Statistics on Crystal Cathedral: ibid.

57 Excerpt from Schuller's TV show: broadcast February 8, 1981, in New York City.

Schuller's estimated $16 million annual revenues: *Time*, February 4, 1980.

58 Swaggart's estimated $20 million annual revenues: ibid.

Excerpt from Swaggart's TV show: broadcast February 8, 1981, in New York City.

59 Billy Graham's renouncing political involvement: Michaels, Marguerite, "Billy Graham Challenges the Moral Majority," *Parade*, February 1, 1981. Graham said, "It would disturb me if there was a wedding between the religious fundamentalists and the political right. The hard right has no interest in religion except to manipulate it." Graham's comments, however, have been contradictory. Days after publication of his *Parade* comments, Moral Majority's Jerry Falwell claimed to have received a letter from Graham saying, "Dear Jerry . . . I am deeply disturbed that there seems to be an attempt to drive a wedge between us. I am deeply grateful for your faithful proclamation of the gospel of Jesus Christ . . . and feel that all of us who know and love our Lord Jesus Christ need to stand together. . . ." (Read by Falwell at the Copacabana in New York City, February 5, 1981.)

60 Robison's charges of "Soviet blackmail," etc.: Robison fundraising letter, dated November 1980.

Robison on planned rapes, animal killings, etc.: See Martin, William, "God's Angry Man," *Texas Monthly*, April 1981.

Robison's railings against local "queer ministry" and subsequent controversy: ibid.; New York *Times*, April 1, 1979.

61 Robison's early documentaries: *Texas Monthly*, op. cit.

"Wake Up America, We're All Hostages!": aired in New York City, June 28, 1980, with appearances by Governor John Connally, Congressman Philip Crane, Pat Robertson, Jerry Falwell and Bill Bright. See also the New York *Times*, June 28, 1980.

Robison's remarks at Religious Roundtable's Dallas national

affairs briefing, August 1980: "Bill Moyers' Journal: Campaign Report #3," broadcast over Public Broadcasting Service, September 26, 1980.

Robison's staff reductions and station cutbacks: New York *Times*, May 20, 1981.

Attempts to raise funds for "Attack on the Family" TV special: Robison fund-raising letter, dated March 1981.

62   Excerpt from Robison's TV show: broadcast February 15, 1981, in New York City.

Bakker's estimated $52-million revenue for 1979: *Combined Financial Statements for 1979 and 1980*, PTL of Heritage Village Church and Missionary Fellowship, Inc.

63   Excerpt from Bakker's TV show: broadcast February 9, 1981, in New York City.

Bakker's crying episode during early fund-raising telethon: Bakker [65], p. 58.

64   Bakker's nervous breakdown: [65], Chapter 8, "Through Valley of Nerves," pp. 77–88.

Bakker's $6 million in debts in 1978: New York *Times*, February 4, 1979.

Newspaper reports of $337,000 diverted to pay domestic bills: Charlotte (N.C.) *Observer*, January 18, 1979.

Bakker's continuing legal battles with the FCC: Washington *Star*, March 22, 1980.

65   Jim and Tammy's $90,000 annual salary and benefits: *Time*, February 4, 1980.

66   Robertson's estimated $60-million revenue for 1980: New York *Times*, September 11, 1981.

Biographical information on Robertson and other facts about CBN: CBN publicity materials.

Bakker's employment and resignation from CBN: [65], p. 106.

67   Excerpt from Robertson's TV show: broadcast February 6, 1981, in New York City.

"700 Club" episode with Senator John Warner: ibid.

70   Robertson's direct-mail activities: Reported to us in personal interviews, and documented in "Preachers in Politics," *U.S. News & World Report*, September 24, 1979.

Details of CBN subsidiaries and CBN University: CBN publicity materials.

71   Excerpts from *Pat Robertson's Perspective:* newsletters dated December 1980, and January / February 1981.

72 Institute for American Church Growth survey: statement by W. Charles Arn, vice-president of the institute. See *U.S. Catholic*, August 1981.

Robertson's statement, "We have enough votes to run the country . . .": in *U.S. News & World Report*, op. cit.

Robertson's resignation from Religious Roundtable: New York *Times*, October 2, 1980.

81 Falwell's comments on abortion as murder: various "The Old-Time Gospel Hour" broadcasts (including one broadcast March 8, 1981, in Washington, D.C.); and Falwell [74], pp. 165–80.

82 Falwell's claimed $60 million revenues in 1980: Los Angeles *Times*, March 4, 1981.

Falwell's 1980 audit showed $23 million in expenses and $19 million in debt: Washington *Post*, June 28, 1981.

Falwell requests doubling contributions to help defeat "enemies": "The Old-Time Gospel Hour," broadcast January 17, 1982, in New York City. Falwell's debts and financial needs: reported in Washington *Post* article, op. cit., and elsewhere.

NOTE: Authors' written request to Falwell's ministry for audited financial statements were never answered, although Falwell's ministry is a charter member of the Evangelical Council for Financial Accountability, which requires members to make such information available on request.

83 Falwell on "Adam and Steve": New York *Times*, November 11, 1980.

Falwell on "noisy Baptist": *The Village Voice*, November 19–25, 1980.

Falwell on "Jesus . . . not a sissy": *Time*, October 1, 1979.

Falwell's battle against *Penthouse:* New York *Times*, February 3, 1981.

Moral Majority book-banning attempts: Winston-Salem *Journal* (N.C.), April 24, 1981, and elsewhere.

Moral Majority lawsuit to obtain library borrowers' lists: In Olympia, Washington, Moral Majority sued to force the state library to disclose names of borrowers of an award-winning sex education film. See the Philadelphia *Inquirer*, March 2, 1981.

Falwell's claim of TV audience of 25 million: Washington *Post*, op. cit.

Falwell's Arbitron rating of only 1.6 million: New York *Times*, May 20, 1981.

Falwell's claim of 70,000 ministers in Moral Majority: New York *Times,* January 21, 1980.

Survey report—only 6.6 percent of Americans in Moral Majority: New York *Times,* June 19, 1981.

Survey report—seven percent had favorable opinion of Falwell and seventy-one percent agreed that religion should not be basis for political action: St. Petersburg *Times* (Fla.), August 22, 1981.

Background on Falwell's humble beginnings: Los Angeles *Times,* March 4, 1981.

84   Falwell quote on early contacts with radio and television: Philadelphia *Inquirer,* September 15, 1980.

Falwell quote on "saturation evangelism": Washington *Post,* June 28, 1981.

1973 U.S. Securities and Exchange Commission charges of "fraud and deceit" and "gross insolvency": ibid.

85   Former U.S. Communist party head Gus Hall's denial of statement attributed to him in Moral Majority presentation: New York *Times,* September 17, 1980.

White House tapes prove Falwell never questioned Carter about presence of practicing homosexuals on White House senior staff: New York *Times,* August 20, 1980.

86   "Ministers and Marches": Sermon delivered by Falwell in Lynchburg, March 21, 1965.

Falwell calls "Ministers and Marches" "false prophecy": FitzGerald, Frances, "A Reporter at Large: A Disciplined, Charging Army." *The New Yorker,* May 18, 1981, p. 114.

Falwell quote on "God . . . calling me to . . . take action": Undated fund-raising letter for Moral Majority.

Listen, America!: Falwell [74].

87   ". . . Communists chop off her parents' heads . . .": ibid., p. 5.

"The teacher . . . tortured by the Communist guard . . .": ibid., p. 93.

Falwell on free-enterprise system: ibid., p. 13.

Falwell on democracy vs. republic: ibid., p. 51.

88   "If a man is not a student of the Word of God . . .": ibid., p. 17.

"We must, from the highest office in the land . . .": ibid., pp. 18–24.

Falwell denies desire to "Christianize" America: San Diego *Union,* October 11, 1980.

"When we as a country . . .": [74], p. 81.

"Each and every man and woman alive today . . .": ibid., p. 63.

89 "A politician, as a minister of God, is a revenger . . . a terror to evildoers within and without the nation.": ibid., p. 98.

90 Falwell's public relations office said that so far, no journalists had balked at signing the agreement: "Rudy Maxa's Front Page," the Washington *Post Magazine,* April 5, 1981.

Examples of Falwell Goosestep: Falwell appearance at the Copacabana in New York City, February 5, 1981.

92 Statistics on Falwell's direct-mail operation: Washington *Post,* June 28, 1981.

93 "I have become the victim . . .": FitzGerald in *The New Yorker,* op. cit., p. 136.

96 Sermons by Rev. John Killinger, First Presbyterian Church in Lynchburg: "Would Jesus Have Appeared on 'The Old-Time Gospel Hour'?" January 11, 1981, and "Could Jesus Belong to the Moral Majority?" March 15, 1981.

97 "I heard that . . . I don't know a real Christian who does subscribe to *Playboy* or any such smut magazine. . . .": "The Old-Time Gospel Hour," broadcast March 8, 1981, in Washington, D.C.

CHAPTER 5: RELIGION AND THE RISE OF THE FUNDAMENTALIST RIGHT

99 Epigraph: Laqueur [50], p. 104.

102 Statistics on Richard A. Viguerie Company: Crawford [39], Chapter 2, and Viguerie [64].

Viguerie's support for Helms, McClure, Hatch, Crane, Edwards, McDonald and Gramm: [64], p. 38.

McDonald's reported link to John Birch Society: McIntyre [53], p. 68.

"devious elitism" and "socialism on the installment plan": [64], p. 6.

"compulsory unionism . . . wives and mothers": ibid., pp. 4–5.

103 Statistics on Viguerie's high fees: [39], pp. 62–63.

Viguerie's six-figure loans to new right groups: [39], p. 55.

Crawford wrote: "In interviews with me in March and May 1979, respectively, Paul Weyrich of the Committee for the Survival of a Free Congress and John T. Dolan of the National Conservative Political Action Committee admitted that each of their organizations owed RAVCO [Viguerie's company] at least $200,000."

"Some people think we are a big conspiracy. . . .": [64], p. 84.

104 Viguerie's rags-to-riches saga: [39], Chapter 2, and [64], Chapter 4.

"the two Macs": [39], p. 43.

"field men" for a "national conservative organization": [64], p. 31.

105 Viguerie's first list copied from Goldwater contributors: ibid., p. 32.

Fund-raising efforts for George Wallace: ibid., p. 37.

Coordinated strategy to counter Jimmy Carter proposals: ibid., pp. 61–62.

106 New right campaign against Panama Canal treaty: ibid., pp. 65–70.

$3 million cost . . . 400,000 new names: ibid., pp. 69–70.

Viguerie on "new technology": ibid., p. 21.

107 Viguerie on direct mail. "Frankly . . . liberals do not control": ibid., pp. 90–91.

"virtual monopoly . . .": ibid., p. 91.

"You can think of direct mail . . .": ibid., p. 92.

"We sell our magazines . . .": ibid., p. 91.

"Raising money is only one . . .": ibid., pp. 92–93.

108 "Dear Friend" letter from Free Congress Research and Education Foundation: [39], p. 52.

Description of "wife letter" by Crawford: [39], p. 73.

Viguerie's seeming attempt to deceive audiences: ibid. Crawford wrote: ". . . company spokesmen admit that they are designed to appear to have been individually handwritten, but, like most fund-raising material, they are mass-produced. . . ."

109 Viguerie mailings displayed names of U.S. congressmen without their authorization: Crawford notes a 1977 mailing by Viguerie for the Citizens Committee for the Right to Keep and Bear Arms, in which 500,000 letters were mailed and attributed to several U.S. congressmen. Representatives Robert S. Walker of Pennsylvania and Bob Carr of Michigan complained, Carr accusing the PAC of "gross and wanton fraud" [39], p. 68.

1970 . . . violation of federal law: In a mailing from Viguerie's company on behalf of Florida Senator Edward J. Gurney: ibid., pp. 67–68.

1977 . . . charged with failing to register and barred from operating in Ohio and Connecticut: in state action against Viguerie's mailing for the Korean Cultural and Freedom Foundation, an organization that has been linked to Rev. Sun Myung Moon's Unification Church: ibid., pp. 62–63.

"unconscionably high" fees: ibid.

Viguerie withdrew children from Catholic schools over films on ecology: [53], pp. 98–99.

Viguerie claims effort "to save the Western world": ibid., p. 99.

"We believe we should be in politics . . . religious concept.": ibid.

"We're going to . . . do an *awful* lot of punishing next election.": ibid., p. 100.

Viguerie on "National Day of Prayer and Fasting": *Conservative Digest*, May / June 1980, and [64], pp. 135–36.

110 Electronic church as new right's "ready-made network": [64], p. 6.

Moral Majority as "most important asset": ibid., p. 8.

Falwell on "godless minority . . .": ibid., introduction.

111 Joseph Coors's reported link to John Birch Society: New York *Times*, August 8, 1980.

John Birch . . . young fundamentalist preacher . . . : [53], p. 108.

Coors's attempt to break the trade union movement in the West: "Do You Know These Godfathers? You Should." *Mother Jones*, February / March 1981.

Weyrich's links with Coors: Crawford [39], pp. 10, 15.

Weyrich's lack of a college degree: ibid., p. 11.

112 Background on Billings: New York *Times*, August 18, 1980. The article quotes Ed McAteer saying, "Billings was inspired to run [for Congress] by the Christian Freedom Foundation. . . ." Also Weyrich claiming, "I persuaded Billings to come back and start an operation in Washington. . . ."

Background on McAteer: ibid. The article cites Christian Freedom Foundation ties to Sun Oil Company founder J. Howard Pew.

Pew's link to John Birch Society: New York *Times*, October 25, 1981.

McAteer's link to Weyrich through Howard Phillips: New

York *Times,* August 18, 1980. The article reports that Phillips hired McAteer as field director for Conservative Caucus.

113   Conservative Caucus, description of purpose and link to Viguerie: [64], p. 58.

Christian Voice: *Time,* April 14, 1980.

Christian Voice congressional advisory committee: Davis, L. J., "Conservatism in America," *Harper's,* October 1980.

Voice link to Weyrich's PACs: ibid.; Davis describes Voice's legislative consultant, David Troxler, as Weyrich's "close associate" at CSFC. He was identified as CSFC associate director in a backgrounder *c.* 1980 by the American Human Rights Fund. Weyrich's other man, Rev. Robert Billings, also served as an early adviser to Voice, which was started in 1978 by two California preachers, Revs. Robert Grant and Richard Zone, before opening its Washington office in early 1979.

Bid to proclaim United States a "Christian nation": American Human Rights Fund backgrounder and address by Sasha G. Lewis, at 19th Unitarian Universalist Association Conference in Albuquerque, New Mexico, June 16, 1980.

Voice subsidiary Christians for Reagan: *Time,* April 14, 1980.

114   McAteer arranges meeting with Falwell, Weyrich and Phillips. New York *Times,* August 18, 1980.

Weyrich, not Falwell, coined the name Moral Majority: Associated Press article on Moral Majority printed in the Albuquerque *Journal,* October 25, 1981, and elsewhere.

Billings becomes Reagan's liaison: New York *Times,* August 18, 1980.

New right people at Roundtable's initial meeting: *Conservative Digest,* November 1979.

Weyrich on Roundtable meeting—"I'm going to make a substantial effort . . .": New York *Times,* August 21, 1980.

Weyrich's remarks at Dallas's First Baptist Church: "Bill Moyers' Journal: Campaign Report #3," op. cit.

115   Viguerie on Weyrich's role with Falwell, Robison and Robertson: [64], p. 53.

Weyrich's quote on "radicals, working to overturn the present power structure of the country": Greene, Johnny, "The Astonishing Wrongs of the New Moral Right." *Playboy,* January 1981, and elsewhere.

Birth of pro-family movement: ibid.

"When the Christian majority takes over . . .": ibid.

116   "If Laxalt will lead . . .": *Conservative Digest,* September 1979.

"This is really . . . if you read, believe in and understand Holy Scripture": *Conservative Digest,* May / June 1980.

117   NCPAC nation's richest PAC: New York *Times,* May 31, 1981.

Reagan endorsement of NCPAC: 1980 NCPAC fund-raising letter signed by Representative Daniel B. Crane.

Helms's endorsement of NCPAC: *Playboy,* op. cit., p. 258. Dolan's views on candidates with no political enemies or public records . . . seeks "stubbornness . . .": "Terry Dolan, Conservative Point Man," *Conservative Digest,* January 1979.

118   "gut-cutting organization": New York *Times,* May 13, 1981. All excerpts from NCPAC's fund-raising letter for "Target '80": undated direct-mail solicitation.

119   NCPAC in South Dakota—McGovern charges NCPAC and Abdnor with collusion: New York *Times,* June 2, 1980.

120   NCPAC's baloney commercials in Indiana: New York *Times,* March 24, 1980.

"There's no question about it . . . we are a negative organization.": ibid.

NCPAC's targets for 1982: *Conservative Digest,* December 1980.

Scathing campaigns against Democrats who opposed Republican budget proposals: New York *Times,* May 31, 1981.

Dolan's comments on Republican party "low ebb," "constitutional libertarianism" and "government shouldn't . . . wipe out sin": ibid.

"make them angry . . . stir up hostilities . . . trying to be divisive . . .": remarks made to Crawford [39], pp. 50, 272.

"A group like ours could lie through its teeth . . .": New York *Times,* May 27, 1981.

CHAPTER 6: TARGET PRACTICE

123   Long before the 1980 election . . . its political potential: Weyrich's views on the political potential of the abortion issue are reflected in his statements in *Time,* April 6, 1981.

A 1980 postelection study by NCPAC: ibid.

124   Scientific debate on the question is . . . heatedly divided . . . : For a summary of medical views, see Nathanson [57], pp. 195–217. A one-time pro-abortion leader, in his book

Nathanson switches camps and is now cited frequently by pro-life activists as an ally.

125 Most Americans disagree: ibid., ABC-Harris polls indicate that by sixty percent to thirty-seven percent Americans approve of the Supreme Court decision legalizing abortion. See also the St. Petersburg *Times* (Fla.), November 16, 1980. According to pollster George Gallup, sixty-five percent of Americans oppose a ban on all abortions.

127 . . . some pro-life sympathizers resorted to more militant . . . means: New York *Times Magazine*, March 30, 1980. The Cleveland incident was reported in the Cleveland *Plain Dealer*, February 17, 1978.

Pro-abortion forces charged . . . "reign of terror": 1980 fund-raising letter for Planned Parenthood.

The pro-life movement pioneered . . . personal intimidation and gruesome scare tactics: statements by Dr. Mildred Jefferson in Right to Life Crusade, Inc., fund-raising letter: "I hope you are shocked by what I am telling you. I hope you are shocked enough to join us. . . ." Also comments by Dr. C. Everett Koop in *Moody Monthly*, May 1980: "Abortion: The whole issue has been foisted upon us through deception. . . . I believe that infanticide, now practiced illegally behind closed doors, will become legal and eventually, for certain types of deformity, may be mandatory. I believe . . . we will adopt active euthanasia. . . . The parallels that can be drawn between Germany with its Holocaust and America here and now are frightening. . . ." See also [57], pp. 184–86, on medical and psychiatric "scare tactics."

Its promotional literature . . . routinely decorated with photographs of aborted fetuses and . . . grisly descriptions . . . : Pictures in fund-raising ad for Monmouth County Right to Life Committee (N.J.) in the *Daily Register*, January 14, 1981 and elsewhere. Descriptions in undated fund-raising letter for STOP the BABY-KILLERS, a Political Action Project of Americans for LIFE. See also [57], p. 183. Nathanson claims most "blood and gore" descriptions are inaccurate.

128 "March for Life": "March for Life" *Program Journal*, January 22, 1981.

By early 1980, nine versions of the proposed amendment . . . : New York *Times Magazine*, March 30, 1980.

Rev. Jerry Falwell . . . prime plank in Moral Majority . . . : [74], pp. 165–80, 253.

Down Library Court . . . : Weyrich's comments in *Time*, op. cit. Also the Greene article in *Playboy*, December 1980. Terry Dolan assigned NCPAC operatives . . . : undated NCPAC "Target '80" fund-raising letter, quoted in Chapter 5. Cornered at its convention in Detroit . . . : New York *Times*, August 18, 1980.

129 Reagan welcomes pro-life leaders to Oval Office: New York *Times*, January 23, 1981.
"white paper" . . . President nominated two pro-life activists: Washington *Post*, March 6, 1981.
A senator and two congressmen quit National Pro-Life PAC: New York *Times*, June 4, 1981.

134 Religious denominations' pro-choice statements: distributed by Religious Coalition for Abortion Rights, Washington, D.C.

143 ACE, Accelerated Christian Education, Inc.: NBC's "Prime-Time Sunday with Tom Snyder," September 9, 1979. See also the New York *Times* of same date.
By 1980, independent Christian schools . . . : statistics claimed by Falwell in [74], p. 219.

144 Public schools still almost ninety percent: New York *Times*, January 4, 1981.
Book-banning attempts: most recent presentation and summary in the New York *Times Book Review*, December 20, 1981. See also the New York *Times*, June 5, 1979.
Mel and Norma Gabler's mom-and-pop foundation: [74], pp. 208–13. See also articles by Professor Edward B. Jenkinson of Indiana University, "How the Mel Gablers Have Put Textbooks on Trial," submitted to NCTE Committee Against Censorship on May 24, 1978; and "Sixty-Seven Targets of the Textbook Protesters," submitted to *Missouri English Bulletin*, May 1980.

145 American Library Association spokeswoman quoted: statement by Judith Krug in Philadelphia *Inquirer*, February 27, 1981.

146 In the passing decades, a surge of scientific knowledge: An excellent presentation of the scientific issues in the creation-evolution battle appears in Asimov, Isaac, "The 'Threat' of Creationism," the New York *Times Magazine*, June 14, 1981. See also *Time*, March 16, 1981.
Criticism of creationist views by scientists and educators: New York *Times*, April 7, 1980; "It is a dangerous view," said Dr. Wayne A. Moyer, executive director of the National

Association of Biology Teachers. "There is not a shred of evidence . . . It is the big lie." Also, "It is a misrepresentation of scientific inquiry. . . ." said Dr. Raymond J. Hannapel, program manager for science education at the National Science Foundation.

147 "Institutes" and "research centers": New York *Daily News*, June 7, 1981.
Textbook publishers retrenched again: *Time*, March 16, 1981. *Biology*, published by Silver Burdett, cut section on Darwin's life from 1,373 words to 45, its text on evolution from 2,750 to 296. *Modern Biology*, published by Holt, Rinehart and Winston, made changes in wording and deleted whole sentences expressing scientific support for evolutionary theory.

148 Statement by Georgia Judge Braswell Dean: *Time*, op. cit.
Darwin "dreamed up" evolution theory: statement attributed to Luther Sunderland, spokesman for creationists in New York. See the New York *Times*, April 7, 1980.
Arkansas creationism trial rulings: New York *Times*, January 6, 1982.

149 Institute for Creation Research was launched by Rev. Tim LaHaye: the ICR's *Impact* bulletin, August 1980, lists Dr. Henry Morris as founder and director of the institute, also as a participating founder and former president of the Creation Research Society of Ann Arbor, Michigan, one of the earliest creationist organizations. However, Christian Heritage *Courier*, August 1980, describes the institute as a branch of Christian Heritage College, founded in 1970 by LaHaye and Morris. LaHaye was president of the college from 1970 to 1978, and Morris was vice-president and professor of apologetics and, later, president from 1978–80. In 1980, ICR announced plans to become a separate organization, with Morris as its head.

151 Bliss was one of the men behind . . . the "two-model approach": *Impact* lists Bliss as former director of science education for the Racine, Wisconsin, Unified School District and co-author of several ICR "published modules" for teaching the two-model approach.

155 He was only partly correct. According to press reports . . . : ABC "Nightline," December 9, 1981, reported that the ICR "drafts legislation" that the Arkansas law was modeled on. An earlier report on "NBC News" identified the head of

the Arkansas Moral Majority as a leader of the creationist fight. The New York *Times,* December 24, 1981, reported that California attorney Wendell Bird, general counsel for the ICR, attempted to dissuade witnesses for the state after the Arkansas attorney general, Steve Clark, refused his request to serve as co-counsel at the highly publicized trial.

157 Background on Rev. Tim LaHaye: Los Angeles *Times,* February 22, 1981; San Diego *Newsline,* January 14–21, 1981; and *San Diego* Magazine, March 1981.

158 *Battle for the Mind:* Sargant, William, *Battle for the Mind: A Physiology of Conversion and Brainwashing,* New York: Perennial Library / Harper & Row, 1957, 1959.
"not only the world's greatest evil . . .": LaHaye [81], p. 57.
LaHaye sent 85,000 copies to fundamentalist pastors . . . : Los Angeles *Times,* February 22, 1981.
"the enemy" . . . "religious evil": [81], p. 10.
"Most people today do not realize . . .": ibid., p. 9.
". . . battle against religious rights . . . goal of . . . world takeover by the year 2000 . . . replace them with pro-moral political leaders": ibid., p. 10.

159 "A major portion of your 1,800-gram brain . . .": ibid., p. 14.
"Your mind has phenomenal potential . . .": ibid., p. 15.
"It is difficult to exaggerate the importance . . .": ibid., p. 16.
"lost their children's minds . . .": ibid., p. 17.
"The second part of your brain is your heart . . .": ibid., pp. 17–18.
"sex crime . . . two thirds of a drawer filled with pornographic filth": ibid., p. 20.
"At a time . . .": ibid.
"Almost every major magazine . . .": ibid., p. 25.
"Today's wave of crime . . .": ibid., p. 26.

160 "vicious in their expressed hatred" . . . "public enemy number one": ibid., pp. 29–30.
"magnificent 'David' stands nude . . .": ibid.
Rousseau . . . "moral degenerate": ibid., p. 69.
"intelligent people . . . Melancholy temperament": ibid., p. 33.
LaHaye's five tenets of humanism: ibid., pp. 59–83.
Humanist Manifestos I and II: Kurtz [48] and [49].

Two elections . . . "could dramatically change the climate . . .": ibid., p. 178.

161   Beverly LaHaye on Reagan administration's Family Policy Advisory Board: Los Angeles *Times*, February 22, 1981.
Mission to Catholics: ibid.
Mormons . . . "posing as Christians" . . . women "totally submissive": ibid.
"I haven't punched anyone's lights out . . .": ibid.

162   Report on LaHaye-Larue dialogue: April 18, 1981, at 40th Annual Meeting of the American Humanist Association, April 17–19, 1981, in San Diego, California.

CHAPTER 7: THE GOSPEL ACCORDING TO BUNKER HUNT

166   Epigraph: Bright [69], p. 213.

167   "the greatest source of manpower . . .": ibid., p. 68.
"leadership people . . . subtle, shaping influence . . .": personal interview John Jones, Jr., director of communications for Campus Crusade.
Background on Bright and details of conversion and start of Campus Crusade: [69] and Jones interview.
"a transaction of the will": [69], p. 6.

168   "as in any expanding business . . .": ibid., p. 11.
"the distilled essence of the gospel": ibid., p. 27.
"The very thought . . . Madison Avenue techniques . . . repugnant and offensive . . .": ibid., p. 22.
"communicated . . . without distorting or diluting": inside cover, "Transferable Concepts," "What is a transferable concept?"
"aggressive evangelism": [69], p. 64.

169   "teaching witnessing disciples . . .": ibid.
Spiritual multiplication . . . developed in the early thirties by . . . the Navigators: Crusade's debt to the Navigators has not been widely acknowledged. Navigators' stated goal, "to help fulfill this Great Commission by making disciples, who will in turn make more disciples," appears to predate Campus Crusade by several decades. Betty Lee Skinner, biographer of Navigators' founder Dawson Trotman, notes several connections in her book *Daws* [88]. "One such visitor [to Navigators' first headquarters in California] was a debonair young man from Oklahoma ranch country who arrived in Los Angeles planning to go into radio. . . . Thus Daws and Lila extended hospitality on his first night in California to Bill

Bright, not yet a believer, but destined to head a worldwide college movement . . ." (p. 190). And later: "He [Trotman] had helped Bill Bright with incorporation of Campus Crusade, to which a half-dozen Nav men were loaned" (p. 354).

"fulfill the Great Commission . . . in this generation": [69], p. 68.

"Maximum Sex": ibid., p. 87.

170   "the fountainhead of the radical movement": ibid., p. 69.

A Berkeley professor told Bright . . . : statement by Dr. Hardin Jones, quoted, ibid., p. 72.

"I am not a religious speaker . . .": ibid., p. 59.

171   ". . . again and again throughout the entire world": ibid., p. 74.

"A select team . . .": ibid., p. 67.

"developing goals, strategies . . . to penetrate and influence the youth culture . . .": ibid., p. 93.

"Here's Life" goals: ibid., p. 165.

172   the brainchild of . . . former ad man for Coca-Cola . . . : "Born Again," "CBS Reports," July 14, 1977, with "CBS News" correspondent Bill Moyers.

"spiritual warfare": [69], p. 166.

"Proclaiming the gospel is like a military offensive . . .": ibid., p. 118.

Bright set a goal of converting 25 million Americans: Denver Post, July 30, 1976.

173   Study of "Here's Life" in Fresno, California, and Indianapolis, Indiana: Time, January 23, 1978.

"God began to chasten us . . .": [69], p. 212.

A 1976 pamphlet urging Christians to elect "men and women of God": Time, January 3, 1977.

Amway Corporation President Richard DeVos: DeVos's links to Campus Crusade are documented in Mechling, Thomas B., "Amway's 'Gold Dust Twins,'" c. 1980 by Interchange Resource Center; and in "The New Right: Fundamentalists & Financiers," press profile No. 4 (Fall 1980) by Data Center Files. According to Mechling, DeVos gave $25,000 to the Christian Freedom Foundation in 1974–75. According to the Data Center, the DeVos Foundation gave $14,500 to Campus Crusade in 1977–78. It also reports that the Coors Foundation, headed by Joseph Coors, gave $10,000 to "Here's Life" of Denver in 1976, and the Pew Memorial

Trust gave $100,000 to Crusade the same year. (Sun Oil Company founder J. Howard Pew was an early backer of the Christian Freedom Foundation and Advisory Board Member of the John Birch Society. See Data Center profile and notes to Chapter 5.)

Art De Moss: Reported by Bright to be a host for thirteen years of Crusade Executive Ministries' evangelistic dinner parties for 150 to 700 guests at his home, and a member of Crusade's board of directors until his death in 1979. See [69], p. 197, and Crusade *Annual Report*, 1980.

Crusade link to Representative Conlon and McAteer of CFF: *Newsweek*, September 6, 1976. The article describes the joint effort by Crusade, CFF and Third Century Publishers.

174   "Christian Embassy": [69], pp. 193–95. See also the Denver *Post*, March 18, 1977.

"the most extensive Christian social and evangelization mission in recorded history . . .": Los Angeles *Times*, August 12, 1978.

175   . . . considered by his father to be a failure: Hurt [46], p. 169.

. . . the richest private individual in the world: ibid., p. 211.

His holdings included . . . : For details of Bunker and Hunt family holdings, see the New York *Times*, January 6, 1980.

Hunt family contributions to "Here's Life": ibid.

176   "You, together with your wife . . .": [46], p. 400.

"hear and discuss plans and strategies . . .": ibid., p. 401.

"History's Handful": "Crusade for Jesus: Billionaire Hunt Signs Up His Rich Friends in Drive to Spread the Gospel," Cleveland *Plain Dealer*, June 2, 1980; and elsewhere.

By early 1981 . . . approaching $220 million: interview with John Jones, op. cit.

177   "task force on technology": Los Angeles *Times*, August 12, 1978.

"diplomatic relations with national governments": ibid.

"We're selling faith . . .": ibid.

Pakistan in "political turmoil": [69], p. 178.

178   Crusade in Malaysia: ibid., p. 180.

"sacrificial mission" in Colombia: ibid., p. 184.

"unexpected impact" in Kenya: headline item in a "Here's Life" newsletter.

179   Quotes on Agape workers in "countries where missionaries are banned . . .": [69], p. 149.

H. L. Hunt on John Birch Society—". . . they should have joined me": [46], p. 195.

Welch as Bunker's political "mentor" and "surrogate ideological father": ibid., p. 221.

Bunker said to be one of its largest contributors: ibid., p. 264.

Bunker on Birch Society national council and reported gifts of $250,000 per year: ibid., p. 369.

Bunker and International Committee for the Defense of Christian Culture: ibid., pp. 264–65.

180   Expedition to find Noah's Ark: ibid., p. 370.

Belief in biblical ratio of gold to silver: ibid., p. 406.

"supernatural ministry": [69], p. 63.

"Miracles must happen . . .": ibid., p. 211.

"think supernaturally" . . . "plan supernatural plans": ibid., pp. 211–13.

"you must . . . turn over your life completely to God": ibid., p. 213.

"Our finances . . . If I understand . . . they have disobeyed God": ibid., pp. 213–14.

181   1980 revenues: See Campus Crusade *Annual Report,* 1980.

"every great movement . . . with just seventeen men": ibid., p. 166.

183   "Nearly everyone responds to love . . . never 'bruise the fruit' ": *Way of Life Discipleship and Evangelism Training* (Crusade handbook), p. M12.

Background on Arrowhead Springs headquarters: [69], pp. 29–32.

CHAPTER 8: LAMENTATIONS

195   Epigraph: Koch [47], p. 322.

196   History of religious freedom in America: Stokes and Pfeffer [62] is the definitive work on church-state relations in the United States, and the primary source of historical material in this chapter.

197   The Great Awakening of the 1740s: Bushman [37].

198   Jefferson's Bill for Establishing Religious Freedom in Virginia: [47], pp. 311–13.

199   "MR. MADISON thought . . . compel others to conform": [62], p. 95.

200   "a wall of separation between church and state": Thomas Jefferson's reply to an address from a committee of the Danbury Baptist Association of Connecticut, January 1, 1802; [62], p. 53.

"For the First Amendment rests upon . . . high and impregnable": statement appeared in two landmark Supreme Court decisions: *Everson* v. *Board of Education* (1947) and *McCollum* v. *Board of Education* (1948). This quote was excerpted from the latter.

201 The "social gospel": For history of the social gospel, see [62], pp. 299–323.

203 Anti-Semitism: [62], pp. 326–28.

204 *The Cross and the Flag:* articles and ads in February 1977 issue.
The *Winrod Letter:* quotes from Issue #179, December 1979.
Rev. Bailey Smith comments: New York *Times,* September 18, 1980.
Israeli Prime Minister Begin presents medal to Falwell: New York *Times,* November 12, 1980.

205 "That miracle called Israel": [74], p. 107.
Falwell quote, "A few of you here today don't like the Jews . . .": FitzGerald's article in *The New Yorker,* op. cit., p. 115.
Rabbi Schindler quotes: from speech before Union of American Hebrew Congregations, San Francisco, California, November 21, 1980.

206 Resurgence of anti-Semitism during AWACS debate in Senate: New York *Times,* October 28, 1981.

207 Rabbi Brickner quotes: "America's Religion: What's Right, What's Left," *Present Tense,* Spring 1981.

209 "Hebrew-Christian" organizations: Proctor [85], pp. 221–29. In this born-again sourcebook, one Hebrew-Christian scholar is quoted to claim that more than 224,000 Jews converted to Christianity in the first half of this century.

210 Background on Jews for Jesus and apparent born-again approval of Hebrew-Christian terms and witnessing tactics: [85], pp. 215–21.

216 Msgr. Higgins quotes: *Face to Face, an Interreligious Bulletin,* Winter 1981.

217 Senator Leahy quotes: Washington *Post,* March 8, 1981.
"Political Responsibility: Choices for the 1980s": statement of the Administration Board of the United States Catholic Conference, November 14, 1979.
"We specifically do not seek the formation of a religious voting bloc . . .": ibid., p. 5.

218 U.S. Church hierarchy takes first official legislative stand in favor of constitutional amendment that would overturn Supreme Court ruling: New York *Times,* November 6, 1981. Anti-Catholicism: [62], pp. 328–37.

222 Kennedy quote, "If I should lose on the real issues . . .": ibid., p. 335.

223 Msgr. Lally quotes: *Church & State,* July / August 1980.

228 William F. Fore quote: from personal interview. See also Fore's article in *TV Guide,* July 19, 1980, op. cit.
Statement by thirteen Christian organizations: New York *Times,* October 21, 1980.

229 Rev. Jimmy Allen quote: New York *Times,* October 25, 1980.
"Only willful ignorance . . . guilty of such heresy": Southern Baptist Bible translator Dr. Robert Bratcher of Chapel Hill, N.C., quoted in the New York *Times,* March 30, 1981.

230 Isaac Backus quote, "And let the history . . . the great single engine of tyranny in the world": [62], p. 45.
Baptist contribution to American religious freedom: ibid., pp. 203–4.

PART II—COVERT OPERATIONS

CHAPTER 9: COVERT OPERATIONS

239 Epigraph: See Ellul [8], p. xvi.

242 "militant opposition of liberalism": Falwell [75], p. 3.
"accommodation to cultural change": ibid., p. 4.
"reactionary evangelicalism": ibid.
"rationalism" and "secularism": ibid.
"Although Falwell and others have attempted . . .": ibid., Chapter 2, "The Roots of Religious Nonconformity."

243 "set forth the fundamentals . . . aggressive Christian work": preface to the paperback edition of *The Fundamentals,* by R. A. Torrey, Los Angeles: Bible Institute of Los Angeles, 1917; [75], pp. 3, 80.
The actual fundamentals . . . : ibid., p. 7.

244 "It was the threat of a common enemy . . .": ibid., pp. 4–5.
The 1925 Scopes "monkey trial" . . . : ibid., pp. 85–89. Falwell's account of the Scopes trial draws liberally from Tierney, Kevin, *Darrow: A Biography,* New York: Crowell,

1979; and Weinberg, Arthur, ed., *Attorney for the Damned,*
New York: Simon & Schuster, 1957.

. . . the movement was not dead but merely . . . forced underground . . . : *The Fundamentals,* op. cit., p. 90.

245   By the late forties . . . : The emergence of fundamentalism
as an openly political force is documented in Clabaugh [38].
Hargis' . . . crusade went down amid allegations [of] . . .
sexual relations with . . . All-American Kids chorus . . . and
. . . young man and young woman . . . : Philadelphia *Inquirer,* January 26, 1981.

246   *Fundamentalism:* Barr [66].

"a pathological condition of Christianity": ibid., p. 5.

"fundamentalism distorts and betrays . . .": ibid., p. v.

"warm, living gospel": ibid., p. 11.

"fossilized . . . fragmented . . . inactive . . . theology-less":
ibid., pp. 160–61.

Barr pointed out the selective nature . . . : ibid., p. 25.

Fundamentalists reject the "social gospel" . . . : ibid., p.
112.

They exalt the political and economic gospels . . . : ibid., p.
108.

"Does it [fundamentalism] really preach . . .": ibid., p. 341.

NOTE: Barr's dissection of fundamentalism appears to have
been a crushing blow to American fundamentalist apologists,
many of whom have been hard-pressed to answer his charges.
Falwell writhes under the critical assault, claiming: "Fundamentalism has often been castigated, maligned and defined in
the most hideous terminology possible" [75], p. 2; and asserts
that Barr has confused American fundamentalism with British
evangelicalism. Writes Falwell: "His [Barr's] statements . . .
reveal that he knows virtually nothing about real American
fundamentalism! It hardly seems appropriate for such a
supposedly careful scholar to make such sweeping statements . . ." ibid. Yet Barr's analysis was not lightly undertaken, and his years of first-hand experience at American
seminaries and universities provided the Oxford theologian
with a unique perspective on the American phenomenon.
Among his other views, too lengthy to be reprinted in full
here: "Modern fundamentalism in many respects falls below
the level of *The Fundamentals,* rather than rising above it"
[66], p. 2; ". . . the actual mode of operation of fundamentalism is in many ways different . . . from the picture of it

drawn by fundamentalist apologists themselves" ibid., p. 9; "Evangelical faith is betrayed by the fundamentalist apparatus of argument" ibid., p. 339. "We do not have to be liberals; but we have to recognize that the liberal quest is in principle a fully legitimate form of Christian obedience within the church, and one that has deep roots within the older church theological tradition and even within the Bible itself" . . . ibid., p. 344.

247 "modern-day 'chosen people' . . .": [75], p. 54.
Militarism is glorified . . . : ibid., p. 56.
"infiltrating the grass roots . . .": ibid., p. 154.

248 "In making friends with people . . .": Henrichsen [78], pp. 55–58.

249 "To a neighbor . . .": *Way of Life Discipleship and Evangelism Training Introductory Course Training Handbook,* Arrowhead Springs: Campus Crusade for Christ International, 1975, p. M9.
"Through the use of simple transitions . . .": ibid., pp. M8–9.
Other transitions include . . . : ibid., pp. M9–10.
"A booklet written by Moishe Rosen" . . . Saved: *How to Witness Simply and Effectively to the Jews,* pp. 20–21.

250 "AVOID DISPLAYING PICTURES OF JESUS . . .": *A Training Manual on How to Share the Messiah,* by Manny Brotman, President, The Messianic Jewish Movement International, c. 1977, pp. 4–5.

251 "Set a definite time and place . . .": *Way of Life* handbook, op. cit., p. M11. NOTE: Other missionary groups appear to copy this formula almost exactly. For example, even the Messianic Jewish Movement International suggests similar transitions: "Do you know how to get 'personal peace' . . . ?" and "Have you ever heard of the Five Jewish Laws?" The same handbook also advises witnesses to "create an interest in spiritual things . . . by playing an 'I Have Found the Messiah' cassette" *How to Share the Messiah* training manual, op. cit., p. 7.

252 "The secret is surrender . . .": Bright [70], pp. 20–21.
The same call is basic . . . to nearly all methods of hypnotic induction: The late Dr. Milton Erickson, pioneer in the indirect induction of hypnosis, detailed more than thirty indirect forms of suggestion in his 1979 work, *Hypnotherapy: An Exploratory Casebook,* co-authored with Dr. Ernest L. Rossi.

Erickson's breakthrough research in hypnosis is pregnant with
insight into the fundamentalist syndrome. NOTE: "The fixation of attention has been the classical approach for initiating
therapeutic trance, or hypnosis. The therapist would ask the
patient to gaze at a spot or candle flame, a bright light, a revolving mirror, the therapist's eyes, gestures, or whatever.
. . . It is even more effective to focus attention on the patient's own body and inner experience . . . on sensations or
internal imagery . . . an interesting story or a fascinating
fact or fantasy can fixate attention just as effectively as a formal induction . . . belief systems are more or less interrupted.
. . . Consciousness has been *distracted* . . . in a manner that
can initiate the altered state of consciousness that has been described as trance or hypnosis" [9], pp. 4–5.
The "carnal" or "self-centered" Christian: "How to be Filled
with the Spirit," *Transferable Concept 3*, by Bill Bright, pp.
19–33.

253   "The only way out. . . . Our wills are surrendered": Cassidy
[73], pp. 19, 35.
"A new control center": ibid., p. 39.
"As we surrender to God . . .": ibid., p. 41.

254   *How to Read the Bible: How to Study the Bible* by Tim
LaHaye, Irvine (CA): Harvest House, 1976.

255   The Navigators' *Topical Memory System:* [83].

256   "overcome reticence . . . mind fixed on Him": ibid., *Guidebook 1*, p. 4.
An explicit plan of "meditation": ibid., *Guidebook 2*, pp.
4–7.
"Here is the secret . . .": *Navlog*, January 1975.
"If you retake the throne of your life . . .": Bright [71], p.
176.

257   "Inhaling and exhaling is an ongoing process . . .": Bright,
Bill, "The Supernatural Power of Spiritual Breathing, Part
III," *Your Guide to Supernatural Living*, July 1981, pp. iv,
40–41.

259   *God Can Make It Happen:* by Russ Johnston with Maureen
Rank, Victor Books, p. 70.

263   "Alas! It is this that deceives you . . .": quote by C. H. Spur-
geon in "Investigating Christian Belief," *Man*, No. 3, *c.* 1976
by the Navigators.
"DO NOT DEPEND ON FEELINGS . . . the promises of His

Word": Bright, Bill, *Have You Heard of the* Four Spiritual Laws? *c.* 1965 by Campus Crusade, p. 12.

264   "Pictures in the mind . . . the eyes and nose . . .": Griffin [77], pp. 140–41.

"The founders of all man-made religions . . .": "Investigating Christian Belief," *Christ*, No. 4, *c.* 1976 by the Navigators.

265   "When He is within you . . .": *Ten Basic Steps Toward Christian Maturity*, Introduction, "The Uniqueness of Jesus," by Bill Bright, *c.* 1968 by Campus Crusade, p. 31.

"What is his occupation . . .": The Navigators, *Studies in Christian Living.*

266   "Christians are engaged in warfare . . .": *Ten Basic Steps*, Step two, "The Christian and the Abundant Life," op. cit., pp. 18–19.

268   "DEADLINE 1981: MOCKERS BEWARE . . .": New York *Times*, January 1981; excerpt from advertisement for book published by The Gospel Truth of St. Pete, St. Petersburg, Fla.

273   "faith imagination": Stapleton [89], pp. 5–6.

CHAPTER 10: BABES IN TOYLAND

279   Epigraph: De Fleur [6], p. 4.

282   Excerpt from Swaggart's TV show: broadcast February 8, 1981, in New York City.

283   Excerpt from Falwell's TV show: broadcast March 8, 1981, in Washington, D.C.

284   Excerpts from CBN's "Another Life": broadcast October 16, 1981, in New York City.

286   Excerpt from Bakker's TV show: broadcast February 10, 1981, in New York City.

288   U.S. Supreme Court "Red Lion" decision: *"Red Lion Broadcasting Co.* v. *FCC,"* 395 U.S. 367 (1969). An overview of the Fairness Doctrine and other public interest standards appears in the *Federal Register*, Vol. 39, Number 139, Part III, July 18, 1974.

289   The FCC's investigation of reports that Jim Bakker's PTL . . . : Charlotte (N.C.) *Observer*, op. cit., January 18, 1979. Details of Bakker's battle with the FCC, including his attacks against the Commission on the "PTL Club" and follow-up campaigns were obtained in authors' interview with FCC counsel L. Bernstein, in talks with other FCC staff

members and from authors' viewing of "PTL Club" broadcasts.

293   "The Electric Church: An FCC-'Established' Institution?":
Lacey, Linda Jo, *Federal Communications Law Journal,* Vol.
31, No. 2, Spring 1979, pp. 235–75.
"a strong argument . . .": ibid., p. 236.
"a substantial amount of proselytizing": ibid., p. 242.
"religion could be ignored . . .": ibid., p. 247.
"halo effect": ibid., p. 250.
"the commission has specifically stated . . .": ibid., p. 261.

294   "represents the type of concentration . . .": ibid., p. 266.
The weight of $600 million a year . . . : According to Ben
Armstrong, executive director of the National Religious
Broadcasters, religious producers spend at least $600 million
annually buying commercial airtime. See *Time,* February 4,
1980. The article notes: "If production, promotion, fund-raising and operation of their own stations are added in, religious
broadcasting is easily a billion-dollar industry."

298   "certainly there would be no New Right": [64], op. cit., p.
90.
"photographs of contorted fetuses matched with . . . U.S.
senators": ad for National Pro-Life Political Action Committee, *Conservative Digest,* January 1980.
Rabid anti-communism . . . hatred of "godless atheists"
. . . : James Robison fund-raising letter, November 1980.

299   Excerpts from Falwell Moral Majority letters: all undated.

300   Excerpts from Robison letter: dated November 1980.

301   Excerpts from McAteer letter: undated.

302   Excerpt from STOP THE BABY-KILLERS letter: undated, signed
by Donald E. Lukens, Senator, Fourth District, Ohio.

303   Excerpts from TAXPAYERS AGAINST SEX EDUCATION letter: undated, signed by Murray Norris.

304   Excerpt from NCPAC letter: undated, signed by Congressman Daniel B. Crane.

306   Background on Tom Mathews: New York *Times,* November
12, 1980, and October 8, 1981.

313   Excerpts from Robison TV show: broadcast February 15,
1981, in New York City.

314   Falwell claims one of the busiest 800 numbers on television:
"The Old-Time Gospel Hour," broadcast November 28,
1981, in New York City.

Excerpt from Falwell TV show: broadcast October 3, 1981, in New York City.

316   "Seven Days Ablaze": "700 Club" programs broadcast during the week of October 5, 1981, in New York City.

CHAPTER 11: TOTAL PROPAGANDA COMES HOME

319   Epigraph: Arendt [35], p. ix.

321   "thousands and even millions into . . . hate and will and hope": Lasswell, Harold D., *Propaganda Techniques in the World War*. New York: Knopf, 1927, pp. 220–21; [6], p. 115.
    the airwaves belong to the people: [6], p. 63.

322   "It was absolutely wrong to make the enemy ridiculous . . .": *Mein Kampf* [45], pp. 181, 145.
    "with amazing skill . . .": ibid., p. 176.

323   "By contrast, the war propaganda of the English and Americans . . .": ibid., p. 181.
    "There was no end to what could be learned . . .": ibid., p. 182.
    "spiritual terror": ibid., p. 43.
    "democracy and humanism": Shirer [61], p. 142. Shirer notes the ideas that "thrashed about in Hitler's mind: the glorification of war . . . and the absolute power of the authoritarian state; the belief in the Aryans . . . as the master race, and the hatred of Jews and Slavs; the contempt for democracy and humanism."
    "Particularly with regard to syphilis . . .": [45], pp. 247–50.

324   "The receptivity of the great masses is very limited . . .": ibid., pp. 180–81.
    ". . . the magnitude of a lie always contains a certain factor . . .": ibid., pp. 231–32.

325   *A New Beginning:* [61], p. 169.
    "At that moment I was reborn . . .": ibid., p. 180.
    "directed a propaganda campaign such as Germany had never seen . . .": ibid., p. 222.
    "I believe," he told Hitler . . . : Doob [7] in [26], p. 521.

326   "There are certain words . . . as the devil does from Holy Water": ibid., p. 532.
    "strategy of terror": ibid., p. 534.

327   "At the moment we cannot change very much through propaganda . . .": ibid., p. 536.
    Their early focus on "attitude change" . . . and . . . "mass

persuasion" . . . : For more on these early communication studies, see Schramm [27].

Also: Hovland, Carl I., Arthur A. Lumsdaine and Fred D. Sheffield, *Experiments on Mass Communication,* Princeton: Princeton University Press, 1949; Lazarsfeld, Paul F., Bernard Berelson and Hazel Gaudet, *The People's Choice,* New York: Columbia University Press, 1948; and Smith, B. L., H. D. Lasswell and R. D. Casey, *Propaganda, Communication, and Public Opinion,* Princeton: Princeton University Press, 1946.

Deep ethical concerns . . . : Klapper [13]; Kris and Leites [14] in [26].

In one of the war's most memorable efforts . . . : Merton, R. K., *Mass Persuasion,* New York: Harper & Bros., 1946.

328   Only after the war . . . ways to "inoculate" people against it: [27], pp. 4–5; see also later studies by Hovland and his colleagues and students at Yale, especially: Hovland, Carl I., Irving L. Janis and Harold H. Kelley.

Communication and Persuasion, New Haven: Yale University Press, 1953; Hovland, et al., *The Order of Presentation in Persuasion,* 1957; and Janis, Hovland, et al., *Personality and Persuasibility,* 1959.

"Bolsheviki" or "majority": *American Heritage Dictionary,* New College Edition—Bolshevik: from [Russian *Bol'shevik,* "one of the majority" . . .].

"The Strategy of Soviet Propaganda": Lasswell [16] in [26].

329   *to economize the material costs* . . . : ibid., p. 538.

"Never have I seen men trying so hard to understand . . .": Reed [58], p. 155.

330   "Form hundreds of circles . . . among the youth . . .": Gourfinkel [44], p. 64.

"direct personal propaganda": [16], p. 541.

genteel women "broken away from their class" . . . : [44], p. 67.

"the output of the Party presses": [16], p. 541.

"In these intellectual 'speakeasies' . . .": ibid., pp. 544–45.

331   Lenin's strategy . . . "was to keep alive an attitude of suspicion . . .": ibid., p. 541.

"The third stage is less subtle . . . spreading of terror": ibid., p. 543.

"impress all with the 'inevitable' triumph . . . beyond the reach of discussion or inquiry": ibid., pp. 546–47.

332 "to permeate every national community . . .": ibid., pp. 545–46.

In the chill of the McCarthy era . . . : Hook [11].

333 "brainwashing": For more, see Lifton, Robert J., *Thought Reform and the Psychology of Totalism*, New York: Norton, 1961; also Schein, Edgar H., *Coercive Persuasion*, New York: Norton, 1961.

"secret action . . .": Ellul [8], pp. x–xi.

"a direct attack against man": ibid., p. xvi.

"Propaganda must be total . . .": ibid., p. 9.

334 "We are here in the presence of an organized myth . . .": ibid., p. 11.

335 "creating ambiguities . . .": ibid., p. 15.

"tends to hide its aims . . .": ibid.

". . . live in a separate world": ibid., p. 17.

"sense of the sacred . . .": ibid., pp. 31–32.

"Even in the actual contact of human relations . . .": ibid., p. 24.

336 "make propaganda in every instance . . . like a fish in water . . . in the midst of the masses": ibid., pp. 306–7.

337 "to drain the opponents . . .": ibid., p. 309.

". . . every person must be placed in the mold . . .": ibid., pp. 309–10.

339 Religious propaganda . . . "not very successful": ibid., p. 49.

"Christians often claim . . .": ibid., pp. 229–30.

341 "It may not be with bullets . . .": [64], p. 55.

342 "At the end of this brief analysis . . .": [8], pp. 231–32.

CHAPTER 12: THE SEIZURE OF POWER

343 Epigraph: *Conservative Digest*, April 1981.

"shadow cabinet": [53], p. 74.

344 Weyrich's Committee . . . claimed thirteen winners in 1978: *Conservative Digest*, June 1979.

By late 1979 . . . 25,000 letters . . . on seventy-two-hour notice . . . : ibid.

345 Moral Majority in Alaska: New York *Times*, June 9, 1980.

Moral Majority in Alabama: New York *Times*, November 1, 1980.

Moral Majority in Oklahoma: New York *Times*, October 11, 1981.

Fundamentalist forces made up more than a third of GOP delegates: Cleveland *Press*, July 25, 1980.

346 Symms nominated "Worst Senator" by Jack Anderson: New York *Daily News,* January 16, 1981.

Grassley . . . "exemplary Christian": *Conservative Digest,* November 1980.

Family Protection Act of 1981 . . . quotes from Jepsen, Moral Majority: Philadelphia *Inquirer,* June 18, 1981.

347 "teen chastity bill": New York *Times,* June 25, 1981.

Denton quote—". . . I'm talking about screwing": Philadelphia *Inquirer,* June 17, 1981.

Background on Jesse Helms: New York *Times Magazine,* February 8, 1981; Elizabeth Drew's article in *The New Yorker,* July 20, 1981; *Time* magazine cover story, September 14, 1981.

348 WHITE PEOPLE WAKE UP: Washington *Post,* July 26, 1981, and elsewhere.

349 "Dr. King's outfit . . .": *The New Yorker,* op. cit., p. 79.

350 "He [Rockefeller] stole another man's wife": *Time,* op. cit., p. 30.

Helms's links to Viguerie and figures on the Congressional Club: ibid., p. 39.

Helms's role in the founding of NCPAC and Conservative Caucus: New York *Times Magazine,* op. cit., p. 75.

"Mr. Integrity" and "the conscience of the conservative movement": *Conservative Digest,* June 1979.

351 "As Americans, we may give our votes to candidates . . .": *The New Yorker,* op. cit., p. 85.

Helms's group . . . worked closely with Dolan and NCPAC: ibid., p. 81.

Helms and Falwell recruited Denton: ibid., p. 82.

Helms's club's efforts for Reagan and Senators East and D'Amato: ibid., p. 81.

Helms's foundations: ibid., pp. 89–90.

352 1979 foreign affairs blowup: New York *Times Magazine,* op. cit., p. 84; Washington *Post,* July 26, 1981.

A "political saint": Washington *Post,* July 26, 1981.

"government-within-a-government": *The New Yorker,* op. cit., p. 91.

Carbaugh "had astonished people . . .": ibid., p. 89.

353 Proxmire quote: New York *Times Magazine,* op. cit., p. 84.

"Every person in the Senate knows . . .": *Time,* op. cit., p. 35.

"This guy really does play a double-dealing game . . .": *The New Yorker,* op. cit., p. 83.

Bumpers quote: ibid., p. 94.

Cranston quote: New York *Times*, July 12, 1981.

"delightful young people": *The New Yorker*, op. cit., p. 90.

"I know almost nothing . . .": ibid., p. 83.

354   "There's nothing wrong with rational analysis . . .": ibid., pp. 85–86.

355   The "Creative Society" and role of Rev. W. S. McBirnie: Boyarsky [36], pp. 84–85.

356   Viguerie quote, Reagan helped "raise millions": [64], p. 47. "The fact is . . . CFTR is in no way a Reagan campaign . . .": [39], p. 17.

357   CFTR nation's fifth-richest PAC: New York *Times*, June 30, 1981.

      Reagan gave creationist movement its first victory . . . : Washington *Post*, September 13, 1980.

358   Reagan's Dallas remarks at Roundtable national affairs briefing: *Conservative Digest*, September 1980.

      "I can only add to that, my friends . . .": "Bill Moyers' Journal: Campaign Report #3," op. cit.

      "Bully pulpit" . . . "moral suasion.": New York *Times*, October 4, 1980.

359   Reagan interview in "PTL Club" *Action* magazine: dated November 1980.

      Excerpt from "700 Club": broadcast February 6, 1981, in New York City.

360   "Hell with them": New York *Times*, November 11, 1980.

      "Nixon-Ford retreads": St. Petersburg *Times* (Fla.), November 21, 1980.

      "country-club . . . very wrong.": New York *Times*, January 25, 1981.

361   A massive infusion of fundamentalist right ideologues: *Time*, March 16, 1981.

      Rev. Robert Billings appointment: Philadelphia *Bulletin*, July 14, 1981.

      Blackwell appointment: St. Petersburg *Times* (Fla.), July 25, 1981.

      Link to *New Right Report* and Youth Politics committee: [39], p. 57.

      Nofziger's role and quotes: *Time*, March 16, 1981.

362   "priority audits" of Planned Parenthood: New York *Times*, December 6, 1981.

      Haig quotes on God: New York *Times*, June 17, 1981, and October 2, 1981.

Watt's "public-interest" law foundation and ties to Coors and oil companies: Jack Anderson's column in Albuquerque *Journal,* June 4, 1981, and elsewhere.

363   "I don't know how many future generations . . .": New York *Daily News,* August 23, 1981.

"I believe there is a life hereafter . . .": Washington *Post,* March 9, 1981.

"a disaster a day": San Diego *Union,* April 4, 1981.

"I am a fundamentalist . . .": Washington *Post,* March 9, 1981.

364   Reagan's first use of behavioral scientists: [36], pp. 95–97.

"the most sophisticated team . . ." ever in White House: Blumenthal, Sidney, "Marketing the President," New York *Times Magazine,* September 13, 1981, p. 43.

365   "open windows . . . proactive": ibid.

366   Pollsters' findings that economy was single most important issue: ibid., p. 110. See also "Budget Ax Becomes a Tool of Social Change," New York *Times,* June 21, 1981; and "Reagan Reversing Many U.S. Policies," New York *Times,* July 3, 1981, which begins: "At a time when public attention has been riveted on President Reagan's tax and budget plans, his Administration has quietly set out to accomplish a sweeping reversal of policy and practice in the way the government deals with business and individual citizens."

Nofziger's "political blitz": Details of coordinated effort in Smith, Hedrick, "Taking Charge of Congress," New York *Times Magazine,* August 9, 1981.

"The way we operate . . .": ibid., pp. 17–18.

367   O'Neill quote—". . . telephone blitz": ibid.

Reagan on "sheer demagoguery": New York *Times,* June 18, 1981.

"We are tired of being manipulated by the White House": ibid.

Bolling quote: New York *Times,* June 17, 1981.

Moynihan quote: New York *Times,* July 7, 1981.

Wright quote: New York *Times,* June 27, 1981.

Jones quote: ibid.

368   The President . . . treaded on veiled prejudices: "The Demons Beneath the AWACS," New York *Times,* November 1, 1981. The editorial notes the anti-Semitic "overtone" and "innuendo" in remarks made by the President and his supporters during the AWACS debate.

The President plied a wavering Southern senator: New York

Times, October 28, 1981. Senator Howell Heflin, Democrat of Alabama, described his conversation with the President during the President's AWACS jawboning effort, noting the President's interpretation that Russia would become involved in a Mideast Armageddon.

"threatened or seduced or suckered": New York *Times,* December 30, 1981.

"What is no longer in doubt . . .": New York *Times,* August 2, 1981.

370   1982 GOP losses: *The New Republic,* December 1982.

Helms, NCPAC figures: *Time,* November 15, 1982.

NCPAC's 1982 targets: *Time,* December 8, 1980.

NCPAC broadcast ban: New York *Times,* December 16, 1981, and April 2, 1982.

371   Cannon defeat attributed partly to Teamsters unsuccessful bribe attempt: New York *Times,* November 7, 1982.

Weyrich disaster quote: ibid.

Weyrich issues quote: *Conservative Digest,* December 1982.

Weyrich on trenches, stacked rules: ibid.

Deukmejian-Bradley race: the National Rifle Association and other groups spent nearly $6 million to rally opposition to the state gun control initiative.

Racism: California pollster Mervin Field noted race as "a major factor" in the close election, New York *Times,* November 4, 1982.

GOP "renegades": Democratic pollster Patrick H. Caddell in the New York *Times,* November 14, 1982.

Overall NCPAC score: *New Republic,* op. cit.

372   Gasper description: *Conservative Digest,* May / June 1980.

Gasper "Gestapo" and actions: New York *Times,* June 21, 1982.

Federal judge blocks "squeal rule": New York *Times,* February 15, 1983.

Administration appointments: New York *Times,* ibid., and Boston *Globe,* November 28, 1982.

373   Moral Majority Bahamas weekend: *New Republic,* op. cit.

Baptist Fundamentalism '84: *Fundamentalist Journal,* December 1982.

374   U.N. forum: Weyrich in *Conservative Digest,* November 1982.

New Populist Revolt: *Conservative Digest,* October, November and December 1982; *New Republic,* op. cit.

DeVos quotes: New York *Times,* November 14, 1981, and New York *Daily News,* August 14, 1982.

DeVos GOP techniques: New York *Times,* August 13, 1982.

Amway indictment: New York *Times,* November 17, 1982.

376 Prescott Bush campaign links to Reagan polltaker Richard Wirthlin and NCPAC cofounder Roger Stone: New York *Times,* January 15, 1982.

377 Weicker reelection results: New York *Times,* November 3, 1982.

NCPAC support for Conservative party candidate Lucien P. Difazio: In reports filed with the Federal Election Commission, NCPAC showed Difazio among its top five Senate race recipients in 1982, with total election contributions of over $3,000.

CHAPTER 13: SPIRITUAL IMPERIALISM

381 Epigraph: New York *Times,* October 15, 1981.

382 Sadat crackdown on "sectarian sedition": New York *Times,* September 6, 1981.

383 "sacred terror": New York *Times,* October 8, 1981.

Sadat helped unleash the movement that destroyed him: New York *Times,* October 27, 1981.

384 Begin coalition with Agudat Israel Party: New York *Times,* August 5, 1981.

Begin and Falwell phone call: Philadelphia *Inquirer,* July 7, 1981.

385 India's Moslems and alleged Persian Gulf connection: New York *Times,* August 14, 1981.

India's Sikhs and Gajender Singh quotes: New York *Times,* August 16, 1981.

Afrikaner Resistance Movement: New York *Times,* August 23, 1981.

387 ". . . it is to the English and American people . . .": Furnas [42], pp. 253–54.

388 "to accept wholeheartedly our duty and our opportunity . . .": Schiller [22], p. 1.

389 American missionary losses: Philadelphia *Bulletin,* June 3, 1981.

390 Israel's anti-missionary laws: *Time,* January 23, 1978.

Charges by Israeli anti-missionary organizations: "In the Shadow of the Cross: A Study of Missionary Activity in Israel," *c.* 1978 by Peylim Yad L'Achim, Israel Torah Activists.

Indian anti-missionary bill: New York *Times,* April 15, 1981.

391   Indonesia and Central African Burundi crackdowns: Albu-
       querque *Journal*, September 17, 1980.

       Morris Cerrullo in Nicaragua: New York *Times*, May 29,
       1981.

       Voronaeff Bible-smuggling: St. Petersburg *Times* (Fla.), Feb-
       ruary 28, 1981.

       Open Doors one million Bibles to China: New York *Times*,
       October 13, 1981.

       Voice of Hope Radio in Lebanon: New York *Times*, August
       15, 1980.

       Maryknoll murders in El Salvador: St. Petersburg *Times*
       (Fla.), June 13, 1981, and Philadelphia *Bulletin*, May 5,
       1981.

392   Bitterman murder in Colombia: Washington *Post*, March 8,
       1981.

       Wycliffe international contracts: Philadelphia *Inquirer*,
       March 5, 1981.

       CIA-related threats to U.S. missionaries abroad: New York
       Times, June 27, 1981, and October 5, 1981. The first article
       is an op-ed piece in which two U.S. Mennonite missionaries
       plead for the CIA to renounce the use of missionaries for
       covert operations.

393   Mexican ban on evangelical broadcasting: *Christianity To-
       day*, September 19, 1980.

       South Korean restrictions: *Worldvision*, January 1981.

       Programs to Change the World and Robertson quotes:
       Flame, Christian Broadcasting Network, undated, early 1981.

396   UNESCO debate over "New International Information Or-
       der": Anthony Smith [29].

       "cultural imperialism" and books by Herbert Schiller:
       [22]–[25].

404   "strange" and "secret" charges against Wycliffe: Philadel-
       phia *Inquirer*, March 5, 1981.

       "Wycliffe Bible Translators believes that to accomplish . . .":
       The World of Wycliffe (pamphlet).

       Wycliffe in Ecuador: Philadelphia *Inquirer*, May 24, 1981.

       Wycliffe and U.S. Agency for International Development
       (AID): Links between the CIA and AID are documented in
       Marchetti and Marks [55]. In their controversial work, the
       authors (respectively, a former executive assistant to the
       deputy director of the CIA and former staff assistant to the
       intelligence director of the State Department) cited instances
       where AID and its divisions served as fronts for CIA opera-

tors, contract mercenaries and other undercover agents around the world (pp. 67, 75). They also reported that AID supplied "cover and additional resources" for CIA counterinsurgency programs in Latin America (pp. 136–37), collaborated in the agency's attempt to influence the 1964 presidential election in Chile (p. 39), and that AID's Public Safety Division "regularly supplies cover to CIA operators all over the world" (p. 71). NOTE: Alleged CIA activities involving clergy or religious groups may be among the agency's most closely guarded operations, but there is evidence that suggests the agency sees religion as a legitimate focus of intelligence work. Marchetti and Marks reported on a secret collaboration between the CIA and troops loyal to the exiled Dalai Lama of Tibet, who received paramilitary training at U.S. Army bases in Colorado before joining CIA contract mercenaries in guerrilla raids into Communist China in the sixties (pp. 129–32). Other reports suggest that, in the wake of damaging leaks and disclosures, the agency may be turning increasingly for its personnel needs to members of the Mormon Church, who are purportedly being recruited for their ardent patriotism, disciplined life-styles and, possibly, for their church's active worldwide missionary program. However, the Mormon Church, which has more than 30,000 missionaries, denies any connection with the agency. See the New York Times, October 5, 1981, and Danforth, Kenneth C., "The Cult of Mormonism," Harper's, May 1980.

Bitterman's "secret, short-term mission": In Other Words, Jubilee Special Edition, Summer 1981, pp. 18–19.

405   Luis Palau article: ibid., "The Lord's Chessboard," pp. 15–17.

406   Campus Crusade booklet: International Personnel Needs, October 1980.

408   Campus Crusade's Military Ministry: [69], pp. 97–100.
      "Besides living in a diverse and challenging community . . .": ibid., p. 98.
      On one Air Force base in Idaho . . . : See the New York Times, June 20, 1980.

412   Colonel Heath Bottomly: Bottomly [68].

CHAPTER 14: REFLECTIONS: ON FAITH, FANATICISM AND THE AMERICAN WAY

416   Epigraph: J. Bronowski, A Sense of the Future: Essays in Natural Philosophy, Cambridge, MIT Press, 1977.

Electronic church growth: Arbitron cites total viewers up again to 22 million weekly. Falwell's show rose from only 373,999 to 458,251 as of November 1981. *Catholic Standard Times,* August 26, 1982.

Freedom Council: *Fact Sheet: The Freedom Council,* October 1981.

Bakker FCC charges: New York *Times,* March 15, 1983.

417 Schuller taxes: New York *Times,* January 26, 1983.

Oral Roberts layoffs: Philadelphia *Inquirer,* July 9, 1982.

Council for National Policy: New York *Times,* May 20, 1981.

Schlafly and ERA defeat: *Time,* July 12, 1982, and the Los Angeles *Times,* July 2, 1982.

Schlafly on God and the bomb: New York *Times,* July 9, 1982.

McAteer quote: "Ed McAteer: Portrait of an American Zealot," on "Crisis to Crisis," with Barbara Jordan, Public Broadcasting Service, July 30, 1982.

Reagan Russia remarks: New York *Times,* March 9, 1983.

418 Radio Marti: New York *Times,* August 20, September 1 and September 12, 1982.

Nicolaides memo and resignation: New York *Times,* November 14, 1981, and March 25, 1982.

419 Reagan secrecy classification: New York *Times,* April 3, 1982.

Interior, State, Defense Dept. and OSHA (Occupational Safety and Health Administration) personnel ordered not to speak to press without official approval: New York *Times,* January 13, July 14 and December 17, 1982.

Pentagon announces lie detector plan: New York *Times,* December 10, 1982.

Freedom of Information Act fees: New York *Times,* January 11, 1983.

Publications slashed: New York *Times,* June 2, 1982.

Critics charge deliberate suppression: New York *Times,* November 15, 1982.

Government efforts to separate abortion from family planning: New York *Times,* December 7, 1982.

420 Harassment and intimidation: the Chicago-based Pro-life Action League picketed abortion clinics and, in one case, hired a private detective to track down the mother of a pregnant 11-

year-old to dissuade her from having an abortion. New York *Times*, June 10, 1982.

Figures on abortion vandalism: ABC "Nightline," September 17, 1982.

Army of God: New York *Times*, August 19, August 21, August 26, August 31, November 1 and November 22, 1982, and January 28, 1983.

Oklahoma fire: *Playboy*, September 1982; New York *Times*, December 12, 1982.

Alabama prayer law: New York *Times*, August 10, September 16, 1982.

Nebraska school closing: New York *Times*, October 23, October 25 and November 26, 1982.

Arizona deaths: New York *Times*, October 24, 1982.

421 Memphis deaths: New York *Times*, January 14 and 15, 1983.

Legion of Zion Army: New York *Times*, December 17, 1980.

Christian Patriots Defense League: Buffalo *Courier-Express*, October 12, 1980.

Committee of 10 Million: Easton *Express* (Pa.), November 29, 1980.

Posse Comitatus: St. Petersburg *Times* (Fla.), March 4, 1981.

Alleged North Dakota Posse Comitatus killings: New York *Times*, February 15 and 16, 1983.

Kahl shoot-out; suspected paramilitary network: New York *Times*, June 11, 1983.

422 Background on Ríos Montt and Guatemalan coup: New York *Times*, June 10 and July 14, 1982; *Time*, June 21, 1982.

Ríos Montt dictatorship and state of siege: New York *Times*, July 2, 1982.

Reports of massacres and other atrocities: New York *Times*, September 28, October 6, 12 and 17, 1982.

423 Ríos Montt press secretary quote: New York *Times*, October 17, 1982.

Ríos Montt "scorched communists" quote: New York *Times*, December 6, 1982.

church elders in government: *Time*, op. cit.

U.S. citizen James DeGolyer Ríos Montt's personal spiritual adviser: CBS News Special Report on Guatemala, broadcast September 1, 1982.

424   Ríos Montt on Robertson and $1 billion: New York *Times*, May 20, 1982.
Ríos Montt interview on "700 Club": April 7, 1982.
Bianchi meetings in U.S.: CBS News Special Report on Guatemala, op. cit.
425   Guatemalan businessmen's campaign: CBS News, op. cit.
Reagan on "bum rap": New York *Times*, December 6, 1982.
State Department loan recommendation: New York *Times*, October 10, 1982.
Ríos Montt planned coup in advance: New York *Times*, July 21, 1982.
Illegal U.S. military aid: New York *Times*, November 15, 1982.
CIA involvement in 1954 Guatemalan coup: CBS News, op. cit.
Reported links between U.S. government, missionaries and counterinsurgency and other covert actions in Latin America: New York *Times*, August 2, 1982.
426   Victores' "courtesy call" to U.S. military officials aboard aircraft carrier *Ranger:* New York *Times*, August 9, 1983.
U.S. admits attaché in national palace but denies involvement in coup: New York *Times*, August 11, 1983.
Guatemalan communiqué announcing Ríos Montt overthrow: New York *Times*, August 9, 1983.
The French *nouvelle droite* and International Societies for the Defense of Tradition, Family and Property: New York *Times*, December 13, 1981.
427   Television sponsors "commitments of intent": Kansas City *Star*, October 25, 1981.
431   *propaganda devices:* Minnick [19] in [12], p. 33.
Haiman quote, "the deliberate use of nonrational . . .": ibid., p. 35.
"It is unethical to falsify . . .": ibid., p. 36.
432   "PR and ad men . . .": Nilsen [20], pp. 75–76.
"Concentration on 'issues' . . .": ibid., pp. 76–77.
"The persuasive techniques we have discussed are inconsistent . . .": ibid., p. 86.

GENERAL NOTE: All quotations from the Bible are reprinted verbatim as told to the authors. Bible references in the text are according to the King James or the Revised Standard Version.

Selected Bibliography

THIS LISTING of books, articles and scholarly papers is not intended to be complete, but it will provide the reader with references to the main sources cited in this book, along with some key texts and seminal works used by the authors in the formulation of their perspective. All newspaper and magazine articles and miscellaneous sources are described in the accompanying Notes.

TOPICS IN COMMUNICATION

1. Ashby, W. Ross, *Design for a Brain: The Origin of Adaptive Behavior*. London: Chapman & Hall, 1952.
2. _____, *An Introduction to Cybernetics*. London: Chapman & Hall, 1956.
3. Bertalanffy, Ludwig von, *General Systems Theory: Foundations, Development, Applications*. Revised edition. New York: George Braziller, 1968.
4. Conway, Flo, and Jim Siegelman, *Snapping: America's Epidemic of Sudden Personality Change*. New York: J. B. Lippincott, 1978; and New York: Delta Books, 1979.
5. _____, "Information Disease: Have Cults Created a New Mental Illness?" *Science Digest*, January 1982.
6. De Fleur, Melvin L., *Theories of Mass Communication*. New York: David McKay, 1966.
7. Doob, Leonard, "Goebbels' Principles of Propaganda." *Public Opinion Quarterly*, 1950; also in [26].
8. Ellul, Jacques, *Propaganda: The Formation of Men's Attitudes*. New York: Knopf, 1965; and New York: Vintage, 1973.
9. Erickson, Milton H., and Ernest L. Rossi, *Hypnotherapy: An Exploratory Casebook*. New York: Irvington, 1979.
10. Fromm, Erika, and Ronald E. Shor, eds., *Hypnosis: Develop-*

ments in Research and New Perspectives. Second edition. New York: Aldine, 1979.

11. Hook, Sidney, "The Ethics of Controversy." *The New Leader,* February 1, 1954; also in [12].

12. Johannesen, Richard L., ed., *Ethics and Persuasion: Selected Readings.* New York: Random House, 1967.

13. Klapper, Joseph T., "Mass Media and Persuasion." *Public Library Inquiry,* 1949; also in [26].

14. Kris, Ernst, and Nathan Leites, "Trends in Twentieth Century Propaganda." *Psychoanalysis and the Social Sciences.* Volume I. New York: International Universities Press, 1947; also in [26].

15. Langer, Susanne K., *Philosophy in a New Key: A Study in the Symbolism of Reason, Rite, and Art.* Third edition. Cambridge, Mass.: Harvard University Press, 1957.

16. Lasswell, Harold D., "The Strategy of Soviet Propaganda." *Proceedings* of the Academy of Political Science, Columbia University, 1961; also in [26].

17. Matson, Floyd W., and Ashley Montagu, eds., *The Human Dialogue: Perspectives on Communication.* New York: The Free Press, 1967.

18. Merton, Robert K., "Mass Persuasion: The Moral Dimension." *Mass Persuasion.* New York: Harper & Brothers, 1946; also in [26].

19. Minnick, Wayne C., "The Ethics of Persuasion." *The Art of Persuasion,* Boston: Houghton Mifflin, 1957; also in [12].

20. Nilsen, Thomas R., "Free Speech, Persuasion, and the Democratic Process." *The Quarterly Journal of Speech.* Volume XLIV, #3 (October 1958); also in [12].

21. Ruesch, Jurgen, and Gregory Bateson, *Communication: The Social Matrix of Psychiatry.* New York: W. W. Norton, 1968.

22. Schiller, Herbert I., *Mass Communications and American Empire.* Boston: Beacon Press, 1969.

23. _____, *The Mind Managers.* Boston: Beacon Press, 1973.

24. _____, *Communication and Cultural Domination.* White Plains, N.Y.: M. E. Sharpe, 1976.

25. _____, "Whose New International Economic and Information Order?" *Communication.* Volume V, 1980.

26. Schramm, Wilbur, ed., *The Process and Effects of Mass Communication.* Urbana, Ill.: University of Illinois Press, 1961. First printing, 1954.

27. _____, ed., *The Science of Human Communication.* New York: Basic Books, 1963.

28. Smith, Alfred G., ed., *Communication and Culture: Readings in the Codes of Human Interaction*. New York: Holt, Rinehart and Winston, 1966.

29. Smith, Anthony, *The Geopolitics of Information: How Western Culture Dominates the World*. New York: Oxford University Press, 1980.

30. Wallace, Karl R., "An Ethical Basis of Communication." *The Speech Teacher*. Volume IV, #1 (January 1955); also in [12].

31. Wiener, Norbert, *Cybernetics: or Control and Communication in the Animal and the Machine*. Cambridge, Mass.: MIT Press, 1948. Second edition, 1961.

32. _____, *The Human Use of Human Beings: Cybernetics and Society*. Boston: Houghton Mifflin, 1950, 1954; and New York: Avon, 1967.

33. _____, *God & Golem, Inc.: A Comment on Certain Points where Cybernetics Impinges on Religion*. Cambridge, Mass.: MIT Press, 1964.

34. Wright, Charles R., *Mass Communication: A Sociological Perspective*. New York: Random House, 1959.

HISTORY, POLITICS AND GENERAL BOOKS

35. Arendt, Hannah, *The Origins of Totalitarianism*. New edition. New York: Harvest / Harcourt Brace Jovanovich, 1973.

36. Boyarsky, Bill, *Ronald Reagan: His Life & Rise to the Presidency*. New York: Random House, 1981.

37. Bushman, Richard L., ed., *The Great Awakening: Documents on the Revival of Religion 1740–1745*. New York: Atheneum, 1970.

38. Clabaugh, Gary K., *Thunder on the Right: The Protestant Fundamentalists*. Chicago: Nelson-Hall, 1974.

39. Crawford, Alan, *Thunder on the Right: The "New Right" and the Politics of Resentment*. New York: Pantheon, 1980.

40. Federal Communications Commission, *The Law of Political Broadcasting and Cablecasting: A Political Primer*. Washington, D.C.: U.S. Government Printing Office, 1980.

41. Felsenthal, Carol, *The Sweetheart of the Silent Majority: The Biography of Phyllis Schlafly*. Garden City, N.Y.: Doubleday, 1981.

42. Furnas, J. C., *Anatomy of Paradise: Hawaii and the Islands of the South Seas*. New York: William Sloane Associates, 1947.

43. Garside, Roger, *Coming Alive: China After Mao*. New York: McGraw-Hill, 1981.

44. Gourfinkel, Nina, *Portrait of Lenin.* New York: Herder & Herder, 1972.
45. Hitler, Adolf, *Mein Kampf.* Translated by Ralph Manheim. Boston: Houghton Mifflin, 1971.
46. Hurt, Harry, III, *Texas Rich: The Hunt Dynasty from the Early Oil Days through the Silver Crash.* New York: W. W. Norton, 1981.
47. Koch, Adrienne, and William Peden, eds., *The Life and Selected Writings of Thomas Jefferson.* New York: Modern Library, 1972.
48. Kurtz, Paul, ed., *Humanist Manifestos I and II.* Buffalo, N.Y.: Prometheus Books, 1973.
49. ———, *A Secular Humanist Declaration.* Buffalo, N.Y.: Prometheus Books, 1980.
50. Laqueur, Walter, *Terrorism: A Study of National and International Political Violence.* Boston: Little, Brown, 1977.
51. ———, ed., *The Terrorism Reader: A Historical Anthology.* New York: Meridian, 1978.
52. Lewis, Sinclair, *Elmer Gantry.* New York: Harcourt, Brace, 1927; and New York: New American Library, 1970.
53. McIntyre, Thomas J., with John C. Obert, *The Fear Brokers: Peddling the Hate Politics of the New Right.* Boston: Beacon Press, 1979.
54. Malone, Dumas, *Jefferson and the Rights of Man.* Boston: Little, Brown, 1951.
55. Marchetti, Victor, and John D. Marks, *The CIA and the Cult of Intelligence.* New York: Knopf, 1974; and New York: Dell, 1975.
56. Mayo, Bernard, ed., *Jefferson Himself.* Charlottesville, Va.: University Press of Virginia, 1970. First edition, 1942.
57. Nathanson, Bernard N., with Richard N. Ostling, *Aborting America.* Garden City, N.Y.: Doubleday, 1979.
58. Reed, John, *Ten Days That Shook the World.* New York: Penguin, 1977. First edition, 1926.
59. Savelle, Max, *The Colonial Origins of American Thought.* Princeton, N.J.: Van Nostrand, 1964.
60. Schoeps, Hans-Joachim, *The Religions of Mankind: Their Origin and Development.* Garden City, N.Y.: Anchor Books, 1968.
61. Shirer, William L., *The Rise and Fall of the Third Reich: A History of Nazi Germany.* First edition. New York: Simon & Schuster, 1960.
62. Stokes, Anson Phelps, and Leo Pfeffer, *Church and State in the*

United States. Revised edition. New York: Harper & Row, 1964.

63. Toland, John, *Adolf Hitler.* Garden City, N.Y.: Doubleday, 1976.

64. Viguerie, Richard A., *The New Right: We're Ready to Lead.* Revised edition. Falls Church, Va.: The Viguerie Company, 1981.

RELIGIOUS BOOKS

65. Bakker, Jim, with Robert Paul Lamb, *Move That Mountain!* Plainfield, N.J.: Logos, 1976.

66. Barr, James, *Fundamentalism.* Philadelphia: Westminster Press, 1977, 1978.

67. Bellah, Robert N., and Phillip E. Hammond, *Varieties of Civil Religion.* New York: Harper & Row, 1980.

68. Bottomly, Colonel Heath, *Prodigal Father: A Fighter Pilot Finds Peace in the Wake of His Destruction.* Glendale, Cal.: G / L Publications, 1975.

69. Bright, Bill, *Come Help Change Our World.* San Bernardino, Cal.: Campus Crusade for Christ, 1979.

70. ———, *Jesus and the Intellectual.* San Bernardino, Cal.: Campus Crusade for Christ, 1968.

71. ———, *A Movement of Miracles.* San Bernardino, Cal.: Campus Crusade for Christ, 1977.

72. Burrows, William R., *New Ministries: The Global Context.* Maryknoll, N.Y.: Orbis Books.

73. Cassidy, Michael, *Christianity for the Open-Minded: An Invitation to Doubters.* Downers Grove, Ill.: InterVarsity Press, 1978.

74. Falwell, Jerry, *Listen, America!* Garden City, N.Y.: Doubleday-Galilee, 1980.

75. ———, ed., with Ed Dobson and Ed Hindson, *The Fundamentalist Phenomenon: The Resurgence of Conservative Christianity.* Garden City, N.Y.: Doubleday-Galilee, 1981.

76. Glover, Rev. Robert Hall, *The Progress of World-Wide Missions.* Revised by J. Herbert Kane. New York: Harper & Brothers, 1939, 1960.

77. Griffin, Em, *The Mind Changers: The Art of Christian Persuasion.* Wheaton, Ill.: Tyndale, 1976.

78. Henrichsen, Walter A., *Disciples Are Made—Not Born: Making Disciples Out of Christians.* Wheaton, Ill.: Victor Books, 1974.

79. *Holy Bible* (King James Version). Nashville, Tenn.: The Gideons International, 1974; and *Holy Bible* (Revised Standard Version). New York: Thomas Nelson, 1952.

80. Kane, J. Herbert, *Understanding Christian Missions.* Grand Rapids, Mich.: Baker, 1974.

81. LaHaye, Tim, *The Battle for the Mind.* Old Tappan, N.J.: Fleming H. Revell, 1980.

82. Mitchell, Basil, *Morality Religious and Secular: The Dilemma of the Traditional Conscience.* Oxford, England: Clarendon Press, 1980.

83. Navigators, *Topical Memory System.* Colorado Springs, Colo.: Navpress, 1969.

84. Orr, J. Edwin, *The Eager Feet: Evangelical Awakenings 1790–1830.* Chicago: Moody Press, 1975.

85. Proctor, William, ed., *The Born-Again Christian Catalog: A Complete Sourcebook for Evangelicals.* New York: M. Evans, 1979.

86. Robertson, Pat, with Jamie Buckingham, *Shout It from the Housetops.* Plainfield, N.J.: Logos, 1972.

87. Sholes, Jerry, *Give Me That Prime-Time Religion: An Insider's Report on the Oral Roberts Evangelistic Association.* Tulsa, Okla.: Oklahoma Book Publishing, 1979.

88. Skinner, Betty Lee, *Daws: The Story of Dawson Trotman, Founder of the Navigators.* Grand Rapids, Mich.: Zondervan, 1974.

89. Stapleton, Ruth Carter, *The Experience of Inner Healing.* New York: Bantam, 1977, 1979.

Index